Early Travels in India

1583-1619

Early Travels in India
1583-1619

Edited By

WILLIAM FOSTER, C.I.E.

GYAN

Published by

Gyan Publishing House
5, Ansari Road
Daryaganj, New Delhi-110002
Phone: 011-47034999, 9811692060
E-mail: books@gyanbooks.com

Distribution Network
gyanbooks.com
India, USA, Canada, UK, Australia, France

ISBN : 978-81-212-2993-7 (PB)
First Published, 1921

2nd Impression 2021

Printed at: Gyan Press, Delhi.

Early Travels in India
1583-1619
Author: William Foster

EARLY TRAVELS IN INDIA

1583—1619

EDITED BY

WILLIAM FOSTER, C.I.E.

HUMPHREY MILFORD
OXFORD UNIVERSITY PRESS
LONDON EDINBURGH GLASGOW COPENHAGEN
NEW YORK TORONTO MELBOURNE CAPE TOWN
BOMBAY CALCUTTA MADRAS SHANGHAI PEKING
1921

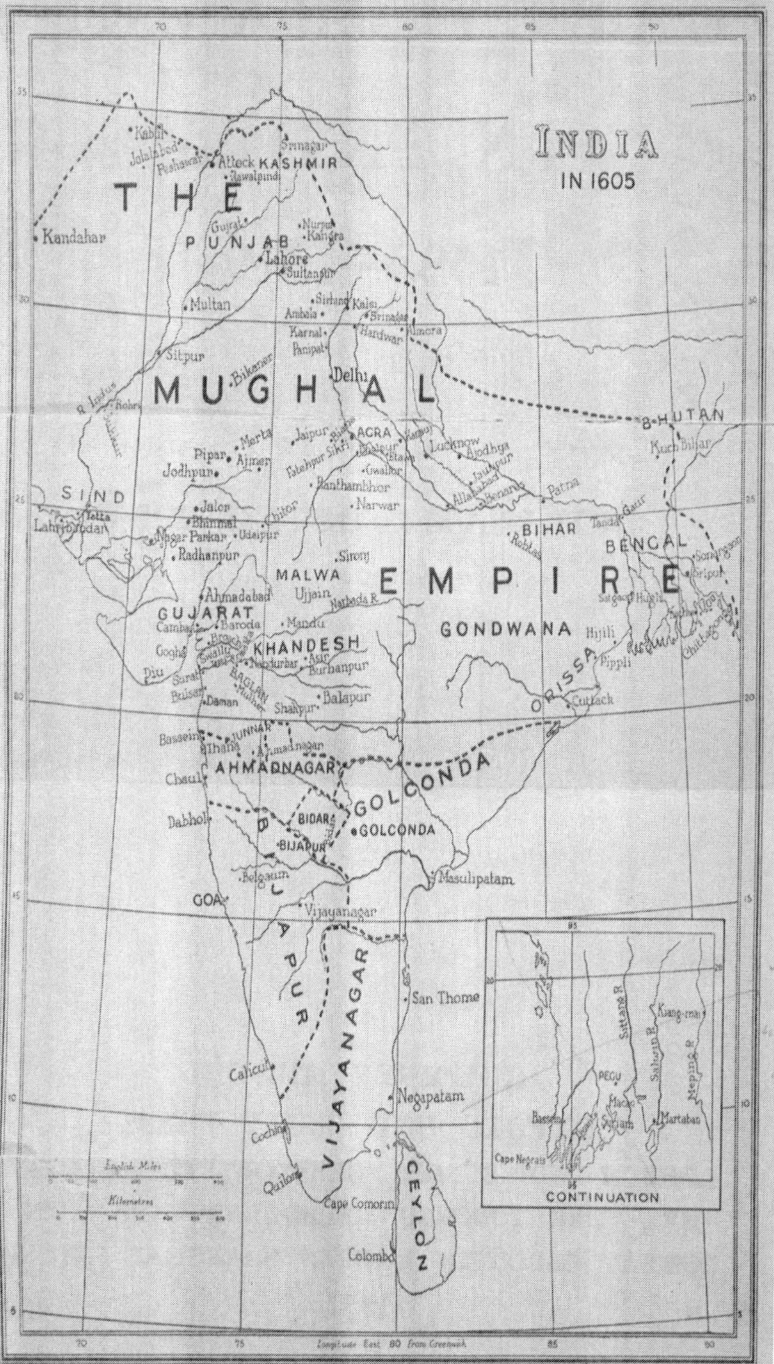
INDIA
IN 1605
THE MUGHAL EMPIRE
KASHMIR
PUNJAB
SIND
MALWA
GUJARAT
KHANDESH
GONDWANA
BIHAR
BENGAL
ORISSA
BHUTAN
AHMADNAGAR
GOLCONDA
BIDAR
BIJAPUR
VIJAYANAGAR
CEYLON
Kandahar
Kabul
Peshawar
Attock
Srinagar
Rawalpindi
Lahore
Multan
Delhi
AGRA
Lucknow
Patna
Jodhpur
Ajmer
Ahmadabad
Ujjain
Surat
Daman
Diu
Burhanpur
Cuttack
Chaul
Dabhol
GOA
Masulipatam
San Thome
Calicut
Negapatam
Cochin
Quilon
Cape Comorin
Colombo
GOLCONDA
Vijayanagar
PEGU
Martaban
Cape Negrais
CONTINUATION
English Miles
Kilometres
Longitude East 80 from Greenwich

LIST OF CONTENTS

PAGE

PREFACE vii

LIST OF CHIEF AUTHORITIES QUOTED . . . xiii

1583–91. RALPH FITCH 1

1599–1606. JOHN MILDENHALL 48

1608–13. WILLIAM HAWKINS 60

1608–11. WILLIAM FINCH 122

1612–16. NICHOLAS WITHINGTON 188

1612–17. THOMAS CORYAT 234

1616–19. EDWARD TERRY 288

INDEX 333

ILLUSTRATIONS

India in 1605 . . . . *Frontispiece*

Mesopotamia . . . . *To face page* 8

The Ghāts at Benares 20
From a photograph by the editor.

Mildenhall's Tomb 50
From a photograph by Miss Milford, reproduced in Mr. E. A. H. Blunt's *Christian Tombs and Monuments in the United Provinces.*

Jahāngīr 80
From a drawing in the Bibliothèque Nationale, Paris.

Surat Castle 134
From a photograph by Mr. V. M. Mehta.

Burhānpur Castle 138
From a photograph by Mr. B. K. Parry, I.C.S.

Ajmer 170
From a photograph by the editor.

Coryat on an Elephant 248
From the 1616 pamphlet.

Edward Terry 288
From his *Voyage to East India* (1655).

PREFACE

The following pages contain the narratives of seven Englishmen who travelled in Northern and Western India during the reigns of the Emperors Akbar and Jahāngīr. Though these do not by any means exhaust the list of English visitors of that period who have left us records of their experiences, they include practically all those of real importance, with the exception of Sir Thomas Roe, whose lengthy account of his embassy is already procurable in a modern edition.

In the case of none of these narratives is a manuscript source available, and it has been necessary to go instead to the earliest printed editions. Ralph Fitch's story of his adventures appeared first in Hakluyt's *Principall Navigations*, from which it is here reprinted. The other six are to be found in the voluminous collection published by the Rev. Samuel Purchas in 1625, and in the case of four of them we follow the text there given. For Nicholas Withington, however, use has also been made of a fuller version (from his original manuscript) given in a scarce eighteenth-century work; while the letters of Thomas Coryat are printed from the contemporary pamphlets in which they first saw the light and from which Purchas made merely a selection.

Since each of the narratives has its own introduction, little need be said here by way of preliminary. It may perhaps be pointed out that at the time (1584) when the earliest of our travellers reached the court of Akbar, the Mughal Empire in India had not yet reached its sixtieth anniversary. It was in 1525 that Bābur, then King of Kābul, crushed at Pānīpat the Afghān dynasty which had ruled at Delhi during the preceding three-quarters of a century. Bābur's son, Humāyūn, was driven from his throne in 1540 by Sher Shāh, the Afghān ruler of Bengal and Bihār, but recovered his kingdom in 1555, only to die in the following year, leaving to his young son Akbar a precarious dominion over a territory which is to-day represented by parts of the Panjāb and the United Provinces of Agra and Oudh. By 1584 Akbar had largely extended his domains. Partly by policy and partly by conquest he had become master of Gujarāt, Mālwa, and the bulk of Rājputāna; while on the east he had subdued, but not yet entirely assimilated, the provinces of Bihār and Bengal. Later in his reign he recovered control of Kābul (which had become practically independent under his brother, Muhammad Hakīm) and added to his empire Kashmīr, Sind, Kandahār, Khāndesh, and parts of Ahmadnagar. On his death in 1605 he was succeeded by his only surviving son, Salīm, who took the title of Nur-ud-dīn Jahāngīr. The latter was Emperor at the time of the visits of all but the first two of our travellers.

Though Southern India has little to do with our story, it may be noted that immediately to the south of the Mughal dominions lay the Muhammadan kingdoms of Ahmadnagar on the western and Golconda on the eastern side of the peninsula. South of Ahmadnagar was a third Muhammadan kingdom, that of Bījāpur; while the rest of the peninsula was still under the rule of petty Hindu princes, the chief of whom was the Rāja of Chandragiri, who represented the once powerful dynasty of Vijayanagar. In contemporary records he is commonly, though incorrectly, described as King of the Carnatic.

The only European nation holding any territorial possessions in India at the time was the Portuguese, whose regular dominions comprised merely the district round Goa and a few other ports on the western coast, though some of their compatriots had established themselves, in a position more or less independent, at various places on the other side of the peninsula and in the delta of the Ganges. The Portuguese had been in India longer than the Mughals, and the control they exercised over the neighbouring seas was accepted without repining by Akbar and his successor. This was not the case with our own countrymen, and the story of the successful endeavours of the English to establish their right to trade with India, notwithstanding the opposition of the Portuguese, forms the underplot of the present volume. Its main purpose, of course, is to give a picture of the Mughal Empire as it appeared to English eyes in the days of Shakespeare.

The accuracy of the picture so presented can be judged by comparison with modern reconstructions of the period. The narratives printed in this volume are individually partial and incomplete, but their general effect is in close accordance with such works as the late Dr. Vincent Smith's *Akbar the Great Mogul*, and Mr. W. H. Moreland's *India at the Death of Akbar*, both of which are based on a much more extensive mass of evidence. In some respects the passing of four centuries has made little difference; Indians are naturally conservative, though we need not go so far as to agree that, as asserted by an Englishman in 1675, they 'preferr an old Hell to a new Heaven'. But in many important respects the change is remarkable. Even physically a great difference may be noted. Large stretches of ground now highly cultivated were then covered with jungle or else left barren. Roads were few and bad, canals scarcely existed, and railways of course had not been dreamt of. Goods were mostly carried from place to place on camels or oxen; and travellers, if they had anything worth taking, could move only in large bodies or with guards, for fear of the outlaws that infested the ways. On the frontiers (of which the southern cut right across Central India) hostilities were almost incessant; while civil wars were of frequent occurrence. Epidemics and famines constantly swept away large numbers, and their advent found the authorities fatalistic and impotent. The Government was a pure despotism, and the lives and property of all subjects, from prince to peasant, were subject to the caprice of the reigning monarch. The revenues of the country were either spent in extravagant display and in maintaining large military forces, or else were hoarded in the imperial treasury. On the other hand justice, if rough and liable to be influenced by bribery, was fairly good; traders of all nations were freely admitted; and in religious matters toleration was more consistently practised than in any European country at that period. On the whole, our travellers, who were of course comparing Indian conditions with those of their own country, were not unfavourably impressed. This was particularly the case with Terry, though his optimistic views are discounted by the fact that he really saw less of India than any of the other narrators whose stories are here given.

One fact it is well to keep in mind is that none of these accounts was designedly written for publication, except possibly that of Withington, who may have intended to issue it for his own justification, though there is no evidence that he did so. Terry's treatise—the only one that deals with the subject in a broad manner—was composed for the edification of the Prince of Wales; Hawkins's for the information of his employers. Fitch's narrative, as Hakluyt tells us in the dedication of his second volume, was presented to Lord Burleigh, who had doubtless taken an interest in the setting forth of the expedition. The section that bears the name of Finch was compiled from his journal after his death by the diligent Purchas. Those dealing with the travels of Mildenhall and Coryat are true letters, and their writers had no hand in their publication. These facts account to some extent for an occasional want of proportion, minor matters being described at length, whilst others, of which we should have been glad to hear full details, are slurred over or omitted. There is compensation, however, in the greater naturalness of the narrative. Most of our travellers are seen, as it were, in undress, and we learn more of their characters than we probably should, had they been conscious that they were addressing a wider audience. Little as we know of them, beyond what we can gather from their writings, the impressions left are favourable. If they appear at times self-assertive, this was natural enough when the English were practically unknown in India and had to encounter a steady stream of disparagement from the Portuguese and their agents, the Roman Catholic missionaries. The hostility thus engendered makes our travellers at times unjust to the latter; but here we must reckon with the sturdy Protestantism of the Englishman, which rendered him quite incapable of recognizing any merit in a Jesuit. For the travellers themselves one feels a genuine admiration. One and all, the men who here write their adventures so soberly and so modestly, with many a shrewd observation and occasionally a flash of humour, ran daily great risks; and in fact three of them found in the East their last resting-place, while a fourth died on the voyage home. Sickness, robbery, threats of violence, were incidents that did not shake their cheerfulness, and there is little reflection in their narratives of the dangers and hardships which were constantly their lot. They had chosen to 'wander to the unfrequented Ynde', and they accepted the consequences, however unpleasant, stolidly and without repining.

The assistance received from many friends in the preparation of the notes, &c., has been acknowledged in the appropriate places. For help in collecting the materials for the illustrations I have to thank Messrs. F. G. H. Anderson, E. A. H. Blunt, B. K. Parry, and A. K. Smith, all of the Indian Civil Service; also M. Henri Omont, of the Bibliothèque Nationale, Paris, who not only gave me permission to reproduce the portrait of the Emperor Jahāngīr, but kindly arranged for the taking of the necessary photograph.

In reprinting the various narratives, the old spelling has been retained, except that the use of *u* for *v*, of *v* for *u*, and of *i* for *j* has not been followed; while as regards punctuation and the employment of capital letters modern practice has also been observed. In the spelling of Oriental names, both of persons and of places, the *Imperial Gazetteer of India* has been mostly adopted as a guide; but vowels occurring at the end of a word have not been marked as long, though they should be understood to be so.

FULLER TITLES OF

CHIEF AUTHORITIES QUOTED

Calendar of State Papers, East Indies, 1513–1616. London, 1862.

Cathay and the Way Thither. By Colonel Yule. Second edition by H. Cordier. 4 vols. Hakluyt Society, 1913–16.

Covert, Robert. *A True and Almost Incredible Report, &c.* London, 1612.

De Laet, Johannes. *De Imperio Magni Mogolis.* Leiden, 1631.

Della Valle, Pietro, Travels of. Translated and edited by Edward Grey. 2 vols. Hakluyt Society, 1891.

Documentos Remettidos da India. 4 vols. Lisbon, 1880–93.

Du Jarric, P. *Thesaurus Rerum Indicarum.* 3 vols. Cologne, 1615.

Fanshawe, H. C. *Delhi Past and Present.* London, 1902.

Federici, Cesare. *Viaggio.* Venice, 1587.

First Letter Book of the East India Company, 1600–19. Edited by Sir George Birdwood and William Foster. London, 1893.

Fryer, John. *A New Account of East India and Persia.* London, 1698.

Gait, Sir Edward. *History of Assam.* Calcutta, 1906.

Galvano, Antonio. *The Discoveries of the World.* Translated and edited by Richard Hakluyt. Hakluyt Society, 1862.

Hakluyt, Richard. *The Principall Navigations, &c.* 3 vols. London, 1598–1600.

Hawkins' Voyages, the. Edited by Sir Clements Markham. Hakluyt Society, 1878.

Herbert, Thomas. *Some Yeares Travels.* London, 1638.

Hobson-Jobson. By Colonel Yule and A. C. Burnell. Second edition (by W. Crooke). London, 1903.

Jourdain, John, the Journal of. Edited by William Foster. Hakluyt Society, 1905.

Lancaster, Sir James, the Voyage of. Edited by Sir Clements Markham. Hakluyt Society, 1877.

Letters Received by the East India Company from its Servants in the East, 1602–17. 6 vols. London, 1896–1902.

Linschoten, J. H. van, the Voyage of. Translated and edited by A. C. Burnell and P. A. Tiele. 2 vols. Hakluyt Society, 1884.

Maclagan, Sir Edward. 'Jesuit Missions to the Emperor Akbar'. *Journal of the Bengal Asiatic Society*, vol. lxv, part i.

——— 'The Earliest English Visitors to the Panjab', 1585–1628. *Journal of the Panjab Historical Society*, vol. i, no. 2.

Manucci, Niccolao. *Storia do Mogor.* Translated and edited by William Irvine. 4 vols. London, 1907–8.

Monserrate, Father. *Mongolicae Legationis Commentarius.* Edited by Father Hosten. Memoirs of the Bengal Asiatic Society, vol. iii, p. 513.

Moreland, W. H. *India at the Death of Akbar.* London, 1920.

Mundy, Peter, the Travels of. Edited by Sir Richard C. Temple. *In progress.* Hakluyt Society, 1907, etc.

Purchas, Samuel. *Purchas His Pilgrimes.* 4 vols. London, 1625.

——— *Purchas His Pilgrimage.* London, 1626.

Roe, Sir Thomas, the Embassy of. Edited by William Foster. 2 vols. Hakluyt Society, 1899.

Smith, Dr. Vincent A. *Akbar the Great Mogul.* Oxford, 1917.

Stein, Sir Aurel. 'Notes on the Routes from the Panjab to Turkestan and China recorded by William Finch'. *Journal of the Panjab Historical Society,* vol. vi.

Stephen, Carr. *The Archaeology and Monumental Remains of Delhi.* Calcutta, 1876.

Teixeira, Pedro, the Travels of, 1604–5. Translated and edited by W. F. Sinclair and D. Ferguson. Hakluyt Society, 1901.

Terry, Edward. *A Voyage to East India.* London, 1655.

Thomas, Edward. *The Revenue Resources of the Mughal Empire.* London, 1871.

Tombs and Monuments in the Bombay Presidency. Bombay, N. D.

Tombs and Monuments in the United Provinces. By E. A. H. Blunt. Allahabad, 1911.

Tūzuk-i-Jahāngīrī, or Memoirs of Jahāngīr. Translated by A. Rogers and edited by H. Beveridge. 2 vols. London, 1909 and 1914.

Yule, Sir Henry. *The Mission to Ava.* London, 1858.

1583–91

RALPH FITCH

The interesting narrative here reprinted belongs of course to a period anterior to the establishment of the English East India Company, though the journey it describes holds a by no means unimportant place among the events leading up thereto. At the date of its inception, namely the end of 1582 or the beginning of 1583, English merchants were striving eagerly to discover some means of securing a share in the rich trade with the East, but so far their endeavours had been unsuccessful. The attempts to find a way to China round the northern coasts of Europe and Asia had ended in failure, while the three expeditions of Martin Frobisher in search of a passage round North America had met with a similar fate. The establishment of a trade with Russia had resulted in several ventures to Persia by that route, but no further attempt was made in this direction after 1581. The sea route by the Cape of Good Hope was not only long and dangerous but was claimed as a Portuguese monopoly, and Queen Elizabeth was not yet prepared to break with Philip II, who since 1580 had been King of Portugal as well as of Spain; and although the return of Sir Francis Drake by this route, from his voyage round the world, had encouraged an attempt under Edward Fenton in June 1582, to pass that way into the Indian Ocean, cautious merchants may well have anticipated the failure that actually ensued.

Attention was thus directed to the possibility of utilizing the long-established trade-route by way of Syria which had already been tapped to some extent by the syndicate of merchants, headed by Edward Osborne and Richard Staper, who had been granted the monopoly of English trade in the Turkish dominions by a royal charter in September 1581. Moreover, a certain John Newbery had just returned from a long and important journey in the desired direction. Starting from Tripoli, in Syria, he had made his way overland to Basra, on the Persian Gulf, and thence by sea to Ormus, the famous island at its mouth, opposite to the present Bandar Abbāsi. After spending some time on the island, during which he carefully concealed his nationality from the Portuguese officials, he returned by land through Persia and Armenia to Constantinople, and thence home by way of Poland and the

Baltic.[1] Evidently he had learnt much about the routes between India and Persia, and had come to the conclusion that commerce by that route was perfectly feasible.

Plans were quickly made for a further experiment in the same direction, and the result was the journey which is here chronicled. The necessary funds were found chiefly by Osborne and Staper, and Newbery was placed in charge of the expedition. The party consisted of a number of merchants (among whom we need only mention John Eldred and Ralph Fitch), together with an expert in gems named William Leeds, and a painter named James Story, who (according to Linschoten) was not employed by the promoters of the venture but joined in order to seek his fortune. It was arranged that two of the merchants should be left at Bagdad with part of the stock, and two more at Basra with a further quantity of goods, while Newbery and Fitch should continue their journey to the Indies. For this purpose they were furnished with letters of introduction from Queen Elizabeth, addressed to the Mughal Emperor Akbar (described as King of Cambay), and also to the Emperor of China. Both letters are among the documents printed by Hakluyt.

The materials for the history of the first portion of the journey are fairly abundant. Besides Fitch's narrative, Hakluyt gives one by Eldred (who did not go farther than Basra), together with six letters from Newbery and one from Fitch; while Purchas supplements these by three more letters from Eldred and two from Newbery. In addition, we have an interesting account (particularly of our travellers' experiences at Goa) by Linschoten in his *Itinerario* (Hakluyt Society's edition, vol. ii, p. 158). These documents are not here reprinted, since we are chiefly interested in that portion of Fitch's narrative which concerns his travels after quitting Goa; use has, however, been made of them to supply a few of the dates which are so conspicuously lacking in Fitch's own account.

Newbery and his companions sailed from London in the *Tiger*[2] in February 1583, and reached Aleppo about May 20. On the last day of that month they started on their adventurous journey, and on August 6 found themselves safe in Basra, the port town of Mesopotamia. Newbery's plan was to go by boat to Bushire on the Persian coast, and thence proceed by land to India; but he was obliged to abandon this idea because an interpreter could not be secured. Forced, therefore, to risk interference on the part of the Portuguese, the little party

[1] Accounts of this and of a previous journey of his in Syria and Palestine will be found in *Purchas His Pilgrimes* (Part ii, bk. ix, ch. 3).

[2] 'Her husband's to Aleppo gone, master of the *Tiger*,' says the First Witch in *Macbeth*, a clear proof (as a previous writer has remarked) that Shakespeare knew his Hakluyt.

embarked for Ormus, which was reached early in September. The Italian merchants resident in the island were quick to note the arrival of fresh trade competitors (concerning whose intentions they had apparently been warned from Aleppo), and on their insinuations that the new-comers were heretics and spies, acting in the interests of the pretender to the Portuguese throne, our travellers were arrested and sent to Goa. At the latter place they were committed to prison, where they remained about a month. They found friends, however, in two Jesuits, one a Dutchman and the other an Englishman, Father Thomas Stevens [1]; also in the young Dutchman Linschoten (already mentioned), who, being in the suite of the Archbishop of Goa, was able to exert some useful influence in their favour. The fact that they all professed to be good Catholics told on their behalf, and just before Christmas 1583 Newbery, Fitch, and Leeds were released on bail.

Story had already obtained his liberty by agreeing to become a lay brother in the Jesuits' convent, where his talents were needed for the decoration of the church. The others now took a shop and commenced to trade, and two letters written by Newbery and Fitch in January 1584 spoke cheerfully of their prospects. Before long, however, matters assumed a different aspect. The Jesuits hinted that the Englishmen would probably be sent to Portugal by the next fleet, and the Viceroy, to whom they applied for the return of the money they had deposited in the hands of their surety, returned a threatening answer. Alarmed at this, they decided to make their escape, and early in April 1584,[2] under pretext of an

[1] It is scarcely necessary to recall that Stevens is famous as the first Englishman known to have set foot on Indian soil. Born in Wiltshire and educated at Winchester, he made his way to Rome and there entered the Jesuit order. Being desirous of serving in India, he obtained a passage at Lisbon in the spring of 1579 and reached Goa in October of that year. A letter to his father, describing the voyage, will be found in the pages of Hakluyt. Stevens laboured in Goa for forty years, dying in 1619, at the age of seventy. He was the first European to make a scientific study of Konkani, and he wrote two religious works, one of which, a long epic in Marāthi, still keeps his memory green in that part of India.

[2] Fitch says 1585, but I imagine that this is a slip, since the narrative is scarcely consistent with their having spent sixteen months in Goa. In the same way, the date he gives for Newbery's departure from Fatehpur Sikri, viz. September 28, 1585, should probably be read as meaning a year earlier. Nothing can be inferred from the Emperor's movements, for he was at Fatehpur Sikri in the summers of both years; but it is clear that the travellers pushed on to Agra through the rainy season (which they would hardly have done unless pressed for time), and once they had seen the Emperor, Newbery would doubtless be anxious to

excursion, they slipped over the border into the territory of the King of Bījāpur. It was well they did so, for, on hearing of the arrival and imprisonment of a party of Englishmen, King Philip wrote to the Viceroy of Goa (February 1585) to punish them if found guilty, and to take special care that neither they nor any of their countrymen should be allowed in Portuguese territory. On being informed, in reply, of the escape of the prisoners, he wrote again, both in 1587 and 1589, urging efforts to apprehend them and punish their abettors; while in 1591 he ordered that the survivor—Story the painter, who had quitted the cloister, married a half-caste woman, and settled down at Goa—should be sent to Lisbon. Whether this was done is not known; but if so, the unlucky artist probably perished in one of the two ships that were lost on their homeward voyage in 1592 (see the Introduction to *The Travels of Pedro Teixeira*, pp. xxvii–xxx).

Newbery and his fellow fugitives made their way first to Bījāpur, the capital of the kingdom of that name. Thence they journeyed to Golconda, the chief city of the Kutb Shāhi kings. At both places they seem to have made special inquiries regarding precious stones, the procuring of which, according to Linschoten, was one of the original objects of the expedition and the reason why a jeweller formed one of the party. It may be surmised that their immediate object was to invest their stock of money in gems, which were easily concealed and could be profitably disposed of at any place of importance. From

start for home. Moreover, Fitch tells us that Newbery promised to meet him in Bengal in two years' time; and, if their parting took place in the autumn of 1584, this would account for Fitch deferring his departure for Pegu until November 1586. On the other hand, if 1585 is correct, it is strange to find that in 1587 Fitch was not in Bengal, but far away in Pegu. As apparently he kept no journal, but wrote the sketch of his journey from memory on his return, it would be easy for him to make such slips in his dates.

Another reason for supposing that we should read 1584 for 1585 is that, while Akbar was at Fatẹhpur Sīkri throughout the former year, in the latter he left that city on August 22. If Fitch was really there at the time of the Emperor's departure—which must have been attended with imposing ceremonial—it seems strange that he should have said nothing about it; and equally strange that he should have stated that in September he left Leeds 'in service with the king Zelabdim Echebar in Fatepore', thus implying that the Emperor was still there. Dr. Vincent Smith suggests (*Akbar*, pp. 228, 231) that the travellers arrived in July or August 1585, that Leeds at once entered Akbar's service, and that Fitch merely meant that the jeweller remained on the imperial establishment at Fatehpur Sīkri after the Emperor's departure. This explanation is plausible, but not quite convincing.

Golconda they started for the court of the Mughal Emperor, whose dominions were entered near Burhānpur; from that place they followed the usual route through Ujjain and got safely to Agra, only to find that Akbar was at his new city of Fatehpur Sīkri, about twenty miles away. Proceeding thither, they presumably waited upon the Emperor, concerning whom Fitch says tantalizingly little. Whether they had succeeded in hiding from the Portuguese Queen Elizabeth's letter, and whether it was now presented, we are not told; nor whether any grant of privileges was secured for future use. At Fatehpur Sīkri the travellers separated: Leeds entered the service of the Emperor, and henceforward nothing more is heard of him; Newbery decided to make his way home overland, and he too disappears from view, dying on the journey, according to Purchas, 'unknown when or where.' Evidently he had come to the conclusion that the project of an overland trade was hopeless, for he promised Fitch to meet him in Bengal within two years 'with a shippe out of England'.

Fitch was to spend the time meanwhile in exploring the eastern parts of India; and so, after his companion's departure he floated slowly down the river from Agra to Tanda in Bengal, stopping on the way at Allahābād, Benares, and Patna. From Tanda he made an excursion northwards to Kuch Bihār; after which he resumed his voyage down the Ganges to the Portuguese settlement at Hūgli, and thence proceeded to Chittagong. At both these places he would find Portuguese traders, and with them he probably established friendly relations without difficulty. They did not recognize the authority of the Viceroy of Goa or any other Portuguese official, and their attitude towards a fellow European would not be influenced by any trouble he had had with the representatives of their government elsewhere. It was in a vessel belonging to one of them that Fitch voyaged to Pegu, and we may infer that it was in association with his Portuguese friends that he now visited Kachua, Srīpur, and Sonārgāon in Eastern Bengal.

In November 1586, there being no sign of Newbery's promised return, our traveller decided to extend his travels in an easterly direction, and accordingly sailed for Pegu. Landing at Kusima (now Bassein), he there took boat and proceeded along the intricate network of inland waterways to a place he calls Macao, whence a short journey by land brought him to the city of Pegu. Of this place, of the royal court, and of the customs, &c., of the people, he gives a lengthy account. His next achievement was an expedition to Kiang-mai, in the Siamese Shan States, nearly two hundred miles north-east of Pegu—a hazardous venture which he relates in the most matter-of-fact manner. Returning to the latter place, he proceeded in January 1588 to Malacca, where he stayed seven weeks, and then made his way back to Pegu and so to Bengal, as the first stage of his homeward journey. He was doubtless able by this time to speak Portuguese fluently; and rather than venture the long and toilsome journey through Northern India and Persia, he decided to risk the sea-route by way of Cochin, in spite of the evident danger of a fresh imprisonment should his identity be discovered. Unfortunately he reached Cochin just too late to catch the last ship of the season, and had, in consequence, to spend nearly eight months there before he could get a passage to Goa. In that dangerous city he remained only three days, and then made his way to Chaul, where he found a ship which carried him to Ormus, another danger point—especially as he had to wait fifty days before he could get a passage to Basra. Once arrived at that port, he was fairly safe, and he managed to reach Aleppo without much trouble. After some delay he embarked for London, where he landed at the end of April 1591, after an absence of just over eight years.

On his arrival in England Fitch found that the charter of the Turkey Company had expired and that negotiations were proceeding for a fresh one. It was doubtless in connexion with these that he presented to Lord Burghley an 'ample relation of his wonderfull travailes', as Hakluyt tells us in the Dedication of the second volume of the *Principall Navigations* (1598–1600). Whether this was identical with the present narrative, or whether the latter was written specially for Hakluyt, we cannot tell. The result of the negotiations was the grant of a charter in January 1592, which united the two associations trading to Turkey and Venice respectively. The new body was known as the Levant Company, and among the privileges granted to it was the monopoly of the trade by land through the Turkish dominions 'into and from the East India', as discovered by Newbery and his companions. Fitch, by the way, is mentioned in this charter as a member of the new Company; as also in the subsequent charter of 1605. It is needless to say that no real attempt was made to develop commerce along this line. It had become evident that the most promising way to the Indies was by the Cape route, and now that England was definitely at war with King Philip there was no need to study the feelings of the Portuguese. James Lancaster had sailed on his first voyage in that direction in 1591; and although he failed to get farther than the Nicobars and Penang, it was proved that the enterprise was at least feasible, and from this period successive expeditions were dispatched from England and Holland until the aim was reached.

Of the rest of Fitch's life but meagre details are available. Evidently he went again to the Levant, for in the autumn of

1596 he was at Aleppo and was elected consul by the English merchants there—an appointment which was disallowed by the Levant Company (British Museum: Lansdowne MSS., no. 241, ff. 52, 294). Probably he thereupon returned to England, for Hakluyt speaks of him (about 1599) as 'living here in London';[1] while the 'Mr. Fitche' whom the East India Company decided, on October 1, 1600, to consult regarding the lading of their ships is certainly our traveller. The Court Minutes of that Company are missing between August 1603 and December 1606, or possibly some further references to him would be forthcoming; but he is clearly mentioned in the minutes for December 31, 1606, when it was directed that the proper titles for the royal letters which were being prepared for various Eastern potentates should be inquired of Ralph Fitch.

Nothing has hitherto been known concerning the rest of our traveller's life, but I was recently fortunate enough to discover at Somerset House two hitherto unnoticed wills which seem to wind up the story and, further, to give us some clues to his family history. In both documents the testator describes himself as Ralph Fitch, citizen and leatherseller[2] of London, and in both he mentions a brother Thomas, a sister Frances, and a niece of the same Christian name. It is evident, therefore, that the two wills were made by the same person; and that this was the Fitch in whom we are interested hardly admits of a doubt. The earlier will (6 *Drury*) is dated February 14, 1583 (the time of our traveller's departure from England), and an interesting feature is that it was duly proved by the executor in February 1590, the testator being described in the Probate Act Book as having died beyond the seas. Evidently, as nothing had been heard of the traveller for several years, his death was presumed and his estate administered; so his reappearance a year later must have been a complete surprise. The second will (81 *Wood*) was made on October 3 and proved on October 15, 1611, and Fitch's death must therefore have occurred between those two dates. The Probate Act Book adds that he belonged to the parish of St. Catherine Cree, and this suggests that he was buried in that church, situated in Leadenhall Street. Unfortunately, the parish registers of the time are not extant. A further point to be noted is that neither will mentions a wife or a child. The presumption is that the testator was a bachelor;

[1] That Hakluyt was personally acquainted with Fitch is suggested also by the passage quoted in a note on p. 40.

[2] Meaning, presumably, that he was a member of the Leathersellers Company. I have not succeeded in obtaining from that body any information on the subject.

and this alone, in a much marrying age, points to his having spent most of his life abroad.

Fitch's story of his experiences was first given to the world by Richard Hakluyt in the second (1598–1600) edition of his *Principall Navigations* (vol. ii, part i, p. 250). Considering the time covered by his wanderings and the many countries he visited, it is disappointingly brief; but probably he kept no journal, and had therefore to rely mainly on his recollections. This, and possibly a distrust of his own literary abilities, may explain why he copied so closely the narrative of Cesar Federici, the Venetian merchant who, starting in 1563, travelled by way of Basra and Ormus to Goa, paid visits to Gujarāt, Vijayanagar, and most of the Portuguese settlements on the coast of India, and then proceeded to Pegu, Malacca, &c., returning to Venice in 1581. His *Viaggio* was published there in 1587, and an English version by Thomas Hickock appeared in London the following year. Hakluyt has printed this translation in juxtaposition to Fitch's own account; and a comparison shows that our English traveller, whenever his route coincided with that of Federici, followed almost slavishly the latter's wording. The narrative of another contemporary traveller, Gasparo Balbi, who was in Pegu about the same time as Fitch, may also have been accessible to our author, since it was published at Venice in 1590; but I can find no convincing evidence that he made use of it.

In 1625 the Rev. Samuel Purchas reprinted the story (with one short omission) in his famous *Purchas His Pilgrimes* (part ii, book x, chap. 6), and a similar compliment has been paid to it in several other collections of travels, both English and foreign. A special volume was devoted to the subject in 1899 by Mr. J. Horton Ryley, entitled *Ralph Fitch: England's Pioneer to India*, containing the traveller's narrative and letters, together with a number of related documents. Though Mr. Ryley's work affords some useful information regarding the historical setting of Fitch's journey, it is weak on the geographical side; but, apart from this, no excuse is necessary for repeating in the present work a narrative of such absorbing interest. The text followed is that given by Hakluyt.

In the yeere of our Lord 1583, I Ralph Fitch of London, marchant, being desirous to see the countreys of the East India, in the company of M. John Newberie, marchant (which had beene at Ormus once before), of William Leedes, jeweller, and James Story, painter, being chiefly set foorth by the

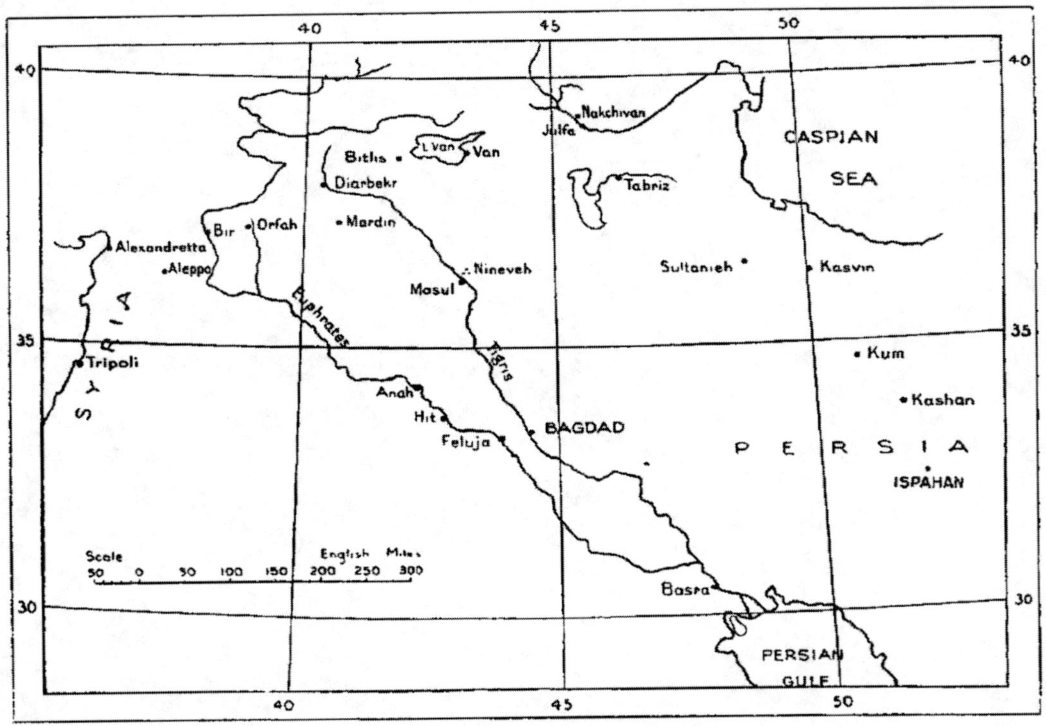

MESOPOTAMIA

right worshipfull Sir Edward Osborne, knight, and M. Richard Staper, citizens and marchants of London, did ship my selfe in a ship of London called the *Tyger*, wherein we went for Tripolis in Syria; and from thence we tooke the way for Aleppo, which we went in seven dayes with the carovan. Being in Aleppo, and finding good company, we went from thence to Birra, which is two dayes and an halfe travaile with camels.

Birra [Bir, or Birijik] is a little towne, but very plentifull of victuals; and neere to the wall of the towne runneth the river of Euphrates. Here we bought a boate and agreed with a master and bargemen, for to go to Babylon. These boats be but for one voiage; for the streame doth runne so fast downewardes that they cannot returne. They carie you to a towne which they call Felugia [Feluja], and there you sell the boate for a litle money, for that which cost you fiftie [1] at Birra you sell there for seven or eight. From Birra to Felugia is sixteene dayes journey. It is not good that one boate goe alone, for if it should chance to breake, you should have much a doe to save your goods from the Arabians, which be alwayes there abouts robbing; and in the night, when your boates be made fast, it is necessarie that you keepe good watch, for the Arabians that bee theeves will come swimming and steale your goods and flee away, against which a gunne is very good, for they doe feare it very much. In the river of Euphrates from Birra to Felugia there be certaine places where you pay custome, so many medines [2] for a some [3] or camels lading, and certaine raysons and sope, which is for the sonnes of Aborise,[4] which is lord of the Arabians and all that great desert, and hath some villages upon the river. Felugia, where you unlade your goods which come from Birra, is a little village; from whence you goe to Babylon in a day.

Babylon [Bagdad] is a towne not very great but very populous, and of great traffike of strangers, for that it is the

[1] In copying from Federici, Fitch has omitted the word *sequins* or (as the English translation has it) *chickens*. This was the gold *zecchino* of Venice, worth about seven shillings English.

[2] A Turkish coin equivalent to about three halfpence.

[3] Probably a misprint for 'seme', a load.

[4] Abu Rish. Balbi speaks of him as living at Anah, on the Euphrates.

way to Persia, Turkia and Arabia ; and from thence doe goe carovans for these and other places. Here are great store of victuals, which come from Armenia downe the river of Tygris. They are brought upon raftes made of goates skinnes blowne full of winde and bordes layde upon them ; and thereupon they lade their goods, which are brought downe to Babylon ; which being discharged, they open their skinnes, and carry them backe by camels, to serve another time. Babylon in times past did belong to the kingdome of Persia, but nowe is subject to the Turke. Over against Babylon there is a very faire village, from whence you passe to Babylon upon a long bridge made of boats, and tyed to a great chaine of yron, which is made fast on either side of the river. When any boates are to passe up or downe the river, they take away certaine of the boates untill they be past.

The Tower of Babel [1] is built on this side the river Tygris, towardes Arabia from the towne about seven or eight miles ; which tower is ruinated on all sides, and with the fall thereof hath made as it were a litle mountaine, so that it hath no shape at all. It was made of brickes dried in the sonne, and certaine canes and leaves of the palme tree layed betwixt the brickes. There is no entrance to be seene to goe into it. It doth stand upon a great plaine betwixt the rivers of Euphrates and Tygris.

By the river Euphrates, two dayes journey from Babylon, at a place called Ait [Hit], in a fielde neere unto it, is a strange thing to see—a mouth that doth continually throwe foorth against the ayre boyling pitch with a filthy smoke ; which pitch doth runne abroad into a great fielde which is alwayes full thereof. The Moores say that it is the mouth of hell. By reason of the great quantitie of it, the men of that countrey doe pitch their boates two or three inches thicke on the out side, so that no water doth enter into them. Their boates be called Danec [*danak*]. When there is great store of water in Tygris, you may goe from Babylon to Basora in 8 or 9 dayes ; if there be small store, it will cost you the more dayes.

Basora in times past was under the Arabians, but now is subject to the Turke. But some of them the Turke cannot

[1] The reference is evidently to the ruined tower called Akerkuf, situated in the desert about nine miles west of Bagdad.

subdue, for that they holde certaine ilandes in the river Euphrates which the Turke cannot winne of them. They be theeves all, and have no setled dwelling, but remove from place to place with their camels, goates, and horses, wives and children, and all. They have large blew gownes; their wives eares and noses are ringed very full of rings of copper and silver, and they weare rings of copper about their legs. Basora standeth neere the Gulfe of Persia, and is a towne of great trade of spices and drugges, which come from Ormus. Also there is great store of wheate, ryce, and dates growing thereabout, wherewith they serve Babylon and all the countrey, Ormus, and all the partes of India. I went from Basora to Ormus downe the Gulfe of Persia in a certaine shippe made of boordes and sowed together with cayro [coir], which is threede made of the huske of cocoes, and certaine canes or strawe leaves sowed upon the seames of the bordes; which is the cause that they leake very much. And so, having Persia alwayes on the left hande, and the coast of Arabia on the right hande, we passed many ilandes, and among others the famous ilande Baharim [Bahrein], from whence come the best pearles, which be round and orient.

Ormus is an island in circuit about five and twentie or thirtie miles, and is the driest island in the world, for there is nothing growing in it but onely salt; for their water, wood, or victuals, and all things necessary come out of Persia, which is about twelve miles from thence. All the ilands thereabout be very fruitfull, from whence all kinde of victuals are sent unto Ormus. The Portugales have a castle here, which standeth neere unto the sea, wherein there is a Captaine for the king of Portugale, having under him a convenient number of souldiers, wherof some part remaine in the castle and some in the towne. In this towne are marchants of all nations, and many Moores and Gentiles.[1] Here is very great trade of all sortes of spices, drugs, silke, cloth of silke, fine tapestrie of Persia, great store of pearles which come from the Isle of Baharim, and are the best pearles of all others, and

[1] This term (from the Portuguese *gentio*) was usually applied to Hindus; but in this narrative it is employed to denote any non-Muhammadan Asiatic.

many horses of Persia, which serve all India. They have a Moore to their king, which is chosen and governed by the Portugales. Their women are very strangely attyred, wearing on their noses, eares, neckes, armes and legges many rings set with jewels, and lockes of silver and golde in their eares, and a long barre of golde upon the side of their noses. Their eares with the weight of their jewels be worne so wide that a man may thrust three of his fingers into them. Here very shortly after our arrivall wee were put in prison, and had part of our goods taken from us by the Captaine of the castle, whose name was Don Mathias de Albuquerque;[1] and from hence the eleventh of October he shipped us and sent us for Goa unto the Viceroy, which at that time was Don Francisco de Mascarenhas. The shippe wherein we were imbarked for Goa belonged to the Captaine, and carried one hundred twentie and foure horses in it. All marchandise carried to Goa in a shippe wherein are horses pay no custome in Goa. The horses pay custome, the goods pay nothing; but if you come in a ship which bringeth no horses, you are then to pay eight in the hundred for your goods.

The first citie of India that we arrived at upon the fift of November, after we had passed the coast of Zindi [Sind], is called Diu, which standeth in an iland in the kingdome of Cambaia, and is the strongest towne that the Portugales have in those partes. It is but litle, but well stored with marchandise; for here they lade many great shippes with diverse commodities for the streits of Mecca, for Ormus, and other places, and these be shippes of the Moores and of Christians. But the Moores cannot passe, except they have a passeport from the Portugales. Cambaietta [Khāmbayat or Cambay] is the chiefe citie of that province, which is great and very populous, and fairely builded for a towne of the Gentiles; but if there happen any famine, the people will sell their children for very little. The last king of Cambaia was Sultan Badu,[2] which was killed at the siege of Diu, and shortly after

[1] Captain of Ormus 1583–6, and afterwards (1591–7) Viceroy at Goa.

[2] Sultān Bahādur, murdered by the Portuguese in 1537. The reference to the conquest of Gujarāt is an inaccurate version of Federici's account. The 'Great Mogor' (*o grão Mogor*) was the Portuguese way of describing the Mughal Emperor.

his citie was taken by the Great Mogor, which is the king of Agra and of Delli, which are fortie dayes journey from the country of Cambaia. Here the women weare upon their armes infinite numbers of rings made of elephants teeth, wherein they take so much delight that they had rather be without their meate then without their bracelets. Going from Diu, we come to Daman, the second towne of the Portugales in the countrey of Cambaia, which is distant from Diu fortie leagues. Here is no trade but of corne and rice. They have many villages under them which they quietly possesse in time of peace, but in time of warre the enemie is maister of them. From thence we passed by Basaim [Bassein], and from Basaim to Tana [Thana], at both which places is small trade but only of corne and rice. The tenth of November we arrived at Chaul, which standeth in the firme land. There be two townes, the one belonging to the Portugales and the other to the Moores. That of the Portugales is neerest to the sea, and commaundeth the bay, and is walled round about. A little above that is the towne of the Moores, which is governed by a Moore king called Xa-Maluco.[1] Here is great traffike for all sortes of spices and drugges, silke, and cloth of silke, sandales [sandalwood], elephants teeth, and much China worke, and much sugar which is made of the nutte called Gagara.[2] The tree is called the palmer [Port. *palmeiro*], which is the profitablest tree in the worlde. It doth alwayes beare fruit, and doth yeeld wine, oyle, sugar, vineger, cordes, coles; of the leaves are made thatch for the houses, sayles for shippes, mats to sit or lie on; of the branches they make their houses, and broomes to sweepe; of the tree wood for shippes. The wine doeth issue out of the toppe of the tree. They cut a branch of a bowe and binde it hard, and hange an earthen pot upon it, which they emptie every morning and every evening, and still it and put in certaine

[1] The Portuguese name for the Kings of Ahmadnagar was 'Nizamaluco', i. e. Nizām-ul-Mulk. Federici missed the first (unaccented) syllable, and wrote 'Zamalucco'; while Fitch, in copying him, gave the term a further twist.

[2] *Jagra* or palm-sugar. Fitch has here misunderstood Federici; but both are wrong in saying that the sugar is made from the coco-nut instead of from the sap extracted from the stem of the tree.

dried raysins, and it becommeth very strong wine in short time. Hither many shippes come from all partes of India, Ormus, and many from Mecca; heere be manie Moores and Gentiles. They have a very strange order among them. They worshippe a cowe, and esteeme much of the cowes doung to paint the walles of their houses. They will kill nothing, not so much as a louse; for they holde it a sinne to kill any thing. They eate no flesh, but live by rootes and ryce and milke. And when the husbande dieth, his wife is burned with him, if shee be alive; if shee will not, her head is shaven, and then is never any account made of her after. They say if they should be buried, it were a great sinne, for of their bodies there would come many wormes and other vermine, and when their bodies were consumed, those wormes would lacke sustenance, which were a sinne; therefore they will be burned. In Cambaia they will kill nothing, nor have any thing killed; in the towne they have hospitals to keepe lame dogs and cats, and for birds. They will give meat to the ants.

Goa is the most principal citie which the Portugals have in India, wherin the Viceroy remaineth with his court. It standeth in an iland, which may be 25 or 30 miles about. It is a fine citie, and for an Indian towne very faire. The iland is very faire, full of orchards and gardens, and many palmer trees, and hath some villages. Here bee many marchants of all nations. And the fleete which commeth every yeere from Portugal, which be foure, five, or sixe great shippes, commeth first hither. And they come for the most part in September, and remaine there fortie or fiftie dayes; and then goe to Cochin, where they lade their pepper for Portugall. Oftentimes they lade one in Goa; the rest goe to Cochin, which is from Goa an hundred leagues southward. Goa standeth in the countrey of Hidalcan,[1] who lieth in the countrey sixe or seven dayes journey. His chiefe citie is called Bisapor. At our comming we were cast into the prison, and examined before the Justice and demanded for letters, and were charged to be spies, but they could proove nothing by us. We continued in prison untill the two and twentie of December, and then we were set at libertie, putting in sureties for two thousand

[1] Ādil Khān (Ādil Shāh), i. e. the King of Bījāpur ('Bisapor').

duckats not to depart the towne; which sureties Father Stevens, an English Jesuite which we found there, and another religious man, a friend of his, procured for us. Our sureties name was Andreas Taborer, to whom we paid 2,150 duckats, and still he demaunded more: whereupon we made sute to the Viceroy and Justice to have our money againe, considering that they had had it in their hands neere five moneths and could proove nothing against us. The Viceroy made us a very sharpe answere, and sayd wee should be better sifted before it were long, and that they had further matter against us. Whereupon we presently determined rather to seeke our liberties, then to bee in danger for ever to be slaves in the country, for it was told us we should have the strapado.[1] Wherupon presently, the fift day of April 1585 [2] in the morning, we ranne from thence. And being set over the river, we went two dayes on foote, not without feare, not knowing the way nor having any guide, for we durst trust none. One of the first townes which we came unto is called Bellergan [Belgaum], where there is a great market kept of diamants, rubies, saphires, and many other soft stones. From Bellergan we went to Bisapor, which is a very great towne where the king doeth keepe his court. Hee hath many Gentiles in his court, and they bee great idolaters. And they have their idols standing in the woods, which they call Pagodes.[3] Some bee like a cowe, some like a monkie, some like buffles, some like peacockes, and some like the devill. Here be very many elephants which they goe to warre withall. Here they have good store of gold and silver. Their houses are of stone, very faire and high. From hence wee went for Gulconda, the king whereof is called Cutup de lashach.[4] Here and in the kingdome of Hidalcan, and in the countrey of the king of Decan [Ahmadnagar], bee the diamants found of the olde water. It is a very faire

[1] A punishment in which the offender was hoisted by a rope and then allowed to fall a considerable distance, thus jerking him violently.

[2] Probably 1584 (see p. 3).

[3] Pagode or Pagoda had in India three meanings: (1) an idol, (2) the temple in which it stood, (3) a coin, so called from the figure of a god impressed upon it.

[4] Kutb Shāh, the title of the kings of Golconda. The city of Golconda, situated about five miles west of Hyderābād, is now in ruins.

towne, pleasant, with faire houses of bricke and timber. It aboundeth with great store of fruites and fresh water. Here the men and the women do go with a cloth bound about their middles, without any more apparell. We found it here very hote. The winter beginneth here about the last of May. In these partes is a porte or haven called Masulipatan, which standeth eight dayes journey from hence toward the Gulfe of Bengala, whether come many shippes out of India,[1] Pegu, and Sumatra, very richly laden with pepper, spices, and other commodities. The countrie is very good and fruitfull.

From thence [i. e. from Golconda] I went to Servidore, which is a fine countrey, and the king is called the King of Bread.[2] The houses here bee all thatched and made of lome. Here be many Moores and Gentiles, but there is small religion among them. From thence I went to Bellapore,[3] and so to Barrampore,[4] which is in the country of Zelabdim Echebar [Jalāluddīn Akbar]. In this place their money is made of a kind of silver, round and thicke, to the value of twentie pence, which is very good silver. It is marveilous great and a populous countrey. In their winter, which is in June, July, and August, there is no passing in the streetes but with horses, the waters be so high. The houses are made of lome and thatched. Here is great store of cotton cloth made, and painted clothes of cotton wooll. Here groweth great store of corne and rice. We found mariages great store, both in townes and villages in many places where wee passed, of boyes of eight or ten yeeres, and girles of five or six yeeres old. They both do ride upon one horse very trimly decked, and are caried through the towne with great piping and playing, and so returne home and eate of a banket made of rice and fruits, and there they daunce the most part of the night, and so make an ende of the marriage. They lie not together untill they be ten yeeres old. They say they marry their children so yoong, because

[1] Here, and in certain other passages, Portuguese India appears to be meant.

[2] Possibly Fitch meant Barīd, the family name of the dynasty of Bīdar, then an independent state. 'Servidore' may be a confused form of Bīdar, the capital, situated about 70 miles NW. of Golconda.

[3] Bālāpur, in Akola district, Berār.

[4] Burhānpur, on the Tāpti, capital of Khāndesh.

it is an order that, when the man dieth, the woman must be burned with him ; so that if the father die, yet they may have a father in lawe to helpe to bring up the children which bee maried ; and also that they will not leave their sonnes without wives, nor their daughters without husbands. From thence we went to Mandoway,[1] which is a very strong towne. It was besieged twelve yeeres by Zelabdim Echebar before hee could winne it. It standeth upon a very great high rocke, as the most part of their castles doe, and was of a very great circuite. From hence wee went to Ugini [Ujjain] and Serringe [Sironj], where wee overtooke the ambassadour[2] of Zelabdim Echebar with a marveilous great company of men, elephants, and camels. Here is great trade of cotton and cloth made of cotton, and great store of drugs. From thence we went to Agra, passing many rivers, which by reason of the raine were so swollen that wee waded and swamme oftentimes for our lives.

Agra is a very great citie and populous, built with stone, having faire and large streetes, with a faire river running by it, which falleth into the Gulfe of Bengala. It hath a faire castle and a strong, with a very faire ditch. Here bee many Moores and Gentiles. The king is called Zelabdim Echebar ; the people for the most part call him the Great Mogor. From thence we went for Fatepore [Fatehpur Sīkri], which is the place where the king kept his court. The towne is greater then Agra, but the houses and streetes be not so faire. Here dwell many people, both Moores and Gentiles. The king hath in Agra and Fatepore (as they doe credibly report) 1,000 elephants, thirtie thousand horses, 1,400 tame deere, 800 concubines : such store of ounces,[3] tigers, buffles, cocks, and haukes, that is very strange to see. He keepeth a great court, which they call Dericcan.[4] Agra and Fatepore are two very great cities,

[1] Māndu, in Dhār state, about thirty miles SW. of Mhow. The story of the siege is mythical.

[2] Presumably this was Abdullah Khān, who was sent by Akbar to Goa in 1582 (see Mr. Vincent Smith's *Akbar*, p. 205). This might have settled the question of the year, but unfortunately the date of the ambassador's return to court is not on record.

[3] Cheetahs (hunting leopards).

[4] Persian *darīkhāna*, a palace.

either of them much greater then London and very populous. Betweene Agra and Fatepore are 12 miles,[1] and all the way is a market of victuals and other things, as full as though a man were still in a towne, and so many people as if a man were in a market. They have many fine cartes, and many of them carved and gilded with gold, with two wheeles, which be drawen with two litle buls about the bignesse of our great dogs in England, and they will runne with any horse, and carie two or three men in one of these cartes; they are covered with silke or very fine cloth, and be used here as our coches be in England. Hither is great resort of marchants from Persia and out of India, and very much marchandise of silke and cloth, and of precious stones, both rubies, diamants, and pearles. The king is apparelled in a white cabie [i. e. a muslin tunic] made like a shirt tied with strings on the one side, and a litle cloth on his head coloured oftentimes with red or yealow. None come into his house but his eunuches which keepe his women. Here in Fatepore we staied all three untill the 28 of September 1585,[2] and then Master John Newberie tooke his journey toward the citie of Lahor, determining from thence to goe for Persia and then for Aleppo or Constantinople (whether hee could get soonest passage unto); and directed me to goe for Bengala and for Pegu, and did promise me, if it pleased God, to meete me in Bengala within two yeeres with a shippe out of England. I left William Leades the jeweller in service with the king Zelabdim Echebar in Fatepore, who did entertaine him very well, and gave him an house and five slaves, an horse, and every day sixe S. S. [shillings] in money.

I went from Agra to Satagam[3] in Bengala, in the companie of one hundred and fourescore boates laden with salt, opium, hinge [asafetida: Hindūstāni *hing*], lead, carpets, and divers other commodities, downe the river Jemena. The chiefe marchants are Moores and Gentiles. In these countries they have many strange ceremonies. The Bramanes, which are

[1] Really twenty-three miles; but Fitch is probably reckoning by the Indian *kos*, each of which is $1\frac{1}{2}$ or 2 miles.

[2] See p. 3 for a suggestion that this was probably 1584.

[3] Sātgāon, on a creek which entered the Hūgli river just above the town of Hūgli. It was the silting up of this creek which transferred the trade to the latter place, called by the Portuguese Porto Piqueno.

their priests, come to the water and have a string about their necks made with great ceremonies, and lade up water with both their hands, and turne the string first with both their hands within, and then one arme after the other out. Though it be never so cold, they will wash themselves in cold water or in warme. These Gentiles will eate no flesh nor kill any thing. They live with rice, butter, milke, and fruits. They pray in the water naked, and dresse their meat and eate it naked, and for their penance they lie flat upon the earth, and rise up and turne themselves about 30 or 40 times, and use to heave up their hands to the sunne, and to kisse the earth, with their armes and legs stretched along out, and their right leg alwayes before the left. Every time they lie downe, they make a score on the ground with their finger, to know when their stint is finished. The Bramanes marke themselves in the foreheads, eares, and throates with a kind of yellow geare which they grind, and every morning they do it. And they have some old men which go in the streetes with a boxe of yellow pouder, and marke men on their heads and necks as they meet them. And their wives do come by 10, 20, and 30 together to the water side singing, and there do wash themselves, and then use their ceremonies, and marke themselves in their foreheds and faces, and cary some with them, and so depart singing. Their daughters be maried at or before the age of 10 yeres. The men may have 7 wives. They be a kind of craftie people, worse then the Jewes. When they salute one another, they heave up their hands to their heads, and say Rame, Rame [*Ram*].

From Agra I came to Prage [Prayāga, now Allahābād], where the river Jemena entreth into the mightie river Ganges, and Jemena looseth his name. Ganges commeth out of the northwest, and runneth east into the Gulfe of Bengala. In those parts there are many tigers and many partriges and turtle-doves, and much other foule. Here be many beggers in these countries which goe naked, and the people make great account of them ; they call them Schesche.[1] Here I sawe one which was a monster among the rest. He would have nothing upon him ; his beard was very long ; and with the haire of his

[1] Possibly, as Dr. Thomas suggests, the Sanskrit *shishya*, a disciple.

head he covered his privities. The nailes of some of his fingers were two inches long, for he would cut nothing from him; neither would he speake. He was accompanied with eight or tenne, and they spake for him. When any man spake to him, he would lay his hand upon his brest and bowe himselfe, but would not speake. Hee would not speake to the king. We went from Prage downe Ganges, the which is here very broad. Here is great store of fish of sundry sorts, and of wild foule, as of swannes, geese, cranes, and many other things. The countrey is very fruitfull and populous. The men for the most part have their faces shaven, and their heads very long, except some which bee all shaven save the crowne; and some of them are as though a man should set a dish on their heads and shave them round, all but the crowne. In this river of Ganges are many ilands. His water is very sweete and pleasant, and the countrey adjoyning very fruitfull. From thence wee went to Bannaras [Benares], which is a great towne, and great store of cloth is made there of cotton, and shashes [turban-clothes] for the Moores. In this place they be all Gentiles, and be the greatest idolaters that ever I sawe. To this towne come the Gentiles on pilgrimage out of farre countreys. Here alongst the waters side bee very many faire houses, and in all of them, or for the most part, they have their images standing, which be evill favoured, made of stone and wood, some like lions, leopards, and monkeis; some like men and women, and pecocks; and some like the devil with foure armes and 4 hands. They sit crosse legged, some with one thing in their hands, and some another. And by breake of day and before, there are men and women which come out of the towne and wash themselves in Ganges. And there are divers old men which upon places of earth made for the purpose, sit praying, and they give the people three or foure strawes, which they take and hold them betweene their fingers when they wash themselves; and some sit to marke them in the foreheads, and they have in a cloth a litle rice, barlie, or money, which, when they have washed themselves, they give to the old men which sit there praying. Afterwards they go to divers of their images, and give them of their sacrifices. And when they give, the old men say certaine prayers, and then is all

P. 20

THE GHĀTS AT BENARES

holy. And in divers places there standeth a kind of image which in their language they call Ada ; and they have divers great stones carved, whereon they poure water, and throw thereupon some rice, wheate, barly, and some other things. This Ada hath foure hands with clawes. Moreover, they have a great place made of stone like to a well, with steppes to goe downe ; wherein the water standeth very foule and stinketh, for the great quantitie of flowers, which continually they throwe into it, doe make it stinke. There be alwayes many people in it ; for they say when they wash themselves in it, that their sinnes be forgiven them, because God, as they say, did washe himselfe in that place. They gather up the sand in the bottome of it, and say it is holy. They never pray but in the water, and they wash themselves overhead, and lade up water with both their handes, and turne themselves about, and then they drinke a litle of the water three times, and so goe to their gods which stand in those houses. Some of them will wash a place which is their length, and then will pray upon the earth with their armes and legs at length out, and will rise up and lie downe, and kisse the ground twentie or thirtie times, but they will not stirre their right foote. And some of them will make their ceremonies with fifteene or sixteene pots litle and great, and ring a litle bel when they make their mixtures tenne or twelve times ; and they make a circle of water round about their pots and pray, and divers sit by them, and one that reacheth them their pots ; and they say divers things over their pots many times, and when they have done, they goe to their gods and strowe their sacrifices, which they thinke are very holy, and marke many of them which sit by in the foreheads, which they take as a great gift. There come fiftie and sometime an hundred together, to wash them in this well, and to offer to these idols. They have in some of these houses their idoles standing, and one sitteth by them in warme weather with a fanne to blowe winde upon them. And when they see any company comming, they ring a litle bell which hangeth by them, and many give them their almes, but especially those which come out of the countrey. Many of them are blacke and have clawes of brasse with long nayles, and some ride upon peacockes and other foules which be evill favoured, with long haukes bils, and some like one thing and some another, but none with a good face. Among the rest there is one which they make great account of; for they say hee giveth them all things both foode and apparell, and one sitteth alwayes by him with a fanne to make wind towards him.

Here some bee burned to ashes, some scorched in the fire and throwen into the water, and dogges and foxes doe presently eate them. The wives here doe burne with their husbands when they die; if they will not, their heads be shaven, and never any account is made of them afterwards. The people goe all naked save a litle cloth bound about their middle. Their women have their necks, armes and eares decked with rings of silver, copper, tinne, and with round hoopes made of ivorie, adorned with amber stones and with many agats, and they are marked with a great spot of red in their foreheads and a stroke of red up to the crowne, and so it runneth three maner of wayes. In their winter, which is our May, the men weare quilted gownes of cotton like to our mattraces and quilted caps like to our great grocers morters, with a slit to looke out at, and so tied downe beneath their eares. If a man or woman be sicke and like to die, they will lay him before their idols all night, and that shall helpe him or make an ende of him. And if he do not mend that night, his friends will come and sit with him a litle and cry, and afterwards will cary him to the waters side and set him upon a litle raft made of reeds, and so let him goe downe the river. When they be maried, the man and the woman come to the water side, and there is an olde man which they call a Bramane (that is, a priest), a cowe, and a calfe, or a cowe with calfe. Then the man and the woman, cowe and calfe, and the olde man goe into the water together, and they give the olde man a white cloth of foure yards long, and a basket crosse bound with divers things in it; the cloth hee laieth upon the backe of the cowe, and then he taketh the cowe by the ende of the taile, and saith certaine wordes; and she hath a copper or a brasse pot full of water, and the man doeth hold his hand by the olde mans hand, and the wives hand by her husbands, and all have the cowe by the taile, and they poure water out of the pot upon the cowes taile, and it runneth through all their hands, and they lade up water with their handes, and then the olde man doeth tie him and her together by their clothes. Which done, they goe round about the cowe and calfe, and then they give somewhat to the poore which be alwayes there, and to the Bramane or priest they give the cowe and calfe, and afterward goe to divers of their idoles and offer money, and lie downe flat upon the ground and kisse it divers times, and then goe their way. Their chiefe idoles bee blacke and evill favoured, their mouthes monstrous, their eares gilded, and full of jewels, their teeth and eyes of gold, silver, and glasse, some having one thing in their handes and some another. You may not come into the houses where they stand with your shooes on. They have continually lampes burning before them.

From Bannaras I went to Patenaw [Patna] downe the river of Ganges; where in the way we passed many faire townes, and a countrey very fruitfull; and many very great rivers doe enter into Ganges, and some of them as great as Ganges, which cause Ganges to bee of a great breadth, and so broad that in the time of raine you cannot see from one side to the other. These Indians when they bee scorched[1] and throwen into the water, the men swimme with their faces downewards, the women with their faces upwards. I thought they tied something to them to cause them to doe so: but they say no. There be very many thieves in this countrey, which be like to the Arabians, for they have no certaine abode, but are sometime in one place and sometime in another. Here the women bee so decked with silver and copper that it is strange to see; they use no shooes by reason of the rings of silver and copper which they weare on their toes. Here at Patanaw they finde gold in this maner: they digge deepe pits in the earth, and washe the earth in great bolles, and therein they finde the gold, and they make the pits round about with bricke, that the earth fall not in. Patenaw is a very long and a great towne. In times past it was a kingdom, but now it is under Zelabdim Echebar, the Great Mogor. The men are tall and slender, and have many old folks among them; the houses are simple, made of earth and covered with strawe; the

[1] He is speaking of corpses partly burnt.

streetes are very large. In this towne there is a trade of cotton and cloth of cotton, much sugar, which they cary from hence to Bengala and India, very much opium and other commodities. He that is chiefe here under the king is called Tipperdas [Tripura Dās], and is of great account among the people. Here in Patenau I saw a dissembling prophet which sate upon an horse in the market place, and made as though he slept, and many of the people came and touched his feete with their hands, and then kissed their hands. They tooke him for a great man, but sure he was a lasie lubber. I left him there sleeping. The people of these countries be much given to such prating and dissembling hypocrites.

From Patanaw I went to Tanda,[1] which is in the land of Gouren [Gaur]. It hath in times past bene a kingdom, but now is subdued by Zelabdim Echebar. Great trade and traffique is here of cotton and of cloth of cotton. The people goe naked, with a litle cloth bound about their waste. It standeth in the countrey of Bengala. Here be many tigers, wild bufs, and great store of wilde foule : they are very great idolaters. Tanda standeth from the river Ganges a league, because in times past the river, flowing over the bankes, in time of raine did drowne the countrey and many villages, and so they do remaine. And the old way which the river Ganges was woont to run remaineth drie, which is the occasion that the citie doeth stand so farre from the water. From Agra downe the river Jemena, and downe the river Ganges, I was five moneths comming to Bengala ; but it may be sailed in much shorter time.

I went from Bengala into the country of Couche,[2] which

[1] Tanda, in Mālda district, became the capital of Bengal upon the decadence of the neighbouring city of Gaur. The old town has been swept away entirely by changes in the course of the Pāgla river.

[2] Fitch's visit to Kuch Bihār is a most interesting incident, and it is much to be deplored that his account of the country is so meagre. 'Suckel Counse', i. e. 'the White (Sanskrit *sukal*) Koch' (or Kuch), was perhaps used as one of the titles of the sovereign, though it should be noted that Sir Edward Gait, in his *History of Assam* (p. 59), is disposed to regard it as equivalent to Sukladhvaj, a title borne by Silarai, the famous brother of King Nar Nārāyan ; there is, however, the difficulty that Silarai had died a few years before Fitch's arrival. The statements about the propinquity of Cochin China and the importation of pepper

lieth 25 dayes journy northwards from Tanda. The king is a Gentile; his name is Suckel Counse. His countrey is great, and lieth not far from Cauchin China; for they say they have pepper from thence. The port is called Cacchegate. All the countrie is set with bambos or canes made sharpe at both the endes and driven into the earth, and they can let in the water and drowne the ground above knee deepe, so that men nor horses can passe. They poison all the waters if any wars be. Here they have much silke and muske, and cloth made of cotton. The people have eares which be marveilous great of a span long, which they draw out in length by devises when they be yong. Here they be all Gentiles, and they will kil nothing. They have hospitals for sheepe, goates, dogs, cats, birds, and for all other living creatures. When they be old and lame, they keepe them until they die. If a man catch or buy any quicke thing in other places and bring it thither, they wil give him mony for it or other victuals, and keepe it in their hospitals or let it go. They wil give meat to the ants. Their smal mony is almonds, which oftentimes they use to eat.

From thence I returned to Hugeli, which is the place where the Portugals keep in the country of Bengala; which standeth in 23 degrees of northerly latitude, and standeth a league from Satagan; they cal it Porto Piqueno. We went through the wildernes, because the right way was full of thieves; where we passed the countrey of Gouren, where we found but few villages, but almost all wildernes, and saw many buffes, swine and deere, grasse longer then a man, and very many tigers. Not far from Porto Piqueno south-westward, standeth an haven which is called Angeli,[1] in the countrey of Orixa. It

from thence must be based on some misunderstanding. 'Cacchegate', according to information kindly furnished by Sir Edward Gait, was the tract of country on the north of Kuch Bihār forming the eastern portion of the present district of Jalpaigūri. The name (Chechakhata) is still borne by a *taluk* in that region, near the town of Alīpur Duar.

Fitch's object in going in this direction was probably to make inquiries into the trade with China by way of Tibet (see *Cathay and the Way Thither*, 2nd ed., vol. iv, p. 176).

[1] Hijili, on the west side of the Hūgli river, at the mouth of the Rāsulpur river. It was for a long time a place of importance, as cargoes were landed there for transport up the Hūgli, but was gradually washed away.

was a kingdom of it selfe, and the king was a great friend to strangers. Afterwards it was taken by the king of Patan,[1] which was their neighbour, but he did not enjoy it long, but was taken by Zelabdim Echebar, which is king of Agra, Delli, and Cambaia. Orixa standeth 6 daies journey from Satagan, southwestward. In this place is very much rice, and cloth made of cotton, and great store of cloth which is made of grasse, which they call Yerva[2]; it is like a silke. They make good cloth of it, which they send for India[3] and divers other places. To this haven of Angeli come every yere many ships out of India, Negapatan, Sumatra, Malacca, and divers other places; and lade from thence great store of rice, and much cloth of cotton wooll, much sugar, and long pepper, great store of butter, and other victuals for India. Satagam is a faire citie for a citie of the Moores, and very plentifull of all things. Here in Bengala they have every day in one place or other a great market which they call Chandeau, and they have many great boats which they cal pericose,[4] wherewithall they go from place to place and buy rice and many other things; these boates have 24 or 26 oares to rowe them; they be great of burthen, but have no coverture. Here the Gentiles have the water of Ganges in great estimation, for having good water neere them, yet they will fetch the water of Ganges a great way off, and if they have not sufficient to drinke, they will sprinkle a litle on them, and then they thinke themselves well. From Satagam I travelled by the countrey of the king of Tippara or Porto Grande, with whom the Mogores or Mogen have almost continuall warres. The Mogen which be of the kingdom of Recon and Rame be stronger then the king of Tippara, so that Chatigan or Porto Grande is oftentimes under the king of Recon.[5]

[1] The Pathān or Afghān kings of Bengal. Orissa was conquered by one of them in 1568, and seven years later became part of Akbar's territories, though it was not definitely subjugated until 1592.

[2] Herba cloth, made from rhea or some similar fibre.

[3] See note 1 on p. 16.

[4] The 'porgos' or 'purgoos' of later writers. The word is possibly a corruption of the Port. *barca*.

[5] Porto Grand was the Portuguese name for Chittagong. 'Tippara' was a kingdom now represented by the small state of Hill Tippera. The 'Mogen' were the 'Mugs' of to-day, belonging to the western part of

There is a country 4 daies journie from Couche or Quicheu before mentioned, which is called Bottanter[1] and the citie Bottia, the king is called Dermain; the people whereof are very tall and strong, and there are marchants which come out of China, and they say out of Muscovia or Tartarie. And they come to buy muske, cambals,[2] agats, silke, pepper, and saffron like the saffron of Persia. The countrey is very great, 3 moneths journey. There are very high mountains in this countrey, and one of them so steep that when a man is 6 daies journey off it, he may see it perfectly. Upon these mountains are people which have eares of a spanne long; if their eares be not long, they call them apes. They say that when they be upon the mountaines, they see ships in the sea sayling to and fro; but they know not from whence they come, nor whether they go. There are marchants which come out of the East, they say, from under the sunne, which is from China, which have no beards, and they say there it is something warme. But those which come from the other side of the mountains, which is from the north, say there it is very cold. These northren merchants are apparelled with woollen cloth and hats, white hosen close, and bootes which be of Moscovia or Tartarie. They report that in their countrey they have very good horses, but they be litle; some men have foure, five, or sixe hundred horses and kine; they live with milke and fleshe. They cut the tailes of their kine, and sell them very deere, for they bee in great request, and much esteemed in those partes. The haire of them is a yard long, the rumpe is above a spanne long; they use to hang them for braverie upon the heades of their elephants; they bee much used in Pegu and China. They buie and sell by scores upon the ground. The people be very swift on foote.

From Chatigan in Bengala, I came to Bacola[3]; the king

Arakan (Fitch's 'Recon'). 'Rame' is supposed to have been the country round the present village of Ramu in the southern part of Chittagong district.

[1] Bhutān. There is no town in it which can be identified as 'Bottia', though the people are known as Bhotiās. 'Dermain' probably represents the Dharma Rājā, the spiritual head of the kingdom.

[2] Blankets or coarse woollen clothes (Sanskrit *kambala*).

[3] Bākla was the old name of much of the present district of Bākarganj, in Eastern Bengal. No town is known of that name, but Mr. H. Beve-

whereof is a Gentile, a man very well disposed and delighteth much to shoot in a gun. His countrey is very great and fruitful, and hath store of rice, much cotton cloth, and cloth of silke. The houses be very faire and high builded, the streetes large, the people naked, except a litle cloth about their waste. The women weare great store of silver hoopes about their neckes and armes, and their legs are ringed with silver and copper, and rings made of elephants teeth.

From Bacola I went to Serrepore which standeth upon the river of Ganges. The king is called Chondery.[1] They be all hereabout rebels against their king Zelabdim Echebar; for here are so many rivers and ilands, that they flee from one to another, whereby his horsemen cannot prevaile against them. Great store of cotton cloth is made here.

Sinnergan [2] is a towne sixe leagues from Serrepore, where there is the best and finest cloth made of cotton that is in all India. The chiefe king of all these countries is called Isacan, and he is chiefe of all the other kings, and is a great friend to all Christians. The houses here, as they be in the most part of India, are very litle, and covered with strawe, and have a fewe mats round about the wals, and the doore to keepe out the tygers and the foxes. Many of the people are very rich. Here they will eate no flesh, nor kill no beast; they live of rice, milke, and fruits. They goe with a litle cloth before them, and all the rest of their bodies is naked. Great store of cotton cloth goeth from hence, and much rice, wherewith they serve all India, Ceilon, Pegu, Malacca, Sumatra, and many other places.

I went from Serrepore the 28 of November 1586 for Pegu, in a small ship or foist of one Albert Caravallos. And so

ridge, in his manual of the district, suggests that Fitch is referring to the old capital, Kachua, on the west bank of the Tītulia river, about twenty-five miles south-east of Barisāl.

[1] Chānd Rai, a petty chief whose head-quarters were at Srīpur, near Rājābāri, at the confluence of the Meghna and the Padma. The latter river has long since washed away Srīpur.

[2] Sonārgāon, the capital of Eastern Bengal, 1351–1608, situated fifteen miles east of Dacca. Isā Khān was an Afghān chief of Khizrpur, near Nārāyanganj in Dacca district, who became leader of the Afghāns throughout Eastern Bengal and at one time ruled over a large tract of country.

passing downe Ganges, and passing by the island of Sundiva,[1] Porto Grande, or the countrie of Tippera, the kingdom of Recon and Mogen, leaving them on our left side with a faire wind at northwest, our course was south and by east, which brought us to the barre of Negrais in Pegu. If any contrary wind had come, we had throwen many of our things over-boord, for we were so pestered with people and goods that there was scant place to lie in. From Bengala to Pegu is 90 leagues. We entred the barre of Negrais, which is a brave barre and hath 4 fadomes water where it hath least. Three dayes after we came to Cosmin,[2] which is a very pretie towne, and standeth very pleasantly, very well furnished with all things. The people be very tall and well disposed; the women white, round faced, with litle eies. The houses are high built, set upon great high postes, and they go up to them with long ladders for feare of the tygers, which be very many. The countrey is very fruitful of all things. Here are very great figs, orenges, cocoes, and other fruits. The land is very high that we fall withall; but after we be entred the barre, it is very lowe and full of rivers, for they goe all too and fro in boates, which they call paroes,[3] and keepe their houses with wife and children in them.

From the barre of Nigrais to the citie of Pegu is ten dayes journey by the rivers. Wee went from Cosmin to Pegu in paroes or boates; and passing up the rivers wee came to Medon, which is a prety towne, where there be a wonderfull number of paroes, for they keepe their houses and their markets in them all upon the water. They rowe too and fro, and have all their marchandizes in their boates with a great sombrero[4] or shadow over their heads to keepe the sunne from them, which is as broad as a great cart wheele made of the leaves of the coco trees and fig trees, and is very light.

From Medon we went to Dela,[5] which is a very faire towne,

[1] The island of Sandwip, off the coast of Chittagong district.

[2] Kusima, the Bassein of to-day, in the Irrawaddy delta.

[3] Port. *parão*, from an Indian word meaning a boat.

[4] Port. *sumbreiro*, an umbrella.

[5] 'Medon' cannot be identified. 'Dela' or 'Dala' was the name of a large district to the west of Rangoon, and it is still applied to the part of the city which lies across the river. Fitch, however, is referring

and hath a faire port into the sea, from whence go many ships to Malacca, Mecca, and many other places. Here are 18 or 20 very great and long houses, where they tame and keep many elephants of the kings; for there about in the wildernesse they catch the wilde elephants. It is a very fruitfull countrey. From Dela we went to Cirion,[1] which is a good towne, and hath a faire porte into the sea, whither come many ships from Mecca, Malacca, Sumatra, and from divers other places. And there the ships staie and discharge, and send up their goods in paroes to Pegu. From Cirion we went to Macao,[2] which is a pretie towne; where we left our boats or paroes, and in the morning taking Delingeges,[3] which are a kind of coches made of cords and cloth quilted, and caried upon a stang [i. e. a pole] betweene 3 or 4 men, we came to Pegu the same day.

Pegu is a citie very great, strong, and very faire, with walles of stone, and great ditches round about it. There are two townes, the old towne and the newe. In the olde towne are all the marchants strangers, and very many marchants of the countrey. All the goods are sold in the olde towne, which is very great, and hath many suburbes round about it, and all the houses are made of canes which they call bambos, and bee covered with strawe. In your house you have a warehouse which they call Godon [godown], which is made of bricke to put your goods in; for oftentimes they take fire and burne in an houre foure or five hundred houses, so that, if the Godon were not, you should bee in danger to have all burned, if any winde should rise, at a trice. In the newe towne is the king, and all his nobilitie and gentrie. It is a citie very great and populous, and is made square and with very faire walles, and a great ditch round about it full of water, with many crocodiles in it; it hath twenty gates, and they bee made of stone, for every square five gates. There are also many turrets

to the old capital of the district, now called Twante, situated at the head of a creek, about sixteen miles south-west of Rangoon.

[1] Syriam, on the Pegu river, about ten miles east of Rangoon.

[2] Federici says that this place was about twelve miles from Pegu. Yule suggests its identification with the pagoda of Mahkau (*Mission to Ava*, p. 211 *n.*).

[3] Talaing (i. e. Peguan) *dalin*, a litter. I have to thank Mr. C. O. Blagden and Sir Richard Temple for explaining these Talaing words.

for centinels to watch, made of wood, and gilded with golde very faire. The streets are the fairest that ever I saw, as straight as a line from one gate to the other, and so broad that tenne or twelve men may ride a front thorow them. On both sides of them at every mans doore is set a palmer tree, which is the nut tree; which make a very faire shew and a very commodious shadow, so that a man may walke in the shade all day. The houses be made of wood, and covered with tiles. The kings house is in the middle of the city, and is walled and ditched round about; and the buildings within are made of wood very sumptuously gilded, and great workemanship is upon the forefront, which is likewise very costly gilded. And the house wherein his pagode or idole standeth is covered with tiles of silver, and all the walles are gilded with golde. Within the first gate of the kings house is a great large roome [i. e. open space], on both sides whereof are houses made for the kings elephants, which be marvellous great and faire, and are brought up to warres and in service of the king. And among the rest he hath foure white elephants, which are very strange and rare; for there is none other king which hath them but he; if any other king hath one, hee will send unto him for it. When any of these white elephants is brought unto the king, all the merchants in the city are commanded to see them, and to give him a present of halfe a ducat, which doth come to a great summe, for that there are many merchants in the city. After that you have given your present you may come and see them at your pleasure, although they stand in the kings house. This king in his title is called the king of the white elephants. If any other king have one, and will not send it him, he will make warre with him for it; for he had rather lose a great part of his kingdome then not to conquere him. They do very great service unto these white elephants; every one of them standeth in an house gilded with golde, and they doe feede in vessels of silver and gilt. One of them, when he doth go to the river to be washed, as every day they do, goeth under a canopy of cloth of golde or of silke carried over him by sixe or eight men, and eight or ten men goe before him playing on drummes, shawmes, or other instruments; and when he is washed and commeth out of the river, there is a gentleman which doth wash his feet in a silver basin ; which is his office given him by the king. There is no such account made of any blacke elephant, be he never so great. And surely there be woonderfull faire and great, and some be nine cubites in height. And they do report that the king hath above five thousand elephants of warre, besides many other which be not taught to fight. This king hath a very large place wherein he taketh the wilde elephants. It standeth about a mile from Pegu, builded with a faire court within, and is in a great grove or wood ; and there be many huntsmen, which go into the wildernesse with she elephants, for without the she they are not to be taken. And they be taught for that purpose, and every hunter hath five or sixe of them ; and they say that they anoint the she elephants with a certaine ointment, which when the wild elephant doth smell, he will not leave her. When they have brought the wilde elephant neere unto the place, they send word unto the towne, and many horsemen and footmen come out and cause the she elephant to enter into a strait way which doeth goe to the palace, and the she and he do runne in, for it is like a wood ; and when they be in, the gate doth shut. Afterward they get out the female ; and when the male seeth that he is left alone, he weepeth and crieth, and runneth against the walles, which be made of so strong trees that some of them doe breake their teeth with running against them. Then they pricke him with sharpe canes, and cause him to go into a strait house, and there they put a rope about his middle and about his feet, and let him stand there three or foure dayes without eating or drinking ; and then they bring a female to him, with meat and drinke, and within few dayes he becommeth tame. The chiefe force of the king is in these elephants. And when they go into the warres they set a frame of wood upon their backes, bound with great cordes, wherein sit foure or sixe men, which fight with gunnes, bowes and arrowes, darts and other weapons. And they say that their skinnes are so thicke that a pellet of an harquebush will scarse pearce them, except it be in some tender place. Their weapons be very badde. They have gunnes, but shoot very badly in them ; darts and swords short without points.

The king keepeth a very great state ; when he sitteth

abroad (as he doth every day twise) all his noble men, which they call Shemines [Talaing *smin*], sit on ech side, a good distance off, and a great guard without them. The court yard is very great. If any man will speake with the king, he is to kneele downe, to heave up his hands to his head, and to put his head to the ground three times, when he entreth, in the middle way, and when he commeth neere to the king; and then he sitteth downe and talketh with the king. If the king like well of him, he sitteth neere him within three or foure paces; if he thinke not well of him, he sitteth further off. When he goeth to warre, he goeth very strong. At my being there, he went to Odia [1] in the countrey of Siam, with three hundred thousand men and five thousand elephants. Thirty thousand men were his guard. These people do eate roots, herbs, leaves, dogs, cats, rats, serpents, and snakes; they refuse almost nothing. When the king rideth abroad, he rideth with a great guard and many noblemen; oftentimes upon an elephant with a fine castle upon him very fairely gilded with gold; and sometimes upon a great frame like an horsliter, which hath a little house upon it covered over head, but open on the sides, which is all gilded with golde, and set with many rubies and saphires, whereof he hath infinite store in his country, and is caried upon sixteene or eighteene mens shoulders. This coach in their language is called Serrion.[2] Very great feasting and triumphing is many times before the king, both of men and women. This king hath little force by sea, because hee hath but very few ships. He hath houses full of golde and silver, and bringeth in often, but spendeth very little, and hath the mines of rubies and saphires, and spinelles. Neere unto the palace of the king, there is a treasure woonderfull rich; the which because it is so neere, he doth not account of it; and it standeth open for all men to see, in a great walled court with two gates, which be alwayes open. There are foure houses gilded very richly, and covered with leade; in every one of them are Pagodes or images of huge stature and great value. In the first is the picture [i. e. image]

[1] Ayuthia, the old capital of Siam, situated on an island in the Menam, about sixty miles from the sea.

[2] Talaing *saren*, pronounced *sarian*.

of a king in golde with a crowne of golde on his head full of great rubies and saphires, and about him there stand foure children of golde. In the second house is the picture of a man in silver, woonderfull great, as high as an house; his foot is as long as a man, and he is made sitting, with a crowne on his head very rich with stones. In the third house is the picture of a man greater then the other, made of brasse, with a rich crowne on his head. In the fourth and last house doth stand another, made of brasse, greater then the other, with a crowne also on his head very rich with stones. In another court not farre from this stand foure other Pagodes or idoles, marvellous great, of copper, made in the same place where they do stand; for they be so great that they be not to be remooved. They stand in foure houses gilded very faire, and are themselves gilded all over save their heads, and they shew like a blacke morian [i. e. helmet]. Their expences in gilding of their images are wonderfull. The king hath one wife and above three hundred concubines, by which they say he hath fourescore or fourescore and ten children. He sitteth in judgement almost every day. They use no speech, but give up their supplications written in the leaves of a tree with the point of an yron bigger then a bodkin. These leaves are an elle long, and about two inches broad; they are also double. He which giveth in his supplication doth stand in a place a little distance off with a present. If his matter be liked of, the king accepteth of his present, and granteth his request; if his sute be not liked of, he returneth with his present, for the king will not take it.

In India there are few commodities which serve for Pegu, except opium of Cambaia, painted cloth of S. Thome or of Masulipatan, and white cloth of Bengala, which is spent there in great quantity. They bring thither also much cotton yarne red coloured with a root which they called Saia [chay-root or Indian madder], which will never lose his colour; it is very wel solde here, and very much of it commeth yerely to Pegu. By your mony you lose much. The ships which come from Bengala, S. Thome, and Masulipatan come to the bar of Nigrais and to Cosmin. To Martavan [Martaban], a port of the sea in the kingdome of Pegu, come many ships from Malacca laden with sandall, porcelanes, and other wares of

China, and with camphora of Borneo, and pepper from Achen in Sumatra. To Cirion, a port of Pegu, come ships from Mecca with woollen cloth, scarlets, velvets, opium, and such like. There are in Pegu eight brokers, whom they call Tareghe,[1] which are bound to sell your goods at the price which they be woorth, and you give them for their labour two in the hundred; and they be bound to make your debt good, because you sell your marchandises upon their word. If the broker pay you not at his day, you may take him home, and keepe him in your house; which is a great shame for him. And if he pay you not presently, you may take his wife and children and his slaves, and binde them at your doore, and set them in the sunne; for that is the law of the countrey. Their current money in these parts is a kinde of brasse which they call Gansa,[2] wherewith you may buy golde, silver, rubies, muske, and all other things. The golde and silver is marchandise, and is worth sometimes more and sometimes lesse, as other wares be. This brasen money doeth goe by a weight which they call a biza[3]; and commonly this biza after our account is worth about halfe a crowne or somewhat lesse. The marchandise which be in Pegu are golde, silver, rubies, saphires, spinelles, muske, benjamin [benzoin] or frankincense, long pepper, tinne, leade, copper, lacca (whereof they make hard waxe), rice, and wine made of rice, and some sugar. The elephants doe eate the sugar canes, or els they would make very much. And they consume many canes likewise in making of their Varellaes[4] or idole temples, which are in great number, both great and small. They be made round like a sugar loafe; some are as high as a church, very broad beneath, some a quarter of a mile in compasse; within they be all earth done about with stone. They consume in these Varellaes great quantity of golde, for that they be all gilded aloft, and many of them from the top to the bottome; and every ten or twelve yeeres they must be new gilded, because the raine consumeth

[1] This is a South Indian term for a broker.

[2] A Malay word meaning bell-metal; but lead and other base metals were frequently used.

[3] Generally termed a 'viss', a weight of about $3\frac{1}{4}$ lb.

[4] This name for a pegoda is thought to be from a Malay word meaning an idol.

off the golde, for they stand open abroad. If they did not consume their golde in these vanities, it would be very plentifull and good cheape in Pegu.

About two dayes journey from Pegu there is a Varelle or pagode, which is the pilgrimage of the Pegues; it is called Dogonne,[1] and is of a woonderfull bignesse, and all gilded from the foot to the toppe. And there is an house by it wherein the Tallipoies[2] (which are their priests) doe preach. This house is five and fifty paces in length, and hath three pawnes[3] or walks in it, and forty great pillars gilded, which stand betweene the walks; and it is open on all sides, with a number of small pillars, which be likewise gilded; it is gilded with golde within and without. There are houses very faire round about for the pilgrims to lie in; and many goodly houses for the Tallipoies to preach in, which are full of images both of men and women, which are all gilded over with golde. It is the fairest place, as I suppose, that is in the world. It standeth very high, and there are foure wayes to it, which all along are set with trees of fruits, in such wise that a man may goe in the shade above two miles in length. And when their feast day is, a man can hardly passe by water or by land for the great presse of people; for they come from all places of the kingdome of Pegu thither at their feast. In Pegu they have many Tallipoies or priests, which preach against all abuses. Many men resort unto them. When they enter into their kiack,[4] that is to say, their holy place or temple, at the doore there is a great jarre of water with a cocke or a ladle in it, and there they wash their feet; and then they enter in, and lift up their hands to their heads first to their preacher, and then to the sunne, and so sit downe. The Tallipoies go very strangely apparelled, with one camboline [see p. 27] or thinne cloth next to their body of a browne colour, another of yellow doubled many times upon their shoulder, and those two be girded to them with a broad girdle; and they have a skinne of leather hanging on a string about their necks, whereupon

[1] The well-known Shwé or Golden Dagon, near Rangoon.
[2] Talaing *tala poe*, 'my lord', a form of address to Buddhist monks.
[3] Covered walks or colonnades.
[4] Talaing *kyāk*, a temple or an object of worship.

they sit, bare headed and bare footed, for none of them weareth shooes; with their right armes bare and a great broad sombrero or shadow in their hands to defend them in the summer from the sunne, and in the winter from the raine. When the Tallipoies or priests take their orders, first they go to schoole untill they be twenty yeres olde or more, and then they come before a Tallipoie appointed for that purpose, whom they call Rowli.[1] He is of the chiefest and most learned, and he opposeth [i. e. questions] them, and afterward examineth them many times, whether they will leave their friends and the company of all women, and take upon them the habit of a Tallipoie. If any be content, then he rideth upon an horse about the streets very richly apparelled, with drummes and pipes, to shew that he leaveth the riches of the world to be a Tallipoie. In few dayes after, he is caried upon a thing like an horsliter, which they call a serion, upon ten or twelve mens shoulders in the apparell of a Tallipoie, with pipes and drummes and many Tallipoies with him, and al his friends, and so they go with him to his house, which standeth without the towne, and there they leave him. Every one of them hath his house, which is very little, set upon six or eight posts, and they go up to them with a ladder of twelve or foureteene staves. Their houses be for the most part by the hie wayes side, and among the trees, and in the woods. And they go with a great pot made of wood or fine earth and covered, tied with a broad girdle upon their shoulder, which commeth under their arme, wherewith they go to begge their victuals which they eate, which is rice, fish, and herbs. They demand nothing, but come to the doore, and the people presently doe give them, some one thing, and some another, and they put all together in their potte; for they say they must eate of their almes, and therewith content themselves. They keepe their feasts by the moone: and when it is new moone they keepe their greatest feast; and then the people send rice and other things to that kiack or church of which they be, and there all the Tallipoies doe meete which be of that church, and eate the victuals which are sent them. When the Tallipoies do preach,

[1] This obscure term is discussed in the *Indian Antiquary*, vol. xxix, p. 28, and vol. xxxv, p. 268.

many of the people cary them gifts into the pulpit where they sit and preach. And there is one which sitteth by them to take that which the people bring. It is divided among them. They have none other ceremonies nor service that I could see, but onely preaching.

I went from Pegu to Jamahey,[1] which is in the countrey of the Langejannes, whom we call Jangomes[2]; it is five and twenty dayes journey northeast from Pegu; in which journey I passed many fruitfull and pleasant countreys. The countrey is very lowe, and hath many faire rivers. The houses are very bad, made of canes and covered with straw. Heere are many wilde buffes [buffaloes] and elephants. Jamahey is a very faire and great towne, with faire houses of stone, well peopled; the streets are very large, the men very well set and strong, with a cloth about them, bare headed and bare footed, for in all these countreys they weare no shooes. The women be much fairer then those of Pegu. Heere in all these countreys they have no wheat. They make some cakes of rice. Hether to Jamahey come many marchants out of China, and bring great store of muske, golde, silver, and many other things of China worke. Here is great store of victuals; they have such plenty that they will not milke the buffles, as they doe in all other places. Here is great store of copper and benjamin. In these countreys, when the people be sicke they make a vow to offer meat unto the divell, if they escape; and when they be recovered they make a banket with many pipes and drummes and other instruments, and dansing all the night, and their friends come and bring gifts, cocos, figges, arrecaes, and other fruits, and with great dauncing and rejoycing they offer to the divell, and say they give the divel to eat and drive him out. When they be dancing and playing, they will cry and hallow very loud; and in this sort they say they drive him away. And when they be sicke, a Tallipoy or two every night doth sit by them and sing, to please the divell that he should not hurt them. And if any die, he is caried upon a

[1] Kiang-mai or Zimmé, in the north-western part of Siam.

[2] Lan-chan is properly Luan Praban, on the Mekong; but it is used here loosely for all the Laos states. 'Jangoma' was the Portuguese form of Kiang-mai.

great frame made like a tower, with a covering all gilded with golde made of canes, caried with foureteene or sixteene men, with drummes and pipes and other instruments playing before him, to a place out of the towne and there is burned. He is accompanied with all his friends and neighbours, all men; and they give to the Tallipoies or priests many mats and cloth; and then they returne to the house and there make a feast for two dayes; and then the wife with all the neighbours wives and her friends go to the place where he was burned, and there they sit a certaine time and cry, and gather the pieces of bones which be left unburned and bury them, and then returne to their houses and make an end of all mourning. And the men and women which be neere of kin do shave their heads; which they do not use except it be for the death of a friend, for they much esteeme of their haire.

Caplan [1] is the place where they finde the rubies, saphires, and spinelles; it standeth sixe dayes journey from Ava in the kingdome of Pegu. There are many great high hilles out of which they digge them. None may go to the pits but onely those which digge them.

In Pegu, and in all the countreys of Ava, Langejannes, Siam, and the Bramas,[2] the men weare bunches or little round balles in their privy members: some of them weare two and some three. They cut the skin and so put them in, one into one side and another into the other side; which they do when they be 25 or 30 yeeres olde, and at their pleasure they take one or more of them out as they thinke good. When they be maried the husband is, for every child which his wife hath, to put in one untill he come to three and then no more; for they say the women doe desire them. They were invented because they should not abuse the male sexe. For in times past all those countries were so given to that villany, that they were very scarse of people. It was also ordained that the women should not have past three cubits of cloth in their nether clothes, which they binde about them; which are so

[1] Kyatpyin, in the Ruby Mines district, about seventy-five miles NNE. of Ava, and six miles south-east of Mogok.

[2] Brama is the Portuguese form of Burma. Fitch uses it both for the country and the people.

strait, that when they go in the streets, they shew one side of the leg bare above the knee. The bunches aforesayd be of divers sorts; the least be as big as a litle walnut, and very round; the greatest are as big as a litle hennes egge. Some are of brasse and some of silver; but those of silver be for the king and his noble men. These are gilded and made with great cunning, and ring like a litle bell. There are some made of leade, which they call Selwy[1] because they ring but litle; and these be of lesser price for the poorer sort. The king sometimes taketh his out, and giveth them to his noblemen as a great gift; and because he hath used them, they esteeme them greatly. They will put one in, and heale up the place in seven or eight dayes.[2]

The Bramas which be of the kings countrey (for the king is a Brama) have their legs or bellies, or some part of their body, as they thinke good themselves, made black with certaine things which they have; they use to pricke the skinne, and to put on it a kinde of anile[3] or blacking, which doth continue alwayes. And this is counted an honour among them; but none may have it but the Bramas which are of the kings kinred.

These people weare no beards; they pull out the haire on their faces with little pinsons [pincers] made for that purpose. Some of them will let 16 or 20 haires grow together, some in one place of his face and some in another, and pulleth out all the rest; for he carieth his pinsons alwayes with him to pull the haires out assoone as they appeare. If they see a man with a beard they wonder at him. They have their teeth blacked, both men and women; for they say a dogge hath his teeth white, therefore they will blacke theirs.

The Pegues, if they have a sute in the law which is so doubtfull that they cannot well determine it, put two long canes into the water where it is very deepe; and both the parties go into the water by the poles, and there sit men to judge,

[1] Talaing *seluy*, bell-metal or some other alloy.

[2] Hakluyt in his edition (1601) of *The Discoveries of the World*, by Antonio Galvano, notes that Fitch 'brought divers of these bels into England'. On the practice see Yule (*op. cit.*, p. 208 *n.*).

[3] Indigo (Port. *anil* from Arabic *al-nil*, pronounced *an-nil*).

and they both do dive under the water, and he which remaineth longest under the water doth winne the sute.

The 10 of January I went from Pegu to Malacca, passing by many of the ports of Pegu, as Martavan, the iland of Tavi [Tavoy], from whence commeth great store of tinne which serveth all India, the ilands of Tanaseri [Tenasserim], Junsalaon [Junkseylon], and many others; and so came to Malacca the 8 of February, where the Portugals have a castle which standeth nere the sea. And the countrey fast without the towne belongeth to the Malayos, which is a kinde of proud people. They go naked with a cloth about their middle, and a litle roll of cloth about their heads. Hither come many ships from China and from the Malucos, Banda, Timor, and from many other ilands of the Javas, which bring great store of spices and drugs, and diamants and other jewels. The voyages into many of these ilands belong unto the Captaine of Malacca; so that none may goe thither without his licence; which yeeld him great summes of money every yeere. The Portugals heere have often times warres with the king of Achem, which standeth in the iland of Sumatra; from whence commeth great store of pepper and other spices every yeere to Pegu and Mecca within the Red Sea, and other places.

When the Portugals go from Macao in China to Japan, they carry much white silke, golde, muske, and porcelanes, and they bring from thence nothing but silver. They have a great caracke which goeth thither every yere, and she bringeth from thence every yere above sixe hundred thousand crusadoes[1]; and all this silver of Japan, and two hundred thousand crusadoes more in silver which they bring yeerely out of India, they imploy to their great advantage in China; and they bring from thence golde, muske, silke, copper, porcelanes, and many other things very costly and gilded. When the Portugals come to Canton in China to traffike, they must remaine there but certaine dayes; and when they come in at the gate of the city, they must enter their names in a booke, and when they goe out at night they must put out their names. They may not lie in the towne all night, but must lie in their boats with-

[1] A Portuguese gold coin, so called from having a cross upon it.

out the towne. And their dayes being expired, if any man remaine there, they are evill used and imprisoned. The Chinians are very suspitious and doe not trust strangers. It is thought that the king doth not know that any strangers come into his countrey. And further it is credibly reported that the common people see their king very seldome or not at all, nor may not looke up to that place where he sitteth. And when he rideth abroad he is caried upon a great chaire or serrion gilded very faire, wherein there is made a little house with a latise to looke out at; so that he may see them, but they may not looke up at him; and all the time that he passeth by them, they heave up their hands to their heads, and lay their heads on the ground, and looke not up untill he be passed. The order of China is, when they mourne, that they weare white thread shoes and hats of straw. The man doth mourne for his wife two yeeres; the wife for her husband three yeeres; the sonne for his father a yeere, and for his mother two yeres. And all the time which they mourne they keepe the dead in the house, the bowels being taken out and filled with chownam [*chunām*] or lime, and coffined; and when the time is expired they carry them out playing and piping, and burne them. And when they returne they pull off their mourning weeds, and marry at their pleasure. A man may keepe as many concubines as he will, but one wife onely. All the Chineans, Japonians, and Cauchin Chineans do write right downwards, and they do write with a fine pensill made of dogs or cats haire.

Laban [Labuan ?] is an iland among the Javas from whence come the diamants of the new water. And they finde them in the rivers; for the king will not suffer them to digge the rocke.

Jamba[1] is an iland among the Javas also, from whence come diamants. And the king hath a masse of earth which is golde; it groweth in the middle of a river, and when the king doth lacke gold, they cut part of the earth and melt it, whereof commeth golde. This masse of earth doth appeare but once in a yere; which is when the water is low, and this is in the moneth of April.

[1] Jambi, in Sumatra, may be meant; but it is not an island.

Bima [1] is another iland among the Javas, where the women travell and labour as our men do in England, and the men keepe house and go where they will.

The 29 of March 1588, I returned from Malacca to Martavan, and so to Pegu, where I remained the second time untill the 17 of September, and then I went to Cosmin, and there tooke shipping; and passing many dangers by reason of contrary windes, it pleased God that we arrived in Bengala in November following; where I stayed for want of passage untill the third of February 1589, and then I shipped my selfe for Cochin. In which voyage we endured great extremity for lacke of fresh water; for the weather was extreme hote, and we were many marchants and passengers, and we had very many calmes, and hote weather. Yet it pleased God that we arrived in Ceylon the sixth of March; where we stayed five dayes to water, and to furnish our selves with other necessary provision. This Ceylon is a brave iland, very fruitfull and faire; but by reason of continuall warres with the king thereof, all things are very deare; for he will not suffer any thing to be brought to the castle where the Portugals be; wherefore often times they have great want of victuals. Their provision of victuals commeth out of Bengala every yere. The king is called Raia [Rāja], and is of great force; for he commeth to Colombo, which is the place where the Portugals have their fort, with an hundred thousand men, and many elephants. But they be naked people all of them; yet many of them be good with their pieces, which be muskets. When the king talketh with any man, he standeth upon one legge, and setteth the other foot upon his knee with his sword in his hand; it is not their order for the king to sit but to stand. His apparell is a fine painted cloth made of cotton wooll about his middle; his haire is long and bound up with a little fine cloth about his head; all the rest of his body is naked. His guard are a thousand men, which stand round about him, and he in the middle; and when he marcheth, many of them goe before him, and the rest come after him. They are of the race of the Chingalayes [Singalese], which they say are the best kinde of all the Malabars. Their eares are very large; for the greater

[1] Possibly the state of that name in the island of Sumbawa.

they are, the more honourable they are accounted. Some of them are a spanne long. The wood which they burne is cinamom wood, and it smelleth very sweet. There is great store of rubies, saphires, and spinelles in this iland; the best kinde of all be here; but the king will not suffer the inhabitants to digge for them, lest his enemies should knowe of them, and make warres against him, and so drive him out of his countrey for them. They have no horses in all the countrey. The elephants be not so great as those of Pegu, which be monstrous huge; but they say all other elephants do feare them, and none dare fight with them, though they be very small. Their women have a cloth bound about them from their middle to their knee, and all the rest is bare. All of them be blacke and but little, both men and women. Their houses are very little, made of the branches of the palmer or coco-tree, and covered with the leaves of the same tree.

The eleventh of March we sailed from Ceylon, and so doubled the cape of Comori. Not far from thence, betweene Ceylon and the maine land of Negapatan, they fish for pearles. And there is fished every yere very much; which doth serve all India, Cambaia, and Bengala. It is not so orient as the pearle of Baharim in the gulfe of Persia. From Cape de Comori we passed by Coulam [Quilon], which is a fort of the Portugals; from whence commeth great store of pepper, which commeth for Portugall, for oftentimes there ladeth one of the caracks of Portugall. Thus passing the coast, we arrived in Cochin the 22 of March, where we found the weather warme, but scarsity of victuals; for here groweth neither corne nor rice, and the greatest part commeth from Bengala. They have here very bad water, for the river is farre off. This bad water causeth many of the people to be like lepers, and many of them have their legs swollen as bigge as a man in the waste, and many of them are scant able to go.[1] These people here be Malabars, and of the race of the Naires of Calicut; and they differ much from the other Malabars. These have their heads very full of haire, and bound up with a string; and there doth appeare a bush without the band wherewith it is bound. The men be tall and strong, and good archers with a long bow and a long arrow, which is their best weapon; yet there be

[1] The reference is to 'Cochin-leg' or elephantiasis.

some calivers [light muskets] among them, but they handle them badly.

Heere groweth the pepper; and it springeth up by a tree or a pole, and is like our ivy berry, but something longer, like the wheat eare; and at the first the bunches are greene, and as they waxe ripe they cut them off and dry them. The leafe is much lesser then the ivy leafe and thinner. All the inhabitants here have very little houses covered with the leaves of the coco-trees. The men be of a reasonable stature; the women litle; all blacke, with a cloth bound about their middle hanging downe to their hammes; all the rest of their bodies be naked. They have horrible great eares, with many rings set with pearles and stones in them. The king goeth incached,[1] as they do all. He doth not remaine in a place above five or sixe dayes. He hath many houses, but they be but litle; his guard is but small; he remooveth from one house to another according to their order. All the pepper of Calicut and course cinamom groweth here in this countrey. The best cinamom doth come from Ceylon, and is pilled from fine yoong trees. Here are very many palmer or coco trees, which is their chiefe food; for it is their meat and drinke, and yeeldeth many other necessary things, as I have declared before.

The Naires which be under the king of Samorin,[1] which be Malabars, have alwayes wars with the Portugals. The king hath alwayes peace with them; but his people goe to the sea to robbe and steale. Their chiefe captaine is called Cogi Alli; he hath three castles under him. When the Portugals complaine to the king, he sayth he doth not send them out; but he consenteth that they go. They range all the coast from Ceylon to Goa, and go by foure or five parowes or boats together; and have in every one of them fifty or threescore men, and boord presently. They do much harme on that coast, and take every yere many foists and boats of the Portugals. Many of these people be Moores. This kings countrey beginneth twelve leagues from Cochin, and reacheth neere unto Goa. I remained in Cochin untill the second of November, which was eight moneths; for that there was no passage that went away in all that time. If I had come two

[1] Encaged, i. e. hidden from view in a litter.

[2] 'Zamorin' was the title of the King of Calicut.

dayes sooner, I had found a passage presently. From Cochin I went to Goa, where I remained three dayes. From Cochin to Goa is an hundred leagues. From Goa I went to Chaul, which is threescore leagues, where I remained three and twenty dayes; and there making my provision of things necessary for the shippe, from thence I departed to Ormus; where I stayed for a passage to Balsara fifty dayes. From Goa to Ormus is foure hundred leagues.

Here I thought good, before I make an end of this my booke, to declare some things which India and the countrey farther eastward do bring forth.[1]

The pepper groweth in many parts of India, especially about Cochin; and much of it doeth grow in the fields among the bushes without any labour, and when it is ripe they go and gather it. The shrubbe is like unto our ivy tree; and if it did not run about some tree or pole, it would fall downe and rot. When they first gather it, it is greene; and then they lay it in the sun, and it becommeth blacke. The ginger groweth like unto our garlike, and the root is the ginger. It is to be found in many parts of India. The cloves doe come from the iles of the Moluccoes, which be divers ilands. Their tree is like to our bay tree. The nutmegs and maces grow together, and come from the ile of Banda. The tree is like to our walnut tree, but somewhat lesser. The white sandol is wood very sweet and in great request among the Indians; for they grinde it with a litle water, and anoynt their bodies therewith. It commeth from the isle of Timor. Camphora is a precious thing among the Indians, and is solde dearer then golde. I thinke none of it commeth for Christendome. That which is compounded commeth from China; but that which groweth in canes, and is the best, commeth from the great isle of Borneo. Lignum aloes commeth from Cauchinchina. The benjamin commeth out of the countreys of Siam and Jangomes. The long pepper groweth in Bengala, in Pegu, and in the ilands of the Javas. The muske commeth out of Tartarie, and is made after this order, by report of the marchants which bring it to Pegu to sell. In Tartarie there is a little beast like unto a yong roe, which they take in snares, and beat him to death with the blood; after that they cut out the bones, and beat

[1] This section is largely copied from Federici.

the flesh with the blood very small, and fill the skin with it; and hereof commeth the muske. Of the amber [ambergris ?] they holde divers opinions; but most men say it commeth out of the sea, and that they finde it upon the shores side. The rubies, saphires, and spinelles are found in Pegu. The diamants are found in divers places, as in Bisnagar,[1] in Agra, in Delli,[2] and in the ilands of the Javas. The best pearles come from the iland of Baharim in the Persian sea, the woorser from the Piscaria [3] neere the isle of Ceylon, and from Aynam [Hai-nan] a great iland on the southermost coast of China. Spodium [4] and many other kindes of drugs come from Cambaia.

Now to returne to my voyage. From Ormus I went to Balsara or Basora, and from Basora to Babylon; and we passed the most part of the way by the strength of men, by halling the boat up the river with a long cord. From Babylon I came by land to Mosul, which standeth nere to Ninive, which is all ruinated and destroyed; it standeth fast by the river of Tigris. From Mosul I went to Merdin, which is in the countrey of the Armenians; but now there dwell in that place a people which they call Cordies, or Curdi [Kurds]. From Merdin [Mardin] I went to Orfa, which is a very faire towne, and it hath a goodly fountaine ful of fish; where the Moores hold many great ceremonies and opinions concerning Abraham; for they say he did once dwell there. From thence I went to Bir, and so passed the river of Euphrates. From Bir I went to Aleppo; where I stayed certaine moneths for company, and then I went to Tripolis; where finding English shipping, I came with a prosperous voyage to London, where by Gods assistance I safely arrived the 29 of April 1591, having bene eight yeeres out of my native countrey.

[1] Vijayanagar, the great Hindu kingdom which once covered the whole of the Indian peninsula south of the Kistna.

[2] Federici says that a certain kind of diamond comes from 'infra terra del Deli'; and Jourdain was told at Agra that the best sorts 'are growne in the countrye of Delly' (*Journal*, p. 164). There seems to be no foundation for the statement.

[3] The Portuguese term for the pearl fishery on the coast of Tinnevelly, already described under Ceylon.

[4] Finch seems to mean *tabāshir*, a substance found in the stems of bamboos and much used by Indians as a medicine. Federici (in Hakluyt's translation) calls it 'the spodiom which congeleth in certaine canes'.

1599–1606

JOHN MILDENHALL

NEARLY twenty years after the visit of Ralph Fitch and his companions to the court of the Great Mogul, another Englishman presented himself there, craving privileges of trade on behalf of himself and his fellow-countrymen. This was John Mildenhall or Midnall, whose experiences are narrated in the two documents printed below, the first of which is a summary of his journey from London to Kandahār, while the second is a letter (addressed to the Richard Staper already mentioned on p. 1) giving an account of his transactions in India and of his return journey as far as Kazvin in Persia.

Of Mildenhall's previous career practically nothing is known, except that, like Fitch, he was a trader in the Levant. From his letter to Staper and subsequent references in the Court Minutes of the East India Company, it may be inferred that he was at one time in the service of that merchant—perhaps apprenticed to him in the first instance. That in making the present venture he had no special mission, least of all from Queen Elizabeth (as has been often asserted), is evident enough from his own narrative. Although in India he did his best to play the part of a messenger from his sovereign, this was clearly a mere pretext, for the purpose of gaining more easily the concessions he was seeking; while the fact that he spent six months at Constantinople engaged in trade, took three years over his journey from Aleppo to Lahore, and was equally leisurely over his return to England, is a further proof that he made the expedition on his own account. Moreover, we learn from a document in the British Museum (Lansdowne MSS., no. 241, ff. 75, 78) that in March 1600 Mildenhall was contemplating a venture to Cairo, but then changed his plans and decided to go to Aleppo. This suggests that his journey to India was an afterthought, prompted, perhaps, by the receipt at Constantinople of the news of the attempt made in the autumn of 1599 to launch an East India Company in London. Though this scheme had failed for the moment, owing to the unwillingness of Queen Elizabeth to jeopardize the success of the negotiations then on foot for peace with Spain, there was every probability that it would become ere long an established fact; and if Mildenhall could in the interim secure a grant of trading privileges in India, he might expect a handsome reward for his pains.

Over the details of his outward journey and his experiences in India itself we need not linger. A point of some interest is the question how long he spent in that country. Of his arrival he tells us only that it was in the year 1603; while of the date of his departure he says nothing, though it may be inferred that he had left Indian territory some time before the death of Akbar in October 1605, since he makes no mention of that important event. A little light is thrown upon the question by a letter from Father Jerome Xavier, written from Agra on September 6, 1604 (N.S.),[1] in which he refers to an unnamed English heretic (doubtless Mildenhall) who had encouraged a discontented Portuguese to make accusations against the Fathers in the preceding June, the Englishman's object being to bring them into discredit and thus facilitate the grant of permission to his fellow-countrymen to frequent the Mogul's ports. Xavier adds that the Englishman bribed heavily but was disappointed, although he had spent two years in soliciting the grant. This would not be consistent (even loosely) with any later date than the spring of 1603 for Mildenhall's arrival; while the time of his departure may be guessed at the summer of 1605, thus making the period of his stay a little over two years. We may note that when Robert Covert, one of the survivors of the *Ascension* (see p. 86), left Agra in January 1610, Father Xavier gave him 'his letters of commendations to one John Midnall, an English merchant or factor *who had lien in Agra three yeeres*'[2]—roughly speaking of course.

It may appear surprising that he should have remained so long, considering that, according to his own account, the Emperor granted at once all his demands except that for permission to attack Portuguese ships and strongholds. The probability is that this was not exactly what Mildenhall required. So long as England was at war with Spain and Portugal, a mere permission for English merchant ships to visit the ports of the Great Mogul may well have appeared useless, unless the Emperor could be induced to go further and to veto any interference with them on the part of the Portuguese. If this was what Mildenhall really solicited, it is easy to understand why he attached so much importance to the point and why he remained so long in order to carry it. Whatever the exact nature of his demand was, it arrayed against him not only the Jesuit missionaries at court, whose

[1] See an excellent article by Sir Edward Maclagan on 'Jesuit Missions to the Emperor Akbar', in the *Journal of the Asiatic Society of Bengal*, vol. lxv, part i; also Father Hosten's article in the Memoirs of the same Society, vol. v, no. 4, p. 174.

[2] Covert adds that he was unable to deliver the letter, because by the time he reached England (April, 1611) Mildenhall had started on his second expedition.

influence was considerable, but also Akbar's principal advisers. The opposition of the latter may well have been due to an unwillingness to risk a breach with the Portuguese, of whose power at sea they were fully conscious; but Mildenhall sets it down partly to bribery on the part of the Jesuits and partly to an acceptance of their contention that the real object of the English was to capture some of the Indian ports. He represents himself as triumphantly refuting this charge and overcoming the scruples of the Emperor, by undertaking that his sovereign would send an ambassador, with rich presents, to reside at the imperial court, where he would be, in effect, a hostage for the good behaviour of his fellow-countrymen. Thereupon, we are told, his demands were granted in full.

Passing over his letter from Kazvin, in which these events are related, the next we hear of our traveller is that, at a meeting of the 'Committees' [Directors] of the East India Company, held on June 21, 1608, letters were read, addressed by him to Mr. Staper, enumerating the privileges he had obtained and offering these, and his own services, in return for a payment of £1500. Evidently he had not yet reached England, for it was decided to adjourn the consideration of his proposals until his arrival either in this country or the Netherlands. In May 1609 the matter was again brought forward and was referred to a special committee, though at the same time his demands were pronounced to be unreasonable and he himself was thought unfit to be employed except as a mere factor. Evidently his concessions were considered to be of small value; while the Company had a further motive for declining to purchase them on extravagant terms, inasmuch as they were expecting to receive at any moment news of the success of the mission of William Hawkins, who had been dispatched to Surat in 1607 with letters from King James to the Great Mogul. However, Mildenhall had another string to his bow. Towards the end of July 1609 the Company learnt with some alarm that he had presented a petition to the King, declaring that he had spent ten years in travel and had obtained, at a cost of three thousand pounds (?), privileges of trade in the dominions of the Great Mogul, and praying that, as the East India Company would pay no attention to his claims, he and his co-adventurers might be permitted to enjoy the said privileges. This petition had been referred by the Lord Treasurer to Sir Walter Cope and three merchants, of whom at least two were friends of Mildenhall. The Company at once appointed four representatives to confer with the referees, and apparently nothing came of the petition. A few months later there was some idea of the Company sending Mildenhall to the East as a factor, but on November 18, 1609, it was decided that he was 'for divers

MILDENHALL'S TOMB

P. 50

respects . . . not fittinge to be ymployed in the service of the Companie'.

For the rest of Mildenhall's career we have to depend chiefly on references in the correspondence of the Company's factors in India, which will be found in *Letters Received*, vols. ii, iii, and v, in Kerridge's letter-book in the British Museum (Additional MSS., no. 9366), &c. From these we learn that, some time before April 1611, he made a second expedition to the East, carrying with him a quantity of goods belonging to Staper and other merchants, intended for sale in Persia. Mildenhall is stated to have betrayed his trust and to have fled with the goods, intending to make his way once again to India. Two Englishmen, named Richard Steel and Richard Newman, were sent in pursuit. They overtook the fugitive near the confines of Persia and forced him to return with them to Ispahān, where he surrendered goods and money to the value of £9,000 and received a full discharge. Being now free, he resumed his journey to India; and Steel, who had quarrelled with Newman, undertook to bear him company. At Lahore Mildenhall fell sick, and Steel went on alone to the court of the Emperor, then at Ajmer, in Rājputāna. By slow stages Mildenhall reached Agra, whence he proceeded to Ajmer, arriving in that town early in April 1614.

He was still very sick. Purchas (*Pilgrimage*, ed. 1626, p. 528) says that he 'had learned (it is reported) the art of poysoning, by which he made away three other Englishmen in Persia, to make himself master of the whole stock; but (I know not by what means) himselfe tasted of the same cup and was exceedingly swelled, but continued his life many moneths with antidotes'. The story, which is evidently based upon Withington's assertions (given later in the present volume), is scarcely a likely one, and Mildenhall's illness was probably due to natural causes. However, after lingering some time, he died in June 1614. As he belonged to the old faith, his body was conveyed to Agra and interred in the Roman Catholic cemetery there. The tombstone marking the spot was discovered in 1909 by Mr. E. A. H. Blunt, who has prefixed a photograph of it to his *Christian Tombs and Monuments in the United Provinces*. It is in good preservation, and the following inscription in Portuguese is still plainly legible: *Joa de Mendenal, Ingles, moreo aos 1[d]e Junhou 1614*. One may say with confidence that it is the oldest English monument in India; and a tablet with an English inscription has now been placed upon it by the orders of the local government.

Just before his death Mildenhall made a will, leaving his property to two children he had had in Persia by an Indian woman during his first expedition. As executor he appointed a Frenchman named Augustin, who had accompanied him in his second journey and had undertaken to marry his daughter and bring up his son. To him, also, he bequeathed his papers, including a diary which would now be of the greatest interest; unfortunately, it was burnt by the executor together with the rest of the documents, immediately after Mildenhall's death. There is reason to believe, by the way, that this Frenchman was none other than the 'Austin of Bordeaux' whose name is often associated with the decoration of the Tāj Mahal (see the *Journal of the Royal Asiatic Society*, April 1910, and the *Journal of the Panjāb Historical Society*, vol. iv, no. 1). Meanwhile, at the instigation of Steel, the East India Company's factors at Surat had dispatched one of their number, Thomas Kerridge (afterwards President at Surat, 1616–21 and 1625–8), to lay claim to Mildenhall's goods on behalf of his employers. Kerridge reached Ajmer on the very day of the fugitive's death, which was at once followed by the sequestration of the estate on behalf of the imperial exchequer, in accordance with the prevailing practice in the case of aliens dying in the country. Then ensued a struggle between Kerridge and the executor, each striving to obtain a grant of the estate from the Emperor. Kerridge had in truth a weak case, being unable to produce any authority from those on whose behalf he was supposed to be acting, and having against him the discharge given by Newman; while his adversary was supported by the Jesuit Fathers, whose sympathies were naturally with the deceased. Kerridge bribed heavily, but without result, for the Emperor, after hearing both sides, concluded that neither had sufficient right thereto and decided to appropriate the estate himself. Nevertheless, Kerridge persevered, and in the end succeeded in recovering most of the money, which was duly transmitted to England for distribution amongst Mildenhall's creditors.

The two documents here printed are taken from *Purchas His Pilgrimes*, part i, book iii, chap. i, § 3. They were found by Purchas among the papers of Richard Hakluyt, who may have obtained them from Staper. In the foregoing account of Mildenhall's career I have drawn freely on an article of my own published in *The Gentleman's Magazine* of August 1906, supplementing this from later information.

I

THE twelfth of February, in the yeere of our Lord God 1599, I, John Mildenhall of London, merchant, tooke upon me a voyage from London towards the East-Indies, in the good ship called the *Hector* of London, Richard Parsons being master, which carried a present to the Grand Seigneur[1] in the same voyage. The seven and twentieth of April, 1599, we arrived at Zante, where I frighted a *satea* [Ital. *saettia*, a swift sailing vessel] and went into the island of Cio [Scio], from thence to Smyrna, and from thence to Constantinople, where I arrived the nine and twentieth of October, 1599; and there I staied about my merchandize till the first of May, 1600, Sir Henry Lillo beeing then Embassador; upon which day I passed from Constantinople to Scanderone [Iskanderun, now Alexandretta] in Asia, where, in company of a *chaus*[2] and some sixe other Turkes, I tooke my voyage for Aleppo overland and arrived in Aleppo the foure and twentieth day of the said May in safetie, without any trouble or molestation by the way, and there abode two and fortie dayes, finding there Master Richard Coulthrust for Consull. And the seventh of July, 1600, I departed from Aleppo, in companie with many other nations, as Armenians, Persians, Turkes, and divers others, to the number of sixe hundred people in our carravan, and onely of English Master John Cartwright, Preacher;[3] from whence we went to Bir, which is within three dayes journey and stands upon the edge of the river Euphrates. From thence we went to Urfa, which is five dayes journey, which we found very hot. From thence we went to Caraemit [Diarbekr], which is foure dayes journey. From thence to Bitelis, a city under the government of a nation called the Courdes [Kurds] yet under the subjection of Constantinople, which is seven dayes journy; and from thence to Van, which is three dayes journy from Bitelis; a city of great strength, and by the side of the castle is a great lake of salt water, navigable, and is in compasse nine dayes journey about, which I my selfe have rowed round about. And once a yeere, at the comming down of the snow waters from the mountaines,

[1] The Sultan of Turkey. The present was an organ built by Thomas Dallam, who was sent out in charge of it. See his journal, published by the Hakluyt Society in 1893.

[2] Turkish *chāush*, a minor official employed in a variety of ways, such as taking charge of a caravan.

[3] In 1611 Cartwright published an account of his experiences under the title of *The Preacher's Travels*. See also *Purchas His Pilgrimes*, part i, lib. ix, cap. 4.

there is abundance of fish, which come of themselves to one end of the lake; which I may compare to our herring-time at Yermouth, where the countrey-people doe resort from divers places and catch the said fish in great abundance, which they salt and dry and keepe them all the yeare for their food; the fish are as big as pilcherds. From thence we went to Nacshian,[1] which is sixe dayes journey; and from Nacshian to Chiulfal, which is halfe a dayes journey; and there we stayed eighteene dayes. From thence we went to Sultania [Sultanieh], and from thence to Casbin [Kazvin] in Persia, which is fifteene dayes journey, and there we abode thirty dayes. From thence to Com [Kum], which is three dayes journey; from thence we went to Cashan [Kashān], which was seven dayes journey. From thence Master Cartwright departed from us and went to Spauhoan [Ispahān], the chiefe citie in Persia. From Cashan to Yesd, which is tenne dayes journey. From thence I went to Curman [Kermān], which is tenne dayes journey; and from thence to Sigistam,[2] which is foureteene daies journey; and from thence to Candahar, which is also foureteene dayes journey.

II

CASBIN, the third day of October, 1606.

Worshipfull Sir, my duty remembred. Not having any other of more auncient love then your selfe, I have thought good to remember the manifold curtesies received, and partly to requite them with the first newes of the successe of this my voyage unto the court of the Great King of Mogor and Cambaia.

At my arrivall in Lahora the of 1603, I dispatched a poste for the Kings court, with my letters to His Majestie that I might have his free leave to come unto him and treat of such businesse as I had to doe with him from my Prince; who foorthwith answered my letters and wrote to the Governour of Lahora to use mee with all honour and curtesie and to send a guarde of horse and foote with me to accompanie me

[1] Nakchivan, an ancient town in Erivan. Julfa, Mildenhall's next stopping-place, is about twenty-six miles farther south, where the road to Tabrīz crosses the Aras river.

[2] Sagistān, the old name of Sistān in Eastern Persia.

to Agra, where his court was, beeing one and twentie dayes journey from Lahora. And beeing neere arrived, I was very well met, and an house with all things necessarie was appointed for mee by the King; where reposing my selfe two dayes, the third day I had audience and presented His Majestie with nine and twentie great horses, very faire and good, such as were hardly found better in those parts (some of them cost me fiftie or threescore pounds an horse), with diverse jewels, rings, and earerings to his great liking. And so I was dismissed with his great favour and content.

The third day after, having made before a great man my friend, he called me into his Councell; and comming into his presence, he demanded of me what I would have and what my businesse was. I made him answere that his greatnesse and renowmed kindnesse unto Christians was so much blased through the world that it was come into the furthermost parts of the westerne ocean and arrived in the court of our Queene of Englands Most Excellent Majestie; who desired to have friendship with him and, as the Portugals and other Christians had trade with His Majestie, so her subjects also might have the same, with the like favours; and farther, because there have beene long warres betweene Her Majestie and the King of Portugall, that if any of their ships or portes were taken by our nation, that he would not take it in evill part, but suffer us to enjoy them to the use of our Queenes Majestie. All this the King commanded to be written downe by his secretarie, and said that in short space he would give me answere. With that I withdrew my selfe (with leave) and went to my house. Within eight or ten dayes after, hee sent me home in money to the value of five hundred pound sterling, the first time with very comfortable speeches. Shortly after, as I was informed, hee sent to certaine Jesuites which lived there in great honour and credit, two in Agra and two others in Lahora,[1] and shewed them my demands; whereat the Jesuites were in an exceeding great rage; and whereas before wee were friends, now we grew to be exceeding great enemies. And the King asking

[1] The two at Agra were Jerome Xavier and Anthony Machado, while those at Lahore were Manoel Pinheiro and Francisco Corsi; see Sir Edward Maclagan's article already mentioned.

their opinion in this matter, they flatly answered him that our nation were all theeves and that I was a spye, sent thither for no other purpose to have friendship with His Majestie but that afterward our men might come thither and get some of his ports, and so put His Majestie to much trouble ; saying withall that they had eleven yeares served His Majestie and were bound by their bread and salt that they had eaten to speake the truth, although it were against Christians. With these and many more such speeches the King and his Councell were all flat against mee and my demands, but made no shew thereof to me in any respect ; but I knew it by friends which I had in his court. Afterward they caused five commandements to bee drawne and sent them mee, with all things that I had written, saving they had left out the taking of the ships and the ports of the Portugals ; which when I had read, I presently went to the court and made demand of the other articles. The King answered that hee would againe speake with his Councell and make answere.

In this manner rested my businesse, and every day I went to the court, and in every eighteene or twentie dayes I put up Ars [Hind. *arz*] or petitions ; and still he put mee off with good words and promised that this day and tomorrow I should have them. In this manner seeing my selfe delayed, and being at exceeding great expenses of eighteene or twentie servants (horsemen and foot), I withdrew my selfe from going to the court, in so much that in thirtie dayes I went not. At length the King, remembring me, sent to call for me. At my comming, he asked the cause why I came not as I was wont. I answered that I had come into his countrey only upon the great renowme of his excellencie and had wasted five yeares in travaile, and could not obtaine so much as a commandement at his hands which was wholly for his profit and nothing for his losse ; adding that if I had asked some greater reward of him, hee would much more have denyed me. With that he presently called for garments for me of the Christian fashion very rich and good, and willed me not to be sad, because every thing that I would have should be accomplished to mine owne content.

So with these sweet words I passed sixe monethes more.

And then, seeing nothing accomplished, I was exceeding wearie of my lingring, and could do nothing; and the rather for that I was out of money. I should have declared before how the Jesuites day and night sought how to work my displeasure. First, they had given to the two chiefest Counsellors that the King had at the least five hundred pounds sterling a piece, that they should not in any wise consent to these demands of mine; so that, when I came to present them, they would not accept of any thing at my hands, although I offered them very largely; and where I had any friendship, they would by all meanes seeke to disgrace me. But God ever kept me in good reputation with all men. Moreover, whereas I had hired in Aleppo an Armenian named Seffur [Safar], to whom I gave twentie duckets the moneth, which served me very well for mine interpreter foure yeares, now, comming neere to the point of my speciall businesse, the Jesuites had soone wrought with him also in such sort that he quarrelled with me and went his way; whereby I was destitute of a drugman[1] and my selfe could speake little or nothing. Now in what case I was in these remote countries without friends, money, and an interpreter, wisemen may judge. Yet afterward I got a schoolemaster, and in my house day and night I so studied the Persian tongue that in sixe monethes space I could speake it something reasonably. Then I went in great discontentment to the King and gave him to understand how the Jesuites had dealt with me in all points, and desired His Majesties licence to depart for mine owne countrey, where I might have redresse for mine injuries received; and withall told him how small it would stand with so great a Princes honour as His Majestie had report to be to delay me so many yeares only upon the reports of two Jesuites, who I would prove were not his friends nor cared not for his profit nor honour; and desired a day of hearing, that now I my selfe might make plaine unto His Majestie (which for want of a drugman before I could not doe) the great abuses of these Jesuites in this his court; beseeching you [him ?] aguine to grant mee licence to depart, and that I might not bee kept any longer with delayes. At these words the King was mooved

[1] Arabic *tārjumān* (an interpreter), whence 'dragoman'.

against the Jesuites, and promised that upon the Sunday following I should bee heard, and that the Jesuites should be present.

This speech I had with the King upon the Wednesday. Comming before the place of Councell the Sunday following, there were met all the great States of the court to heare the controversie betweene us. At the first the King called me and demanded what injuries I had received of the Jesuites. I answered that they had abused my Prince and countrey, most falsly calling us all theeves; and if they had beene of another sort and calling, I would have made them eate their words or I would have lost my life in the quarrell. Secondly, in saying that under colour of marchandise wee would invade your countrey and take some of your forts and put Your Majestie to great trouble. Now, that Your Majestie may understand the untruth of these mens false suggestions, know you all that Her Majestie hath her ambassadour leiger in Constantinople, and everie three yeeres most commonly doth send a new and call home the old; and at the first comming of every ambassadour shee sendeth not them emptie, but with a great and princely present; according whereunto Her Highnesse intent is to deale with Your Majestie. This profit of rich presents and honour like to redound to Your Majestie by having league of amitie and entercourse with Christian Princes, and to have their ambassadours leigers in your court, these men by their craftie practices would deprive you of. And our ambassadours being resident as pledges in your court, what dare any of our nation doe against Your Highnesse or any of your subjects? Upon these and other such like speeches of mine, the King turned to his nobles and said that all that I said was reason; and so they all answered. After this I demanded of the Jesuites before the King: In these twelve yeeres space that you have served the King, how many ambassadours and how many presents have you procured to the benefit of His Majestie? With that the Kings eldest sonne[1] stood out and said unto them (naming them) that it was most true that in a eleven or twelve yeares not one came, either upon ambassage or upon any other profit unto His

[1] Prince Salim, afterwards the Emperor Jahāngir.

Majestie. Hereupon the King was very merrie and laughed at the Jesuites, not having one word to answer. Then I said: If it please Your Majestie, I will not onely procure an ambassadour but also a present at my safe returne againe into your countrie. Divers other demands and questions were at that time propounded by the King and his nobles unto me; and I answered them all in such sort as the King called his Vice-Roy[1] (which before was by the Jesuites bribes made my great enemy) and commanding [*sic*] him that whatsoever priviledges or commandements I would have hee should presently write them, seale them, and give them me without any more delay or question. And so within thirtie dayes after I had them signed to my owne contentment and (as I hope) to the profit of my nation, Afterwards I went and presented them unto the Prince his eldest sonne, and demanded of him the like commandements; which he most willingly granted, and shortly after were delivered unto me. And so departing from the court, I brought them with me into Persia; which are here in Casbin with my selfe, readie to doe you any service. And I would have come my selfe when I wrote this letter, save that there were two Italian marchants in Agra[2] that knew of all my proceedings; whom I doubted (as I had good cause) least they would doe mee some harme in Bagdet or some other places, they alwayes being enemies to our nation, that they should find any new trade this way, as to you it is well knowne. And within foure moneths I meane to depart by the way of Moscovia; where arriving, I will not faile but satisfie you at large of all matters.

[1] Mr. Vincent Smith (*Akbar*, p. 294) suggests that this was Aziz Koka (Khān Azam).

[2] Sir E. Maclagan thinks that one of these was João Battista Vechieto

1608–13

WILLIAM HAWKINS

At the time of the establishment of the East India Company (1600) and for the next few years, England was at war with the united kingdoms of Spain and Portugal; and it was largely for this reason that the fleets of the First and Second Voyages made no attempt to visit the coasts of India itself, where the Portuguese were known to be in strong force, but went instead to the ports of Java, Sumatra, and the Far East. By the time, however, that a Third Voyage was under preparation, hostilities had been terminated by the Treaty of London (August 1604), and there was some hope that the Portuguese would not offer active opposition to the extension of English trade to the realm of the Great Mogul. Not that the negotiations preceding the treaty had afforded much ground for confidence in this respect. The Spanish commissioners had, in fact, pressed hard for a recognition of the illegality of English trade in the Indies, both East and West; but the utmost that the English negotiators would offer was that commerce with places actually occupied by King Philip's subjects should be forbidden, provided that no attempt were made to exclude the English from trading with independent countries. This proposal proving unacceptable, matters were left as before, the whole subject being ignored in the treaty.

In deciding to put to the proof the intentions of the Portuguese, the 'Committees' of the East India Company were largely influenced by the consideration that the markets of the Far East afforded little opening for English goods, which might, however, find ready sale in India itself or at an Arabian port frequented by Indian traders. The latter seemed the safer alternative, as offering less opportunity or justification for Portuguese interference. When, therefore, the instructions for the Third Voyage[1] were drafted, in March 1607, it was laid down that the fleet should make in the first instance for the island of Sokotra, to glean information and obtain the services of a pilot. Then, if the season permitted, a visit was to be paid to Aden, to see whether trade could be opened up there and a factory established. If a sufficient cargo could be obtained, the *Hector* was to be sent home direct; while the

[1] For these, and the royal commission for the venture, see *The First Letter Book*, pp. 111, 114.

other two vessels were to proceed to Bantam, calling, if time permitted, on the coast of Gujarāt to inquire into the possibility of 'a mayntenance of a trade in those parts heereafter in saffetie from the daunger of the Portingalls or other enymies, endevouring alsoe to learne whether the Kinge of Cambaya or Suratt or any of his havens be in subjection to the Portugalls, and what havens of his are not'. Should it prove, however, that the monsoon would not permit of the fleet going to Aden, all three ships were to repair to the Gujarāt coast; there, if such a course appeared safe, the *Hector* and the *Consent* were to be left to open up trade, for which purpose a letter was provided from King James to the Great Mogul, soliciting the grant of 'such libertie of traffique and priviledges as shall be resonable both for their securitie and proffitt'. In the event of a favourable reception, one ship was to remain at Surat to lade a cargo for England, while the other was to proceed to Aden to carry out the original plan. In any case, the *Dragon*, the flagship of the 'General' or commander of the fleet, William Keeling, was to go on to Bantam as soon as possible.

The 'Lieutenant-General' of the fleet and captain of the *Hector* (in which vessel, by the way, Mildenhall had voyaged to the Levant in 1599) was William Hawkins, whose narrative we are now considering. Of his previous history we know but two facts—first, that he had been in the West Indies, and secondly, that he had spent some time in the Levant and was well acquainted with Turkish. The first of these two facts may have been Mr. Noel Sainsbury's reason for suggesting (in the index to his *Calendar of State Papers, East Indies*, 1513–1616) the possibility of his identity with the William Hawkins who was a nephew of the famous Sir John Hawkins and acted as second in command in Fenton's abortive expedition of 1582–3—a conjecture adopted as a certainty by Sir Clements Markham in his work on *The Hawkins' Voyages*. In reality (as noted by Sir John Laughton in the *Dictionary of National Biography*, s.n.), what little evidence exists points rather the other way; and the only fact in his family history of which we can be sure is that he had a brother Charles. Possibly the general impression that Hawkins was a sailor by profession—'a bluff sea-captain', as one modern writer calls him—accounts for the ready acceptance of this theory. Such, of course, was not the case; the position of commander of a vessel in those days did not necessarily imply an expert knowledge of navigation—that was the business of the master—and no argument can be based thereon. In all probability Hawkins had been a Levant merchant, like so many of the East India Company's servants at this time. Evidently it was his acquaintance with the Turkish language and his experience of Eastern ways that procured him his employment in the present expedition, for he was expressly designated as the person who was to deliver the royal letters to the Governor of Aden or (if available, for he might be going home direct from Aden with his ship) to the Great Mogul,[1] and to take charge of the negotiations in either case. In order that he might appear with becoming splendour he was furnished with scarlet apparel, his cloak being lined with taffeta and embroidered with silver lace ; while suitable presents of plate and broadcloth to the value of £133 were provided, with a stipulation that anything received in return was to be considered the property of the Company.

The vessels started on their voyage early in March 1607.[2] The *Consent* quickly lost company and never rejoined. The other two met with baffling winds near the equator and were forced to seek supplies at Sierra Leone, with the result that they did not reach Table Bay until the middle of December. Their next port of call was St. Augustine's Bay (Madagascar), whence they proceeded to Sokotra, arriving there in April 1608, more than a year from the commencement of the voyage. An attempt to get to Aden was foiled by contrary winds, and it was then decided that the *Dragon* should proceed direct to Bantam, while the *Hector* (with a pinnace which had been put together at Sokotra) should make the venture to Surat. Keeling sailed accordingly on June 24, and Hawkins departed on August 4. His vessel—the first to display the English flag on the coast of India—anchored at the entrance to the Tāpti River on August 24.

Surat, situated on the left bank of that river, about 14 miles from its mouth, was now one of the chief ports of India, and the centre of trade with the Red Sea. The harbour of its more northerly rival, Cambay, was fast silting up, and sea-going ships of any size could no longer lade there, but had to embark their goods from lighters at Gogha, on the opposite side of the Gulf

[1] For these letters see *The First Letter Book*, pp. 105, 106. The one intended for the Great Mogul was addressed to the Emperor Akbar, in ignorance of the fact that he had been dead for some time.

[2] Purchas prints two narratives of the voyage, by Keeling and Finch respectively. Sir Clements Markham, in his *Voyages of Sir James Lancaster, &c.*, has summarized three manuscripts now in the India Office, one of which is an abstract of Keeling's journal ; and besides these the India Office possesses two fragments, one being the first leaf of Keeling's journal and the other a portion of a journal kept on board the *Hector*. The British Museum has two manuscripts, viz. an incomplete diary kept by Anthony Marlow (*Titus*, B viii, ff. 252–279) and what seems to be a copy (possibly holograph) of Hawkins's own journal as far as Surat (*Egerton* 2100). The latter has been printed in *The Hawkins' Voyages.*

of Cambay. Surat possessed the further advantage that vessels frequenting it were spared the voyage up that dangerous gulf, which was full of sandbanks; but, on the other hand, the only roadstead available for ships of any size was the exposed anchorage outside the bar at the mouth of the river, and this was safe merely during the period of fair weather. For customs purposes it was under the control of a certain Mukarrab Khān, who was also in charge of the port of Cambay—the customs of Gujarāt going thus directly into the royal treasury. This individual was a great favourite with the reigning Emperor Jahāngīr (the son of Akbar, whom he had succeeded in 1605), having won his regard by his skill in surgery and by his usefulness in the field sports to which that monarch was so much addicted. This esteem Mukarrab Khān took care to maintain by seeking out and presenting curiosities of all sorts, and it was doubtless for such purposes that he had obtained charge of the Gujarāt ports, where the trade carried on with the Portuguese gave him many opportunities of acquiring rarities of every description. In these circumstances the arrival of a ship belonging to an unfamiliar European nation was naturally of great interest to him, and he quickly dispatched his brother to Surat to examine the cargo, himself following a little later. In the meantime Hawkins prepared for the further voyage of the *Hector* by buying goods suitable for Bantam, much to the annoyance of the Surat merchants trading to those parts, who feared the competition of the new-comers. Hawkins himself had decided to remain behind and proceed to Agra with King James's letters; so he handed over the command of the ship to Anthony Marlow (one of the merchants who had come with him) and sent him down the river with the goods in two boats, manned by about thirty men. On their way they were attacked by some Portuguese frigates [1] and many of their number, with all the goods, were captured. Hawkins at once demanded their restitution, but was answered only with insults and a declaration that the Indian seas belonged exclusively to Portugal. The captives were sent to Goa and thence to Lisbon; while the merchandise was confiscated. On October 5 the *Hector* departed for Bantam, leaving Hawkins with only William Finch and two English servants.

Two days earlier Mukarrab Khān had reached Surat. He was at first extremely gracious to Hawkins; but once he had got into his possession all the goods he specially coveted, his behaviour changed. He dared not prevent the Englishman from going to Agra, since the latter claimed (without any authorization) to be an ambassador and undoubtedly had

[1] *Fragatas*, i. e. small armed coasting vessels, fitted to sail or row. The Portuguese regularly sent a fleet (termed a *kāfila* or caravan) of such vessels from Goa to Cambay to sell and buy goods.

royal letters to deliver to the Emperor; but he refused to pay for the goods he had bought (except at his own price) and, according to Hawkins, at the instigation of a Jesuit he plotted to have him murdered on the way. All the time of Hawkins's stay in Surat he was troubled by the threats and intrigues of the Portuguese, who, as he asserts, made several attempts to assassinate him.

However, on February 1, 1609, Hawkins got safely away from Surat, leaving Finch in charge of the remaining stock of merchandise; and on April 16 he reached Agra. He had meant to keep his arrival secret for a while; but the news soon spread that an ambassador from England was in the city, and Jahāngīr, who perhaps remembered the scene in his father's Court a few years earlier, when Mildenhall promised so confidently that his sovereign would dispatch an envoy with rich presents, was all eagerness to see the new-comer; and Hawkins was accordingly hurried into his presence. He had nothing but broadcloth to offer by way of gift, for Mukarrab Khān had taken possession of the articles sent out for that purpose; but notwithstanding this, he had an excellent reception from the Emperor, who, finding that the Englishman could speak Turkish, held frequent conversations with him about the countries of the West. So pleased was Jahāngīr with his visitor that he pressed him to remain as a resident ambassador, promising in that case to permit English trade with his ports on favourable terms. To this Hawkins readily agreed; whereupon he was made captain of four hundred horse, with a handsome allowance, was married to an Armenian maiden, and took his place among the grandees of the court. According to the Jesuits, he now assumed the garb of a Muhammadan noble; and Jourdain adds that 'in his howse he used altogether the custome of the Moores or Mahometans, both in his meate and drinke and other customes, and would seeme to bee discontent if all men did not the like'.

Meanwhile, his enemies had not been idle. The Jesuits at court did their best to disgrace him; while the Portuguese authorities at Goa stirred up Mukarrab Khān and other persons of influence in Gujarāt to represent the serious injury which the trade of that province would suffer if the English were allowed to gain a footing in India. Naturally, many of the courtiers, envying the favour with which Hawkins was regarded by the Emperor, joined willingly in these attempts to shake his position; and his hopes were beginning to decline when, at the end of October 1609, he was apprised, by letters from Finch, that an English ship, the *Ascension*, had reached Indian waters and was daily expected at Surat. This was excellent news, for, as Hawkins at once guessed, the vessel was bringing a fresh supply of presents for the Great Mogul.

He hastened to Court with the intelligence, begging that a *farmān* (order) might be granted for the establishment of a factory at Surat, and that he might be allowed to carry this down himself. The latter request was refused; but the *farmān* was at once made out and dispatched to Surat. Before it could arrive, however, tidings reached Agra that the *Ascension* had struck a sandbank and had become a wreck, and that her crew had landed in their boats at Gaṇdevi, proceeding thence to Surat.[1] Alarmed at the advent of so many Englishmen, the local authorities had insisted on their taking up their quarters in a village outside the city, where their conduct was anything but creditable to their nation. Hawkins appears to have represented to the Emperor that this exclusion was a grievance; whereupon another *farmān* was issued, directing that the Englishmen should be well treated and that assistance should be given towards recovering the cargo of the wrecked vessel. Evidently Jahāngīr was hoping that the presents he had been led to expect might still be forthcoming; in this, however, he was disappointed, and the influence of Hawkins commenced to diminish in consequence.

Early in December a number of the survivors from the *Ascension* arrived at Agra and were presented to the Emperor by Hawkins. Their disorderly behaviour lent colour to the representations of the Portuguese as to the undesirability of admitting such a nation to the Gujarāt ports; and it is clear that the 'ambassador's' position was not improved by their advent, though he was still treated with respect and consideration. Covert, who left Agra in January 1610, says that Hawkins was then 'in great credit with the King, being allowed one hundred ruckees [rupees] a day, which is ten pound sterling, and is intituled by the name of a Can [Khān], which is a knight, and keepeth company with the greatest noblemen belonging to the King; and he seemeth very willing to doe his country good'.

Towards the end of March 1610 Mukarrab Khān arrived from Gujarāt, bringing a large array of presents for the Emperor, including a number of European articles, among which Hawkins recognized some of his own goods. According to the text, Mukarrab Khān had been recalled in consequence of complaints made against his administration, and his goods had been seized by Jahāngīr's orders; but there is no hint of this in the Emperor's own memoirs.[2] Soon after, however,

[1] Details are given in *The Journal of John Jourdain*, where will also be found Jourdain's account of his journey to court and much other information bearing on the present subject. Robert Covert's *True and Almost Incredible Report* (1612) should also be consulted.

[2] The *Tūzuk-i-Jahāngīri*, vol. i, p. 167. It may be noted that there is no allusion to Hawkins or his embassy in this work.

Mukarrab Khān did fall into disgrace for a time, owing to a serious accusation brought against him; and Hawkins felt safe in pressing him to pay what was still due for the broadcloth he had bought. The account in the text may be compared with that given by Jourdain, who manifestly thought the attitude of Hawkins unwise. According to him Mukarrab Khān was willing to pay the greater part of the debt, but contended for the remission of the rest, on the ground that the original price was too high; Hawkins, however, demanded the full amount and threatened to complain to the Emperor. Khwāja Abūl Hasan, 'the Kings chiefe Vizir,' endeavoured to persuade the Englishman to accept the money offered, but in vain. The complaint was duly made, and Jahāngīr angrily ordered Abūl Hasan to see the debt discharged; whereupon the latter paid Hawkins the amount Mukarrab Khān had previously tendered, and added threats which effectually deterred him from applying again to the Emperor; so by his obstinacy he had gained nothing but the ill-will of Abūl Hasan, who took care to make him feel its effect by docking the pay due to him from the royal treasury.

The prospects of the English were now far from bright. A rich present arrived from Goa accompanied by a letter complaining that another European nation should be allowed to endanger the friendship that had so long existed between Portugal and the Mogul; while the effect of this was enhanced by the declaration of certain Surat merchants (then at court) that any encouragement of the English would mean the ruin of the trade of Gujarāt, owing to the reprisals threatened by the Portuguese. Moreover, Jahāngīr had long entertained the idea of sending Mukarrab Khān to Goa, and his actual departure on this errand had only been deferred until it should be known that the long-expected Viceroy had arrived from Portugal and would welcome the presence of such an emissary. The letter now received settled both points, and mentioned also that a merchant at Goa had for sale a particularly fine ruby, a model of which was sent. The Emperor was of course eager to acquire this gem, and accordingly Mukarrab Khān, now restored to favour, was ordered to proceed on his mission. He represented, however, that it was necessary that he should be able to assure the Viceroy that the English would be definitely excluded from trade in India; and this promise Jahāngīr at once gave.

Hawkins waited until the envoy was well on his way, and then applied afresh to the Emperor, with the result that the latter changed his mind and declared that the English should be freely admitted; but on hearing of this, Mukarrab Khān wrote that it would be useless in that case for him to proceed to Goa, and thereupon the promised *farmān* was withheld, in spite of all the entreaties of Hawkins. Another mortification for the Englishman was his exclusion from the place of honour he had hitherto enjoyed at court. This he ascribes to the malice of Abūl Hasan. The latter, however, would not have dared to take such a step without the Emperor's sanction, and the real reason was probably that given by Jourdain, which is as follows. From time to time Jahāngīr made attempts to abstain from his usual indulgence in strong drink, and in one of these fits of temperance he ordered that none of his courtiers should come into his presence smelling of liquor. Hawkins, who had a weakness in that direction, offended against this regulation, and in consequence he was one day denounced in the presence of the court; 'whereat the Kinge pauzed a little space and, consideringe that he was a stranger, he bid him goe to his howse, and when hee came next, he should not drinke. Soe, beeing disgraced in publique, he could not be suffred to come into his accustomed place neere the Kinge; which was the cause that he went not soe often to courte' (*Journal of John Jourdain*, p. 156). Evidently Jahāngīr was by this time tired of his troublesome visitor, and an appeal from Hawkins 'either to establish me as formerly or give me leave to depart', produced only an immediate order for his passports to be made ready. He then applied for an answer to the letter he had brought from King James, but this was contemptuously refused.

The few Englishmen remaining in India now began to make plans for their departure. Finch, who had joined Hawkins early in 1610 but was now at Lahore, decided to go home overland. Jourdain, who had reached Agra in February 1611, left again towards the end of July for the coast, accompanied by three other Englishmen. At their farewell audience they presented Jahāngīr with 'a peece of gould of our Kings quoyne, which he looked earnestlie upon and putt itt in his pockett' (*Jourdain*, p. 166).[1] Hawkins himself was in a difficulty, as he had his wife to consider, whose friends objected strongly to her quitting India. He decided to apply to the Jesuits (whom he had so persistently reviled) and to beg them to procure a pass from the Viceroy to enable him to proceed by way of Cambay to Goa (to which place his wife's friends would allow her to accompany him), hoping then to obtain a passage to Lisbon. This the Fathers willingly agreed to effect; and so he continued his preparations for departure.

[1] Covert on quitting Agra gave the Emperor 'a small whistle of gold, weighing almost an ounce, set with sparks of rubies; which hee tooke and whistleled therewith almost an houre. Also I gave him the picture of St. Johns head cut in amber and gold, which he also received very gratiously. The whistle hee gave to one of his great women, and the picture to Sultan Caroone, his yongest sonne'.

However, the end was not yet. In the early summer of 1611 Khwâja Abûl Hasan was sent to the Deccan, and Ghiyâs Beg, father of the celebrated Nûr Jahân (whom Jahângîr had just espoused), was made Wazîr in his place. His son, known later as Âsaf Khân, was also in great favour; and as he was on very friendly terms with Hawkins, the envoy began to build fresh hopes upon this change of ministers, particularly as he had learned that an English fleet, under Sir Henry Middleton, was on its way to the Gujarât coast. These vessels reached the bar of Surat on September 26, and as soon as the news arrived at court, Hawkins presented himself before Jahângîr, with a handsome ruby ring by way of offering, and once more requested a *farmân* for the establishment of English trade at Surat. The Emperor, probably in expectation of the curiosities likely to be brought by the ships, at once ordered the desired document to be drawn up; but here one of his chief favourites interposed, representing that this was in flat contradiction to the promises made to the Portuguese and would entail 'the utter overthrow' of the trade of Gujarât. Thereupon Jahângîr retracted his concession, at the same time assuring Hawkins that if he would remain in India, he should receive in full the allowance previously assigned to him. The Englishman, however, replied with dignity that he could not remain if his fellow-countrymen were refused the liberty of commerce which had been promised to them; and, after another ineffectual attempt to procure an answer to the letter he had brought, he quitted Agra early in November 1611.

He and his wife got safely to Cambay; and from thence, in the following January, managed to reach Middleton's fleet, bringing with them goods to the value of about £1,800. Having been finally refused by Mukarrab Khân, in view of the menaces of the Portuguese, permission to establish a factory at Surat, the English departed on February 11, 1612, for the Red Sea, where Middleton found Captain Saris with a fresh fleet from England, including Hawkins's old ship the *Hector*. The Indian vessels trading to Mokha and Aden were now held up and forced to exchange their goods for English commodities, and finally those belonging to Diu and Surat were required to pay a heavy ransom, as a punishment for the action of the Gujarât officials in excluding the English at the dictation of the Portuguese. These measures had a great effect in India, showing as they did that it was as dangerous to injure the one nation as to defy the other; and wnen, a little later, Best and Downton demonstrated that their countrymen were as powerful at sea as the Portuguese, the Gujarât seaports were duly opened to English trade.

Having finished his business in the Red Sea, Middleton departed in August 1612 for Sumatra and Java. Hawkins and his household were on board the *Trade's Increase*, which, after running aground near Tiku (in Sumatra), reached Bantam four days before Christmas. There they found the *Hector*, the *Solomon*, and the *Thomas*, all preparing to start for England. Hawkins and his wife embarked on the last-named, and the vessels sailed in January 1613. The *Hector* and *Thomas* reached the Cape of Good Hope in April, and after a month's respite the voyage was resumed on the 21st of May. Next day the two ships lost company, and of the rest of the voyage we know but little. Sickness broke out on board the *Thomas*, with the result that most of the crew died; while at one time the vessel was in danger of being plundered by 'certain Newfoundland men'—probably rough traders tempted by the sight of a richly laden ship weakly manned. Fortunately, this danger was averted by the appearance of the *Pearl*, an interloping vessel homeward bound from the East. Her captain not only rescued the *Thomas* from the danger that threatened her, but also supplied her with much needed provisions. With this assistance she staggered home, arriving some time in the autumn of 1613; but Hawkins did not see his native land, for it was his fate to 'dye on the Irish shoare in his returne homewards' (*Purchas His Pilgrimage*, p. 521). When, and exactly where, this happened we are not told.

His widow came on to London in the *Thomas*. Besides her claim to her late husband's property, she was reputed to have many valuable jewels; and these considerations probably had a share in leading to her second marriage, early in 1614, to Gabriel Towerson, who had been captain of the *Hector* in the recent voyage. There was some haggling with the East India Company over the settlement of Hawkins's accounts. The 'Committees' who examined these reported that they included heavy charges for housekeeping, presents, 'goeinge to the campe with 60 horse,' and so on; and that, after allowing his full salary of £200 a year up to the day of his death, with £300 for the expense of bringing his household down to the coast, there still remained a balance due from his estate of £600. However, the Company, considering that the widow was 'a straunger', and that liberal treatment of her might have a good effect in India, agreed to forgo all claims; while in addition they presented her with a wedding gift of 200 jacobuses (about £240) as a 'token of there love'. In 1617 Mr. and Mrs. Towerson obtained permission from the Company to proceed to India in a private capacity, hoping to improve their fortunes by the aid of her relatives. From the journal of Sir Thomas Roe (who was much vexed by their vagaries) we learn that these hopes were disappointed. Towerson himself returned to England with the ambassador in 1619, leaving his wife with her friends at Agra, where, a couple of years later, we find her pestering the Company's factors for maintenance. Her second husband had evidently no intention of rejoining her, for in 1620 he obtained employment from the Company as a principal factor for the Moluccas. Three years later, while holding this post, he was put to death by the Dutch in what is termed 'the Massacre of Amboyna'.

The narrative here reprinted from *Purchas His Pilgrimes* (part i, book iii, chap. 7) represents Hawkins's own report to the East India Company. The reverend gentleman tells us, in his companion work the *Pilgrimage* (p. 520), that the traveller's 'booke or large journall, written by himselfe, was communicated to me by the Right Worshipfull Sir Thomas Smith' (the Governor of the Company); and elsewhere he describes it as 'written at sea-leasure, very voluminous, in a hundred sheets of paper'. This account Purchas edited freely, omitting, as he frankly tells us, 'many advices of the authour touching forts, Indian factories, &c.,' which he regarded 'as not so fitting every eye'. Unfortunately, the manuscript is no longer extant, and we are unable therefore to assess the value of what was thus excised.

Hawkins's story should be read in conjunction with the narrative of William Finch, which supplements it in many ways. It is a characteristic production and gives a vivid idea of the writer—enterprising and resourceful, but somewhat arrogant and blustering. Upon his contemporaries he made an impression not altogether favourable. Finch quarrelled with him; Jourdain, as we have seen, gives rather a hostile account of his behaviour, and declares that 'his promises weare of little force, for he was very fickle in his resolucion, as alsoe in his religion' (*Journal*, p. 162); and Roe, though he did not know him personally, wrote of him: 'For Hawkings, I fynd him a vayne foole' (British Museum, Addl. MSS., no. 6115, f. 148). But, at all events, we owe to him a most valuable account of the Court of the Emperor Jahāngīr, second only to that given by Roe himself; while his picturesque account of his adventures has an interest which is all its own.

At my arrivall unto the bar of Surat, being the foure and twentieth of August, 1608, I presently sent unto Surat Francis Buck, merchant, with two others, to make knowne unto the Governour[1] that the King of England had sent me as his embassadour unto his king, with his letter and present. I received the Governours answere, both by them and three

[1] His name appears to have been Mirza Nūruddīn.

of his servants sent me from Surat, that he and what the countrey affoorded was at my command, and that I should be very welcome if I would vouchsafe to come on shore. I went, accompanied with my merchants and others, in the best manner I could, befitting for the honour of my king and country. At my comming on shore, after their barbarous manner I was kindly received, and multitudes of people following me, all desirous to see a new come people, much nominated but never came in their parts. As I was neere the Governors house, word was brought me that he was not well; but I thinke rather drunke with affion [Hind. *afiyun*, opium] or opion, being an aged man. So I went unto the Chiefe Customer,[1] which was the onely man that seafaring causes belonged unto (for the government of Surat belonged unto two great noblemen, the one being Viceroy of Decan, named Chanchana,[2] the other Viceroy of Cambaya and Surat, named Mocreb-chan,[3] but in Surat hee had no command, save onely over the Kings customes), who was the onely man I was to deale withall. After many complements done with this Chiefe Customer, I told him that my comming was to establish and settle a factory in Surat, and that I had a letter for his king from His Majesty of England tending to the same purpose, who is desirous to have league and amitie with his king, in that kind that his subjects might freely goe and come, sell and buy, as the custome of all nations is; and that my ship was laden with the commodities of our land which, by intelligence of former travellers, were vendible for these parts. His answere was that he would dispatch a foot-man for Cambaya unto the nobleman his master, for of himselfe he could doe nothing without his order. So taking my leave, I departed to my lodging appointed for mee, which was at the customehouse.

In the morning I went to visit the Governour and, after

[1] The Shāhbandar, who had control of all matters relating to the port, including the customs.

[2] Khān-khānān, the highest military title. It was borne at this time by Mīrza Abdurrahīm, son of Bairām Khān, Akbar's celebrated general. He was in charge of the operations against the Deccan kings, with headquarters at Burhānpur.

[3] Mukarrab Khān (for whom see p 63).

a present given him, with great gravity and outward shew of kindnesse he entertained me, bidding me most heartily welcome, and that the countrey was at my command. After complements done, and entring into the maine affaires of my businesse, acquainting him wherefore my comming was for these parts, he answered me that these my affaires did not concerne him, because they were sea-faring causes, which did belong unto Mocrebchan, unto whom hee promised me to dispatch a foot-man unto Cambaya and would write in my behalfe, both for the unlading of my shippe, as also concerning a factorie. In the meane while, he appointed me to lodge in a merchants house that understood the Turkish, being at that time my trouch-man [interpreter (see p. 57)], the captaine of that shippe which Sir Edward Michelborne tooke.[1]

It was twentie daies ere the answer came, by reason of the great waters and raines that men could not passe. In this time the merchants, many of them very friendly, feasted me, when it was faire weather that I could get out of doores; for there fell a great raine, continuing almost the time the messengers were absent, who at the end of twenty daies brought answer from Mocrebchan with licence to land my goods and buy and sell for this present voyage, but for a future trade and setling of a factorie he could not doe it without the Kings commaundement, which he thought would be effected, if I would take the paines of two moneths travell to deliver my kings letter. And further, he wrote unto his Chiefe Customer that all whatsoever I brought should be kept in the custome-house till his brother, Sheck Abder Rachim [Shaikh Abdurrahīm], came, who should make all the hast that possibly could bee, for to chuse such goods as were fitting for the King (these excuses of taking goods of all men for the King are for their owne private gaine). Upon this answere I made all the hast I could in easing our shippe of her heavy burthen of lead and iron, which of necessitie must be landed.

[1] This was in 1605, during an interloping voyage, for which Michelborne had obtained a licence from James I. His high-handed proceedings with the native vessels he met much alarmed the East India Company.

The goods being landed and kept in the Customers power till the comming of this great man, perceiving the time precious and my ship not able long to stay, I thought it convenient to send for three chests of money, and with that to buy commodities of the same sorts that were vendible at Priaman and Bantam,[1] which the Guzerats carry yearely thither, making great benefit thereof. I began to buy against the will of all the merchants in the towne, whose grumbling was very much, and complaining unto the Governour and Customer of the leave that was granted me in buying those commodities, which would cut their owne throates at Priaman and Bantam, they not suspecting that I would buy commodities for those parts, but onely for England.

At the end of this businesse this great man came, who gave me licence to ship it; before the shipping of which I called a councell, which were the merchants I had and those that I thought fitting for the businesse I pretended [i. e. intended], demanding every ones opinion according to his place what should be thought convenient for the delivery of His Majesties letter, and the establishing of a trade. So generally it was agreed and concluded that for the effecting of these waighty affaires it neither would nor could be accomplished by any but by myselfe, by reason of my experience in my former travels and language; as also I was knowne to all to be the man that was sent as embassadour about these affaires. After it was concluded, and I contented to stay, I made what hast I could in dispatching away the ship, and to ship the goods. This done, I called Master Marlow and all the company that was on shore before mee, acquainting them with my pretence [intention], and how they should receive for their commander Master Marlow, willing them that they obey and reverence him in that kind as they did me. This done, I brought them to the water side and, seeing them imbarke themselves, I bad them farewell.

The next day, going about my affaires to the great mans brother, I met with some tenne or twelve of our men, of the better sort of them, very much frighted, telling me the heaviest

[1] Priaman, a pepper port on the west coast of Sumatra. Bantam, on the north-east coast of Java.

newes (as I thought) that ever came unto me, of the taking of the barkes by a Portugal frigat or two, and all goods and men taken, onely they escaped.[1] I demanding in what manner they were taken and whether they did not fight, their answer was no: M[aster] Marlow would not suffer them, for that the Portugals were our friends, and Bucke, on the other side, went to the Portugall without a pawne [hostage], and there he betrayed us, for he never came unto us after. Indeed, Bucke went upon the oath and faithfull promise of the Captaine, but was never suffered to returne. I presently sent a letter unto the Captaine Major, that he release my men and goods, for that we were Englishmen, and that our kings had peace and amity together, and that we were sent unto the Mogols countrey by our king, and with his letter unto the Mogol for his subjects to trade in his countrey, and with His Majesties commission for the government of his subjects, and I made no question but in delivering backe His Majesties subjects and goods, that it would be well taken at his kings hands; if the contrary, it would be a meanes of breach. At the receit of my letter, the proud rascall braved so much, as the messenger told me, most vilely abusing His Majestie, tearming him King of Fishermen, and of an iland of no import, and a fart for his commission, scorning to send me any answer.

It was my chance the next day to meete with a captaine of one of the Portugal frigats, who came about businesse, sent by the Captaine Major. The businesse, as I understood, was that the Governour should send me as prisoner unto him, for that we were Hollanders. I, understanding what he was, tooke occasion to speake with him of the abuses offered the King of England and his subjects. His answere was that these seas belonged unto the King of Portugall, and none ought to come here without his license. I told him that the King of Englands license was as good as the King of Spaines, and as free for his subjects as for the King of Spaines, and he that saith the contrary is a traytor and a villaine, and so tel your

[1] 'Our two barks taken by the Portugals, and thirtie men in them. This not fighting was upbrayded to our men by the Indians with much disgrace, since recovered with interest by our sea-fights with the Portugals.' (*Marginal note by Purchas.*)

great captaine that in abusing the King of England he is a base villaine and a traytor to his king, and that I will maintaine it with my sword, if he dare come on shore. I sending him a challenge, the Mores, perceiving I was much mooved, caused the Portugal to depart. This Portugal, some two houres after, came to my house, promising me that he would procure the libertie of my men and goods, so that I would be liberall unto him. I entertained him kindly and promised him much, but before he departed the towne my men and goods were sent for Goa.

I had my goods readie some five dayes before I could be cleare and have leave, for they would not let them be shipped untill this great man came, which was the third of October; and two dayes after, the ship set sayle, I remaining with one merchant, William Finch, who was sicke the greater part of his time and not able to stirre abroad to doe any businesse; the rest were two servants, a cooke and my boy. These were the companie I had to defend our selves from so many enemies, which lay daily lurking to destroy us, aiming at me for the stopping of my passage to the Great Mogol; but God preserved me, and in spight of them all I tooke heart and resolution to goe forwards on my travels. After the departure of the ship, I understood that my goods and men were betrayed unto the Portugal by Mocreb-chan and his followers; for it was a plot laid by the Jesuite [1] and Mocreb-chan to protract time till the frigats came to the bar, and then to dispatch me, for till then this dogge Mocreb-chan his brother came not, and the comming of these frigats was in such secrecy that, till they had taken us, we heard no newes of them. After the departure of my ship I was so misused that it was unsufferable, but so long as my ship was at the bar I was flattered withall. But howsoever, well used or ill, it was not for mee to take thought for any thing, although remaining in an heathen countrey, invironed with so many enemies, who daily did nothing else but plot to murther me and cosen me of my goods, as hereafter you shall understand. First, misused by Mocreb-chan as to have possession of my goods, taking what he pleased and leaving what he pleased, giving me such a price

[1] This was Father Manoel Pinheiro (see p. 55).

as his owne barbarous conscience afforded, that from thirtie five would give but eighteene, not regarding his brothers bil, who had full authoritie from him; and how difficult it was to get money from his chiefe servant, after the time expired, as it is best knowne to us who tooke the paines in receiving a small part thereof before his comming to Surat; and after his comming I was barred of all, although he outwardly dissembled and flattered with me almost for three moneths, feeding me with faire promises of payment and other kindnesses. In the meane time he came to my house three times, sweeping me cleane of all things that were good; so that, when he saw that I had no more good things left, he likewise by little and little degraded me of his good lookes. Almost all this time William Finch was extreame sicke of the fluxe [dysentery], but, thankes be to God, recovered past all hope. I, on the other side, could not peepe out of doores for feare of the Portugals, who in troops lay lurking in by-wayes to give me assault to murther me, this beeing at the time that the armada[1] was there.

The first plot laid against me was: I was invited by Hogio Nazam [Khwāja Nizām] to the fraughting of his ship for Mocha, as the custome is they make at the fraughting of their ships great feasts for all the principallest of the towne. It was my good hap at that time, a great captaine belonging to the Vice-Roy of Guzerat, resident in Amadavar [Ahmadābād], being sent about affaires unto Surat, was likewise invited to this feast, which was kept at the water side; and neere unto it the Portugals had two frigats of their armada, which came to receive their tribute of the shippes that were to depart, as also refreshment. Out of these frigats there came three gallant fellowes to the tent where I was, and some fortie followers, Portugals, scattering themselves along the sea side ready to give an assault when the word should be given. These three gallants that came to the tents, armed with coats of buffe downe to the knees, their rapiers and pistols by their sides, demaunded for the English captaine; upon the hearing of which I arose presently and told them that I was the man,

[1] The Portuguese fleet of frigates trading between Goa and Cambay (see p. 63).

and perceiving an alteration in them I laid hand on my weapon. The Captaine Mogol perceiving treason towards me, both he and his followers drew their weapons and, if the Portugals had not been the swifter, both they and their scattered crew (in retiring to their frigats) had come short home. Another time they came to assault me in my house with a friar, some thirty or fortie of them. The friars comming was to animate the souldiers and to give them absolution. But I was alwaies wary, having a strong house with good doores. Many troopes at other times lay lurking for me and mine in the streetes, in that kind that I was forced to goe to the Governour to complaine that I was not able to goe about my businesse for the Portugals comming armed into the citie to murther me; which was not a custome at other times for any Portugals to come armed, as now they did. He presently sent word to the Portugals that, if they came into the city armed againe, at their owne perils be it. At Mocreb-chan his comming, with a Jesuite named Padre Pineiro in his company (who profered Mocreb-chan fortie thousand rials of eight [1] to send me to Daman, as I understood by certaine advise given me by Hassun Ally [2] and Ally Pommory), I went to visit him, giving him a present, besides the present his brother had; and for a time, as I have above written, I had many kind outward shewes of him, till the time that I demanded my money. After that his dissembling was past and he told me plainely that he would not give mee twentie mamadies per vare,[3] but would deliver me backe my cloath. Upon which dealings I dissembled as wel as I could with him, intreating leave for Agra to the King, telling him that William Finch was the man that I left as my chiefe in this place, and in what kind soever his pleasure was to deale with me, he was the man to receive either money or ware; upon which answer he gave me his license and letter to the King, promising me fortie horsemen to goe with me. which hee did not accomplish. After license received, the Father put into Mocreb-chan his head

[1] The rial of eight was worth about 4*s*. 6*d*.

[2] Khwāja Hasan Ali, afterwards Shāhbandar of Surat.

[3] 'Vare' is probably a misprint for 'yard'. The *mahmūdi* was a small silver coin (equivalent to about 11*d*. or 12*d*. English), which was still the favourite currency in Gujarāt, side by side with the rupee.

that it was not good to let me passe, for that I would complaine of him unto the King. This he plotted with Mocreb-chan to overthrow my journey, which he could not doe because I came from a king; but he said that he would not let me have any force to goe with me. And what else hee would have him to doe, either with my treuch-man [see p. 72] and coachman, to poyson or murther me, if one should faile, the other to doe it. This invention was put into Mocreb-chans head by the Father, but God for His mercie sake afterward discovered these plots, and the counsell of this Jesuite tooke not place. Before the plotting of this, the Jesuite and I fell out in the presence of Mocreb-chan for vile speaches made by him of our king and nation to bee vassals unto the King of Portugall; which words I could not brooke, in so much that, if I could have had my will, the Father had never spoken more, but I was prevented.

Now finding William Finch in good health, newly recovered, I left all things touching the trade of merchandizing in his power, giving him my remembrance and order what he should doe in my absence. So I began to take up souldiers to conduct mee, being denyed of Mocrebchan, besides shot and bow-men that I hired. For my better safety I went to one of Chanchanna his captaines to let me have fortie or fiftie horsemen to conduct me to Chanchanna, being then Vice-roy of Decan, resident in Bramport [Burhānpur], who did to his power all that I demanded, giving me valiant horsemen, Pattans [Pathāns], a people very much feared in these parts; for if I had not done it, I had beene over-throwne. For the Portugalls of Daman had wrought with an ancient friend of theirs, a Raga [Rāja], who was absolute lord of a province (betweene Daman, Guzerat and Decan) called Cruly,[1] to be readie with two hundred horsemen to stay my passage; but I went so strong and well provided, that they durst not incounter with us; so likewise that time I escaped.

Then at Dayta,[2] another province or princedome, my

[1] This has been identified as the district round Karoli, four miles south-east of Sālher (for which see Finch's narrative).

[2] Dhāita, on the Surpini River. The 'province' referred to is Bāglān, a mountainous district to the south of the Tāpti, which still maintained

coachman being drunke with certaine of his kindred, discovered the treason that hee was to worke against mee, which was that hee was hiered to murther me ; he being overheard by some of my souldiers, who at that present came and told me and how it should be done in the morning following, when we begin our travell (for wee use to travell two houres before day) ; upon which notice I called the coachman unto me, examining him and his friends before the captaine of the horsemen I had with mee ; who could not deny ; but hee would never confesse who hired him, although hee was very much beaten, cursing his fortune that he could not effect it, for he was to doe it the next morning. So I sent him prisoner unto the Governour of Suratt. But afterward by my broker or truchman I understood that both hee and the coachman were hired by Mocrebchan, but by the Fathers perswasion, the one to poyson me, and the other to murther me ; but the truchman received nothing till he had done the deed, which hee never meant to doe, for in that kind hee was alwayes true unto mee ; thus God preserved me. This was five dayes after my departure from Suratt, and my departure from Suratt was the first of February, 1608 [1609]. So following on my travels for Bramport, some two dayes beyond Dayta the Pattans left me, but to be conducted by another Pattan captaine, governour of that lordship, by whom I was most kindly entertained. His name was Sherchan [Sher Khān]. Beeing sometime a prisoner unto the Portugall and having the Portugall language perfect, was glad to doe me any service, for that I was of the nation that was enemie unto the Portugall. Himselfe in person, with fortie horsemen, went two dayes journey with mee till hee had freed mee from the dangerous places ; at which time he met with a troupe of out-lawes and tooke some foure alive and slew and hurt eight ; the rest escaped. This man very kindly writ his letter for me to have his house at Bramport, which was a great curtesie ; otherwise I could not tell where to lodge my selfe, the towne being so full of souldiers, for then began the warres with the Decans.

its independence. The chief's headquarters were at Jaitāpur, near Mulher ; and he levied tolls on travellers from Surat to Burhānpur, the road passing through his territories. See also Finch's account.

The eighteenth of the said moneth, thankes be to God, I came in safetie to Bramport, and the next day I went to the court to visit Chanchanna, being then Lord Generall and Vice-Roy of Decan, giving him a present, who kindly tooke it; and after three houres conference with him, he made me a great feast, and being risen from the table, invested me with two clokes, one of fine woollen, and another of cloth of gold, giving mee his most kind letter of favour to the King, which avayled much. That done, he imbraced me, and so we departed. The language that we spoke was Turkish, which he spake very well. I remayned in Bramport unto the second of March; till then I could not end my businesses of monies that I brought by exchange, staying likewise for a carravan. Having taken new souldiers, I followed my voyage or journey to Agra, where after much labour, toyle, and many dangers I arrived in safety the sixteenth of Aprill, 1609.

Being in the citie, and seeking out for an house in a very secret manner, notice was given the King that I was come, but not to bee found. He presently charged both horsemen and footmen in many troupes not to leave before I was found, commanding his Knight Marshall to accompany mee with great state to the court, as an embassador of a king ought to be; which he did with a great traine, making such extraordinary haste that I admired [i. e. wondered] much, for I could scarce obtayne time to apparell my selfe in my best attyre. In fine I was brought before the King. I came with a slight present, having nothing but cloth, and that not esteemed; for what I had for the King Mocreb-chan tooke from me, wherwith I acquainted His Majestie. After salutation done, with a most kinde and smiling countenance he bade me most heartily welcome; upon which speech I did my obeysance and dutie againe. Having His Majesties letter in my hand, he called me to come neere unto him, stretching downe his hand from the seate royall, where he sate in great majestie something high for to be seene of the people; receiving very kindly the letter of me. Viewing the letter a prettie while, both the seale and the manner of the making of it up, he called for an old Jesuite[1] that was there present to reade it.

[1] Probably Father Xavier (see p. 55).

JAHĀNGĪR

P. 80

In the meane space, while the Jesuite was reading it, hee spake unto mee in the kindest manner that could bee, demanding of mee the contents of the letter, which I told him ; upon which notice presently granting and promising me by God that all what the King had there written he would grant and allow with all his heart, and more if His Majestie would require it. The Jesuite likewise told him the effect of the letter, but discommending the stile, saying it was basely penned, writing *Vestra* without *Majestad*.[1] My answere was unto the King: And if it shall please Your Majestie, these people are our enemies ; how can this letter be ill written, when my king demandeth favour of Your Majestie ? He said it was true.

Perceiving I had the Turkish tongue, which himselfe well understood, hee commanded me to follow him unto his chamber of presence,[2] being then risen from that place of open audience, desiring to have further conference with me ; in which place I stayed some two houres, till the King came forth from his women. Then calling mee unto him, the first thing that hee spake was that he understood that Mocrebchan had not dealt well with mee ; bidding mee bee of good cheere, for he would remedie all. It should seeme that Mocrebchans enemies had acquainted the King with all his proceedings, for indeed the King hath spies upon every nobleman. I answered most humbly that I was certaine all matters would goe well on my side so long as His Majestie protected me ; upon which speech he presently sent away a post for Suratt, with his command to Mocrebchan, writing unto him very earnestly in our behalfes, conjuring him to bee none of his friend if hee did not deale well with the English in that kind as their desire was. This being dispatched and sent, by the same messenger I sent my letter to William Finch, wishing him to goe with this command to Mocrebchan ; at the receit of which hee wondred that I came safe to Agra and was not murthered or poysoned by the way, of which speech William Finch advertised me afterward.

[1] According to Du Jarric (vol. iii, p. 194), Hawkins had brought with him a Spanish version of the royal letter.

[2] The *Diwān-i-khās*. Hawkins had been received in the *Diwān-i-ām*, or public audience chamber.

It grew late, and having had some small conference with the King at that time, he commanded that I should daily be brought into his presence, and gave a captaine named Houshaberchan[1] charge that I should lodge at his house till a house were found convenient for me, and when I needed anything of the King, that he should bee my solicitor. According to command I resorted to the court, where I had daily conference with the King. Both night and day his delight was very much to talke with mee, both of the affaires of England and other countries, as also many demands of the West Indies, whereof hee had notice long before, being in doubt if there were any such place till he had spoken with me, who had beene in the countrey.

Many dayes and weekes being past and I now in great favour with the King, to the griefe of all mine enemies, espying my time, I demanded for his commandement or commission with capitulations for the establishing of our factory to be in mine owne power. His answere was whether I would remayne with him in his court. I replyed, till shipping came; then my desire was to goe home with the answere of His Majesties letter. Hee replyed againe that his meaning was a longer time, for he meant to send an embassador to the King of England at the comming of the next shipping, and that I should stay with him untill some other bee sent from my king to remayne in my place, saying this: Thy staying would be highly for the benefit of thy nation; and that he would give me good maintenance, and my being heere in his presence would bee the cause to right all wrongs that should be offered unto my nation; and further, what I should see beneficiall for them, upon my petition made, hee would grant; swearing by his fathers soule that, if I would remayne with him, he would grant me articles for our factorie to my hearts desire, and would never goe from his word. I replyed againe, that I would consider of it. Thus daily inticing me to stay with him, alleaging as is above written, and that I should doe service both to my naturall king and to him, and likewise he would

[1] Probably Khūshkhabar Khān, the title given by Jahāngīr to the man who brought him the news of the defeat of his rebel son Khusrau (*Tūzuk*, vol. i, p. 63).

allow me by the yeare three thousand and two hundred pounds sterling[1] for my first, and so yeerely hee promised mee to augment my living till I came to a thousand horse. So my first should be foure hundred horse; for the nobilitie of India have their titles by the number of their horses, that is to say, from fortie to twelve thousand, which pay belongeth to princes and his sonnes. I trusting upon his promise, and seeing it was beneficiall both to my nation and my selfe, beeing dispossessed of that benefit which I should have reaped if I had gone to Bantam, and that after halfe a doozen yeeres, Your Worships would send another man of sort in my place, in the meane time I should feather my neast, and doe you service; and further perceiving great injuries offered us, by reason the King is so farre from the ports; for all which causes above specified, I did not thinke it amisse to yeeld unto his request. Then, because my name was something hard for his pronuntiation, hee called me by the name of English Chan, that is to say, English lord, but in Persia it [i. e. Khān] is the title for a Duke; and this went currant throughout the countrey.

Now your Worships shall understand that I being now in the highest of my favours, the Jesuites and Portugalls slept not, but by all meanes sought my overthrow; and, to say the truth, the principall Mahumetans neere the King envyed much that a Christian should bee so nigh unto him. The Jesuite Peniero being with Mocrebchan, and the Jesuites here, I thinke did little regard their masses and church matters for studying how to overthrow my affaires; advice being gone to Goa by the Jesuites here, I meane in Agra, and to Padre Peneiro at Surat or Cambaya, hee working with Mocrebchan to be the Portugals assistance, and the Vice-Roy sending him a great present, together with many toyes [i. e. curiosities] unto the King with his letter. These presents and many more promises wrought so much with Mocrebchan that he writeth his petition

[1] The Jesuit accounts give Hawkins's stipend as 30,000 rupees, which would amount to about the sum here stated. Equal credit cannot be accorded to their statement that the Englishman gave the Emperor presents worth 25,000 gold pieces, four-fifths of which sum was represented by a single gem. (Du Jarric, vol. iii, p. 194.) The gold piece was doubtless the Venetian sequin (see p. 9).

unto the King, sending it together with the present, advertising the King that the suffring of the English in his land would be the cause of the losse of his owne countries neere the sea-coasts, as Suratt, Cambaya, and such like, and that in any case he entertaine me not, for that his ancient friends the Portugalls murmured highly at it, and that the fame is spread amongst the Portugalls that I was generall of ten thousand horsemen, readie to give the assault upon Diu when our shipping came.[1] The Vice-Royes letter likewise was in this kind. The Kings answere was that he had but one English-man in his court, and him they needed not to feare, for hee hath not pretended any such matter, for I would have given him living neere the sea parts but he refused it, taking it neere me heere. This was the Kings answere; upon which answere the Portugalls were like madde dogges, labouring to worke my passage out of the world. So I told the King what dangers I had passed, and the present danger wherein I was, my boy, Stephen Gravener, instantly departing this world, my man, Nicholas Ufflet,[2] extreame sicke, and this was all my English company, my selfe beginning to fall downe too. The King presently called the Jesuites and told them that if I dyed by any extraordinary casualtie, that they should all rue for it. This past, the King was very earnest with me to take a white mayden out of his palace; who would give her all things necessary, with slaves, and he would promise mee shee should turne Christian, and by this meanes my meates and drinkes should be looked unto by them, and I should live without feare. In regard she was a Moore, I refused; but if so bee there could bee a Christian found, I would accept it. At which my speech I little thought a Christians daughter could bee found. So the King called to memorie one Mubarique Sha [Mubārak

[1] Du Jarric (vol. iii, p. 196) repeats the allegation that Hawkins proposed to the Emperor the blockade by land of the Portuguese settlement at Diu, promising the help of fourteen ships to cut off relief from the sea.

[2] Ufflet returned to England with Hawkins, and then came out again in Downton's fleet. In 1617 we find him in Java, and two years later he died on board one of the vessels of Sir Thomas Dale's fleet. An account he appears to have written of Agra and the chief routes thither is referred to on a later page.

Shāh] his daughter, who was a Christian Armenian, and of the race of the most ancient Christians, who was a captaine and in great favour with Ekber Padasha [Hind. *Pādshāh*, Emperor], this kings father. This captaine dyed suddenly and without will, worth a masse of money, and all robbed by his brothers and kindred, and debts that cannot be recovered, leaving the child but only a few jewels. I, seeing shee was of so honest a descent, having passed my word to the King, could not withstand my fortunes; wherefore I tooke her and, for want of a minister, before Christian witnesses I marryed her.[1] The priest was my man Nicholas [Ufflet], which I thought had beene lawfull, till I met with a preacher that came with Sir Henry Middleton and, hee shewing me the error, I was new marryed againe. So ever after I lived content and without feare, she being willing to goe where I went, and live as I lived.

After these matters ended, newes came hither that the *Ascention* was to come, by the men of her pinnasse, that was cast away neere Suratt; upon which newes I presently went to the King and told him, craving his licence, together with his commission for the setling of our trade; which the King was willing to doe, limiting me a time to returne and be with him againe. But the Kings chiefe Vizir, Abdal Hassan,[2] a man envious to all Christians, told the King that my going would be the occasion of warre, and thus harme might happen unto a great man [i. e. Mukarrab Khān] who was sent for Goa to buy toyes for the King. Upon which speach the Kings pleasure was I should stay, and send away his commission to my chiefe factor at Surat; and presently gave order that it should be most effectually written. In fine, under his great seale with golden letters his commission was written, so firmely for our good and so free as heart can wish. This I obtained presently and sent it to William Finch. Before it

[1] According to Du Jarric, Hawkins applied to the Jesuit Father to perform the ceremony, but was told that this could only be done if he would acknowledge that the Pope was the head of the Church; whereupon he got his servant to officiate.

[2] Khwāja Abūl Hasan. In the *Tūzuk* (vol. i, p. 202) his office is spoken of as the chief Diwanship; while Jourdain terms him the King's secretary.

came there, newes came that the *Ascention* was cast away and her men saved, but not suffered to come into the citie of Surat. Of that likewise I told the King, who seemed to be very much discontented with that great captaine Mocreb-chan, my enemy, and gave me another commandement for their good usage and meanes to be wrought to save the goods, if it were possible. These two commandements came almost together, to the great joy of William Finch and the rest, admiring much at these things.

And now continuing these great favours with the King, being continually in his sight, for the one halfe of foure and twentie houres serving him day and night, I wanted not the greater part of his nobles that were Mahumetans to be mine enemies, for it went against their hearts that a Christian should be so great and neere the King ; and the more, because the King had promised to make his brothers children Christians, which two yeares after my coming he performed, commanding them to be made Christians.[1] A while after came some of the *Ascentions* company unto me (whom I could have wished of better behaviour, a thing pryed into by the King). In all this time I could not get my debts of Mocrebchan, till at length he was sent for up to the King to answere for many faults and tyrannicall injustice which he did to all people in those parts, many a man being undone by him, who petitioned to the King for justice. Now this dogge to make his peace sent many bribes to the Kings sonnes and noblemen that were neere the King, who laboured in his behalfe. After newes came that Mocrebchan was approached neere, the King presently sent to attach all his goods, which were in that abundance that the King was two moneths in viewing of them, every day allotting a certaine quantitie to be brought before me [him ?] ; and what he thought fitting for his owne turne he kept, and the rest delivered againe to Mocrebchan. In the viewing of these goods there came those peeces and costlet and head-peece, with other presents that he tooke from me for the King of mine owne, not suffering mee to bring them my selfe ; at the sight whereof I was so bold to tell the King what was mine. After the King had viewed these goods, a very great

[1] See the account of this given by Finch.

complaint was made by a Banian [Hindu trader], how that Mocrebchan had taken his daughter, saying she was for the King; which was his excuse, deflowring her himselfe, and afterwards gave her to a Brammen [Brahmin] belonging to Mocrebchan. The man who gave notice of this child protested her to passe all that ever he saw for beautie. The matter being examined, and the offence done by Mocrebchan found to be true, hee was committed to prison in the power of a great nobleman, and commandement was given that the Brammene his privy members should be cut off.[1]

Before this happened to Mocrebchan, I went to visite him divers times, who made me verie faire promises that he would deale very kindly with mee and be my friend, and that I should have my right. Now being in this disgrace, his friends daily sollicitng for him, at length got him cleere, with commandement that he pay every man his right, and that no more complaints be made of him if he loved his life. So Mocrebchan by the Kings command paid every one his due excepting me, whom he would not pay but deliver me my cloath, whereof I was desirous and to make (if it were possible) by faire meanes an end with him; but he put me off the more, delaying time till his departure, which was shortly after. For the King had restored him his old place againe, and he was to goe for Goa about a faire ballace ruby[2] and other rare things promised the King.

All my going and sending to Mocrebchan for my money or cloath was in vaine, I being abused so basely by him that I was forced to demaund justice of the King, who commanded that the money be brought before him; but for all the Kings commaund he did as he listed, and, doe what I could, he cut me off twelve thousand and five hundred mamadies. For the greatest man in this kingdome was his friend, and many others

[1] According to the *Tūzuk* (vol. i, p. 172), the complaint was made by a widow woman, whose daughter had been done to death in Mukarrab's Khān's house at Cambay. On investigation it was found that the outrage had been perpetrated by one of Mukarrab Khān's attendants, who was thereupon put to death and an allowance granted to the complainant; while Mukarrab Khān himself had his pay reduced by one half.

[2] Really a rose-red spinel. 'Balass' is said to mean *Badakhshi*, from Badakhshān, their place of origin.

holding on his side, murmuring to the King the suffering of English to come into his countrey, for that we were a nation that, if we once set foot, we would take his countrey from him. The King called me to make answere to that they said. I answered His Majestie that, if any such matter were, I would answer it with my life, and that we were not so base a nation as these mine enemies reported; all this was because I demaunded my due and yet cannot get it. At this time those that were neere favourites and neerest unto the King, whom I daily visited and kept in withall, spake in my behalfe; and the King, holding on my side, commanded that no more such wrongs be offred me. So I thinking to use my best in the recovery of this, intreting the head Vizir that he would be meanes that I receive not so great a losse, he answered me in a threatning manner, that if I did open my mouth any more hee would make me to pay an hundred thousand mamadies, which the King had lost in his customes by entertaining mee, and no man durst adventure by reason of the Portugall. So by this meanes I was forced to hold my tongue, for I know this money was swallowed by both these dogges. Now Mocrebchan being commaunded in publicke that by such a day he be ready to depart for Guzerat, and so for Goa,[1] and then come and take his leave, as the custome is: in this meane time three of the principallest merchants of Surat were sent for by the Kings commaundement and come to the court about affaires wherein the King or his Vizir had imployed them, being then present there when Mocrebchan was taking his leave, this being a plot laid both by the Portugals, Mocrebchan, and the Vizir, for some six daies before a letter came unto the King from the Portugall Vice-roy, with a present of many rare things. The contents of this letter were, how highly the King of Portugall tooke in ill part the entertaining of the English, he being of an ancient amitie, with other complements; and withall, how that a merchant was there arrived with a very

[1] Mukarrab Khān had been dispatched on this mission as early as September 1607, but had halted at Cambay to await news of the arrival at Goa of the expected Viceroy, the Conde de Feyra. The death of the latter and the disputes over the admission of the English had further delayed matters, and nothing had been done at the time of Mukarrab Khān's return to court. (Du Jarric, vol. iii, pp. 192, &c.)

faire ballace ruby, weighing three hundred and fiftie rotties,[1] of which stone the pattern was sent. Upon this newes Mocreb-chan was to be hastened away; at whose comming to take his leave, together with Padre Pineiro that was to goe with him, the above named merchants of Surat being then there present, Mocrebchan began to make his speech to the King, saying that this and many other things he hoped to obtaine of the Portugall, so that the English were disanulled; saying more, that it woud redound to great losse unto His Majestie and subjects if hee did further suffer the English to come into his parts. Upon which speech he called the merchants before the King to declare what losse it would be, for that they best knew. They affirmed that they were like to be all undone because of the English, nor hereafter any toy could come into this countrey, because the Portugal was so strong at sea and would not suffer them to goe in or out of their ports, and all their excuse was for suffering the English. These speeches now and formerly, and lucre of this stone, and promises by the Fathers of rare things were the causes the King overthrew my affaires, saying: Let the English come no more; presently giving Mocreb-chan his commandement to deliver the Viceroy to that effect, that he would never suffer the English to come any more into his ports.

I now saw that it booted me not to meddle upon a sudden, or to make any petition unto the King till a prety while after the departure of Mocreb-chan; and seeing my enemies were so many, although they had eaten of me many presents. When I saw my time, I made petition unto the King. In this space I found a toy to give, as the order is, for there is no man that commeth to make petition who commeth emptie-handed. Upon which petition made him, he presently graunted my request, commanding his Vizir to make me another commandement in as ample manner as my former, and commanded that no man should open his mouth to the contrary, for it was his pleasure that the English should come into his ports. So this time againe I was afloate. Of this alteration at that instant the Jesuite had notice; for there is no matter passeth in the Mogols court in secret, but it is knowne halfe an houre

[1] *Rati*, the seed of *Abrus precatorius*, used as a jeweller's weight.

after, giving a small matter to the writer of that day, for there is nothing that passeth but it is written, and writers appointed by turnes, so that the Father nor I could passe any businesse, but when we would we had notice. So the Jesuite presently sent away the most speedy messenger that could be gotten, with his letter to Padre Pineiro and Mocreb-chan, advertising them of all that had passed. At the receit of which they consulted amongst themselves not to goe forward on their voyage for Goa till I were overthrown againe. Wherefore Mocreb-chan wrote his petition unto the King, and letters unto his friend the head Vizir, how it stood not with the Kings honour to send him, if he performed not what he promised the Portugal, and that his voyage would be overthrowne, if he did not call in the commandement he had given the Englishman. Upon the receiving and reading of this, the King went againe from his word, esteeming a few toyes which the Fathers had promised him more then his honour.

Now beeing desirous to see the full issue of this, I went to Hogio Jahan,[1] Lord General of the Kings Palace (the second man in place in the kingdome), intreating him that he would stand my friend. He very kindly presently went unto the King, telling him that I was very heavy and discontent that Abdall Hassan would not deliver me my commandement, which His Majestie had graunted me. The King answered him (I being present and very neere him), saying, it was true that the commandement is sealed, and ready to be delivered him : but upon letters received from Mocreb-chan and better consideration by me had on these my affaires in my ports in Guzerat, I thought it fitting not to let him have it. Thus was I tossed and tumbled in the kind of a rich merchant adventuring all he had in one bottome, and by casualtie of stormes or pirates lost it all at once. So that on the other side, concerning my living, I was so crossed that many times this Abdall Hassan his answere would be unto me : I knowe wel enough you stand not in such need, for your master beareth your charges, and the King knew not what he did in giving to you, from whom

[1] Khwāja Jahān, the title given to Dost Muhammad of Kābul, whose daughter Jahāngīr had married. He was much employed by the Emperor in superintending architectural work at Agra and Lahore.

he should receive.[1] My answer was that it was the Kings pleasure and none of my request, and seeing it is His Majesties gift, I had no reason to loose it. So that from time to time he bad mee have patience and he would find out a good living for me. Thus was I dallied withall by this mine enemie, in so much that in all the time I served in court I could not get a living that would yeeld any thing, giving me my living still in places where out-lawes raigned. Only once at Lahor, by an especiall commandement from the King; but I was soon deprived of it, and all that I received from the beginning was not fully three hundred pounds, a great part whereof was spent upon charges of men sent to the lordships. When that I saw that the living which the King absolutely gave me was taken from me, I was then past all hopes; for before, at the newes of the arrivall of shipping, I had great hope that the King would performe former grants, in hope of rare things that should come from England. But when I made arse [see p. 56] or petition unto the King concerning my living, he turned me over to Abdal Hassan, who not onely denied me my living, but also gave order that I be suffered no more to enter within the red rayles, which is a place of honour where all my time I was placed very neere unto the King, in which place there were but five men in the kingdome before me.

Now perceiving that all my affaires were overthrowne, I determined with the councell of those that were neere me to resolve whereto to trust, either to be well in or well out. Upon this resolution I had my petition made ready, by which I made known unto the King how Abdall Hassan had dealt with me, having himselfe eaten what His Majestie gave me; and how that my charges of so long time (being by His Majestie desired to stay in his court, upon the faithfull promises he made me) were so much that it would be my utter overthrow; therefore I besought His Majestie that he would consider my cause, either to establish me as formerly, or give me leave to depart. His answere was that he gave me leave, commanding

[1] According to Jourdain, Khwāja Abūl Hasan told Hawkins that, 'beeinge a marchannt, he might plye his marchandizinge and not looke for any thinge att the Kings hands'.

his safe conduct to bee made mee to passe freely without molestation throughout his kingdomes. When this commandement was made, as the custome is, I came to doe my obeysance and to take my leave, intreating for an answere of my kings letter. Abdall Hassan, comming unto me from the King, in a disdainfull manner utterly denyed me, saying that it was not the custome of so great a monarch to write in the kind of a letter unto a pettie prince or governour. I answered him that the King knew more of the mightinesse of the King of England then to be a petty governour. Well, this was mine answere, together with my leave taken.

I went home to my house, studying with all my endeavours to get all my goods and debts together, and to buy commodities with those monies that were remayning, using all the speed I could to cleere my selfe of the countrey, staying only for Nicholas Ufflet to come from Lahor with a remainder of indico that was in William Finches power, who determined to goe overland, being past all hopes for ever imbarking our selves at Surat; which course I also would willingly have taken, but that (as it is well knowne) for some causes I could not travell thorow Turkie, and especially with a woman; so I was forced to currie favour with the Jesuites to get mee a safe conduct or seguro from the Vice-Roy to goe for Goa, and so to Portugall, and from thence to England, thinking (as the opinion of others was) that, the Vice-Roy giving his secure[1] royall, there would be no danger for me. But when my wifes mother and kindred saw that I was to carry her away, suspecting that they should never see her any more, they did so distaste me in these my travels that I was forced to yeeld unto them that my wife go no further then Goa, because it was India, and that they could goe and come and visit her, and that, if at any time I meant to goe for Portugall, or any other-where, that I leave her that portion that the custome of Portugall is to leave to their wives when they dye; unto which I was forced to yeeld, to give them content to prevent all mischiefes. But knowing that, if my wife would goe with me, all would bee of no effect, I effected with the Jesuite to send for two secures, the one concerning my quiet being and free libertie

[1] Port. *seguro* (as just above), 'assurance'.

of conscicnee in Goa, and to bee as a Portugall in all tradings and commerce in Goa (this was to shew my wifes parents), the other was an absolute grant for free passage into Portugall, and so for England, with my wife and goods, without any disturbances of any of my wives friends: and what agreements I made with them to be void and of none effect, but I should stay or goe when I pleased, with free libertie of conscicnce for my selfe. This last securo I should receive at Cambaya, which at my departure for our shippes was not yet come, but was to come with the carravan of frigats. This and much more the Fathers would have done for me, only to rid me out of the country; for being cleere of me, they should much more quietly sleepe. About this time I had notice of the comming of three English shipps, that were arrived at Mocha, and without faile their determination was to come for Surat at the time of the yeare; having this advertisement by Nicholas Bangham from Bramport, who departed from me some six weekes before, both for the recovery of certaine debts, as also with my letter to our shipping (if it were possible to send it) advertising them of my proceedings.

In this time of my dispatching, newes came of Mocreb-chans returne from Goa with many gallant and rare things, which he brought for the King.[1] But that ballace ruby was not for his turne, saying it was false, or at the least made his excuse, for feare that if he should give the Portugall his price and when it came into the Kings power it should bee valued much lesse (which overplus he should be forced to pay, as hee had done in former times for other things), hee left it behind him. And besides I understood that Mocrebchan had not his full content as he expected of the Portugalls. And likewise at this instant the Vizir, my enemy, was thrust out of his place for many complaints made of him by noblemen that were at great charges and in debt, and could not receive their livings in places that were good, but in barren and rebellious places, and that he made a benefit of the good places himselfe and robbed them all. For these complaints and others he had much ado to escape with life, being put out of his place and

[1] See the *Tūzuk*, vol. i, p. 215. One of the curiosities he brought was a turkeycock, in which Jahāngīr was much interested.

sent to the wars of Decan.[1] Now one Gaihbeig,[2] being the Kings chiefe treasurer (a man that in outward shew made much of me and was alwayes willing to pleasure me when I had occasion to use him), was made chiefe Vizir, and his daughter marryed with the King, being his chiefe queene or paramor. This Vizirs sonne and myselfe were great friends, he having beene often at my house, and was now exalted to high dignities by the King. Perceiving this alteration, and being certified of the comming of shipping by certaine advise sundry wayes, knowing the custome of these Moores that without gifts and bribes nothing would either goe forward or bee accomplished, I sent my broker to seeke out for jewels fitting for the Kings sister[3] and new paramour, and likewise for this new Vizir and his sonne.

Now after they had my gifts, they beganne on all sides to solicite my cause; at which time newes came to Agra by Banians of Diu how that of Diu three English ships were seene, and three dayes after other newes came that they were at the barre of Surat. Upon which newes the Great Vizir asked me what toy I had for the King. I shewed him a ruby ring that I had gotten, at the sight of which he bade me make readie to goe with him at court time and he would make my petition to the King, and told me that the King was alreadie wonne. So once more comming before His Greatnesse, and my petition being read, he presently granted mee the establishing of our factorie, and that the English come and freely trade for Surat; willing the Vizir that with all expedition my commandement be made; upon which grant the Vizir made signe unto mee to make obeysance, which I did according to the custome. But now what followed? A great

[1] There is nothing in the *Tūzuk* to support these accusations, and the fact that Abūl Hasan was put in charge of the province of the Deccan shows that the Emperor was not really displeased with him.

[2] Ghiyās Beg, Itimāduddaula. His daughter, Nūr Mahal (better known by her later title of Nūr Jahān) was married to the Emperor in May 1611. Her brother shared in the family honours by receiving the title of Itikād Khān. He is familiar to readers of Sir Thomas Roe's journal by his later style of Āsaf Khān, bestowed upon him in March 1614.

[3] Probably Shakarunnisa Begam, to whom Jahāngīr was much attached.

nobleman and neerest favourite of the King, being the dearest friend that Mocrebchan and likewise Abdall Hassan had, brought up together from their childhood, and pages together unto the King, began to make a speech unto the King, saying that the granting of this would be the utter overthrow of his sea coasts and people, as His Majestie had beene informed by petition from divers of his subjects: and besides, that it stood not with His Majesties honour to contradict that which he had granted to his ancient friends the Portugals, and whosoever laboured for the English knew not what he did; if knowing, hee was not His Majesties friend. Upon the speech of this nobleman my businesse once againe was quite overthrowne, and all my time and presents lost; the King answering that, for my nation, hee would not grant trade at the sea ports, for the inconvenience that divers times had beene scanned upon; but, for my selfe, if I would remayne in his service, he would command that what he had allowed me should be given me to my content; which I denyed, unlesse the English should come unto his ports according to promise, and, as for my particular maintenance, my King would not see me want. Then desiring againe answere of the Kings letter, he consulted awhile with his Vizirs and then sent me his denyall. So I tooke my leave, and departed from Agra the second of November, 1611, being of a thousand thoughts what course I were best to take; for I still had a doubt of the Portugalls that for lucre of my goods they would poyson me. Againe, on the other side, it was dangerous by reason of the warres to travell thorow Decan unto Masulipatan. By land, by reason of the Turkes, I could not goe; and to stay I would not amongst these faithlesse infidels.

I arrived at Cambaya the last of December, 1611,[1] where I had certaine newes of the English ships that were at Surat. Immediately I sent a footman unto the ships with my letter, with certaine advice, affirmed for a truth by the Fathers of Cambaya unto me, that the Vice-Roy had in a readinesse prepared to depart from Goa foure great ships, with certaine gallies and frigats, for to come upon them, and treasons plotted against Sir Henry Middletons person; of which newes I was

[1] This date appears to be a little too late: see Jourdain, p. 188.

wished by the Fathers to advise Sir Henry; which I found afterward to bee but their policie to put him in feare, and so to depart; and withall I wished them to be well advised. And as for me, my shifts were to goe home by the way of the Portugalls, for so I had promised my wife and her brother, who at that present was with me, and to delude him and the Fathers till I had notice for certaine that I might freely get aboord without feare, which I was assured to know at the returne of my letter. In the meane time I did all that I could to dispatch her brother away; who within two dayes after departed for Agra, not suspecting that I had any intent for the ships. Nicholas Ufflet now departing from mee to survey the way, beeing two dayes journey on his way, met with Captaine William[1] Sharpeigh, Master Fraine and Hugh Greete, sent by Sir Henry to Cambaya unto mee, which was no small joy unto mee. So understanding of the place (which was miraculously found out by Sir Henry Middleton, and never knowne to any of the countrey),[2] I admired and gave God thankes: for if this place had not beene found, it had beene impossible for mee to have gotten aboord with my goods. Wherefore making all the haste that I could in dispatching my selfe away, I departed from Cambaya the eighteenth of January, 1611 [1612] and came unto the ships the six and twentieth of the said moneth, where I was most kindly received by Sir Henry Middleton.

From this place we departed the eleventh of February, 1611 [1612] and arrived at Dabul [Dābhol] the sixteenth of the same; in which place we tooke a Portugall ship and frigat, out of which we tooke some quantitie of goods. And from thence we departed the fift of March, 1611 [1612] for the Red Sea, with an intent to revenge us of the wrongs offered us, both by Turkes and Mogols; at which place wee arrived the third of Aprill, 1612. Here we found three English ships; their Generall was Captaine John Saris.[3] Having dispatched our businesse in the Red Sea, wee set sayle from thence the

[1] A mistake for Alexander.

[2] This refers to the discovery of a safe anchorage in 'Swally Hole', for which see Jourdain's narrative, pp. xxxvi, 177, &c.

[3] See *The Voyage of John Saris*, Hakluyt Society, 1900.

sixteenth of August, 1612, and arrived in Tecu [Tiku] in Sumatra the ninteenth of October, 1612. And having ended our businesse there, we departed in the night the twentieth of November, 1612, and came on ground the same night, three leagues off, upon a bed of corall in three fathome water, or thereabouts ; and by the great mercie of God we escaped, but were forced to returne backe againe to stop her leakes, the goods being taken out and some damage received. Now her leakes being somewhat stopped, and her goods in, not losing an houre of time, wee departed from thence the eight of December, 1612, and arrived at Bantam the one and twentieth of the same ; where Sir Henry Midleton, not finding the *Trade* sufficient to goe home that yeare, was forced to stay and carine her. Having ended account with him, as himselfe liked best, I tooke my goods and shipped them in the *Salomon*, which came for our Voyage, for saving of a greater fraight ; but I could not be admitted to goe in her myselfe. Captaine Saris, I thanke him, accommodated me in the *Thomas*, and it was agreed that the *Salomon* and wee should keepe company together.

From thence we set sayle on the thirtieth of January, 1612 [1613], and arrived in Saldania Roade [Table Bay] the one and twentieth of Aprill, 1613 ; and comming neere some two hundred leagues from the Cape, we had much foule weather and contrary windes. Here we found foure sayle of Hollanders, that departed Bantam a moneth before us. There was great kindnesse betwixt us, especially to me, in regard that they had heard much of my great estate in India by an agent of theirs that was lieger [resident] at Masulipatan. Some eight dayes after, the *Expedition* [1] came in, and brought mee a letter from Your Worships and delivered it unto me two dayes after their arrivall. The wind comming faire we departed from Saldania the one and twentieth of May, 1613.

[1] This was the Twelfth Voyage, under Christopher Newport. An account of it, written by Walter Peyton, will be found in *Purchas His Pilgrimes* (part i, bk. iv, chap. 9).

A briefe discourse of the strength, wealth, and government with some customes of the Great Mogol, which I have both seene and gathered by his chiefe officers and over-seers of all his estate.

First, I begin with his princes, dukes, marquesses, earles, viscounts, barons, knights, esquires, gentlemen, and yeomen. As Christian princes use their degrees by titles, so they have their degrees and titles by their number of horses; unlesse it bee those that the King most favoureth, whom he honoureth with the title of Chan and Immirza [Mīrza]. None have the title of Sultan but his sonnes. Chan in the Persian language is as much as a duke. Immirza is the title for the Kings brothers children. They that be of the fame of twelve thousand horsemen belong to the King, and his mother,[1] and eldest sonne,[2] and one more, who is of the bloud royall of Uzbeck, named Chan Azam.[3] Dukes be nine thousand fame, marquesses five thousand fame, earles three thousand, viscounts two thousand, barons a thousand, knights foure hundred, esquires an hundred, gentlemen fifty, yeomen from twentie downwards.[4] All they that have these numbers of horsemen are called mansibdars,[5] or men of livings or lordships. Of these there be three thousand, that is to say; foure be of twelve thousand horse a-piece, and they be the King, his mother, Sultan Pervis, Prince, and Chan Azam. Of nine thousand horsemen there bee three, that is to say, Sultan Chorem,[6] the Kings third sonne, Chanchanna, and Kelich Chan [Kilīj Khān]. Of five thousand there bee eighteene, named Hasuff Chan, Chan Ichan, Abdula Chan, Raga Manging, Ray Durga, Raga Sursing, Ramadas Rechuva, Raga Bassu, Emirel Umera, Mahabet Chan, Chan Dowran, Sedris Chan,

[1] Maryam-zamāni. She was a daughter of Rāja Bihāri Mal.

[2] As shown below, Hawkins means Sultān Parwīz, who was Jahāngīr's second son. Khusrau, the eldest, was at this time a prisoner, owing to his rebellion.

[3] Azīz Koka, Khān Azam, a foster-brother of Akbar, in whose reign he had been a conspicuous figure. The allegation about his descent from a chief of the Uzbeg Tartars is not borne out by other evidence.

[4] This comparison with English degrees is rather fanciful, and the enumeration of the various grades is incomplete.

[5] *Mansab*, an office or rank; *-dār*, the holder thereof.

[6] Khurram, afterwards the Emperor Shāh Jahān.

Hogio Bey Mirza, Mirza Cazi, Ettebar Chan, Abulfet Dekenny, Jelam Cully Chan, Sheik Ferid. Of three thousand there bee two and twentie, to wit, Chan Alem, Imirza Ereg, Imirza Darab, Hogio Jahan, Hogio Abdal Hassan, Mirza Gaysbey, Mirza Shemchadin, Mirza Chadulla, Seffer Chan, Kazmy Chan, Mirza Chin Kelich, Saif Chan, Lalla Bersingdia, Mirza Zeady, Mirza Ally Ecberchuly, Terbiat Chan, Mirza Laschary, Mirza Charucogly, Mirza Rustem, Ally Merdon Badur, Tasbey Chan, Abulbey.[1] The rest bee from two thousand downwards till you come to twentie horses, two thousand nine hundred and fiftie. Of horsemen that receive pay monethly, from sixe horse to one, there be five thousand; these bee called haddies [*ahadi*]. Of such officers and men as belong to the court and campe there bee thirtie sixe thousand, to say, porters, gunners, watermen, lackeyes, horse-keepers, elephant-keepers, small-shot, frasses [*farrāsh*] or tent men, cookes, light bearers, gardiners, keepers of all kind of beasts. All these be payd monethly out of the Kings treasurie; whose wages be from ten to three rupias. All his captaines are to maintaine at a seven-nights warning from twelve thousand to twentie horse, all horsemen three leckes [*lakhs*], which is three hundred thousand horsemen, which of the incomes of their lordships allowed them they must maintayne.

The Kings yeerely income of his crowne land is fiftie crou [*kror*] of rupias.[2] Every crou is an hundred leckes, and every leck is an hundred thousand rupiae.

[1] Apart from misprints, these two lists appear to be both incomplete and incorrect. The persons named are probably: (i) Āsaf Khān (Jafar Beg), Khān Jahān Lodi, Abdullah Khān, Rāja Mān Singh of Jaipur, Rāy Dūrga, Rāja Sūrsing of Jodhpur, Rām Dās Kachhwāha, Rāja Bāso, the Amīrulumara (Sharīf Khān), Mahābat Khān, Khān Daurān, Idrīs Khān (?), Khwāja Beg Mīrza Safawi, Mīrza Kāsim (?), Itibār Khān, Abūlfath Dekhani, Jahāngīr Kuli Khān (?), Shaikh Farīd Bukhāri; (ii) Khān Ālam, Mīrza Īraj (Shāhnawāz Khān), Mīrza Dārāb, Khwāja Jahān, Khwāja Abūl Hasan, Mīrza Ghiyās Beg, Mīrza Shamsuddīn, Mīrza Sadullah, Zafar Khān, Kāzmi Khān (?), Mīrza Chīn Kilīj, Saif Khān Bārha, Lāla Bīr Singh Deo of Orchha, Mīrza Zāhid (?), Mīrza Ali Akbar Kuli, Tarbiyat Khān, Mīrza Lashkari, Mīrza Shāhrukh Oglu (?), Mīrza Rustam, Ali Mardān Khān Bahādur, Tāsh Beg Khān, Abūlbi Uzbeg.

[2] At 2*s*. 3*d*. the rupee, this would equal 56¼ millions of pounds sterling. Edward Thomas, in his *Revenue Resources of the Mughal Empire* (p. 23),

The compasse of his countrey is two yeares travell with carravan, to say, from Candahar to Agra, from Soughtare [1] in Bengala to Agra, from Cabul to Agra, from Decan to Agra, from Surat to Agra, from Tatta in Sinde to Agra. Agra is in a manner in the heart of all his kingdomes.

His empire is divided into five great kingdomes. The first named Pengab [Panjāb], whereof Lahor is the chiefe seate; the second is Bengala, the chiefe seate Sonargham [Sonārgaon]; the third is Malva [Mālwa], the chiefe seate is Ugam [Ujjain]; the fourth is Decan, the chiefe seate Bramport [Burhānpur]; the fifth is Guzerat, the chiefe seat is Amadavar [Ahmadābād]. The chiefe citie or seate royall of the Kings of India is called Delly, where hee is established king, and there all the rites touching his coronation are performed.

There are sixe especiall castles, to say, Agra, Guallier [Gwalior], Nerver, Ratamboore, Hassier, Roughtaz.[2] In every one of these castles he hath his treasure kept.

In all his empire there are three arch-enemies or rebels, which with all his forces cannot be called in, to say, Amberry Chapu [3] in Decan; in Guzerat the sonne of Muzafer that was king (his name is Bahador); [4] of Malva, Raga Rahana.[5] His sonnes be five, to say, Sultan Coussero, Sultan Pervis, Sultan Chorem, Sultan Shariar, and Sultan Bath.[6] Hee hath

accepts this statement as authoritative, with the reservation that Hawkins must have meant it to include receipts from all sources, not merely from land revenue. It should be noted, however, that Salbank, writing from Agra in 1617, declared that Hawkins had exaggerated the amount (*Letters Received*, vol. vi, p. 187). The impression likely to be made on the Englishmen of that day by such figures may be gauged by the fact that the public revenue in England was then only about £425,000 per annum.

[1] Possibly meant for Kiyāra Sundar, near Sonārgaon. Roe mentions this place as the easternmost limit of the empire.

[2] The last four are Narwar (now in Gwalior State), Ranthambhor (in Jaipur), Asīr (near Burhānpur), and Rohtās (in the Shāhābād district, Bihār).

[3] Malik Ambar, for whom see p. 130. 'Chapu' is possibly a misreading of some form of 'Habashi' (Abyssinian).

[4] Bahādur, son of Muzaffar Shāh III, the last king of Gujarāt.

[5] The Rāja Rāna of Udaipur (Amar Singh).

[6] Jahāngīr's sons were Khusrau, Parwīz, Khurram, Shahryār, and Jahāndār. Terry calls the last named Takht, and possibly 'Bath' is

two yong daughters,[1] and three hundred wives, whereof foure be chiefe as queenes, to say, the first, named Padasha Banu,[2] daughter to Kaime Chan ; the second is called Noore Mahal, the daughter of Gais Beyge ; the third is the daughter of Seinchan [3] ; the fourth is the daughter of Hakim Hamaun, who was brother to his father, Ecber Padasha.[4]

His treasure is as followeth : the first is his severall coine of gold.[5]

Inprimis, of seraffins Ecberi,[6] which be ten rupias a piece, there are sixtie leckes. Of another sort of coyne of a thousand rupias a piece,[7] there are twentie thousand pieces. Of another sorte of halfe the value there are ten thousand pieces. Of another sort of gold of twenty toles [8] a piece there are thirtie thousand pieces. Of another sort of tenne toles a piece there bee five and twenty thousand pieces. Of another sort of five toles, which is this kings stampe, of these there be fiftie thousand pieces.

a misprint for this. Similarly, Salbank in *Letters Received*, vol. vi, p. 189, speaks of ' Sultan Take '.

[1] Sultānunnisa and Bihār Bānu Begam.

[2] Pādshāh Bānu Begam, daughter of Kāim Khān.

[3] Zain Khān Koka, Akbar's foster-brother.

[4] Nothing seems to be known of this consort of Jahāngīr. Hakim Humām was a favourite officer of Akbar, but not his brother. Perhaps he is confused with Mīrza Muhammad Hakīm, governor of Kābul, who was a brother of that monarch.

[5] Purchas, in his *Pilgrimage* (p. 522), says that Withington ' received of the Jesuites which reside there this same story of the Mogols treasures '. Probably Hawkins obtained his information from the same source.

[6] Mohurs of Akbar's coinage. ' Xerafim ' was the Portuguese form of *Ashrafi*, which was frequently used for the gold mohur.

[7] The Mughals coined pieces of 200, 100, and 50 mohurs, but they seem to have been used chiefly for presentation by or to the Emperor on ceremonial occasions. An account of them will be found in Lane Poole's *Coins of the Moghul Emperors* (p. lxxxvii). Manucci (*Storia do Mogor*, vol. i, p. 206) speaks of pieces of 100, 500, and 1,000 mohurs, adding ' the king gave them as presents to his ladies. When I was attending as physician on one of these, she made me a present of one of these coins.'

[8] ' A tole is a rupia challany [*chalani*, current] of silver, and ten of these toles are the value of one of gold ' (*marginal note*). The *tola* was a goldsmith's weight, equivalent to 96 *ratis*. The rupee weighed about a *tola*.

Of silver, as followeth.

Inprimis, of rupias Ecbery, thirteene crou (every crou is an hundred leckes and every leck an hundred thousand rupias), is one thousand three hundred leckes. Of another sort of coine of Selim Sha,[1] this king, of an hundred toles a piece, there are fiftie thousand pieces. Of fiftie toles a piece there is one lecke. Of thirtie toles a piece there are fortie thousand pieces. Of twentie toles a piece there are thirtie thousand pieces. Of ten toles a piece there are twentie thousand pieces. Of five toles a piece there are five and twentie thousand pieces. Of a certaine money that is called savoy,[2] which is a tole ¼, of these there are two leckes. Of jagaries,[3] whereof five make sixe toles, there is one lecke. More should have been coyned of this stampe, but the contrary was commanded.

Here followeth of his jewells of all sorts.

Inprimis, of diamantes 1½ battman ; these be rough, of all sorts and sizes, great and small, but no lesse then 2½ caratts. The battman[4] is fifty five pound waight, which maketh eightie two pounds ½ weight English.[5] Of ballace rubies little and great, good and bad, there are single two thousand pieces. Of pearle of all sorts there are twelve battmans. Of rubies of all sorts there are two battmans. Of emeraudes of all sorts, five battmans. Of eshime,[6] which stone commeth from Cathaia [China], one battman. Of stones of Emen,[7] which is a red stone, there are five thousand pieces. Of all other sorts, as corall, topasses, etc., there is an infinite number.

[1] Jahāngīr's birth-name was Salīm, after Shaikh Salīm, the hermit of Fatehpur Sīkri, who had prophesied his birth.

[2] Rupees called *sawāi*, 'an excess of one fourth.'

[3] Jahāngīri rupees, five of which (as Ufflet confirms) were worth six ordinary rupees. Roe values them at 2*s.* 7*d.* each. This account of Jahāngīr's coins should be compared with that given in the *Tūzuk*, vol. i, p. 10.

[4] The *bātmān*, a Turkish weight, is here used for the Indian maund (cf. p. 105). Finch employs the term in the same way (*Letters Received*, vol. i, p. 28).

[5] For the total weight of the diamonds.

[6] Jade (Persian *yashm*).

[7] Cornelian (*yamani*).

Here followeth of the jewels wrought in gold.

Of swords of Almaine [German] blades, with the hilts and scabberds set with divers sorts of rich stones of the richest sort, there are two thousand and two hundred. Of two sorts of poniards there bee two thousand. Of saddle drummes, which they use in their hawking, of these there are very rich ones of gold set with stones, five hundred. Of brooches for their heads [i. e. the *sarpesh*], whereinto their feathers be put, these be very rich, and of them there are two thousand. Of saddles of gold and silver set with stones there are one thousand. Of teukes[1] there be five and twentie; this is a great launce covered with gold and the fluke set with stones, and these, instead of their colours, are carryed when the King goeth to the warres; of these there are five and twentie. Of kittasoles [Port. *quitasol*, a sunshade] of state, for to shaddow him, there bee twentie. None in his empire dareth in any sort have any of these carryed for his shadow but himselfe; of these, I say, there are twentie. Of chaires of estate there bee five, to say, three of silver and two of gold; and of other sorts of chaires there bee an hundred of silver and gold; in all an hundred and five. Of rich glasses there bee two hundred. Of vases for wine very faire and rich, set with jewels, there are an hundred. Of drinking cuppes five hundred, but fiftie very rich, that is to say, made of one piece of ballace ruby, and also of emerods [emeralds], of eshim, of Turkish stone [turquoises], and of other sorts of stones. Of chaines of pearle, and chaines of all sorts of precious stones, and ringes with jewels of rich diamants, ballace rubies, rubies, and old emerods, there is an infinite number, which only the keeper thereof knoweth. Of all sorts of plate, as dishes, cups, basons, pots, beakers of silver wrought, there are two thousand battmans. Of gold wrought, there are one thousand battmans.

Here followeth of all sorts of beasts.

Of horses there are twelve thousand; whereof there bee of Persian horses foure thousand, of Turkie horses six thousand,

[1] Turkish *toq* or *togh*, a flag or standard. Blochmann gives an illustration of one in his translation of the *Āīn-i-Akbari*.

and of Kismire [Kashmīr] two thousand; all are twelve thousand. Of elephants there be twelve thousand, whereof five thousand bee teeth elephants and seven thousand of shee ones and yong ones; which are twelve thousand. Of camels there be two thousand. Of oxen for the cart and all other services there bee tenne thousand. Of moyles [mules] there be one thousand. Of deere like buckes, for game and sport, there be three thousand. Of ounces [see p. 17] for game there be foure hundred. Of dogges for hunting, as grey-hounds and other, there be foure hundred. Of lions tame there are an hundred. Of buffalaes there be five hundred. Of all sorts of hawkes there bee foure thousand. Of pidgeons for sport of flying there bee ten thousand. Of all sorts of singing birds there be foure thousand. Of armour of all sorts, at an houres warning, in a readinesse to arme five and twentie thousand men.

His daily expences for his owne person, that is to say, for feeding of his cattell of all sorts, and amongst them some few elephants royall, and all other expences particularly, as apparell, victuals, and other petty expences for his house, amounts to fiftie thousand rupias a day. The expences daily for his women by the day is thirtie thousand rupias.[1]

All this written concerning his treasure, expences, and monethly pay is in his court or castle of Agra; and every one of the castles above nominated have their severall treasure, especially Lahor, which was not mentioned.

The custome of this Mogoll Emperour is to take possession of his noblemens treasure when they dye, and to bestow on his [their] children what he pleaseth; but commonly he dealeth well with them, possessing them with their fathers land, dividing it amongst them; and unto the eldest sonne he hath a very great respect, who in time receiveth the full

[1] Jourdain says (p. 164): 'The Kinge is at greate charge in expence of his howse and for his beasts, as horses, camells, dromedaries, coaches, and elaphannts. It was crediblie reported to Captaine Hawkins in my presence by the Kings purveyour for his beasts, that every daie in the yeare he spent in meate for them 70,000 ripeas, which is 35,000 rialls of eight. His wives, there slaves, and his concubines doe spend him an infinite deale of money, incredible to bee believed, and therefore I omitt itt.'

title of his father. There was in my time a great Indian lord or prince, a Gentile named Raga Gaginat,[1] upon whose goods the Kings seizing after his death, he was found (besides jewels and other treasure) to have sixtie maunes [maunds] in gold, and every maune is five and fiftie pound waight. Also his custome is that of all sorts of treasure excepting coine, to say, of all sorts of beasts, and all other things of value, a small quantitie is daily brought before him. All things are severally divided into three hundred and sixtie parts; so that hee daily seeth a certaine number, to say, of elephants, horses, camels, dromedaries, moyles, oxen, and all other; as also a certaine quantitie of jewels, and so it continueth all the yeere long; for what is brought him to day is not seene againe till that day twelve moneth.

He hath three hundred elephants royall, which are elephants whereon himselfe rideth; and when they are brought before him they come with great jollitie, having some twentie or thirty men before them with small stremers. The elephants cloth or covering is very rich, eyther of cloth of gold or rich velvet; hee hath following him his shee elephant, his whelpe or whelpes, and foure or five yong ones as pages, which will bee in number some sixe, some seven, and some eight or nine. These elephants and other cattell are dispersed among his nobles and men of sort to oversee them, the King allowing them for their expences a certaine quantitie; but some of them will eate a great deale more then their allowance commeth unto. These elephants royall eate tenne rupias every day in sugar, butter, graine, and sugar canes. These elephants are the goodliest and fairest of all the rest, and tame withall, so managed that I saw with mine eyes when the King commanded one of his young sonnes named Shariar (a childe of seven yeeres of age) to goe to the elephant to bee taken up by him with his snout; who did so, delivering him to his keeper that commanded him with his hooke; and having done this unto the Kings sonne, he afterwards did the like to many other children. When these elephants are shewed, if they who have the charge of them bring them leane, then are they checked and in disgrace,

[1] Rāja Jagannāth, son of Rāja Bihāri Mal.

unlesse their excuse bee the better. And so it is with all things else in that kind, that every man striveth to bring his quantitie in good liking, although hee spend of his owne.

When hee rideth on progresse or hunting, the compasse of his tents may bee as much as the compasse of London and more; and I may say that of all sorts of people that follow the campe there are two hundred thousand, for hee is provided as for a citie. This king is thought to be the greatest emperour of the East for wealth, land, and force of men, as also for horses, elephants, camels, and dromedaries. As for elephants of his owne and of his nobles, there are fortie thousand, of which the one halfe are trayned elephants for the warre; and these elephants of all beasts are the most understanding. I thought good here to set downe this one thing, which was reported to me for a certainty, although it seemed very strange. An elephant having journyed very hard, being on his travell, was misused by his commander; and one day finding the fellow asleepe by him, but out of his reach, having greene canes brought him to eate, split the end of one of them with his teeth, and taking the other end of the cane with his snowt, reached it toward the head of the fellow, who being fast asleepe and his turbant fallen from his head (the use of India being to wear their haire long like women) he tooke hold with the cane on his haire, wreathing it therein and withall haling him unto him untill he brought him within the compasse of his snowt; he then presently killed him. Many other strange things are done by elephants.

He hath also infinite numbers of dromedaries, which are very swift, to come with great speed to give assault to any citie; as this kings father did, so that the enemies thought he had beene in Agra when he was at Amadavar, and he came from Agra thither in nine daies upon these dromedaries with twelve thousand choyce men, Chan-channa being then his generall. The day being appointed for the battell, on a suddaine newes came of the Kings arrivall, which strucke such a present feare into the Guzerats that at that time they were overthrowne and conquered.[1] This king hath diminished his chiefe captaines, which were Rasbootes [Rājputs] or Gentiles,

[1] This was in the autumn of 1573.

and naturall Indians, and hath preferred the Mahumetans (weak spirited men, void of resolution) in such sort that what this mans father, called Ecber Padasha, got of the Decans, this king, Selim Sha, beginneth to loose. He hath a few good captaines yet remaining, whom his father highly esteemed, although they be out of favour with him, because that upon his rebellion against his father they would not assist him, considering his intent was naught, for he meant to have shortned his fathers daies and before his time to have come to the crowne. And to that purpose being in Attabase,[1] the regall seate of a kingdome called Porub, hee arose with eighty thousand horse, intending to take Agra and to have possession of the treasury, his father being then at the warres of Decan; who, understanding of his sonnes pretence, left his conquering there and made hast to come home to save his owne. Before the Kings departure to the warres, hee gave order to his sonne to goe with his forces upon Aranna [see p. 100], that great rebell in Malva; who comming to parle with this rebell, he told the Prince that there was nothing to bee gotten by him but blowes, and it were better for him, now his father was at Decan, to goe upon Agra and possesse himselfe of his fathers treasure and make himselfe king, for there was no man able to resist him. The Prince followed his counsell and would have prosecuted it but his fathers hast before (upon notice given) prevented his purpose; at whose arrivall at Agra hee presently sent unto his sonne, that he make choyce either to come and fall at his feete and be at his mercy to doe with him as he pleased, or to fit himselfe for the battell and fight it out. He, well considering the valour of his father, thought it meetest to submit himselfe and stand to his fathers mercy; who, after affronts shewed him and imprisonment, was soone released and pardoned by reason of many friends, his mother, sisters, and others.[2]

This Selim Padasha being in his rebellion, his father dispossessed him and proclaimed heire apparant his eldest sonne

[1] Ilahābās, the old name for Allahābād. 'Porub' (Hind. *Purb*, 'the east') was the country east and north of the Ganges, including Oudh and part of Bihār.

[2] This account of Salīm's rebellion contains several inaccuracies.

Cossero,[1] being eldest sonne to Selimsha ; for his owne sonnes [Murād and Dāniyāl], younger brothers to Selim, were all dead in Decan and Guzerat. Yet shortly after his father dyed, who in his death-bed had mercy on Selim, possessing him againe. But Cossero, who was proclaimed heire apparant, stomached his father, and rose with great troopes, yet was not able to indure after the losse of many thousand men on both sides, but was taken and remaineth still in prison in the Kings pallace, yet blinde, as all men report, and was so commaunded to be blinded by his father.[2] So since that time, being now eight yeares after, he had commanded to put all his sonnes confederates to death, with sundry kinds of death, some to bee hanged, some spitted, some to have their heads chopped off, and some to bee torne by elephants. Since which time hee hath raigned in quiet, but ill beloved of the greater part of his subjects, who stand greatly in feare of him. His custome is every yeare to be out two moneths on hunting, as is before specified. When he meaneth to begin his journey, if comming forth of his pallace hee get up on a horse, it is a signe that he goeth for the warres ; but if he get up upon an elephant or palankine, it will bee but an hunting voyage.

My selfe, in the time that I was one of his courtiers, have seene many cruell deeds done by him. Five times a weeke he commaundeth his brave elephants to fight before him ; and in the time of their fighting, either comming or going out, many times men are killed or dangerously hurt by these elephants. But if any be grievously hurt which might very well escape, yet neverthelesse that man is cast into the river, himselfe commaunding it, saying : dispatch him, for as long as he liveth he will doe nothing else but curse me, and therefore it is better that he dye presently. I have seene many in this kind. Againe, hee delighteth to see men executed himselfe and torne in peeces with elephants. He put to death in my time his secretary, onely upon suspicion that Chan-channa should write unto the Decan king ; who, being sent for and examined about this matter, denied it ; whereupon the King,

[1] Khusrau. The statement that Akbar recognized him as his heir is incorrect.

[2] See Finch's account

not having patience, arose from his seate and with his sword gave him his deadly wound, and afterwards delivered him to bee torne by elephants.

Likewise it happened to one who was a great friend of mine (a chiefe man, having under his charge the Kings ward-robe and all woollen cloath, and all sorts of mercery, and his China dishes), that a faire China dish (which cost ninetie rupias or fortie five rials of eight) was broken in this my friends time by a mischance (when the King was in his progresse), being packed amongst other things on a cammell, which fell and broke all the whole parcell. This nobleman, knowing how deerely the King loved this dish above the rest, presently sent one of his trusty servants to China-machina [China] over land to seeke for another, hoping that, before he should remember that dish, he would returne with another like unto it; but his evill lucke was contrarie, for the King two yeares after remembred this dish, and his man was not yet come. Now when the King heard that the dish was broken, he was in a great rage, commanding him to be brought before him and to be beaten by two men with two great whips made of cords; and after that he had received one hundred and twenty of these lashes, he commanded his porters, who be appointed for that purpose, to beate him with their small cudgels, till a great many of them were broken; at the least twenty men were beating of him, till the poore man was thought to bee dead, and then he was haled out by the heeles and commaunded to prison. The next day the King demaunded whether he was living; answer was made that he was; whereupon he commanded him to be carried unto perpetuall prison. But the Kings sonne, being his friend, freed him of that and obtained of his father that he might bee sent home to his owne house and there be cured. So after two moneths he was reasonably well recovered and came before the King, who presently commanded him to depart the court and never come againe before him untill he had found such a like dish, and that hee travell for China-machina to seeke it. The King allowed him five thousand rupias[1] towards his charges, and besides

[1] Jourdain, who tells the story with some variations, says 50,000 (p. 166). Terry has a brief reference to the anecdote (p. 338).

returning one fourth part of his living that he had before, to maintaine him in his travell. He being departed and fourteene moneths on his travell, was not yet come home; but newes came of him that the King of Persia had the like dish and for pitties sake hath sent it him; who at my departure was on his way homeward.

Likewise in my time it happened that a Pattan, a man of good stature, came to one of the Kings sonnes, named Sultan Pervis, to intreat him to bestow somewhat on him, by petition delivered to one of the Princes chiefe men; at the delivery whereof the Prince caused him to come neere; and demanding of him whether hee would serve him, he answered no, for he thought that the Prince would not grant him so much as he would aske. The Prince, seeing him to be a pretty fellow and meanely apparelled, smiled, demanding what would content him. Hee told him plainly that hee would neither serve his father nor him under a thousand rupias a day, which is 100 pound sterling. The Prince asked what was in him that he demanded so much. He replyed: make tryall of me with all sorts of weapons, either on horsebacke or on foote; and for my sufficient command in the warres, if I do not performe as much as I speake, let mee dye for it. The houre being come for the Prince to go to his father, he gave over his talk, commanding the man to be forth comming. At night the Kings custome being to drinke, the Prince, perceiving his father to be merry, told him of this man. So the King commaunded him to be brought before him. Now while he was sent for, a wilde lyon was brought in, a very great one, strongly chained, and led by a dozen men and keepers; and while the King was viewing this lyon, the Pattan came in, at whose sight the Prince presently remembred his father. The King demanding of this Pattan whence he was, and of what parentage, and what valour was in him that he should demand so much wages, his answer was that the King should make tryal of him. That I will, saith the King; goe wrastle and buffet with this lyon. The Pattans answere was that this was a wild beast, and to goe barely upon him without weapon would be no triall of his manhood. The King, not regarding his speech, commanded him to buckle with the lion; who did so, wrastling and buffeting with the lyon a pretty while; and then the lyon, being loose from his keepers, but not from his chaines, got the poore man within his clawes and tore his body in many parts, and with his pawes tore the one halfe of his face so that this valiant man was killed by this wilde beast.[1] The King, not yet contented, but desirous to see more sport, sent for ten men that were of his horse-men in pay, being that night on the watch; for it is the custome of all those that receive pay or living from the King to watch once a weeke, none excepted, if they be well and in the citie. These men, one after another, were to buffet with the lyon; who were all grievously wounded, and it cost three of them their lives. The King continued three moneths in this vaine when he was in his humors, for whose pleasure sake many men lost their lives and many were grievously wounded. So that ever after, untill my comming away, some fifteene young lyons were made tame and played one with another before the King, frisking betweene mens legs and no man hurt in a long time.

Likewise he cannot abide that any man should have any precious stone of value, for it is death if he know it not at that present time, and that he hath the refusall thereof. His jeweller, a Bannian, named Herranand [Hīra Nand], had bought a diamond of three mettegals,[2] which cost one hundred thousand rupias; which was not so closely done but newes came to the King. Herranand likewise was befriended, beeing presently acquainted therewith; who, before the King sent for him, came unto him and challenged the King that he had often promised him that he would come to his house. The King answered that it was true. Herranand therefore replyed that now was the time, for that he had a faire present to bestow upon His Majestie, for that he had bought a stone of such a weight. The King smiled and said: thy lucke was good to prevent me. So preparation was made, and to the Bannians house he went. By this means the King hath ingrossed all faire stones, that no man can buy from five carats upwards with-

[1] This anecdote is also told by Jourdain (p. 160).
[2] Arabic *mithkāl*, a weight of about 73 grains.

out his leave[1]; for he hath the refusall of all, and giveth not by a third part so much as their value. There was a diamant cutter of my acquaintance that was sent for to cut a diamant of three mettegals and a halfe, who demanded a small foule diamant to make powder, wherewith to cut the other diamant. They brought him a chest, as he said, of three spannes long and a spanne and half broad, and a spanne and halfe deepe, full of diamants of all sizes and sorts; yet could he find never any one for his purpose, but one of five rotties, which was not very foule neither.

He is exceeding rich in diamants and all other precious stones, and usually weareth every day a faire diamant of great price; and that which he weareth this day, till his time be come about to weare it againe he weareth not the same; that is to say, all his faire jewels are divided into a certaine quantitie or proportion to weare every day. He also weareth a chaine of pearle, very faire and great, and another chaine of emeralds and ballace rubies. Hee hath another jewell that commeth round about his turbant, full of faire diamants and rubies. It is not much to bee wondered that he is so rich in jewels and in gold and silver, when he hath heaped together the treasure and jewels of so many kings as his forefathers have conquered, who likewise were a long time in gathering them together, and all came to his hands. Againe, all the money and jewels which his nobles heape together, when they die come all unto him, who giveth what he listeth to the noblemens wives and children; and this is done to all them that receive pay or living from the King. India is rich in silver, for all nations bring coyne and carry away commodities for the same; and this coyne is buried in India and goeth not out; so it is thought that once in twentie yeeres it commeth into the Kings power. All the lands in his monarchie are at his disposing, who giveth and taketh at his pleasure.[2] If I have lands at Lahor, being sent unto

[1] Jourdain (p. 164) says the same, but adds that dealings took place secretly.

[2] 'Those lands which are let pay to the king two thirds of the profit; and of those which he giveth in fee, one third remaineth to the King. In all the world is not more fertile land then in some great parts of his dominions.' (*Marginal note.*)

the warres at Decan, another hath the lands, and I am to receive mine in Decan, or thereabouts, neere the place where I am, whether it be in the warres, or that I be sent about any other businesse for any other countrey. And men are to looke well unto their doings ; for if they be found tardie in never so little a matter, they are in danger of loosing their lands ; and if complaints of injustice which they doe be made unto the King, it is well if they escape with losse of their lands.

He is very severe in such causes, and with all severitie punisheth those captaines who suffer out-lawes to give assault unto their citie, without resisting. In my time there were some eight captaines who had their living upon the borders of Bengala, in a chiefe citie called Pattana [Patna], which was suffered to be taken by out-lawes, and they all fled ; but that citie was againe restored by a great captaine, who was commander of a countrey neere thereabouts, who tooke all those captaines that fled and sent them to the King to use punishment upon them at his pleasure. So they were brought before the King in chaines and were presently commanded to be shaven, both head and beard, and to weare womens apparell, riding upon asses with their faces backwards, and so carried about the citie. This being done, they were brought before the King againe and there whipped, and sent to perpetuall prison ; and this punishment was inflicted upon them in my sight.[1] He is severe enough, but all helpeth not, for his poore riats [*raīyat*, a cultivator] or clownes complaine of injustice done them and cry for justice at the Kings hands. They come to a certaine place where a long rope is fastened unto two pillars, neere unto the place where the King sitteth in justice.[2] This rope is hanged full of bels, plated with gold, so that the rope beeing shaken the bels are heard by the King; who sendeth to know the cause and doth his justice accordingly. At his first comming to the crowne he was more severe than now he is ; which is the cause that the country is so full of outlawes and theeves that almost a man cannot stirre out of doores throughout

[1] For this outbreak, and the punishment of the officials who failed in their duty, see the *Tūzuk*, vol. i, p. 173.

[2] See Jahāngīr's own account of this chain in the *Tūzuk*, vol. i, p. 7.

all his dominions without great forces, for they are all become rebels.

There is one great Ragane [see p. 100] betwixt Agra and Amadavar, who commandeth as much land as a good kingdome, and all the forces the Mogol hath cannot bring him in, for his forces are upon the mountaines. He is twentie thousand strong in horse, and fiftie thousand strong in foote. And many of these rebels are in all his dominions; but this is one of the greatest. There are many risen at Candahar, Cabul, Moldun [Multān], and Sinde, and in the kingdome of Boloch [Balkh]: Bengala likewise, Decan, and Guzerat are full, so that a man can travell no way for out-lawes. Their government is in such a barbarous kind, and cruell exacting upon the clownes, which causeth them to be so headstrong. The fault is in the chiefe, for a man cannot continue halfe a yeere in his living but it is taken from him and given unto another; or else the King taketh it for himselfe (if it be rich ground and likely to yeeld much), making exchange for a worse place; or as he is befriended of the Vizir. By this meanes he racketh the poore to get from them what he can, who still thinketh every houre to be put out of his place. But there are many who continue a long time in one place, and if they remaine but sixe yeeres their wealth which they gaine is infinite, if it be a thing of any sort. The custome is, they are allowed so much living to maintaine that port which the King hath given them; that is to say, they are allowed twentie rupias of everie horse by the moneth, and two rupias by the moneth for every horse fame, for the maintenance of their table. As thus: a captaine that hath five thousand horse to maintaine in the warres hath likewise of fame other five thousand, which he is not to maintaine in the warres, but onely for his table, allowed upon every horse by the moneth two rupias, and the other five thousand, twenty rupias by the moneth; and this is the pay which the greater part of them are allowed.[1]

Now here I meane to speake a little of his manners and customes in the court. First, in the morning about the breake of day he is at his beades, with his face turned to the west-ward. The manner of his praying, when he is in Agra, is in a private

[1] Roe (*Embassy*, p. 110) gives the rate as £25 per annum per horse.

faire roome, upon a goodly jet stone,[1] having onely a Persian lamb-skinne under him; having also some eight chaines of beads, every one of them containing foure hundred. The beads are of rich pearle, ballace rubyes, diamonds, rubyes, emeralds, lignum aloes, eshem, and corall. At the upper end of this jet stone the pictures of Our Lady and Christ are placed, graven in stone; so he turneth over his beads, and saith three thousand two hundred words, according to the number of his beads, and then his prayer is ended. After he hath done, he sheweth himselfe to the people, receiving their salames[2] or good morrowes; unto whom multitudes resort every morning for this purpose. This done, hee sleepeth two houres more, and then dineth and passeth his time with his women, and at noone hee sheweth himselfe to the people againe, sitting till three of the clocke, viewing and seeing his pastimes and sports made by men, and fighting of many sorts of beasts, every day sundry kinds of pastimes. Then at three of the clocke, all the nobles in generall (that be in Agra and are well) resort unto the court, the King comming forth in open audience, sitting in his seat-royall, and every man standing in his degree before him, his chiefest sort of the nobles standing within a red rayle, and the rest without. They are all placed by his Lieutenant-Generall. This red rayle is three steppes higher then the place where the rest stand; and within this red rayle I was placed, amongst the chiefest of all. The rest are placed by officers, and they likewise be within another very spacious place rayled; and without that rayle stand all sorts of horsemen and souldiers that belong unto his captaines, and all other commers. At these rayles there are many doores kept by many porters, who have white rods to keepe men in order. In the middest of the place, right before the King, standeth one of his sheriffes, together with his master hangman, who is accompanied with forty hangmen wearing on their heads a certaine quilted cap, different from all others, with an hatchet on their shoulders; and others with all sorts of whips being there, readie to doe what the King commandeth.

[1] The famous black (slate) throne still to be seen at Agra on the terrace of the fort. An account of it is given in the *Tūzuk*, vol. i, p. 177.

[2] Salutations (Arabic *salām*, 'peace').

The King heareth all causes in this place, and stayeth some two houres every day (these Kings of India sit daily in justice every day, and on the Tuesdayes doe their executions). Then he departeth towards his private place of prayer. His prayer beeing ended, foure or five sorts of very well dressed and roasted meats are brought him, of which, as hee pleaseth, he eateth a bit to stay his stomacke, drinking once of his strong drinke. Then hee commeth forth into a private roome, where none can come but such as himselfe nominateth (for two yeeres together I was one of his attendants here). In this place he drinketh other five cupfuls, which is the portion that the physicians alot him. This done, he eateth opium, and then he ariseth; and being in the height of his drinke he layeth him downe to sleepe, every man departing to his owne home. And after he hath slept two houres, they awake him and bring his supper to him; at which time he is not able to feed himselfe, but it is thrust into his mouth by others; and this is about one of the clocke, and then he sleepeth the rest of the night.

Now in the space of these five cups he doth many idle things; and whatsoever he doth, either without or within, drunken or sober, he hath writers who by turnes set downe everything in writing which he doth, so that there is nothing passeth in his lifetime which is not noted, no, not so much as his going to the necessary, and how often he lieth with his women, and with whom; and all this is done unto this end, that when he dieth these writings of al his actions and speeches which are worthy to be set downe might be recorded in the chronicles. At my being with him he made his brothers children Christians; the doing whereof was not for any zeale he had to Christianitie, as the Fathers and all Christians thought, but upon the prophecie of certain learned Gentiles, who told him that the sonnes of his body should be disinherited and the children of his brother should raigne; and therefore he did it to make these children hatefull to all Moores, as Christians are odious in their sight, and that they beeing once Christians, when any such matter should happen, they should find no subjects. But God is omnipotent and can turne the making of these Christians unto a good ende, if it be His pleasure.

This King amongst his children hath one called Sultan Shariar, of seven yeeres of age; and his father on a day, being to goe some whether to solace himselfe, demanded of him whether hee would goe with him. The child answered that if it pleased His Highnesse he would either goe or stay, as the pleasure of his father was. But because his answer was not that with all his heart he would waite upon His Majestie, he was very well buffeted by the King, and that in such sort that no child in the world but would have cryed, which this child did not. Wherefore his father demanded why he cryed not. He answered that his nurses told him that it was the greatest shame in the world for princes to cry when they were beaten; and ever since they nurtured me in this kind, saith he, I never cryed, and nothing shall make me cry to the death. Upon which speech his father, being more vexed, stroke him againe, and caused a bodkin to bee brought him, which he thrust through his cheeke; but all this would not make him cry, although he bled very much; which was admired of all that the father should doe this unto his child, and that he was so stout that hee would not crie. There is great hope of this child to exceed all the rest.

This emperour keepeth many feasts in the yeare, but two feasts especially may be nominated. The one called the Nourous [*Nauroz*], which is in honour of the New-Yeares day. This feast continueth eighteene daies, and the wealth and riches are wonderfull that are to be seene in the decking and setting forth of every mans roome or place where he lodgeth when it is his turne to watch; for every nobleman hath his place appointed him in the palace. In the middest of that spacious place I speake of, there is a rich tent pitched, but so rich that I thinke the like cannot bee found in the world. This tent is curiously wrought and hath many seminans [Hind. *shamiyāna*, an awning] joyning round about it of most curious wrought velvet, embroidered with gold, and many of them are of cloath of gold and silver. These seminans be shaddowes to keepe the sunne from the compasse of this tent. I may say it is at the least two acres of ground, but so richly spread with silke and gold carpets and hangings in the principall places, rich as rich velvet imbroydered with gold, pearle, and precious stones can make it. Within it five chaires of estate are placed, most rich to behold, where at his pleasure the King sitteth. There are likewise private roomes made for his Queenes, most rich, where they sit and see all, but are not seene. So round about this tent the compasse of all may bee some five acres of ground. Every principall nobleman maketh his roome and decketh it; likewise every man, according to his ability, striveth who may adorne his roome richest. The King, where he doth affect, commeth to his noble-mens rooms, and is most sumptuously feasted there, and at his departure is presented with the rarest jewels and toyes that they can find; but because he will not receive any thing at that time as a present, he commandeth his Treasurer to pay what his praysers valew them to bee worth; which are valewed at halfe the price. Every one and all of his nobles provide toyes and rare things to give him at this feast; so commonly at this feast every man his estate is augmented. Two daies of this feast the better sort of the women come to take the pleasure thereof; and this feast beginneth at the beginning of the moone of March. The other feast[1] is some foure moneths after, which is called the feast of his birth-day. This day every man striveth who may be the richest in apparell and jewels. After many sports and pastimes performed in his palace, he goeth to his mothers house with all the better sort of his nobles, where every man presenteth a jewell unto his mother, according to his estate. After the bancket is ended, the King goeth into a very faire roome, where a ballance of beaten gold is hanged, with one scale emptie for him to sit in, the other scale being filled with divers things, that is to say, silver, gold, divers sorts of grains a little, and so of every kind of mettall a little, and with all sorts of precious stones some. In fine, he weigheth himselfe with these things, which the next day are given to the poore, and all may be valued to be worth

[1] Both festivals are fully described in Roe's journal (see the *Embassy*, pp. 252, 411). Jahāngīr kept both lunar and solar birthdays, the latter at the beginning of September.

ten thousand pounds. This day, before he goeth unto his mothers house, every man bringeth him his present, which is thought to be ten times more worth then that which he giveth to the poore. This done, every man departeth unto his home.

His custome is that when you petition him for any thing, you must not come empty handed, but give him some toy or other, whether you write or no. By the gift you give him he knoweth that you would demand some thing of him; so after enquiry is made, if he seeth it convenient, he granteth it.

The custome of the Indians is to burne their dead, as you have read in other authors, and at their burning many of their wives will burne with them, because they will bee registred in their bookes for famous and most modest and loving wives, who, leaving all worldly affaires, content themselves to live no longer then their husbands. I have seene many proper women brought before the King, whom (by his commandment) none may burne without his leave and sight of them; I meane those of Agra. When any of these commeth, hee doth perswade them with many promises of gifts and living if they will live, but in my time no perswasion could prevaile, but burne they would. The King, seeing that all would not serve, giveth his leave for her to be carried to the fire, where she burneth herselfe alive with her dead husband.

Likewise his custome is, when any great noble-man hath been absent from him two or three yeares, if they come in favour and have performed well, hee receiveth them in manner and forme following. First, the noble-man stayeth at the gate of the pallace till the Vizir and Lieutenant-Generall and Knight Martiall come to accompany him unto the King. Then he is brought to the gate of the outermost rayles, whereof I have spoken before, where hee standeth in the view of the King, in the middest betweene these two nobles. Then he toucheth the ground with his hand and also with his head, very gravely, and doth thus three times. This done, he kneeleth downe touching the ground with his forehead; which being once done, he is carried forward towards the King, and in the midway he is made to doe this reverence againe. Then he commeth to the doore of the red rayles, doing the like reverence the third time; and having thus done, he commeth within the red rayles and doth it once more upon the carpets. Then the King commandeth him to come up the staires or ladder of seaven steppes that he may embrace him; where the King most lovingly embraceth him before all the people, whereby they shall take notice that he is in the Kings favour. The King having done this, he then commeth downe, and is placed by the Lieutenant-Generall according to his degree. Now if he come in disgrace, through exclamations made against him, he hath none of these honours from the King, but is placed in his place till he come to his tryall. This King is very much adored of the heathen comminalty, insomuch that they will spread their bodies all upon the ground, rubbing the earth with their faces on both sides. They use many other fopperies and superstitions, which I omit, leaving them for other travellers which shall come from thence hereafter.

After I had written this, there came into my memory another feast, solemnized at his fathers funerall, which is kept at his sepulchre,[1] where likewise himselfe, with all his posterity, meane to be buried. Upon this day there is great store of victuals dressed, and much money given to the poore. This sepulchre may be counted one of the rarest monuments of the world. It hath beene this foureteene yeares a building, and it is thought it will not be finished these seaven yeares more,[2] in ending gates and walls and other needfull things for the beautifying and setting of it forth. The least that worke there daily are three thousand people; but thus much I will say, that one of our worke-men will dispatch more then three of them. The sepulchre is some three-quarters of a mile about, made square. It hath seaven heights built, every height narrower then the other, till you come to the top where his herse is. At the outermost gate

[1] Akbar's famous tomb at Sikandra, about six miles NW. of Agra (cf. Finch's account).

[2] The mausoleum and south gate were finished A. H. 1021 (A. D. 1612-13), but the remaining gates probably took some years to complete.

before you come to the sepulchre there is a most stately palace building. The compasse of the wall joyning to this gate of the sepulchre and garding, being, within, may be at the least three miles.[1] This sepulchre is some foure miles distant from the citie of Agra.

[1] Hawkins is not very accurate in his statements. The base of the central building measures about 500 feet on each of the four sides. There are five stories, not seven. Each side of the garden is about 3½ furlongs, making 1¾ miles in all. The 'stately palace' is presumably the principal gateway of the enclosure.

1608–11

WILLIAM FINCH

Much of what has been already said concerning Captain Hawkins and his experiences will serve also as an introduction to the narrative of his colleague, William Finch. Not that the latter account is in any way a repetition of the same story in other words; on the contrary, it deals principally with experiences in which Hawkins had no share, and its chief feature is the topographical information gleaned by the writer either in his own journeyings or by diligent inquiry from others. Its interest in this respect it would be difficult to exaggerate. Purchas says of it that it is 'supplied in substance with more accurate observations of men, beasts, plants, cities, deserts, castles, buildings, regions, religions, then almost any other; as also of waies, wares, warres'. Based upon a carefully kept journal and giving a detailed description of a large extent of the country, it is a most valuable contribution to our knowledge of the dominions of the Great Mogul in the early years of the seventeenth century. It has, however, to a large extent been lost sight of in the mass of Purchas's unwieldy collection, and much of the information it contains is known chiefly at secondhand from the works of two slightly later authors, viz. Johannes de Laet, who, in his *De Imperio Magni Mogolis* (1631), availed himself freely of the materials provided by Finch, and Thomas Herbert, who copied De Laet in the second edition (1638) of his account of his own travels. The fact that Herbert had actually made a voyage to India and Persia has perhaps assisted to give the impression that his descriptions of the former country were from his own observation; but in reality he saw scarcely anything of India outside the immediate vicinity of Surat, and the bulk of his work is a medley of information gathered from previous writers.

Of Finch himself, previous to our finding him among the merchants on board the *Hector* in the outward voyage, we know only that he had been 'servant to Master Johnson in Cheapside'—a detail we owe to Robert Covert, the author of *A True and Almost Incredible Report*; but of the rest of his short career we have a fairly full account, mainly from his own pen. He landed with Hawkins at Surat in August 1608, and remained there in charge of a small stock of goods when the

Captain himself proceeded to Agra. Finch's experiences while at the port are fully related in his Journal, supplemented by a letter from him to Hawkins in July 1609, printed at p. 23 of vol. i of *Letters Received by the East India Company.*[1] In January 1610, in obedience to a summons from Hawkins, he left Surat for Agra, where he arrived early in April. Towards the close of the year he was dispatched on a short expedition to Bayāna for the purpose of buying a stock of indigo. Here, according to Jourdain (*Journal*, p. 156), an incident happened which gave some offence at court. The Emperor's mother, or others acting under her protection, carried on extensive trading operations, and at this time a vessel belonging to her was being laden for a voyage to Mokha. A merchant had accordingly been sent to Bayāna to buy indigo, and he had nearly concluded his bargain when Finch arrived. No Indian would have dared to compete in such a case, but the Englishman did not scruple to bid against the Queen-Mother's agent and so 'had awaie the indico', with the result that the aggrieved lady complained to the Emperor, and Hawkins's position at court suffered accordingly.

Finch's return to Agra was quickly followed by his departure for Lahore to make sale on the Company's behalf of the indigo he had purchased at Bayāna. Travelling by way of Delhi, Ambāla, and Sultānpur, he reached his destination early in February 1611. Lahore was at that time second only to Agra in importance (it will be remembered that Milton couples them together as the chief seats of the Great Mogul); and our author's description of the palace, before it was altered by Shāh Jahān, is of great interest. In this city Finch remained until at least August 18 of the same year, which is the last date given in his narrative. Its sudden breaking off suggests that at this point he found that he had filled up the last blank sheet of his note-book, and was consequently obliged to make his further jottings in a second book or on loose paper, unfortunately lost or destroyed at the time of his death. The rest of our text is occupied with notes which Finch had doubtless inserted from time to time on the back pages of his journal—a common practice among the factors. Purchas printed them in the order in which he found them; but in all probability they were entered in the reverse order. Thus the account of routes from Agra to places lying to the eastwards (p. 175), and the descriptions of that city and of Sikandra, were doubtless written during Finch's stay in the capital. Next he inserted the details obtained from Nicholas Ufflet of the route from Agra to Surat by way of Ajmer (p. 170). These must have

[1] The document printed at p. 28 of the same volume, without any name attached, is undoubtedly by Finch.

been communicated when the two were together at Lahore in 1611. Finally, while at Lahore, he gathered the information entered at p. 167 concerning the routes from that city to Kābul and to Srīnagar.

Hawkins had instructed Finch to return to Agra as soon as he had disposed of his goods; but the latter had come to the conclusion that the prospects of English trade in India were hopeless;[1] and, learning that a caravan was about to set out from Lahore for Aleppo, he resolved to take the opportunity to go home by that route. Accordingly he wrote to Hawkins, acquainting him with his intention, and asking either to be allowed to go as the Company's servant, carrying with him for sale the indigo in his charge, or to be paid his wages and released from the service. Hawkins conceived the idea that Finch might abscond with the indigo, and so he dispatched secretly a power of attorney to a Jesuit at Lahore, authorizing him, in the event of Finch attempting to leave with the caravan, to seize him and his goods. Nicholas Ufflet was then sent to Lahore to take over the indigo. The implied distrust of his honesty cut Finch to the quick, and when the secret of the power of attorney leaked out, the breach between him and Hawkins was complete. Jourdain wrote to Finch, telling him that an English fleet was on its way to India, and urging him to come to Agra in order that they might journey down to Surat in company; but Finch replied that 'he knewe well the Companie would never send more shipps for Suratt . . . exclaymeinge very much on Captaine Hawkins and his disconfidence, sayinge that he would not come to Agra because he would not see the face of him' (*Journal of John Jourdain*, p. 158).

The rest of the story is contained in a letter written to the East India Company by Bartholomew Haggatt, the English consul at Aleppo, in August 1613.[2] Travelling in company with a Captain Boys and their respective servants, Thomas Styles and Laurence Pigot, Finch made his way overland to Bagdad. There the whole party were seized with sickness, due, it is said, to their having drunk some infected water; and all but Styles died soon after their arrival. Finch's goods were at once confiscated by the Bāsha, who also imprisoned the survivor in the hope of making him disclose the hiding place of further articles; but with the aid of the Venetian vice-

[1] Sir Henry Middleton notes (*Purchas His Pilgrimes*, part i, bk. ix, chap. xi) that in October 1611 he received a letter written by Finch at Lahore, addressed to the commander of any of the Company's ships arriving off Surat, and announcing that he was going home overland, as there was no hope of the establishment of English trade in India.

[2] Printed in *Letters Received*, vol. i (p. 273). See also Kerridge's letter at p. 286 of the same volume.

consul, Styles effected his escape, and after a dangerous journey succeeded in reaching Aleppo at the beginning of October 1612. The friendly vice-consul at Bagdad did his best to induce the Bāsha to disgorge his prey, and with much trouble managed to get from him a portion of it, which seems, however, to have been scarcely more than sufficient to defray the expenses of the suit and the claims of certain creditors. Finch's apparel and the bulk at least of his papers were also saved and delivered to Haggatt, who forwarded them to the East India Company. This explains how the Rev. Samuel Purchas, when searching the Company's archives for materials, came across Finch's 'large journall' and, recognizing its value, printed it almost in full, as the fourth chapter of the fourth book of part one of the *Pilgrimes*. The subsequent fate of the manuscript is unknown.

Finch's narrative is here printed as given by Purchas, except that the voluminous account of the outward voyage is omitted, as having no bearing upon India. It may be added that the portion relating to the Punjab has been reproduced by Sir Edward Maclagan in the *Journal of the Panjāb Historical Society* (vol. i, no. 2), accompanied by some useful notes; while (as mentioned in the text) still more recently Sir Aurel Stein has examined in the same periodical Finch's references to Kashmīr and Central Asia.

Mr. W. H. Moreland, C.S.I., C.I.E., has been good enough to read this section and make some useful suggestions for its annotation.

The eight and twentieth of August, 1608, Captaine Hawkins with the merchants and certaine others landed at Surat, where the Captaine was received in a coach and carryed before the Dawne [Dīwān]. Wee had poore lodging alloted us, the porters lodge of the custome house; whither the next morning came the Customers, who searched and tumbled our trunkes to our great dislike, which had yet brought ashore only necessaries. We were invited to dinner to a merchant, where wee had great cheere, but in the midst of our banquet sowre sawce, for hee was the man that had sustayned almost all the losse in a ship that Sir Edward Michelborne tooke. The captaine also of that ship dined with us. Which when it was there told us, the Captaine [Hawkins] answered that hee never heard of such a matter, and rather judged it done by Flemmings; but they said that they knew certainely that they were English, deploring their hard fortunes and affirming that there were theeves in all countries, nor would they impute that fault to honest merchants. This speech somewhat revived us. The day after, Mede Colee [Mahdi Kuli], the captaine of that ship aforesaid, invited us to supper.

The second of October wee imbarqued our goods and provisions, gave Shek Abdelreheime [see p. 72] a present, and got dispatch to depart; the Customers denying leave, till they had searched the ship whether she had discharged all her goods, to ship any new; but meeting with frigats, they, supposing them Malabars,[1] durst not adventure their own river. These frigats were Portugals, which desired one to come talke with them, and Master Bucke rashly doing it, they detayned him, and after (I and Nicholas Ufflet being ashoare) Master Marlow and the rest beganne to flee. The cockson would have fought, which he would not permit; but running aground through ignorance of the channell, they were taken going on the sandie iland by Portugall treacherie, and the fault of some of themselves, nineteene with Master Bucke. But the ginne [i.e. ging or crew] put off the pinnace and, notwithstanding the Portugall bullets, rowed her to Surat. Foure escaped by swimming and got that night to Surat, besides Nicholas Ufflet and my selfe, neere twentie miles from the place. Yet had we resisted we wanted shot, and in number and armour they very much exceeded us. The fourth, the captaine of the frigats sent a reviling letter to the Governour of the towne, calling us Lutherans and theeves, and said we were Flemmings and not English; charging him (on continuance of their friendship) to send aboord the Captaine with the rest of us; which Abdelreheime not only denied, but in the Mogols name commanded him to render the goods and men. The fifth, came a captaine of one of the frigats, which used peremptorie words and before the Governour stood upon it that the King of Spaine was lord of those seas, and that they had in commission from him to take all that came in those parts without his passe.

[1] The pirates of the Malabar Coast, whose widespread depredations were a trouble to commerce down to the middle of the eighteenth century.

The thirteenth, the Governour called all the chiefe merchants of the towne upon their conscience to value our cloth (before carryed to his house), which they did at a farre under rate; the Governour affirming that hee must and would have it, the Captaine [Hawkins] denying his consent. On the sixteenth, we were forced to accept, for some of our cloth in their hands, promise of a little more, and were permitted to carrie away the rest, causing us to leave fiftie pieces and fourteene Devonshire kersies for the King, with nine and twentie other kersies, and fifteene clothes for Shek Ferred [Shaikh Farīd], keeping also the foure clothes which wee reserved for presents for the King. We were otherwise molested by a contention betwixt Shek Ferred and Mocrow Bowcan (or Mocreb Can) about the custome-house, that wee could not get our goods from thence. Wee heard that the Portugals sold our goods for halfe that they cost. Our men were sent to Goa.

The fifteenth of December, came Mo. Bowcan with a Jesuite, Padre Peniero. To this our captaine shewed kindnesse, for hope of his men; to the other he gave presents. Both dealt treacherously in requitall, the Jesuite (as it was reported by Mo. Bowcan himselfe) offering a jewell, which he said was worth two hundred thousand rials, to betray us. This day came to us R. Carelesse, an Englishman, who had long lived amongst the Portugals, from whom hee now fledde for fear of punishment forcarring necessaries to the Dutch at Muselpatan; desiring to bee entertayned, which we did with much circumspection.[1]

The seven and twentieth, Mo. Bowcan desired great abatements upon our cloth, or else hee would returne it, and (will wee nill wee) abated two thousand seven hundred and fiftie mamudies before hee would give us licence to fetch up the rest of our goods to make sales. My selfe was very ill of the bloudy fluxe (whereof Master Dorchester[2] dyed), of which that Englishman Carelesse (next under God) recovered me. I learned of him many matters, as namely of the great

[1] Jourdain mentions this man and says that 'there v ate doubt of his honestie'.

[2] John Dorchester, a merchant who had

spoile done the last yeere[1] to the Portugals by the Hollanders, who lying before Malacca with sixteene ships, inclosing the towne with helpe of other kings by sea and land, newes was carryed to the Vice-Roy,[2] then before Achen, accompanied with all the gallants of India, having with him a very great fleet of ships, gallies and frigats, and foure thousand souldiers, being commanded by the King to take Achen, and there to build a castle and appoint an Alphandira,[3] and thence to goe and spoile Jor [Johor] and chastise the Moluccas for giving the Hollanders traffique, being minded to roote out the Holland name in those parts, for which purpose came two thousand Castilians from the Manilias. Andrew Hurtado[4] then governed within Malacca, and sent word of their present distresse; upon which the Vice-Roy weighed from Achen (which otherwise had beene spoyled); whereof the Dutch Generall advertised, got his men and artillery aboord, and went forth to meete him; where after a long and bloudie fight, with much losse on both sides, the Dutch departed, enforced to stop the leakes of their admirall, likely otherwise to perish. The Portugals let slip this opportunitie, and fell to merriments and bragges of their victorie, not looking any more for the Hollanders, who, having stopped their leakes at Jor, new rigged and returned upon the Portugals, whom they found disordered and feasting ashoare; where they sunke and burned the whole fleet, making a cruell execution; and had not the Vice-Roy before sent sixe shippes on some other service, they had beene all heere utterly extinguished. After this fell such sicknesse in the city that most of them dyed, amongst which the Vice-Roy was one, and shortly after the Governour of the Spaniards in the Moluccas; so that their strength was laid in the dust, and the Archbishoppe [Aleixo de Menezes] made and yet remayneth Vice-Roy.

This last yeere the Malabarres vexed the Portugals and tooke or sunke of them at times sixtie saile[5] or more. This yeere

[1] Most of the events here related took place in 1606.

[2] Dom Martim Affonso de Castro.

[3] 'Alphandica' is meant, i. e. 'a customhouse' (Port. *alfandega*).

[4] André Furtado de Mendonça.

[5] These were, of course, small vessels (see note on p. 63).

also was expected a Vice-Roy to come with a strong fleet to drive the Hollanders out of India. This fleet consisted of nine shippes of warre, and sixe for the voyage; they were separated in the calme of Guinea, and never met together after. Two of them came to Mosambique, where they were fired of the Hollanders, who also much distressed the castle but could not take it, and the time of the yeere requiring their departure, they set sayle for Goa, to the number of fifteene shippes and one pinnasse, where they rode at the barre challenging the great captaine Andrew Hurtado, who durst not visit them. Another of that voyage having advise that the Hollanders rode at the barre, put to the northward, where they presently landed their money and goods and set fire of their shippe to save the Dutch a labour; and lastly, the souldiers fell together by the eares for the sharing of the money. This fleet departing from Goa sailed alongst the coast of Malabar, spoyling and burning all they could meet with. There was report of leave given them by the Samorine [see p. 45], to build a castle at Chaul [*sic*].

This moneth here was also newes of an Ormus ship taken by the Malabarres, and three frigats; and shortly after of a fleet of twentie five frigots from Cochen, whereof sixteene were taken and burnt by the Malabars, which the rest escaped, if miserable spoile be an escape; also of fiftie frigats and galiots of the Malabars spoiling on their coast. In January [1609] came other newes of thirtie frigats, which put for Diu richly laden, taken by the Malabars, beeing at this time masters of these seas. They are good souldiers and carry in each frigat one hundred souldiers, and in their galiots two hundred.

The first of February, the Captaine [Hawkins] departed with fiftie peons[1] and certaine horsemen. About this time was great stirre touching the Queene Mothers ship, which was to be laden for Mocha. The Portugals then riding at the barre, with two and twentie frigats, threatned to carry her to Diu. At length they fell to compounding, the Portugals demanding an hundred thousand mamudies for her cartas [Port. *cartaz*; cf. p. 135] or passe, and after twentie thousand; at last taking one thousand rialls and odde money, with divers presents

[1] Foot-men (Port. *peão*). As Hawkins tells us (p. 78), these were foot-soldiers hired for purposes of defence.

which the Mogolls were faine to give them. Mo. Bowcan gave me faire words, but the divell was in his heart; he minded nothing lesse indeed then paiment of his debts, seeking also to deduct some, others imbeselled, striking off by new accounts seventeene thousand of one and fortie thousand. I thought he meant to shift if hee could and pay nothing, secretly departing the towne, owing much to certaine Banians, who must get it when they can. At last I got his cheet [order: Hind. *chitthi*] for some, though with great abatements; esteeming halfe better secured then to endanger all.

The six and twentieth of March, 1609, it was here reported that Malacca was besieged with thirtie ships of Holland; in succour of which the Vice-Roy assembled all these his northerne Indian forces, appointing Andrew Hurtado generall, being the more cranke by newes of a new Vice-Roy [see p. 131] with fourteene saile to winter at Mosambique. Meane while a ship of Cambaya, which had been at Queda, came for Goga, which the Portugalls finding without cartas made prize of. The Customers at that time by new prices and reckonings sought to make prize in great part of us. I was also in the beginning of Aprill taken with a burning fever, which drew from me much blood, besides ten dayes fasting with a little rice; and after my fever miserable stitches tormented me. The next moneth I was visited againe with a burning fever.

The twelfth of May came newes that Melik Amber, King of Decan, had besieged the citie of Aurdanagar [1] (which had been the metropolitan of that kingdome, conquered by the Acabar) with two and twentie thousand horse, and that after divers assaults the Mogolls made shew to deliver up the citie, upon condition that hee would withdraw his armie some foure or five cose [*kos*: see p. 18] from thence, that they might passe with more assurance with bagge and baggage; which being done, they suddenly issued forth with all their forces upon the unprovided enemie and made a great slaughter; but feared

[1] Finch no doubt wrote 'Amedanagar', i. e. Ahmadnagar. Malik Ambar (an Abyssinian by birth) was not the King but the chief minister and generalissimo. Akbar had subdued Ahmadnagar in the year 1600. For an account of the capitulation mentioned in the text see the *Tūzuk*, vol. i, p. 181.

hee would bee revenged on those parts which were lesse able to resist. The Canchanna gathered great forces, and demanded of Surat three hundred thousand m[ahmūdis] towards the charge, sending also for the Governour, an expert Decan souldier.

The twentieth of June came newes of the arrivall of five shippes at Goa, and of the Vice-Royes death;[1] whereupon Andrew Hurtado was chosen Vice-Roy, being the only stay left of all those parts, and reported a brave souldier. He presently gave order for shipping to be built, intending after the breaking up of winter to make a bolt or shaft with the Hollanders, which were now reported to lye before Malacca with eighteene ships. The Portugall ships in the way had met with one of this towne and, finding her without cartas, brought her with them as prize for Goa, where on the barre shee was cast away; whereupon the Governour for Can-Channa, and the Customer for Mo. Bowcan, seised on Tappidas the owner, a Banian, for money owing to them; whereby also we lost his debt to us, for which we may thanke the Portugall.

The twentieth of July, Sha Selim commanded Can Channa and Manisengo,[3] two great commanders of his, to invade all the kingdomes from hence to the south, even to Cape Comori; for which a huge armie was assembling. In resistance of whom, three great kings were combined, the King of Decan [Ahmadnagar] (whose chiefe citie is Genefro[4]), the King of Visapor [Bījāpur], and the King of Golcunda (whose chiefe citie is Braganadar[5]), who also gathered great forces, making head neare Bramport [Burhānpur], upon the Mogolls frontiers, expecting the breaking up of winter [i.e. the rainy season], both armies lying abroad in tents.

In August I received flying newes of an English pinnasse at Gandove,[6] which, departing thence, was againe forced

[1] The Conde de Feyra, who was coming out as Viceroy, died on his way.

[2] See Finch's letter to Hawkins mentioned on p. 123.

[3] Rāja Mān Singh. Prince Parwiz was nominally in command.

[4] This seems to be intended either for Junnar (in Poona District) or for Jālnapur (see p. 137).

[5] Bhāgnagar, the original name of the city of Hyderābād, the present capital of the Nizām's dominions.

[6] Gandevi, about twelve miles up the Ambika River, and twenty-eight miles south-east of Surat.

thither by three Portugall frigats. I supposed that it might belong to some of our shipping which, standing for Socatora, might not be able to fetch in, and so be forced to fall on this coast; which proved accordingly, it being the *Ascensions* pinnasse, wanting water, wood, and victuall, the master John Elmer, with five men and two boyes. The master and foure of the company came hither on the eight and twentieth, but I had no small adoe with the townsmen of Surat for bringing them into the towne, they taking them from me, pretending we were but allowed trade (indeed fearing the Portugalls), till I should send to the Nobob [1] foure course [*kos*: see p. 18] off, fearing force. To which evill was added a worse of the Portugalls comming into the river with five frigats and carrying away the pinnasse, weighing also the two falcons [2] which they had cast by the boord. And yet a worse report came the fifth of September, of the casting away of the *Ascension*, the company (about seventie persons) being saved; which the next day came to Surat, but were forced by the towne to lye without amongst the trees and tombes, I being not able to procure leave for the Generall [3] himselfe (notwithstanding divers letters of recommendation which hee brought from Mocha, besides letters from the King himselfe) into the towne; such is their slavish awe of the Portugalls, two Jesuits threatning fire, faggot, and utter desolation, if they received any more English thither. That which I could doe was to send them refreshing and carry them to the Tanke,[4] where they were conveniently lodged, yet amongst tombes, till the Governor appointed them a more convenient place at a small aldea [5] two course off; and with much adoe got leave for Master Rivet,[6] Master Jordan [Jourdain] and the surgion to come hither to provide necessaries for the rest. I had other trouble by the disorder and riot committed by some of them,

[1] The Nawāb, i. e. Mukarrab Khān.

[2] A small cannon.

[3] Alexander Sharpeigh. For all this see the *Journal of John Jourdain*, pp. 127 *et seq.*

[4] The Gopi Talāo, near the Nausāri gate of Surat. 'Tank' is commonly applied in India to a pool or reservoir.

[5] Portuguese for a village.

[6] William Revett, one of the merchants of the *Ascension*.

especially one Thomas Tucker, which in drinke had killed a calfe (a slaughter more then murther in India), which made mee glad of their departure, fifteene staying behind sicke, or unwilling to goe for Agra; and some returned againe.

The sixt of October, came letters from Captaine Hawkins, importing his mariage with the daughter of an Armenian; and others in the latter end of the next moneth, for my comming to Agra. In December we stood much in feare of Badur [see p. 100] his comming upon Surat, he lying within two dayes journey with sixe hundred horse and many foote; for which cause the Governour cessed all men with the entertainment of souldiers, setting upon my head ten men. I went to him and told him that I had twentie English at his command; for which hee thanked mee, and freed mee of further charge. During this time the Banians were forced to labour to barricado all the streets of the citie, great watches were appointed at the gates, certaine peeces drawne from the castle, and from Carode [see p. 136] garrison fiftie horse; which had not sufficed, had not the Governour of Amadavar [Ahmadābād] sent one thousand horse and two thousand foot to our succour; upon newes of which forces Badur withdrew to his holds. Two yeeres before our comming had this man sacked Cambaya, whereof his grandfather had been king.

The eighteenth of January [1610], I departed out of Surat towards Agra, willing yet to leave some notice thereof before I leave it. The citie is of good quantitie, with many faire merchants houses therein, standing twentie miles within the land up a faire river. Some three miles from the mouth of the river (where on the south side lyeth a small low island over-flowed in time of raine) is the barre, where ships trade and unlade, whereon at a spring tide is three fathome water. Over this the channell is faire to the citie side, able to beare vessels of fiftie tunnes laden. This river runneth to Bramport, and from thence, as some say, to Musselpatan.[1] As you come up the river, on the right hand stands the castle, well walled, ditched, reasonable great and faire, with a number of faire peeces [pieces of ordnance], whereof some of exceeding great-

[1] Masulipatam. The statement was of course absurd.

nesse. It hath one gate to the green-ward, with a draw-bridge and a small port [i. e. gate] on the river side. The Captaine hath in command two hundred horse. Before this lyeth the medon [Hind. *maidān*, an open space], which is a pleasant greene, in the middest whereof is a may-pole to hang a light on, and for other pastimes on great festivalls. On this side the citie lyeth open to the greene, but on all other parts is ditched and fenced with thicke hedges, having three gates, of which one leadeth to Variaw,[1] a small village, where is the ford to passe over for Cambaya way. Neare this village on the left hand lieth a small aldea on the rivers banke very pleasant, where stands a great pagod, much resorted to by the Indians. Another gate leadeth to Bramport; the third to Nonsary,[2] a towne ten cose off, where is made great store of calico, having a faire river comming to it. Some ten cose further lyeth Gondoree [Gandevi: see p. 131], and a little further Belsaca,[3] the frontire towne upon Daman. Hard without Nonsary gate is a fair tanke sixteene square,[4] inclosed on all sides with stone steppes, three quarters of an English mile in compasse, with a small house in the middest. On the further side are divers faire tombes, with a goodly paved court pleasant to behold, behind which groweth a small grove of manga [mango] trees, whither the citizens goe forth to banquet. Some halfe cose behind this place is a great tree much worshipped by the Banians, where they affirme a dew [Hind. *deo*, a spirit] to keepe [i. e. dwell], and that it hath beene oftentimes cut downe and stocked up by the rootes at the Moores command, and yet hath sprung up againe.[5] Neare to the castle is the alphandica [see p. 128], where is a paire of staires for lading and unlading of goods; within are roomes for keeping goods till they be cleared, the custome being two and an halfe for goods, three for victualls, and two for money.

[1] Variāo, on the Tāpti, two miles north of Surat.

[2] Nausāri, on the Purna, about twenty miles south of Surat.

[3] Here, as elsewhere, Purchas has mistaken Finch's 'r' for a 'c'. Bulsār, forty miles south of Surat, is meant.

[4] The Gopi Talāo (see p. 132). Mundy (vol. ii, p. 31) describes it as 'made into sixteen squares'.

[5] See *The Travels of Peter Mundy*, vol. ii, p. 34, for an account of this tree; also Fryer's *New Account*, p. 105.

SURAT CASTLE

Without this gate is the great gondoree[1] or bazar. Right before this gate stands a tree with an arbour, whereon the fokeers [fakīrs] (which are Indian holy men) sit in state. Betwixt this and the castle, on the entrance of the greene, is the market for horse and cattell. A little lower on the right hand over the river is a little pleasant towne, Ranele,[2] inhabited by a people called Naites, speaking another language, and for the most part sea-men. The houses are faire therein, with high steps to each mans doore, the streets narrow. They are very friendly to the English. Heere are many pleasant gardens, which attract many to passe there their time; and on the trees are infinite number of those great bats which wee saw at Saint Augustines [in Madagascar], hanging by the clawes on the boughes, making a shrill noise. This fowle, the people say, ingendreth in the eare; on each wing it hath a hooke and giveth the yong sucke.

The winter heere beginneth about the first of June and dureth till the twentieth of September; but not with continuall raines, as at Goa, but for some sixe or seven dayes every change and full, with much wind, thunder, and raine. But at the breaking up commeth alway a cruell storme, which they call the tuffon,[3] fearefull even to men on land; which is not alike extreame every yeare, but in two or three at the most. Monsons [i.e. monsoon winds] heere for the south serve in Aprill and September, and for Mocha in February and March. From the south ships come hither in December, January, and February, and from Mocha about the fifth of September, after the raines; from Ormus for the coast of India in November. But none may passe without the Portugalls passe, for what, how much, and whither they please to give licence, erecting a custome on the sea, with confiscation of shippe and

[1] Mr. Motiram Advani explains this as *gojri*, the Gujarāti word for a bazar. It is possible that Finch wrote 'goudoree'.

[2] Rānder, two miles above Surat, on the other side of the river. For an account of the Nāyatas, a body of Arab merchants and sailors who settled there early in the twelfth century, see the *Bombay Gazetteer: Surat*, p. 299.

[3] Our 'typhoon', which comes (through the Portuguese) from the Arabic *ṭūfān*. For the periodic storm mentioned in the text and known locally as 'the Elephant', see Roe's *Journal* (vol. i, p. 247).

goods not shewing it in the full quantitie to the taker and examiner.

The second [1] of January [1610] I departed from Comvariaw [Khumbāria] (a small village three cose from Surat) to Mutta [Mota], a great aldea, seven c[os]. [January] 21, eight c. to Carode [Karod], a great countrey towne, by which on the north runneth Surat river ; it hath a castle with two hundred horse, Patans, good souldiers. [January] twentie two, to Curka [2] 12 c. ; it is a great village, with a river on the south side. In the way (7 c.) is Beca [Viāra], a castle with a great tanke and a pleasant grove. [January] 23, ten c. to Nacampore [Nārāyanpur], a great towne under the Pectopshaw.[3] In this way on the right hand beginneth a great ridge of mountaines which come from Amadavar-wards, neare which Badur keepeth, holding divers strong holds thereon, that the King with all his force cannot hurt him. These mountaines runne to Bramport ; on them are bred many wilde elephants. [January] 24, to Dayta [Dhāita], 8 c., a great towne ; in the mid-way you passe a stony troublesome river. This towne hath a castle, and is almost encompassed with a river, seated in a fertile soyle. [January] 25, to Badur [Bhadwar], 10 c., a filthy towne and full of theeves ; heere is made much wine of a sweete fruit called mewa,[4] but I found it not wholesome except it be burnt. This towne is the last of note in Pectopshaws land, who is a small king or rajaw, a Gentile, keeping on the top of inaccessible mountaines, which beginne at Curka and extend many courses. He holdeth two faire cities, Salere, and the other Muliere,[5] where the mamudees are coyned ; each having two mightie castles, which have way to them but for

[1] This date is clearly wrong. Perhaps the 20th is intended.
The route from Surat to Burhānpur is described by Roe, Jourdain, Mundy, Tavernier, and other travellers, to whose narratives the reader is referred for details.

[2] On this place see a note in *The Journal of John Jourdain*, p. 142.

[3] Partab Shāh, ruler of Bāglān (see p. 78).

[4] The Mhowa or Mahua tree (*Bassia latifolia*), from the flowers of which a spirit is distilled.

[5] Mulher (already mentioned on p. 79 *n.*) and Sālher are both hill forts in the Bāglān district. The latter is about 15 miles NNW. of Kalvan ; and Mulher is about twelve miles east of Sālher, for a description of which see the *Bombay Gazetteer*, vol. vii, p. 585.

two men abrest, or for an elephant at most to get up; having also in the way eightie small fortresses dispersed on the mountaines to guard the way. Upon the top of these mountaines is good pasture and abundance of graine, fountaines running thence into the plaines. The Acabar besieged him seven yeeres, and in the end was forced to compound with him, giving him Narampore, Dayta, and Badur, with divers other aldeas, for the safe conducting of his merchants alongst this plaine; so that he now remaineth this kings friend, sends presents yeerely, leaves one of his sonnes at Bramport, for pledge of his fealtie. He is said to have alway in readinesse foure thousand mares of a strange breed and excellent, and one hundred elephants. [January] 26, seven c. to Nonderbar [Nandurbār], a citie, short of which are many tombes and houses of pleasure, with a castle and a faire tanke. [January] seven and twentie, to Lingull [Nimgul], 10 c., a beastly towne, with theevish inhabitants and a dirtie castle; a deepe sandie way neare the towne. [January] 28, ten c. to Sindkerry [Sindkhera], a great dirtie towne. In the way the Governour of Lingull (with others as honest as himselfe) would have borrowed some money of me; but, seeing it prove powder and shot, gave over, and wee drew on our carts without trouble. On the further side of Sindkerry runneth a river of brackish water [the Buray], with drinking whereof I got the bloody fluxe, which accompanied me to Bramport. [January] 29, ten c. to Taulneere ([Thālner], a theevish way, the towne faire, with a castle and a river, in time of raine not passable without boat. [January] 30, fifteen c. to Chupra [Chopra], a great towne. I rested two dayes by reason of raine; in which time came the Governour of Nonderbar with foure hundred horse, without whose company I could not have proceeded without danger, Can-Canna having been beaten and retired to Bramport, after the losse of the strong and rich towne of Joulnapoure;[1] whereupon the Decanes grew so insolent that they made roades [i. e. raids] into this way and spoyled many passengers. The second of February, 6 c. to Rawd [Arāvad], a countrey village.

[1] Probably the Jālna of to-day, about thirty-five miles east of Aurangābād. It appears to be the 'Jenaport' of *Purchas His Pilgrimes*, part i, bk. iii, chap. ix.

The unseasonable thunder, wind, and raine, with my disease, almost made an end of me; which made us make mukom [*makām*, a halt] the third and fourth. The fifth, to Beawle [Byāval], 10 c., a great towne with a faire castle. [February] 6: stayed by foule weather. [February] 7, sixteen c. to Ravere [Rāver], a great towne. [February] 8, ten c. to Bramport [Burhānpur], where I pitched my tent in the Armenians yard, not being able for money to get an house, the towne was so full of souldiers. Some 2 c. short of this citie lyeth Badurpore [Bahādurpur], a faire citie, and betwixt these two cities the campe of Can-Canna under tents, 2 c. in length (having some fifteene thousand horse, two hundred faire elephants, an hundred peeces of ordnance of all sizes) on the north side. On the other side, within twentie or thirtie course, lay Amber-chapon, an Abashed [Arabic *Habashi*, an Abyssinian: see p. 130] and generall of the King of Decans forces, with some ten thousand of his owne cost,[1] all brave souldiers, and som forty thousand Decanees; in so much that the citie of Bramport had certainly been lost, had not the Prince Sultan Pervis and Rajaw Manisengo come instantly downe with great forces. For at this time he had sent to the Can-Canna to yeeld up the citie upon composition, deeming him not able to hold it against him. This citie is very great, but beastly, situate in a low, unholsome aire, a very sickly place, caused especially by the bad water. On the north-east is the castle on the rivers bank (comming from Surat), large and well fortified. By the castles side in the river lyeth an elephant of stone, so lively [i.e. lifelike] that a living elephant, comming one day to drinke, ranne against it with all his force and brake both his teeth. The head is painted red in the fore-head, and many simple Indians worship it.[2] Some two cose forth of the citie is Can Cannas garden, called Loll bage,[3] the whole way thereto being under shadie trees, very pleasant. Within it are divers faire walkes, with a stately small tanke standing square betweene

[1] Probably 'cast' in the manuscript. This word was often used in the sense of 'race'.

[2] Several travellers have described this figure: see Mundy, vol. ii, p. 51, and the works there cited.

[3] The *Lāl Bāg*, now a public garden.

BURHĀNPUR CASTLE

P. 138

foure trees, all shaded and inclosed with a wall; at the entrance without, a faire banketting house built aloft betweene foure trees.

I rested to the twelfth [February] for recovery (which God sent) under my tent. Two dayes after my comming came newes of the sacking of Ravere by fifteene hundred Decan horse, with other places neere thereto, we blessing God for our safe arrivall, the way now not passable with one thousand horse. I was here certified also by an Armenians letters of a great overthrow given to the Portugall armada upon the Mallabar coast, consisting of fiftie frigats and two gallies, which being dispersed with foule weather were sudainly out of divers creekes assailed by the Malabars; which was attended with spoile, fire, taking, the rest fleeing. On the twelfth I rode to visit the Prince [Parwīz]; and on the thirteenth gave him a present, found him courteous, promising what I desired. The Prince had with him twentie thousand horse and three hundred faire elephants, and with him Asaph Can [1] with some three thousand, and Emersee Rastein,[2] late King of Candhar, with some thousand old souldiers. And during my abode in the campe came also Raja Manisengo with ten thousand horse, all Resboots [Rājputs], and neere a thousand elephants; so that all the plaines for a great distance were covered with tents very brave to behold. With the armie came divers great boats for the transportation of forces over waters. The Prince removing, I returned to Bramport, and on the sixe and twentieth, hee being advanced 3 c. towards the enemie, I went to him to take my leave; where newes came of the overthrow of certaine of Manisengos forces.

The first of March, the Governour of Bramport departed for Agra, and I with him 12 c. to Barre,[3] a great village, stonie and steepe way, being the passage over the great ridge of

[1] Āsaf Khān (Jafar Beg).

[2] Mīrza Rustam, a Persian prince who with his brother at one time controlled Kandahār and the neighbouring districts. Finding their position precarious, they made over their territory to Akbar and entered his service.

[3] Borgāon, about twenty miles north-west of Burhānpur. For the rest of the journey to Agra the notes on Jourdain's and Mundy's routes will be found useful.

mountaines which come from Amadavarwards. About some 4 c. of this way lyeth the strong and invincible castle of Hassere,[1] seated on the top of a high mountaine, large and strong, able to receive (as is reported) fortie or fiftie thousand horse ; and on the top are many faire tankes and good pasture grounds. It hath had in the dayes of Badur Sha, late king thereof, some sixe hundred peeces of ordnance. The Acabar besieged it a long time, circling it on all sides, and at length tooke it by composition ; for it is said that there bred such an innumerable sort of emmets [i. e. ants] or other small worms in all the waters that the people swelled and burst with drinking thereof ; which mortalitie caused him to compound and deliver it, being by meere humane force invincible. The third [March], 11 c. to Camla, a small aldea ; stonie, troublesome way. The fourth, to Magergom [Mogargāon] 4 c., a great aldea ; bad way. The fifth, 10 c. to Kergom [Khargon], a great village ; steepe way. The sixth, 13 c. to Berkul [Balkhar], a small village. The seventh, 8 c. to Taxapore [Tarapur], a small towne. At 2 c. on the way you passe a faire river called Nervor [Narbada], which comes from Baroche [Broach] ; upon the banke is a prettie towne [Akbarpur] and faire castle, and under it the ferrie place. To passe over with camels is a way a c. lower on the left hand, where is an overfall and not above three foot in the passage, but neere a mile over. The eight, 5 c. to Mandow [Māndu ; see p. 17], 3 c. whereof is up a steepe, stonie mountaine, having way but for a coach at most. This ridge of mountaines extendeth north-east and south-west. On the top at the edge of the mountaine standeth the gate or entrance of the citie, over which is built a faire fort and house of pleasure, the walls extending all along the mountaines side for many coses. On the left hand at the entrance, some two or three miles distant, on the toppe of a picked [peaked] mountaine standeth a strong fort, and in other places dispersed some ten or twelve more. For 2 c. or better within this gate the citie is ruined all save only tombes and meskites [mosques],

[1] Asīr (Asīrgarh), the famous fortress which was taken by Akbar in 1600 from Bahādur Khān, the last of the Fāruki kings of Khāndesh. For accounts of the siege see Du Jarric, vol. iii, p. 43, and the *Nīmār District Gazetteer*, p. 202.

which remayne in great numbers to this day, with some tottered walls of great houses. The olde citie is from gate to gate 4 c. long north and south, but east and west ten or twelve coses;[1] and yet to the east-ward of all lyeth good pasture ground for many courses. Aloft on this mountaine are some sixteene faire tankes here and there dispersed about the citie. That which is now standing is very faire, but small in comparison of the former, with divers goodly buildings all of firme stone, and faire high gates, that I suppose the like not to be in all Christendome. At the entrance on the south within the gate of the city now inhabited, as you passe along on the left hand, stands a goodly meskite, and over against it a faire palace, wherein are interred the bodies of foure kings, with exceeding rich tombes.[2] By the side thereof standeth a high turret[3] of one hundred and seventie steps high, built round with galleries and windowes to every roome, all exceeding for goodly ports [i. e. gates], arches, pillars; the walls also all interlayed with a greene stone much beautifying. On the north side where I came forth lyeth a piece [of ordnance], of a foot and an halfe bore in the mouth, but the breech was in the ground. The gate is very strong, with a steepe descent; and without this sixe other, all very strong, with great walled places for courts of guard betweene gate and gate. On this side is also a small port, but the way thereto is exceeding steepe. All alongst on the side also runneth the wall, with flankers ever here and there among; and yet is the hill so steepe of it selfe, that it is not almost possible for a man to climbe up on all foure to any part of it. So that to mans judgement it is altogether invincible; and yet was taken, partly by force, partly by treason, by Hamawne, this mans grandfather, forcing Seic Sha Selim, whose ancestors had conquered it from the Indians some foure hundred yeeres agoe.[4]

[1] These figures are exaggerated. The ruins are 3¾ miles from north to south and 5¼ from east to west.

[2] The mosque is the Jāma Masjid, built by Hoshang Shāh. The tombs are those of the Khalji kings. See the reports of the Archaeological Survey for 1902–3 and subsequent years.

[3] The Tower of Victory, erected by Sultān Mahmūd I in 1443 to commemorate his defeat of the Rāna of Chitor.

[4] 'The first of name that took it was Can John, a Potan, who built the

This Sha Selim was a very powerfull king of Dely, and on
forced Hamawne to flye into Persia for ayde; from when
returning with Persian forces, he put him againe to the worst
who yet held out against him all his life time, as also a lo
time of Ecabars raigne, flying from one mountaine to anothe
Without the wals of the city on this side the suburbs entr
[extend ?] 4 c. long, but all ruinate, save certaine tombe
meskits, and goodly seraies,[1] no man remayning in them.

The way exceeding stony and bad. At 4 c. end lyeth Lun
heira [Lunera], a small saray, where wee pitched [March] t
ninth. Betweene this and the ruines, about 8 c. of the way,
a goodly tanke inclosed with stone, and a banketting house
the middest; on the south whereof are faire houses of pleasur
now ruinated, from whence goeth an arched bridge to t
banketting house in the tanke. Some halfe a cose beyo
Luneheira, on the right hand are foure or five faire tankes wi
a great pagode, a very pleasant place. The tenth, to Dupa
pore [Dipālpur], 14 c. good way; a small towne. The elevent
to Ouglue [Ujjain], a faire city, twelve long coses. Th
countrey is called Malva [Mālwa], a fertile soile, aboundi
with opium. Here the cose or course is two miles Englis
The twelfth, wee made mukom [see p. 138]. The thirteent
to Conoscia [Kanasia], 11 c. good way; a little village.
enquired the price of opium. They give the head thr
scratches, from whence issue small teares, at the first whit
which with the cold of the night turneth reddish; which th
daily scrape, not without infinite trouble, the head bee
very small and yeelding little. The fourteenth, to Sunenar
[Sunera], 8 c. way much stony and theevish, a people call

turret, and lyeth buried in the palace adjoyning, with three of h
successors. This citie was built by an Indian some thousand yeeres ago
(*marginal note*). The Mogul Emperor Humāyūn took Māndu in 15
from Bahādur Shāh of Gujarāt, who had captured it eight years befo
from the last of the Khalji kings. When the revolt of Sher Shāh forc
Humāyūn to flee to Persia, Māndu passed under the rule of the rebe
but the latter had no personal connexion with the city. Finch h
mixed up Sher Shāh and his son Salīm Shāh; also Khān Jahān and h
father, Mahmūd I.

[1] A shortened form of *karwānsarāi*, a building for the reception
caravans.

Graciae[1] inhabiting the hils on the left hand, which often ungraciously entertayn caravans. A hundred of them had done the like to a caffila [*kāfila*, a caravan] now, had not our comming prevented. It is a small towne, short of which is a great tanke full of wilde fowle. The fifteenth, 10 c. to Pimpelgom [Pipliagāon], a ragged aldea. At 4 c. end of this way lyeth Sarampore [Sarangpur], a great towne with a castle on the south-west side, with a faire towne-house. Here are made faire turbants and good linnen. Short of this towne we met Caun John,[2] a great minion [i. e. favourite] of the Kings, with ten thousand horse, many elephants, and boats carryed on carts, going for Bramport. On the way also we passed divers of Manisengos men, hee having in all some twenty thousand; so that it was deemed there were one hundred thousand horse assembled.

The sixteenth, 7 c. to Cuckra,[3] a great countrey towne abounding with all sorts of graine, victuall, and Mewa wine; at 4 c. lyeth Berroul [Bora], a great aldea. The seventeenth, 12 c. to Delout, a great aldea; the way for the five last coses theevish, hilly, stony; the other pleasant plaines. The eighteenth, 7 c. to Burrow [Barrai], a small towne, but plentifull of victuall, except flesh, which is scarse all this way; the way dangerous. The nineteenth, 7 c. to Sukesera, a small ragged towne. The twentieth, to Syrange [Sironj] 9 c., a very great towne, where are many betele[4] gardens. The one and twentieth and two and twentieth, wee make mukom. The three and twentieth, to Cuchenary Saray [Kachner Sarāi] 8 c. The foure and twentieth, to Sadura [Shāhdaura] 5 c. The five and twentieth, to Collebage [Kālabāg] 7 c. The sixe and twentieth, 12 c. to Qualeres [Kulhāras], a pretty small towne

[1] *Grās* was a kind of blackmail levied by Rājputs and Kolis, and *grassia* was the term given to the person who received this toll. It thus came to mean a robber.

[2] The dispatch of Khān Jahān to the Deccan is described at p. 161 of the *Tūzuk* (vol. i).

[3] Apparently Kakarwar, on the Dudi River. Finch seems to have turned east at Pipliagāon, until he struck a main road again at Barrai, twelve miles north-east of Bersia and thirty miles south-west of Sironj.

[4] The *pān* or *piper betel*, the leaf of which is used for chewing with the betel-nut.

encompassed with tamarind and manga trees. The seven and twentieth, to Cipry [Sipri], seven of Surat couses (a mile and an halfe); way theevish, stony, full of trees, a desart passage; a walled towne, faire houses covered with slate. Two nights before, some sixtie or seventie theeves (mistaking for a late passed caravan) assayled in a darke night one hundred and fiftie Potan souldiers, and fell into the pit they digged for others, ten being slaine and as many taken, the rest fled. The eight and twentieth, to Norwar [Narwar] 12 c., a desart rascally way full of theeves. In the woods sate divers chuckees[1] to prevent robbing, but the foxe is often made the goose-heard. One pretty neat meskite, and in one place at the foot of the gate a few poore inhabitants, wee saw in this dayes journey, and nineteene faire saraies ruinated. The towne at the foot of the hill hath a castle on the top of a stony steepe mountaine, with a narrow stone causey leading to the top, some mile or better in ascent. In the way stand three gates very strong, with places for corps du guard. At the top of all is the fourth gate, which leads into the castle, where stands a guard, not permitting any stranger to enter without order from the King. The towne within is faire and great, with a descent thereto, being situate in a valley on the top of a mountaine very strangely. As it is reported, this cliffe is in circle some 5 or 6 c., and walled round with towers and flankers here and there dispersed, without treason invincible. This hath been the gate or border of the kingdome of Mandow, and hath been beautifull, and stored with ordnance, but now is much gone to ruine. The twenty ninth to Palacha [Paraich] 7 c. The thirtieth, to Antro [Antri], a great towne, 12 c. The thirty one, to Gualere [Gwalior] 6 c., a pleasant citie with a castle. On the east side is on the top of a steepe piked hill a ruinous building, where divers great men have been interred. On the west side is the castle, which is a steep craggy cliffe of 6 c. compasse at least (divers say eleven), all inclosed with a strong wall. At the going up to the castle, adjoyning to the citie is a faire court enclosed with high walls and shut in with strong gates, where keeps a strong guard, not permitting any to enter without publike order. From hence to the top leads a stone

[1] Guards: Hind. *chauki*.

narrow cawsey, walled on both sides; in the way are three gates to be passed, all exceeding strong, with courts of guard to each. At the top of all, at the entrance of the last gate, standeth a mightie elephant of stone very curiously wrought. This gate is also exceeding stately to behold, with a goodly house adjoyning,[1] whose wals are all set with greene and blue stone, with divers gilded turrets on the top. This is the Governours lodging, where is place to keepe nobles that offend. He [i. e. the Great Mogul] is said to have three such noble-prisons or castles, this, and Rantimore [see p. 100], 40 c., to which are sent such nobles as he intends to put to death, which commonly is some two moneths after their arrivall, the Governour then bringing them to the top of the wall and giving them a dishe of milke,[2] which having drunke, he is cast downe thence on the rockes; the third is Rotas [see p. 100], a castle in the kingdome of Bengala, whither are sent those nobles which are condemned to perpetuall imprisonment, from whence very few returne againe. On the top of this mountaine of Gualere is very good ground, with three or foure faire tankes, and many other faire buildings. On the towne side are many houses cut out of the maine rocke, for habitation and sale of goods. On the north-west side, at the foot of the hill is a spacious meadow inclosed with a stone wall, within which are divers gardens and places of pleasure, fit also to keepe horses in time of warre. This castle was the gate or frontier of the kingdome of Dely, bordering on Mandow, and is neere a mile of ascent.

The first of Aprill 1610, to Mendaker [perhaps Mundiākhera], 9 c. The second, 10 c. to Doulpore [Dholpur]. Within 2 c. of the towne, you passe a faire river called Cambere [the Chambal], as broad as the Thames, short of which is a narrow passage with hills on both sides, very dangerous. The castle is strong, ditched round, and hath foure walls and gates one within an other, all very strong, with steep ascents to each, paved with stone; the citie is inhabited most-what with Gentiles. The castle is three quarters of a mile through, and

[1] The palace of Mān Singh. The gate is the Hāthīya Pol; or Elephant Gate.

[2] Rather, a decoction of the milky juice of the poppy.

on the further side hath like gates to be passed againe. The third, to Jajow [Jaju], 9 c. The fourth, to Agra, 9 c. In the afternoone, the Captaine [i. e. Hawkins] carried me before the King. I here found at my comming Captaine Thomas Boys,[1] with three French souldiours, a Dutch inginer, and a Venetian merchant with his sonne and a servant, newly come by land out of Christendome.

In May and part of June, the towne was much vexed with fires night and day, flaming in one part or other, whereby many thousands of houses were consumed, besides men, women, children and cattell, that we feared the judgement of Sodome and Gomorrha upon the place. I was long dangerously sicke of a fever; and in June the heat so exceeded that we were halfe rosted alive. June the twenty eighth arrived Padre Peniero, an arch-knave (a Jesuite, I should say), who brought letters from the Viceroy, with many rich presents, tending only to thwart our affaires. In this time Mo. Bowcan was complained of by the Captaine to the King, who commaunded Abdel Hassan, the Chiefe Vizier, to doe justice; but birds of a feather will flie together, and Mo. Bowcan partly mis-reckoned, partly turned us over to a bankrupt Bannian, so that of thirty two thousand five hundred one m[ahmūdis] and an halfe due, he would pay but eleven thousand; neither would he pay that present [i. e. at once].

In July came newes of the ill successe of the Kings forces in Decan, who, beeing within some foure dayes journey of Amdananager [Ahmadnagar], hoping to raise the siege thereof, were forced through famine and drought to make their retrait for Bramport; whereupon the citie, after much miserie indured, was lost. This armie consisted of one hundred thousand horse at the least, with infinite numbers of cammels and elephants; so that with the whole baggage there could not bee lesse then five or sixe hundred thousand persons, insomuch that the waters were not sufficient for them; a

[1] A soldier of fortune who had come out by way of Turkey and Persia. Two letters from him at Ispahān to Lord Salisbury are noted in the *Calendar of State Papers, East Indies*, s. d. June 10, 1609. As already mentioned, he started for England with Finch and died, like him, at Bagdad.

mussocke [Hind. *mashak*, a goatskin water-bag] of water being sold for a rupia, and yet not enough to be had, and all victualls at an excessive rate. For the Decan army still spoyled the countrey before them, and cut betwixt them and supplies for victualing them out of Guzerate and Bramport, daily making light skirmishes upon them to their great disadvantage, that without retiring the whole army had been endangered. At their returne to Bramport there were not to bee found thirty thousand horse, with infinite number of elephants, cammels, and other cattell dead. This moneth also came newes of the sacking of Potana [see p. 113], a great citie in Purrop [see p. 107], and surprising of the castle where the Kings treasure lay, the citizens flying without making resistance. But upon this Cavalero [1] presently came a great Ombra [2] adjoyning, and tooke him in the castle. The citizens returning, he sent twelve of the chiefe of them to the King, who caused them to be shaven, and in womens attire to bee carried on asses through all the streets of Agra, and on the next day (as it is said) cut off their heads. All this moneth also was much stirre with the King about Christianitie, hee affirming before his nobles that it was the soundest faith, and that of Mahomet lies and fables. He commanded also three princes, his deceassed brothers sonnes,[3] to be instructed by the Jesuites, and Christian apparell to be made for them, the whole city admiring. And yet at the same time Abdel Hassans judgement was that it was not justice to pay debts to Christians, in Mo. Bowcans case, wherof againe we had reference from the King to him. Perhaps on like ground as some Europæans thinke it lawfull to make price [i. e. prize] of the goods and ships of Ethnikes [heathen], *eo nomine*; therefore setting out men of warre, so to make the Christian *name*, not *as an ointment powred out, that the virgin soules* may be converted and *love Christ*, but as filthy

[1] Properly a knight, but used in the sense of a dashing adventurer.

[2] *Umara*, a noble (really the plural of *amīr*).

[3] Tahmūras, Bāyasanghar, and Hoshang, the three sons of the late Prince Dāniyāl. Their conversion is referred to by Hawkins (see pp. 86, 116), Roe, Terry, and Bernier, but the last three say that only two of them were made Christians. They soon renounced their new profession, on the ground that the Jesuits had refused to provide them with Portuguese wives (Roe, p. 316; Terry, p. 425).

matter running out of rotten hearts and poisoned lips, yea, with force and armes to exoccupate the kingdome of Christ in those parts. At least let reformed professors reforme this *man-of-warre-profession* against innocents, that the *name of God through them be not blasphemed among the Gentiles.* But to returne to this dissimulation (as since it hath to the world appeared), those three princes were christened solemnly, conducted to church by all the Christians of the citie to the number of some sixtie horse, Captaine Hawkins being in the head of them, with St. Georges colours carried before him, to the honour of the English nation, letting them flie in the court before Sha Selim himselfe. The eldest was named Don Philippo,[1] the second Don Carlo, the third Don Henrico; and on the ninth of September was christened another young prince, the Acabars brothers[2] sonnes sonne, by the name Don Duarte; the King giving daily charge to the Fathers for their instruction, that they might become good Christians.

October the twelfth we were certified by letters of M. Jourdaine from Surat that thirtie frigats of the Portugals were cast away on the barre of Surat, hasting before the winter was broken up to catch more English; many of the men escaped and were glad to beg releefe at the English doore.

The first of November I was sent to buy nill [see p. 40] or indigo at Byana [see p. 151]. I lodged that night at Menhapoore,[3] a great saray, 7 c., by which is a garden and moholl [*mahal*, palace] or summer house of the Queene Mothers, very curiously contrived. The second at Cannowa [Khānwa], 11 c.; at 4 c. end is a moholl of the Kings. And at every cose end from Agra is erected a stone pillar for 130 c. to Asmere, where lieth interred the body of a great Moorish saint called Hoghee Mondee,[4] whereto the Acabar, wanting children, made

[1] No doubt after the King of Spain and Portugal. The ceremony of baptism was performed by Father Xavier and the task of instruction was committed to Father Corsi. Bāyasanghar was the one christened Don Carlos (see the *Journal of the Panjāb Historical Society*, vol. iv, part i, p. 15).

[2] Mīrza Muhammad Hakīm (see p. 101).

[3] Probably Mundiāpura, near Kiraoli. Traces of the garden still exist (see the *Tūzuk*, vol. ii, p. 64 *n.*).

[4] The celebrated shrine of Khwāja Muīnuddīn Chishti at Ajmer.

a foot-pilgrimage to beg for issue, and caused a pillar at each course to be set up, and a moholl with lodgings for sixteene great women at every eighth course alongst, and after his returne obtained three sonnes. At 7 c. on this way, and 12 c. from Agra, is seated the famous citie of Fetipore [Fatehpur Sikri], built by the Acubar, and inclosed with a faire stone wall, which yet standeth fresh, having foure faire and strong gates, it being some three English miles betwixt gate and gate. In the middest it is all ruinate, lying like a waste desart, and very dangerous to passe through in the night, the buildings lying wast without inhabitants; much of the ground beeing now converted to gardens, and much sowed with nill and other graine, that a man standing there would little thinke he were in the middest of a citie. To the entrance of the gate from Agra, some course in length upon a stony ascent, lie the ruines of the suburbs; as also without the southwest gate for two English miles in length, many faire buildings being fallen to the ground; and on the left hand are many faire enclosed gardens, three miles alongst from the citie. At the entrance of the northeast gate is a goodly bazar (market place) of stone, halfe a mile long, being a spacious, straight-paved street, with faire buildings on either side. Close within the gate is the Kings saray, with large stone lodgings, but much ruined. At the head of this street stands the Kings house and moholl, with much curious building; and on the further side hereof, upon an ascent, stands the goodliest meskite of the East [the Jāma Masjid]. It hath some twentie foure or thirty steps of ascent to the gate [the Baland Darwāza], which is one of the highest and fairest (I suppose) in the whole world; on the top are a number of clustering pinnacles, curiously disposed. The top of this gate may be plainely seene eight or tenne miles distance. Within is a goodly spacious court, very curiously paved with free stone, about sixe times the largenesse of Londons Exchange, with faire large walkes alongst the side more then twice as broad and double the height of those about the Burse of London [the Royal Exchange], the pillars upholding them beeing of one intire stone; and round about are entrances into many goodly roomes, neatly contrived. Opposite to the gate toward the further side stands a faire and sumptuous tombe, artificially inlaied with mother of pearle and inclosed with a grating of stone curiously carved. Over head is rich pargetting and paynting. Herein lyeth the body of a great Kalender,[1] at whose cost the whole meskite was builded. Under the court yard is a goodly tanke of excellent water; none other being to be had through the citie, but brackish and fretting [corrosive], by drinking whereof was caused such mortality that the Acubar, before it was quite finished, left it, and remooved his seat to Agra; so that this goodly citie was short lived, in fifty or sixty yeares space beeing built and ruinate. It was at the first called Sykary, which signifieth seeking or hunting; but after the Acabar was returned from his Asmere pilgrimage and was father of this Sha Selim, hee named it Fetipore, that is, a *towne of content*, or *place of hearts desire obtained.*[2]

The north north-west side of the citie, without the walles, is a goodly lough for 2 or 3 c. in length, abounding with good fish and wilde fowle; all over which groweth the herbe which beareth the hermodactyle, and another bearing a fruit like a goblet, called camolachachery,[3] both very cooling fruits. The herbe which beareth the hermodactyle [4] is a weed abounding in most tankes neare Agra, spreading over all the water; the leafe I observed not, but the fruit is inclosed with a three cornered shell of a hard woodie substance, having at each angle a sharpe picked pricking point and is a little indented on both the flat sides like two posternes. The fruit, being greene, is soft and tender, white, and of a mealish taste, much eaten in India, being exceeding cold in my judgement, for alwayes after it I desired aqua-vitae. It is called by the people Singarra.[5] The other beareth a fruit in maner of a goblet, flat

[1] Shaikh Salīm Chishti (see p. 102 *n.*). A *kalandar* is strictly a wandering mendicant. On p. 164 it is used as equivalent to *fakīr*.

[2] Finch's etymology is at fault. Fatehpur signifies 'the city of victory'; while Sīkri is the name of the original village and has nothing to do with *shikār*, 'hunting'.

[3] *Kānwal kakri*, a name given in the Punjab to the sacred Lotus (*Nelumbium speciosum*).

[4] This is a mistake; the hermodactyle is usually identified as the root of some species of *colchicum*.

[5] Hind. *singhāra*, the caltrop or water-chestnut (*Trapa bispinosa*). Both the kernels and the flour made from them are largely used as food

on the toppe and of a soft greenish substance, within which a little eminent stand sixe or eight small fruits like akornes, divided from each other and inclosed with a whitish filme, at the first of a russettish greene, tasting like a nut or akorne; in the middest is a small greene sprigge naught to be eaten.

Cannowa is a small countrey towne, round about which is made very good nill, by reason of the fastnesse [denseness] of the soile and brackishnesse of the water; it maketh yeerely some five hundred m[aunds]. Ouchen [Uchen], 8 c. distant, makes very good; besides which no towne but Byana itselfe compares with this. I remained heere to the two and twentieth; and three and twentieth, 6 c. to Candere, a roguish, dirtie aldea. At 2 c. on this way is one of those mohol1s before mentioned. It is a square stone building; within the first gate is a small court with a place for the King to keepe his darsany,[1] and two or three other retiring roomes, but none of note. Within the second court is the moholl, being a foure-square thing, about twice as bigge or better then the Exchange, having at each corner a faire open devoncan [*dīwānkhāna*, hall], and in the middest of each side another, which are to bee spread with rich carpets and to sit in to passe the time; and betwixt each corner and this middle-most are two faire large chambers for his women (so that each moholl receiveth sixteene) in severall lodgings, without doores to any of them, all keeping open house to the kings pleasure. Round by the side goeth a faire paved walke, some eight foote broad; and in the middest of all the court stands the Kings chamber, where he, like a cocke of the game, may crow over all. At Candere I remained till the eight and twentieth, and returned to Bachuna [Pichuna], 4 c. backe in the way.

The twentieth of December I went to Byana,[2] 8 c., a backe way thorow the fields. This citie hath beene great and faire, but is now ruinate, save two sarayes and a long bazar, with a

and medicine. On the cultivation of this plant see Sleeman's *Rambles* (ed. 1915, p. 76).

[1] *Darshani*, 'appearing'. The reference is to the Emperor showing himself in public.

[2] Bayāna or Biāna, in Bhartpur State, fifty miles south-west of Agra.

few stragling houses; many faire ones being fallen and many others not inhabited (except by rogues or theeves), so that many streets are quite desolate. On the north-west, some three or four cose off, are the ruines of a kings house, with many other faire buildings. The like ruines are to bee seene on the south-west side, over against a towne called Scanderbade,[1] in like distance upon the height of the rocky mountaines. The way leading up is a narrow steepe stony cawsey, not to be passed on horse-backe, some quarter of a mile the ascent; the entrance is thorow a small wicket, passing the lips of the mountaines in a narrow gutte. On the right hand, upon the very edge, stands a pleasant building where are divers tombes; from each side the way may be made good with stones against millions of men. Passing a mile hence on a faire cawsey, you come to the kings house, sometimes faire, now ruinate, where a few poore Googers[2] remaine in the ruines. Many tombes and monuments yet remaine. At the foote of the hill toward Scanderbade is a pleasant valley inclosed with a wall, and therein many gardens of pleasure. This city hath been in ancient times the seate of a great Potane king,[3] and hath had the walles extending on the cliffes 8 c. in length, in those places where is any possibilitie of getting up, the rockes otherwhere over-hanging; the fortifications on the other side I saw not. It hath beene a goodly city, inhabited now only with Googers, which are keepers of cattell and makers of butter and cheese. From hence, notwithstanding all this strength, did the Acabar force Sha Selim [see p. 142 *n.*] the Tyrant, and then laid it waste, as he hath done Mandow and most of the strongholds which he tooke. The countrey which affordeth that rich nill which takes name of Byana is not above twenty or thirtie cose long.

The herbe Nill groweth in forme not much unlike cives [the chive or *Allium*] or cich-pease [chickpea], having a small leafe like that of Sena, but shorter and broader and set on a very

[1] Sikandarābād, now called Sikandra, three miles to the south of Bayāna.

[2] Hind. *Gūjar*, a pastoral caste, formerly notorious for cattle-stealing.

[3] Sikandar Shāh Lodi, according to Mundy, who also describes the fort (Bījāgarh or Sāntipur).

short foot-stalke, the branches hard and of a woodie substance like unto broome. It usually groweth not above a yard high and with a stalke at the biggest (which is at the third yeare) not much exceeding a mans thumbe. The seede is included in a small round codde about an inch long, resembling Foeni-graecum, save that it is more blunt at both ends, as if it had been cut off with a knife. It carryeth a small flower like that of Hearts-ease; the seed is ripe in November, and then gathered. The herbe once sowne dureth three yeeres, being cut every yeere in August and September after the raines. That of one yeere is tender and thereof is made Notee,[1] which is a weighty reddish nill, sinking in water, not come to his perfection; that of the second yeere is rich, and called Cyeree,[2] very light and of a perfect violet colour, swimming on the water; in the third yeere the herbe is declining, and this nill is called Catteld,[3] being a weightie blackish nill, the worst of the three. This herbe, being cut the moneth aforesaid, is cast into a long cisterne, where it is pressed downe with many stones, and then filled with water till it be covered; which so remaineth for certaine dayes, till the substance of the herbe be gone into the water. Then they let the water forth into another round cisterne, in the middest of which is another small cisterne or center; this water being thus drawne forth, they labour with great staves, like batter or white starch, and then let it settle, scumming off the cleare water on the toppe; then labouring it afresh, and let it settle againe, drawing forth the cleare water; doing this oft, till nothing but a thicke substance remaine, which they take foorth and spread on cloth to dry in the sunne; and being a little hardened, they take it in their hands and, making small balls, lay them on the sand to dry (for any other thing would drinke up the colour); this is the cause of the sandy foot. So if raine fall, it looseth his colour and glosse, and is called Aliad.[4] Some deceitfully will

[1] Sir George Watt concludes that this term is derived from *naudha*, the young plant.

[2] *Jari*, 'sprouting from the root'.

[3] *Khutiyāl* or *khūnti*. With this account of the various crops cf. that in *Letters Received*, vol. vi, p. 241.

[4] This seems to be connected with the Hind. *āla*, 'moist'.

take of the herbe of all three crops and steepe them all together, hard to be discerned, very knavishly. Fowre things are required in nill : a pure graine, a violet colour, his glosse in the sunne, and that it be dry and light, so that swimming in the water or burning in the fire it cast forth a pure light violet vapour, leaving a few ashes.

About the sixt of January [1611] the King, being on hunting, was assailed by a lyon, which hee had wounded with his peece, with such fiercenesse that, had not a captaine of his, a Resboot, tutor of the late baptized princes, interposed himselfe, thrusting his arme into the lions mouth as hee ramped against His Majestie, he had in all likelihood been destroyed. In this strugling Sultan Corom, Rajaw Ranidas,[1] and others came in and amongst them slew the lyon, that captaine having first received thirty two wounds ; whome therfore the King tooke up into his owne palanke, with his owne hands also wiped and bound up his wounds, and made him a captaine of five thousand horse, in recompence of that his valourous loyaltie.

The Kings manner of hunting is this : about the beginning of November, accompanied with many thousands, he goeth forth of his castle of Agra and hunteth some thirty or forty course round about the citie ; so continuing till the ende of March, when the heat drives him home againe. He causeth, with choise men, a certain wood or desart place to bee incircled, so contracting themselves to a neerer compasse till they meet againe ; and whatsoever is taken in this inclosure is called the Kings sikar [Hind. *shikār*] or game, whether men or beasts ; and whosoever lets ought escape without the Kings mercy must loose his life. The beasts taken, if mans meat, are sold and the money given to the poore ; if men, they remaine the Kings slaves, which he yearely sends to Cabull to barter for horse and dogs ; these beeing poore, miserable, theevish people that live in woods and desarts, little differing from beasts.

This moneth the King was providing more forces for Decan,

[1] A mistake for Rāja Rām Dās : see Jahāngīr's own account of the incident in the *Tūzuk* (vol. i, p. 185), where the animal is described as a tiger. The Rājput captain was named Anūp Rāi. Jourdain says that he was rewarded with '1000 horse per yeare, which is as good as 1000*l.* sterlinge' (p. 161).

notwithstanding the Decanees required his peace, offering to restore what they had taken. Caun Asom [see p. 98] was sent Generall, and with him twentie thousand horse, accompanied with Matrobet Caun [Mahābat Khān], another great captaine, together with infinite treasure. With these forces went John Frenchman [1] and Charles Charke,[2] entertained in his service for the warres.

January the ninth, I departed from Agra for Lahor to recover debts, and carried twelve carts laden with nil [indigo] in hope of a good price. The places I passed were Rownocta [Rankata], twelve courses: Badeg Sara,[3] 10: Acabarpore [Akbarpur], 12 c., formerly a great city, still famous for the antiquities of Indian gobins [4] or saints. A little short of this place is a faire deury [*deura*, temple] inclosed with a stone wall, in which is a devoncan, and round about a little distance in vaults (or cloisters)are to be seen many pagods [see p. 15 *n*.], which are stone images of monstrous men feareful to behold, but adored by the Indians with flowers and offerings. Houdle [Hodal], 13 c.; at the entrance of the saray is a faire fountaine [i.e. well], three stories and one hundred steps. Pulwooll [Palwal], 12 c. Ferreedabade [Farīdābād], 12 c. Dely, 10 c. On the left hand is seene the carkasse of old Dely,[5] called the nine castles and

[1] Jourdain and Covert call him 'Frencham'. He was one of the survivors from the *Ascension*, and later proceeded to Agra with Covert. At Burhānpur they were asked by the Khānkhānān to serve him in the Deccan war. On their declaring that they were only merchants, he replied (according to Covert) that 'there was no Englishman, merchant nor other, but he was a souldier'. Frencham left Agra with Covert, but fell ill and had to remain behind at Bukkur, whence no doubt he returned to Agra on recovery.

[2] 'This Ch. Charke I have spoken with since in London after divers yeares service' (*marginal note by Purchas*).

[3] Bād-ki-sarāi. It is suggested in Growse's *Mathura* (p. 28) that the *sarāi* intended is the one at Jamālpur, about three *kos* from Bād.

[4] 'Gosains' is probably intended.

[5] Tughlakābād, which according to tradition had fifty-two gates (Carr Stephen's *Archaeology of Delhi*, p. 91). The following marginal note is appended to the passage in the text: 'There are said to bee foure Delyes within 5 c.; the eldest built by Rase [i. e. Rāja Anang Pāl], who by his ponde [pundit] or magicians counsell tried the earth by an iron stake, which he pulled out bloody with the blood of a snake, which his ponde said was signe of good fortune. [This is a well-known story

fiftie two gates, now inhabited onely by Googers. A little short is a stone bridge of eleven arches,[1] over a branch of Gemini [the Jumna]; from hence a broad way shaded with great trees leading to the sepulchre of Hamaron [Humāyūn], this kings grandfather, in a large roome spread with rich carpets, the tombe itselfe covered with a pure white sheet, a rich semiane [see p. 117] over head, and a front certaine bookes on small tressels, by which stand his sword, tucke [turban] and shooes.[2] At the entrance are other tombes of his wives and daughters. Beyond this, under like shaded way, you come to the Kings house and moholl, now ruinous. The city is 2 c. betweene gate and gate, begirt with a strong wall, but much ruinate, as are many goodly houses. Within and about this citie are the tombes of twenty Potan kings, all very faire and stately. The kings of India are here to be crowned, or else they are held usurpers. It is seated in a goodly plaine, environed with goodly pleasant gardens and monuments.

Nalero [Narela] is hence 14 c. About 2 c. without Dely is the remainder of an auncient mole [*mahal*?] or hunting house, built by Sultan Berusa,[3] a great Indian monarch, with much curiositie of stoneworke. With and above the rest is to be

relating to the iron pillar near the Kutb Minār (*op. cit.*, p. 17).] The last of his race was Rase Pethory [Rāi Pithora or Prithwi Rāj], who, after seven times taking a Potan king, was at last by him taken and slaine. He began the Potan kingdome. They came from the mountaines between Candahar and Catull [Kābul]. The second built by Togall Sha [Tughlak Shāh], a Potan king. The third little of note. The fourth by Shershaselim [Sher Shāh], where is that tomb of Hamaron' [Humāyūn].

The last named was the Delhi of Finch's day. It lay to the south of the modern city, and occupied part of the site of Firozābād.

[1] The Bāra Pala bridge, near the shrine of Nizām-uddīn.

[2] Cf. Peter Mundy's description (*Travels*, vol. ii, pp. 100, 181) of the tomb of Prince Khusrau.

[3] Sultān Firoz Shāh, who laid out a hunting park on the Ridge and built therein a palace. The pillar referred to by Finch is the Asoka *lāt* brought by Firoz Shāh from Meerut and erected on the same spot, where it still stands. The earliest European account of it seems to be that given by Monserrate. Some writers have supposed that Finch meant to describe the other Asoka pillar at Delhi—that in the Kotila of Firozābād, but this is evidently wrong.

seen a stone pillar,[1] which, passing through three stories, is higher then all twenty foure foot, having at the top a globe and a halfe moone over it. This stone, they say, stands as much under the earth, and is placed in the water, being all one entire stone; some say Naserdengady,[2] a Potan king, would have taken it up and was prohibited by multitude of scorpions, and that it hath inscriptions. In divers parts of India the like are to be seene, and of late was found buried in the ground about Fettipore a stone piller of an hundred cubits length, which the King commanded to bring to Agra, but was broken in the way, to his great griefe.[3] It is remarkeable that the quarries of India, specially neere Fettipore (whence they are carryed farre) are of such nature that they may be cleft like logges and sawne like plancks to seele chambers and cover houses of a great length and breadth. From this monument is said to bee a way under ground to Dely castle.[4] Now here remaine onely Googers, and there are store of deere. We saw in the way the ruines of divers places [palaces ?], and neere the same the ruines of a wall 20 c. in circuit, being a parke for game. Some part of this way was theevish, and, some report being given out of the Kings death, many rogues with that false alarme were abroad. We met the Fosder [*faujdār*, military commandant] of Dely with some two thousand horse and foot in their pursuit, who burnt their townes and tooke them and theirs, whatsoever he could get; and the next day at breakfast we were like to be surprized by theeves.

Gonowre [Ganaur], 14 c. Panneput [Pānīpat], 14 c.; at the entry whereof was placed a manora [5] with the heads of some

[1] 'A stately obeliske with Greeke or Hebrew inscriptions (as some affirme), supposed to be set there by Alexander' (*marginal note, probably by Purchas, based on Coryat*).

[2] Sir Edward Maclagan thinks this Nāsiruddīn Ghāzi may have been Nāsiruddīn Tughlak, son of Firoz Shāh.

[3] Nothing seems to be known concerning this pillar.

[4] For references to this and other subterranean passages see Mon serrate (p. 590), Jarrett's *Āīn* (vol. ii, p. 279), and Father Hosten's articles in the *Journal of the Bengal Asiatic Society*, 1911 (p. 102) and 1912 (p. 279).

[5] *Mīnār*, or pillar. For the practice of cementing the heads of criminals or rebels in pillars erected for the purpose, see Mundy, pp. 72, 90, &c.

hundred theeves newly taken, their bodies set on stakes a mile in length. Carmall [Karnāl], 14 c.; the way theevish, where but for our peece language we had been assaulted. On the north-west extend mountaines neere to Lahor from hence, with snow on the tops. Tanassar [Thānesar], 14 c.; here is a castle, a goodly tanke, and by it pagods, much reverenced by all the Gentiles throughout India. Neere it also are the salarmoniake pits. Shabad [Shāhābād] or Goobade, 10 c. Amballa [Ambāla], 12 c. Hollowa Saray [Alūwa sarāi], 14 c. Syrinam [Sirhind], 7 c.; it hath a faire tanke with a summerhouse in the middest, to which leads a bridge of fifteene stone arches, very pleasant. From hence is a small river cut to the Kings garden,[1] a corse distant, with a cawsey of forty foot broad, planted with trees on both sides to it. The garden is fowre square, each square a cose in length or better, inclosed with a bricke-wall, richly planted with all sorts of fruits and flowers, rented yeerely (as I was told) for fifty thousand rupias; crossed with two maine walkes, forty foot broad and eight high, with water running alongst stone channells in the middest, and planted on both sides thicke with faire cypresses; one of these cawseys is also paved with peble, curiously inter-wrought. At the crossing stands an eight square mohol with eight chambers for women, in the midst thereof a faire tank; over these, eight other roomes, with faire galleries round about; on the top of all a faire jounter;[2] the whole building curiously wrought in stone, with faire painting, rich carving, and pargetting; and on two sides two faire tankes in the midst of a faire stone chounter, planted round with cypresse trees; a little distant is another mohol, but not so curious.

From hence we passed to Dorapy [Dorāha], 15 c. Pulloceque Saray [Phillaur-ki-sarāi], 18 c. Nicoder [Nakodar], 12 c. Sultanpoore [Sultānpur], 11 c. Fetipore,[3] 7 c.; a saray built (if it were finished) by Sha Selim in memoriall of the overthrow given Sultan Cusseroom [Khusrau], his eldest sonne, the occa-

[1] 'Some say it was made An. Dom. 1580' (*marginal note*).

[2] 'Jounter' or 'chounter' is the Hind. *chautri* or *chabūtara*, a terrace for recreation.

[3] Vairowāl, on the Beās, named Fatehpur ('town of victory') in memory of Khusrau's defeat.

sion whereof was this.[1] Sha Selim, upon some disgust, tooke armes in his fathers lifetime and fled into Purrop, where he kept the strong castle of Alobasse [Allahābād] (but came in some three moneths before his fathers deceasse); whereupon Acubar gave the crowne to Sultan Cusseroom his sonne. But after Acabars death, Selim, by his friends, seized on the castle and treasure, and his sonne fled for Lahor, where hee gathered some twelve thousand horse, all good souldiours and Mogols, possessing the suburbs twelve daies, and proclaimed king in the kasse,[2] and his father in the castle. In this place he gave battell to Strek Fereed [Shaikh Farīd], and disordered his three hundred horse and put them to the sword. To the second [i.e. assistance] of him came Melec Ale Cutwall [Khwāja Malik Ali, the *kotwāl*] (the King being some 20 c. behind) with some two hundred horse, beating up the Kings drummes, and giving a brave assault, shouting God save King Selim; upon which the Princes souldiours fainted and fled, the Prince himselfe fleeing only with five horse, and got 30 c. beyond Lahor for Cabull; which if he had gotten, he would have put his father to further trouble; but beeing to passe a river where hee gave mohors of gold, the boate-man grew in distrust, and in the middest of the channell leapt overboord and swamme to the shoare, where hee gave notice to the governour of the towne adjoyning, who presently with fiftie horse came downe to the river, where the boat was still floting, imbarqued himselfe in another, and saluted him by the name of king, dissemblingly offering his aide and inviting him to his house; which the Prince accepting, was locked up with his company and guarded till hee had sent the King word; who sent Germaunabeg[3] to fetch him fettered on an elephant. From hence his father proceeded to Cabul, punishing such as he found tardie in this revolt; carrying his sonne with

[1] See Hawkins's account (p. 107).

[2] Perhaps he means the *ām-khās*, a term sometimes used for the *dīwān-i-ām*. The city and the castle would have separate governors, and it would seem that one declared for Jahāngīr and the other for Khusrau.

[3] Zamāna Beg, i. e. Mahābat Khān. For other accounts of Khusrau's capture see the *Tūzuk* (vol. i, p. 66), the *Āīn* (vol. i, p. 414), and Du Jarric (vol. iii, p. 141).

him prisoner; and returning by this place where the battell was fought (as some say) caused his eyes to be burned out with a glasse; others say onely blind-folded him with a napkin, tying it behind and sealing it with his owne seale, which yet remaineth, and himselfe prisoner in the castle of Agra.[1] All alongst on both sides the way from Cabul to Agra, a reasonable distance, the King caused trees to be planted to shade the way in remembrance of this exploit, and called this place Fetipoore, that is, *Hearts content*, as ye before heard of the citie [see p. 150], which for his birth was named so by his father Accubar; these, as any decay, must by the peoples toyle be supplied.

From hence to Hoghe Moheede,[2] 10 c. Cancanna saray, 12 c. Lahor, 7 c.; where I arrived February the fourth. On the

[1] That Khusrau was blinded by his father was evidently very generally believed at the time (see *supra*, p. 108, and Du Jarric, vol. iii, p. 169). The question is discussed by Mr. Beveridge in a note on p. 174 of vol. i of the *Tūzuk* and in an article in the *Journal of the Bengal Asiatic Society*, vol. 39 (p. 597). He inclines to accept the story, mainly because the impostor who afterwards personated the Prince pretended that he had marks of the blinding. This, however, was a very natural artifice, given the prevailing impression; and against such an argument may be set the fact that Sir Thomas Roe, who both saw and talked with the Prince in 1617, makes no mention of any injury to his sight, and moreover speaks of him as destined to succeed to the throne—an event hardly to be contemplated in the case of a blind man. Terry, who also saw Khusrau more than once, says explicitly that 'his eyes were sealed up (by something put before them which might not be taken off) for the space of three years; after which time that seal was taken away'; and this agrees with one of the rumours noted by Finch. Della Valle's version is that the eyes were sewn up for a time, without injuring the sight. The story given in Elliot's *History of India*, vol. vi (p. 448), that the Prince was deprived of his sight by having a wire thrust into his eyes, but that his vision was afterwards restored by the skill of a surgeon, is not only improbable in itself but is obviously an attempt to reconcile the current belief in the blinding with the fact that Khusrau could see quite well in later years. Mundy, it may be noted, has a tale (p. 104) that one eye was 'eaten out with applyeinge to it a certaine venemous hearbe', but fixes the date of this as a little before the Prince's murder in 1622.

[2] The position given seems to answer to Tarn Tāran; but Finch's distances are not to be trusted. Khānkhānān-sarāi has not been identified.

twentie eighth arrived here a Persian embassadour [1] allied to Sha Abash, with a great caravan accompanying him. I by them learned that the way to Candahar was now cleere, the warres being ended which the Turkish Gelole [2] had caused, who the former yeare had fled to the Persian with some ten thousand Turkes and had obtained some jaggere [*jāgīr*, an assignment of land] neere thereto ; whereof he purposing to make himselfe king, was overthrowne, and being sent for by the Persian refused to come ; till, deluded by promise of a mariage, he was got to the court, and there lost his head. We heard also of the Persians taking from the Turke the strong castle of Curdes after a yeeres siege, with other Asian and Europæan newes.

Lahor is one of the greatest cities of the East, containing some 24 c. in circuit by the ditch which is now casting up about it, and by the Kings command now to be inclosed with a strong wall. In the time of the Potans it was but a village, Multan then flourishing, till Hamawn [Humāyūn] enlarged this. The towne and suburb is some 6 c. thorow. The castle or towne is inclosed with a strong bricke wall, having thereto twelve faire gates, nine by land and three openings to the river ; the streets faire and well paved ; the inhabitants most Baneans and handicrafts men, all white men of note lying in the suburbs. The buildings are faire and high, with bricke and much curiositie of carved windowes and doores ; most of the Gentiles doores of sixe or seven steps ascent and very troublesome to get up, so built for more securitie and that passengers should not see into their houses. The castle is seated on Ravee, a goodly river which falleth into Indus, downe which go many boats, of sixtie tunne or upwards, for Tatta in Sind, after the fall of the raine, being a journey of some fortie dayes alongst by Multan, Seetpore,[3] Buchur [Bukkur], Rauree [Rohri] etc.

[1] Yādgār Ali Sultān. For this embassy, see the *Tūzuk*, vol. i, pp. 193, 237, &c.

[2] A letter from Persia of June, 1609, refers to the defeat of 'Jouile, the great Geloly' (*Cal. State Papers, E. Indies*, 1513–1616, no. 446), but who he was is not evident, unless he is to be identified with the Turkish general Jāghāl-āghli mentioned by Malcolm (*History of Persia*, vol. i, p. 538). In that case, however, Malcolm's dates must be wrong.

[3] Sītpur, an ancient town on the Indus, in the Muzaffargarh district.

This river commeth from the east and runneth westerly by the north side of the citie; upon which, within the castle, is the Kings house,[1] passing in at the middle gate to the river-ward. Within the citie on the left-hand you enter thorow a strong gate, and a musket shot further another smaller, into a faire great square court, with atescanna [2] for the Kings guard to watch in. On the left-hand thorow another gate you enter into an inner court, where the King keepes his darbar, and round about which court are atescanna's also for great men to watch in. In the middest there stands a high pole to hang a light on. From hence you go up to a faire stone jounter or small court, in the middest whereof stands a faire devoncan, with two or three other retiring rooms wherein the King sits out all the first part of the night, commonly from eight to eleven. On the walles is the Kings picture, sitting crosse-legged on a chaire of state; on his right hand Sultan Pervese, Sultan Caroone, and Sultan Timoret,[3] his sonnes; next these Sha Morat [Shāh Murād] and Don Sha [Dāniyāl Shāh], two of his brothers (the three baptized before spoken were sonnes of this later): next them Emersee Sheriff [Mīrza Sharīf], eldest brother to Caun Asom (of whom it is reported his estate to be such that, of one hundred chiefe women which he kept, he never suffred any of their clothing after their first wearing to be ever touched by any stranger, but caused them to bee buried in the ground, there to rot; as also that he alway had in service five hundred massalgees [torchbearers: *mashalchi*], in so much that whensoever he went from court to his house in Agra, which was at least a corse, no man removed foote with his torch but stood all alongst to his house): next this man, Emersee Rostene [Mīrza Rustam], late King of Candhar; then Can Canna [see p. 71] (which signifieth prince of the Cannes): then Cuttûp Caun [Kutbuddīn Khān Koka], Rajaw Manisengo [Rāja Mān Singh], Caun Asom [Khān Azam],

[1] The palace was altered and enlarged by Shāh Jahān, and in later times suffered much at the hands of the Sikhs and the British. See the *Archaeological Survey Report* for 1902–1903 and an article by Dr. Vogel in the *Journal of the Panjāb Historical Society*, vol. i, no. 1.

[2] *Yātish-khāna*, a guard-room (see Monserrate, p. 645).

[3] Parwiz, Khurram, and Tahmūras. The last was a nephew, not a son.

Asoph Caun [Āsaf Khān (Jafar Beg)], Sheck Fereed [Shaikh Farid], Kelish Caun [Kilīj Khān], and Rajaw Juggonat [Rāja Jagannāth] (who at his death had seven of his friends that burned themselves with him, besides one of his sisters, and a brothers childe). On the left hand of the King stands Rajaw Bowsing [Bhāo Singh], who beats away flyes, then Rajaw Ramdas [Rām Dās], who holds his sword, Cleriff Caun, Caun John, Jemana Lege or Mawbet Caun, Mocrow Bowcan, Rajaw Bossow, Rajaw Ransing, Majo Kesso, and Lala Bersing.[1] Note also that in this gallery, as you enter, on the right-hand of the King over the doore is the picture of our Saviour; opposite on this left-hand, of the Virgin Mary. This devoncan is very pleasantly seated, over-looking the Ravee. From hence passing thorow a small entrie to the west, you enter another small court, where is another open chounter of stone to sit in, covered with rich semianes [see p. 117]. From hence you enter into a small gallery, at the end of which, next the river, thorow a small window the King looks forth at his dersanee [see p. 151] to behold the fights of wilde beasts on the medow by the river. On the wall of this gallery is drawne the picture of the Acabar sitting in his state, and before him Sha Selim his sonne standing with a hawke on his fist, and by him Sultan Cusseroom, Sultan Pervis, Sultan Coroome, his three sonnes. At the end is a small devoncan where the King useth to sit; behind which is his lodging chamber, and before it all open into a paved court, alongst the right-hand whereof runneth a small moholl of two stories, each containing eight faire lodgings for severall women, with galleries and windowes looking to the river and to the court. All the doores of these chambers are to bee fastened on the out-side, and none within. In the gallery where the King useth to sit are drawne over-head many pictures of angels, with pictures of Banian dews [see p. 134], or rather divels, intermixt in most ugly shape with long hornes, staring eyes, shagge haire, great fangs, ugly pawes, long tailes, with such horrible difformity and deformity that I wonder the poore women are not frighted

[1] These are Sharīf Khān, Khān Jahān, Zamāna Beg or Mahābat Khān, Mukarrab Khān, Rāja Bāso, Rāja Rāi Singh, Rāja Keshu Dās (?), and Lāla Bīr Singh.

therewith. Within this court is a pleasant devoncan and lodgings, and the way to another moholl for the King to passe, but none other.

Now to returne to the former court, where the Adees [see p. 99] or guard keepe their watch, there is also on the left hand the new Derbar ; beyond it another small court with atescanna, and passing thorow another gate a faire large square moholl, called the New Moholl, of that largenesse that it may lodge two hundred women in state, all severall. Likewise returning to the great court, passing right on, you enter another small paved court on the left hand and into another moholl, the stateliest of the three, contrived into sixteene severall great lodgings, each having faire lodgings, a devoncan (or hall), a small paved court, each her tanke, and enjoying a little world of pleasure and state to herselfe ; all seated very pleasantly upon the river. Before the moholl of Sultan Casserooms mother [1] is placed an high pole to hang a light on, as before the King ; for that shee brought forth his first sonne and heire. In the midst stands a goodly gallery for the King to sit in, with such ugly pictures over-head as before. At the end are drawne many portraitures of the King in state sitting amongst his women, one holding a flaske of wine, another a napkin, a third presenting the peally [*piyāli*, a small cup] ; behind, one punkawing [fanning : *pankha*], another holding his sword, another his bow and two or three arrowes etc. Before this gallery is a faire paved court, with stone gratings and windowes alongst the waters side ; at the end a faire marble jounter, convexed over-head, looking over the river ; beneath it a garden of pleasure ; behind, the Kings lodgings, very sumptuous, the walles and seelings all over-laid with pure gold, and round alongst the sides, about a mans height, some three foote distant, are placed faire Venice looking-glasses, three and three, each above other ; and below these, alongst the walles, are drawne many pictures of this mans ancestors, as of Acabar his father, Hamowne his grand-father, Babur his great grand-father, who first set foote into India with thirtie of his nobles, all clad like kalendars or fookeers, which so came

[1] The Shāh Begam. She was a daughter of Rāja Bhagwān Dās and sister of Rāja Mān Singh.

to Dely to Secanders [Sikandar Lodi, 1489–1517] court then raigning; where by his very countenance he was discovered, yet found mercy and returned upon his oath not to attempt anything during the said Secanders raigne, which he performed; but after his death he sent his sonne Hamawne upon his successor Abram [Ibrāhīm Lodi, 1517–26], from whom he tooke the whole kingdome.[1] Yet at length rose up a great captaine [Sher Shāh] of the blood-royall in Bengala, who fought a great battel with Hamawne neare Ganges, put him to flight, and so closely followed him that he drave him forth of the kingdome to the Persian Shaw; of whom hee obtained new forces (with whom came Byram, Caun Canna his father [see p. 71 *n.*], for generall) and reconquered all, living after that in security. This king dying left Acabar very yong, appointed Byram Caun Protector; whom the Acabar, comming to yeares, cast off, and on a roomery [Spanish *romeria*] or pilgrimage to Mecca, as is said, made away with him. His sonne Can Canna (or Caun of the Caunces) doth also much curbe Sha Selim the King, with his friends and allyes being able to make better then an hundred thousand horse. Sha Selim affirmeth himselfe to be the ninth lawfully descended from the loynes of Tamerlane the Great, being the great-grand-child of Babur, King of Cabull.

But to returne to the entrance of this moholl: passing forth of that court thorow a strong gate, you enter into the city againe; this house and appurtenances of mohols being at the least two English miles in circuit. On the east-side of the castle, hard without the wall, is the garden of Asoph Caun [Āsaf Khān (Jafar Beg)], small, neat, with walkes (planted with cypresse trees), divers tankes and jounters; as you enter, a faire devoncan supported with stone pillars, with a faire tanke in the midst, and in the midst of that, on foure stone pillars, a jounter for coolenesse. Beyond are other galleries and walkes, divers lodgings for his women neatly contrived, and behind, a small garden and garden-house. In the midst of the garden is a very stately jounter with faire buildings over-

[1] There seems to be no truth in this story of Bābur's visit to India in disguise; and it was he, and not Humāyūn, who made the invasion of 1526.

head, and a tanke in the center with large and goodly galleries alongst the foure sides thereof, supported with high stone pillars. Adjoyning to this is a garden of the Kings, in which are very good apples, but small, toot [*tūt*, mulberry] white and red, almonds, peaches, figges, grapes, quinces, orenges, limmons, pomgranats, roses, stock-gellow-flowers,[1] marigolds, wall-flowers, ireos,[2] pinkes white and red, with divers sorts of Indian flowers.

On the west side of the castle is the ferry to passe over to Cabul (and so to Tartary or Cascar [Kāshgar]), a very great road-way, and the further side of the river is a goodly countrey. Infinit numbers of gardens full of rarity exceeds [i. e. project beyond], two or three c. in length.

Passing the Sugar Gonge[3] is a faire meskite built by Shecke Fereed;[4] beyond it (without the towne, in the way to the gardens) is a faire monument for Don Sha his mother, one of the Acabar his wives, with whom it is said Sha Selim had to do (her name was Immacque Kelle,[5] or Pomgranate kernell); upon notice of which the King [Akbar] caused her to be inclosed quicke within a wall in his moholl, where shee dyed, and the King [Jahāngīr], in token of his love, commands a sumptuous tombe to be built of stone in the midst of a foure-square garden richly walled, with a gate and divers roomes over it.[6] The convexity of the tombe he hath willed to be wrought in workes of gold, with a large faire jounter with roomes over-head. Note that most of these monuments which I mention are of such largeness that, if they were otherwise contrived, would have roome to entertaine a very good man with his whole houshold. Without the Dely Droware,[7] where the nolat [*naubat*] or great drum beats, is a goodly streight

[1] The white stock (*Mathiola incana*).

[2] The Florentine iris.

[3] The shrine of Bāwa Farīd Shakarganj, to the south-west of the city.

[4] Shaikh Farīd erected several buildings in Lahore, but this mosque does not appear in the list.

[5] *Anārkīkali* (pomegranate blossom). There is no corroboration of Finch's story that she was the mother of Dāniyāl.

[6] The tomb, which is still one of the sights of Lahore, was not finished till 1615.

[7] The Delhi Gate (*darwāza*).

street, about three quarters of a mile long, all paved ; at the end of which is the Bazar ; by it the great saray ; besides which are divers others, both in the city and suburbs, wherein divers neate lodgings are to be let, with doores, lockes, and keyes to each. Hence to the north-east lyeth Ambere,[1] the place of hospitality ; from hence to the south-east the habitation of divers loving etc.

The seventeenth of May came newes of the sacking of Cabul by the Potan theeves, which kept in the mountains, being eleven thousand foot and one thousand horse ; the Governour thereof being at Gelalabade [Jalālābād] about other affaires, and the garrison so weak that they were able only to maintaine the castle. In six houres they spoiled the city and retired with great booty. The King, for better awing of these rebels, hath placed twenty three ombraes betwixt Lahor and Cabul ; and yet all will not serve, they often sallying from the mountains, robbing caravans, and ransacking townes. The eighteenth of August arrived a great caravan from Persia, by whom we had newes from an Armenian, which had served M. Boys, of the French kings death,[2] and of affaires betwixt the Turk and Persian ; he having destroyed the countrey about Tauris [Tabrīz], raced the citie, and filled up the wells to hinder the Turks armie ; the merchants by this means (to our griefe) not daring to adventure beyond Candhar.

Of divers wayes in the Mogols Kingdome, to and from Lahor and Agra, and places of note in them.[3]

From Lahor to Cabull, passing the Ravee, at 10 c. stands Googes saray [Kacha sarāi] ; beyond which 8 c. Emenbade [Amīnābād], a faire city ; thence to Chumaguckur [Chīma Gakkhar] 12 c., a great towne. To Guzurat [Gujrāt] 14 c., a faire citie of great trade ; at 7 c. of this way you passe the river Chantrow [Chenāb], neare a corse over. To Howaspore

[1] This may possibly refer to some *āmbāgh* (mango-garden) in which there may have been a *dharmsāla* or rest-house ; but no trace of such a place can be found in modern maps.

[2] Henri IV was assassinated in May, 1610.

[3] This heading was doubtless supplied by Purchas.

[Khawāsspur] 12 c. To Loure Rotas [Rohtās][1] 15 c., a citie with a strong castle on a mountaine, the frontier of the Potan kingdome. To Hattea [Hatya] 15 c. To Puckow [Pakka] 4 c. To Raulepende [Rāwalpindi] 14 c. To Collapanne [Kālapāni] 15 c. To Hassanabdall[2] 4 c., a pleasant towne with a small river and many faire tanks in which are many fishes with gold rings in their noses, hung by Acabar; the water so cleare that you may see a penny in the bottome. To Attock 15 c., a citie with a strong castle, by which Indus passeth in great beautie. To Pishore [Peshāwar] 36 c. To Alleek Meskite [Ali Masjid] 10 c., the way dangerous for rebels, which are able to make ten or twelve thousand men. To Ducka [Daka] 12 c. To Beshoule [Basāwal] 6 c. To Abareek [Bariku] 6 c. To Aleboga [Ali Boghan] 9 c.; by which runneth Cow [the Kābul River], a great river which comes from Cabul (way still theevish). To Gelalabade [Jalālābād] 4 c. To Loure-Charebage 4 c. To Budde-Charbag 6 c. To Nimla [Nīmla] 8 c. To Gondoma [Gandamak] 4 c. To Surcrood [Surkhāb] 4 c.; a saray with a small river which lookes red and makes to have a good stomack. To Zagdelee [Jagdalak] 8 c. To Abereek [Āb-i-bārīk] 8 c. To Dowaba [Doāba] 8 c.; a great mountain in the way, 4 c. ascent. To Butta Cauke [Butkhāk] 8 c. To Camree [Bikrāmi] 8 c. To Cabul 8 c. It is a great and faire citie, the first seate of this kings great grand-father, with two castles and many sarayes. 20 c. beyond is Chare-cullow [Chārīkār], a pleasant faire citie; and 20 c. beyond, Gorebond [Ghorband], a great citie bordering upon Usbeke. 150 c. beyond Cabul is Taul Caun [Talikhān], a citie in Buddocsha [Badakhshān].

From Cabull to Cascar [Kāshgar] with the caravan is some two or three monethes journey.[3] It is a great kingdome and

[1] From this point the road may be traced in the *Tūzuk* (vol. i, p. 96).

[2] Hasan Abdāl. Jahāngīr records that he caught some fish here and released them after fastening pearls in their noses (*Tūzuk*, vol. i, p. 99).

[3] 'Beyond Cabull 60 c. runne mountaines, at the foote of which lyeth the way to Cascar' (*marginal note*).

Finch's references to Central Asia and Kashmīr in this and the succeeding paragraph form the subject of an interesting article contributed by Sir Aurel Stein, K.C.I.E., to the *Journal of the Panjāb Historical Society*, 1917, to which the reader may be referred for details. Sir Aurel Stein notes that the time allowed by Finch for the journeys from Kābul

under the Tartar. A chiefe citie of trade in his territorie is Yar Chaun [Yārkand], whence comes much silke, purslane [porcelain], muske, and rheubarb, with other merchandize; all which come from China, the gate or entrance whereof is some two or three monethes journey from hence. When they come to this entrance, they are forced to remaine under their tents, and by license send some ten or fifteene merchants at once to doe their businesse, which being returned they may send as many more; but by no means can the whole caravan enter at once.

From Lahor to Cassimere [Kashmīr, i. e. Srīnagar] the way is as in Cabull way to Guzerat [Gujrāt]; from thence north or somewhat easterly withall, 16 c. to Bimbar [Bhimbar]; to Joagek Hately 14 c.; to Chingesque Hately[1] 10 c.; to Peckly[2] 10 c.; to Conowa 12 c.; thence 8 c. you ascend a mountaine called Hast Caunk Gate,[3] on the top of which is a goodly plaine, from whence to Cassimer is 12 c. thorew a goodly countrey. The city is strong, seated on the river Bahat [Bihat or Jhelum]; the countrie is a goodly plaine, lying on the mountaines, some 150 c. in length and 50 c. in breadth, abounding with fruits, graine, saffron, faire and white women. Heere are made the rich pomberies [shawls: *pamri*] which serve all the Indians. This countrey is cold, subject to frosts and great snowes; neare to Cascar, but seperated with such mountaines that there is no passage for caravans; yet there commeth oft-times musk, with silke and other merchandize,

to Kāshgar, and from thence to China, still holds good. The 'gate' of the latter country he identifies with the present-day Chia-yü-kuan, near Su-chou. The route described from Lahore to Kashmīr is, he points out, that regularly used by the Mughal emperors and now known as the Pīr Panjāl route; and the stages given by Finch, so far as they can be traced, are roughly correct.

[1] The present Chingas Sarāi.

[2] The reference seems to be to the hilly district known as Pakhli; but as this is a considerable distance from the Pīr Panjāl route, being in fact on the alternative route via the Hāji Pīr pass, Sir A. Stein suggests that Finch's informant really meant to convey that from Chingas Sarāi there was a branch route to the road coming through Pakhli to Kashmīr.

[3] The Pīr Panjāl pass. Sir A. Stein explains 'Hast Chaunk' as a reference to the mountain ridge of Hastivanj, overlooking the Pīr Panjāl pass from the south.

this way by men, and goods are faine to be triced up, and let downe often by engines and devices. Upon these mountaines keepes a small king called Tibbot, who of late sent one of his daughters to Sha Selim to make affinitie.[1]

Nicholas Uphet [Ufflet] made another way from Agra to Surat[2] by Fetipore [Fatehpur Sīkri], Scanderbade [Sikandarābād], Hindoine [Hindaun], Cheningom [Chandangāon], Mogoll Saray, Nonnigong, at the foote of a mountaine, which with others adjoyning are held by two Rajaws of no note. Opposite to these on the left hand beginne the mountaines of Marwa [Mārwār], which extend neare Amadaver. Upon these mountaines stands an impregnable castle called Gur Chitto,[3] the cheefe seat of Rana, a very powerfull Rajaw, whom neither Potan or the Acabar himselfe could ever subdue; which comes to passe by reason that all India hath beene Gentiles and this prince hath bin and still is esteemed in like reverence by them as the Pope of Rome by the Papists. And for this cause the Rajaws which have been sent against him frame some excuses that they may not indamage much his territories, which extend hence alongst Amadaver way an hundred and fifty great corses, and in breadth toward Ougen [Ujjain] 200 c., inclosed for the most part with inaccessible mountaines and fortified well by art in places accessible. He is able to make twelve thousand good horse upon any occasion, and holds many faire townes and goodly cities. The way followeth by Gamgra [Jampda]; Charsoot [Chātsu] (chiefe seat of Rajaw Manisengo his prigonies):[4] Ladaney [Ladāna]: Mousalde [Mozābād]: Banderamde.[5] Asmere [Ajmer], seated

[1] As Sir Edward Maclagan points out, Jahāngīr in 1590–91 married a daughter of Ali Rāi, the ruler of Baltistān or Little Tibet (*Āīn*, vol. i, p. 310).

[2] This is the route described also by Jourdain, Mundy, Tavernier, &c. Ufflet's journey seems to have been made in the autumn of 1610 (see *Jourdain*, p. 139)

[3] Chitorgarh, the ancient capital of Mewār until it was captured by Akbar in 1568, when the Rāna founded a new capital at Udaipur.

[4] '*Prigonies* are lordships' (*marginal note*). The word is really *parganas*, the old-established territorial divisions of Northern India, commonly adopted as administrative units by the Moguls and later rulers.

[5] Probably Bandar Sindri, which Mundy calls Bandersunder.

AJMER

upon the top of an inaccessible mountaine of 3 c. ascent, being a fort invincible ; the citie at the foot not great, inclosed with a stone wall, ditched round, the buildings reasonable faire ; without the wals are many antiquities, amongst which, some 2 c. toward Agra, is a very faire tanke.[1] This place is only famous for the sepulchre of Hoghee Mundee [see p. 148], a saint much respected by the Mogols, to whom (as is said before) the Acabar made a romery on foot from Agra to obtayne a sonne. Before you come to this tombe you passe three faire courts, of which the first contayneth neere an acre of ground, paved all with blacke and white marble, wherein are interred many of Mahomets cursed kindred ; on the left hand is a faire tanke inclosed with stone. The second court is paved like the former, but richer, twice as bigge as the Exchange in London ; in the middest whereof hangs a curious candlesticke with many lights. Into the third you passe by a brazen gate curiously wrought ; it is the fairest of the three, especially neere the doore of the sepulchre, where the pavement is curiously interlayed ; the doore is large and inlayed with mother of pearle, and the pavement about the tombe of inter-laid marble ; the sepulchre very curiously wrought in worke of mother of pearle and gold, with an epitaph in the Persian tongue. A little distant stands his seate in a darke obscure place, where he sat to fore-tell of matters, and is much reverenced. On the east-side stand three other courts, in each a faire tanke ; on the north and west stand divers faire houses, wherein keepe their sides[2] or church-men. Note that you may not enter any of these places but bare-foot.

From hence the way lieth to Cairo [Garao] : Mearta [Merta], which hath a stone castle with many faire turrets, a faire tanke, and three faire pagodes richly wrought with inlayd workes, adorned richly with jewels, and maintayned with rich offerings : Pipera [Pīpar] ; Jouges gong [Jogikāgāon] ; Settrange [Sutu-lāna ?] ; Canderupe [Khandap] ; Jeloure [Jālor]. This last is a castle seated on the height of a steepe mountaine, 3 c. in ascent, by a faire stone cawsey, broad enough for two men to

[1] The lake called the Ana Sāgar.

[2] Arabic *saiyid*, 'a lord' ; the designation in India of those who claim to be descendants of Muhammad.

passe abrest. At the first cose end is a gate and place of armes; there the cawsey is inclosed with wals on both sides; and at the 2 c. end is a double gate; at the 3 c. stands the castle, where you must enter three severall gates, the first very strongly plated with iron; the second not so strong, with places over it to throw downe scalding lead or oyle; the third strongly plated with pikes sticking forth, like harping irons. Betwixt each of these gates are spacious courts for armes, and within the further gate is a faire portcullis. Being entred, on the right hand stands a faire meskite, with divers devoncans adjoyning, both to doe justice and to take the aire. On the left hand stands the Governours house on the height of the hils, over-looking all. A flight-shot [bow-shot] within the castle is a faire pagode built by the founders of the castle, ancestors of Gidney Caun,[1] which were Indians. He turned Moore and bereaved his elder brother of this hold by this stratageme. He invited him and his women to a banket; which his brother requiting with like invitation of him and his, in steed of women he sends choice souldiers well appointed and close covered, two and two in a dowle[2]; who, beeing entred after this manner, possest themselves of the ports [gates] and held it for the Great Mogoll, to whom it now appertayneth, being one of the strongest seated forts in the world. Some halfe cose within the gate is a goodly tanke foure square, cut directly downe into the rocke, affirmed to bee fiftie fathome deepe, of cleere and good water. A little further is a faire plaine shaded with many goodly trees, beyond which, on the top of a little piqued mountayne, is the sepulchre of King Hassward,[3] while he lived a great souldier, since his death a great saint, honoured in these parts. Here lye also interred two sonnes of Gillould, a Potan king of Dely;[4] neere to which is a wall which divides the castle neere a cose in circuit (the whole castle beeing

[1] Possibly Ghazni or Ghaznīn Khān of Jālor, for whom see the *Āīn* (vol. i, p. 493).

[2] 'A *dowly* or *dowle* is a chaire or cage wherein they carry their women on mens sholders' (*marginal note*). It is of course the familiar *dhooly*.

[3] Can he mean Malik Shāh, a noted Muhammadan saint, whose tomb is still to be seen in the castle?

[4] Possibly Jalāl-uddīn Fīroz (1290–96), the first of the Khalji kings of Delhi.

about 8 c. in compasse), nigh whereto is said to keepe a huge snake of five and twentie foot long and as bigge as a man in the waste, which the people will by no meanes hurt, holding it a good fortune, for it hurts no man, but keepes amongst the bushes and bryars of this piqued mountaine. This castle is called the gate or frontire of Guzurate. From hence you come to Mudre [Modra]; Billmall [Bhīnmāl], the foundations of whose ancient wall are yet seene (they have beene 24 c. in circuit); many goodly tankes also going to ruine, by one of which is the founders sepulchre, whither the Indians resort to worship. From hence to Amadabade is a deepe sandy desart countrey. Rodeapore [Rādhanpur] in this way hath many sepulchres (I let passe it and the rest).

Amadabade or Amadavar is a goodly city and scituate on a faire river, inclosed with strong wals and faire gates, with many beautifull turrets. The castle is large and strong; where resideth Caun Asom his sonne [Jahāngīr Kuli Khān], the Vice-Roy in these parts. The buildings comparable to any citie in Asia or Africa, the streets large and well paved, the trade great (for almost every ten dayes goe from hence two hundred coaches richly laden with merchandise for Cambaya), the merchants rich, the artificers excellent for carvings, paintings, inlayd workes, imbroydery with gold and silver. At an houres warning it hath in readiness sixe thousand horse; the gates perpetually strong guarded; none suffered without license to enter, nor to depart without certificate. The cause of this is Badurs [see p. 100] neighbourhood in his strong hold, within 50 c. of this citie to the east, where nature, with some helpe of art and industry, hath fortified him against all the Mogolls power; and whence some foure yeeres since (proclaiming liberty and lawes of good fellowship) hee sacked Cambaya with a sudden power (combined by hope of spoile) of one hundred thousand men, which for fourteene dayes continued possessors there and sharkers. There is also betwixt this and Trage [1] a certaine Rajaw on the mountaines able to make seventeene thousand horse and foot, the people called Collees [Kolis] or Quullees, keeping in a desart wildernesse which secures him from conquest; and on the right hand is

[1] There is a Trāj about seven miles south-west of Kaira.

another able to make tenne thousand horse, holding in a desart plaine a castle impregnable, whose land is subject to Gidney Cauns government, but these seven yeeres he hath denyed him tribute, and stands on his defence. This Rajaw is said to have a race of horses not equalled in all the East, each valued at fifteene thousand r[upees], reported to bee much swifter then the Arabian, and able to continue with reasonable speed a whole day without once drawing bitte; of which he is said to have one hundred mares. From Geloure to this citie is all a sandy, woody countrey, full of theevish beastly men and of mankind, savage beasts, lions, tygres etc. Thirty c. about this city is made nill [indigo] called Cickell [Sarkhej], of a towne 4 c. from Amadavar, not so good as that of Biana.

Cambaya is hence 38 c.; sandy, wooddie, theevish way. It stands by the sea, encompassed with a strong bricke wall; the houses high and faire; the streets paved in a direct line with strong gates at the end of each; the bazar large. About the citie are such infinite numbers of munkeyes, leaping from house to house, that they doe much mischiefe and, untyling the houses, are readie to braine men as they passe in the streets with the stones that fall. On the south is a goodly garden with a watch-tower of an exceeding height; on the north are many faire tankes. It is the mart of Guzurat, and so haunted by the Portugals that you shall often finde two hundred frigats at once riding there. It aboundeth with all sorts of cloth and rich drugges. The bay is 8 c. over, dangerous to passe by reason of the great bore which drownes many, and therefore requires guides skilfull of the tydes (in the neap tydes is least perill). Theeves also, when you are over the channell, are not a little dangerous, forcing you (if not the better provided) to quit your goods, or in long bickerings betraying you to the tydes fury, which comes so swift that ten to one you escape not. Foure coses beyond this bay is Joumbeser [Jāmbusar], now much ruined, and from thence eighteene to Boroche [Broach], a woodie, dangerous passage, in which are many wilde peacockes. Within 4 c. of Boroche is a great mine of agats.[1] It is a faire castle, seated on a river twice as broad

[1] Doubtless the reference is to the mines at Ratanpur, in the Rājpīpla

as the Thames, to the mouth of which is hence 12 c. Here are made the rich baffatas,[1] in finenesse surpassing Holland cloth, for fiftie rupias a booke, which contayneth fourteene English yards, and are not three quarters broad. Hence to Variaw [Variāo] 20 c., a goodly countrey and fertile, full of villages, abounding with wild date trees, which generally are plentifull by the sea-side in most places; whence they draw a liquor called tarrie [*tāri*, toddy] or sure [Sanskrit *sura*], as also from another wild coco-tree called tarrie. Three c. hence is Surat.

In a towne betweene Boroche and Amadavar lyeth a great saint of the Moores called Polle-Medomy,[2] much resorted to out of all places of India for wealth, children, or what else they desire. Divers in the way goe with great chaines on their legges, and with their hands chained together and their mouthes locked up (only opening them for food), and when they come before him in this manner of their humble devotion, they affirme that presently their chaines and lockes fly open, not one returning in vaine; if themselves bee not vaine in their hopes, and in these and other like affections, which *wayting on lying vanities, forsake their owne judge.*

From Agra to Cannowes [Kanauj] is 130 c.[3] east; the citie great and unwalled, seated on an ascent, and the castle on the height well fortified; at the foot whereof anciently Ganges tooke his course, but hath now broken a passage thorow the valley some 4 c. distant, notwithstanding as yet a small branch remayneth there. Ganges is within his bounds three quarters of a mile broad, but with great raines swels over his bankes, covering the whole vale neere 10 c. It hath thirtie rivers of note which fall into it, as doth he himselfe into the Gulfe of Bengala. In it are innumerable alagaters or crocodiles, there called murgurmach [*magarmachh*, crocodile-fish]. It hath eighteene faire branches. Thence to Lacanowes [Lucknow]

state, about fourteen miles east of Broach. They are still the chief source of supply for agates.

[1] Cotton clothes (*bāfta*, 'woven').

[2] Probably some such name as Pīr Ali Madini; the shrine has not been traced.

[3] The distance is about half this; and Finch's figures for the other distances are not reliable.

is 30 c.; a towne of great traffique for linnen and other merchandize. To Oude [Ajodhya] from thence are 50 c.; a citie of ancient note, and seate of a Potan king, now much ruined; the castle built foure hundred yeeres agoe. Heere are also the ruines of Ranichand[s] [1] castle and houses, which the Indians acknowled[g]e for the great God, saying that he tooke flesh upon him to see the tamasha [2] of the world. In these ruines remayne certaine Bramenes, who record the names of all such Indians as wash themselves in the river running thereby; which custome, they say, hath continued foure lackes of yeeres (which is three hundred ninetie foure thousand and five hundred yeeres before the worlds creation). Some two miles on the further side of the river is a cave of his with a narrow entrance, but so spacious and full of turnings within that a man may well loose himselfe there, if he take not better heed; where it is thought his ashes were buried. Hither resort many from all parts of India, which carry from hence in remembrance certaine graines of rice as blacke as gun-powder, which they say have beene reserved ever since. Out of the ruines of this castle is yet much gold tryed.[3] Here is great trade, and such abundance of Indian asse-horne [4] that they make hereof bucklers and divers sorts of drinking cups. There are of these hornes, all the Indians affirme, some rare of great price, no jewell comparable, some esteeming them the right unicornes horne.

From Oudee to Acabarpore [Akbarpur, in Fyzābād district] 30 c., some 80 c. from whence lyeth Bonarce [Benares], the principall mart of Bengala goods. From Acab[arpore] to Jounpore [Jaunpur] 30 c.; seated on a small river, over which is a bridge with houses like London Bridge, but nothing so good. The castle hath beene a seat of the Potan kings, there yet remayning two faire meskites, with many other ancient monuments; the houses are like those of Amadavar; the

[1] Rāma Chandra, the hero of the *Rāmāyana*. The reference is to the mound known as the Rāmkot or fort of Rāma.

[2] Hind. *tamāsha*, a show or spectacle.

[3] This practice is mentioned in the *Āīn* (Blochmann and Jarrett's transln., vol. ii, p. 171).

[4] Rhinoceros horn. The bucklers were made from the hide of the animal.

circuit some 8 or 10c. Hence come excellent sweete oyles, carpets, hangings embrodered with silke, all sorts of fine linnen, etc.

Thus much from Agra to Jounpore this way; from thence (returning that way to Agra) to Alabasse is 110 c.,[1] 30 c. all [of ?] which are thorow a continuall forrest. The towne and castle stand out on the further side of Ganges pleasantly seated, called anciently Praye [see p. 19], and is held one of the wonders of the east. Divers Potan kings have sought to build here a castle, but none could doe it till Acabar layd the foundation and proceeded with the worke. It stands on a point or angle, having the river Gemini [Jumna] on the southside falling into Ganges. It hath beene fortie yeeres abuilding, and is not yet finished; neither is like to bee in a long time. The Acabar for many yeeres had attending this worke by report twentie thousand persons, and as yet there continue working thereon some five thousand of all sorts. It will be one of the most famous buildings of the world. In this castle Sha Selim kept, when he rebelled against his father. The outward wals are of an admirable height, of a red square stone, like Agra Castle; within which are two other wals nothing so high. You enter thorow two faire gates into a faire court, in which stands a piller of stone [2] fiftie cubits above ground (so deeply placed within ground that no end can be found), which by circumstances of the Indians seemeth to have beene placed by Alexander or some other great conquerour, who could not passe further for Ganges. Passing this court you enter a lesse; beyond that a larger, where the King sits on high at his dersane to behold elephants and other beasts to fight. Right under him within a vault are many pagodes, being monuments of Baba Adam and Mama Havah [Adam and Eve] (as they call them) and of their progenie, with pictures of Noah and his descent. The Indians suppose that man was heere created, or kept heere at least for many yeeres, affirming themselves to be of that religion whereof these fathers were. To this place resort many

[1] He means that the distance to Agra from Jaunpur via Allahābād is 110 *kos* (a gross under-estimate), of which the stage from Jaunpur to Allahābād represents thirty.

[2] The Asoka pillar in Allahābād fort. It is really only thirty-five feet in length.

thousands from all parts to worship ; but before they approch these reliques, they wash their bodies in Ganges, shaving their heads and beards, thereby deeming themselves clensed from all their former sins. Out of this court is another richly paved where the King keepes his derbar ; beyond it another, whence you enter into the moholl, large, divided into sixteene severall lodgings for sixteene great women with their slaves and attendants. In the middest of all, the Kings lodgings of three stories, each contayning sixteene roomes ; in all eight and fortie lodgings, all wrought over-head with rich pargetting and curious painting in all kind of colours. In the midst of the lowest storie is a curious tanke.

In this moholl is a tree which the Indians call the tree of life (beeing a wilde Indian figge tree), for that it could never bee destroyed by the Potan kings and this mans ancestors, which have sought to doe it by all meanes, stocking it up and sifting the very earth under it to gather forth the sprigs ; it still springing againe, insomuch that this king lets it alone, seeking to cherish it.[1] This tree is of no small esteeme with the Indians. In the waters side within the moholl are divers large devoncans, where the King with his women often passe their times in beholding Gemini paying his tribute to Ganges. Betweene them and the waters side at the foote of the wall is a pleasant garden, shaded with cypresse trees and abounding with excellent fruits and flowres, having in the midst a faire banquetting house, with privie staires to take boate. From hence in October or November, when the great frost [freshet ?] is past, you may passe by boats for Bengala, but the passage is dangerous ; 4 c. downe are two castles opposite on the bankes, Harrayle and Gussee,[2] seated on two hils raysed by industry, built by the Potans.

From Alabasse to Menepore [Manihpur] is 20 c. alongst the river Ganges. At 2 c. on this way is a sumptuous tombe for this kings first wife,[3] mother to Sultan Cusseroon and sister to

[1] This is the *Akshaivat,* or undying fig tree, for which see the *Allahâbâd Gazetteer*, p. 210.

[2] Arãil and Jhũsi, just below the junction of the Ganges and the Jumna. There are ruins of forts at both places.

[3] See note on p. 164. She poisoned herself before Khusrau actually rebelled (*Tũzuk*, vol. i, p. 55).

Raja Manisengo, who upon the newes of her sonnes revolt poysoned her selfe. From hence passing Ganges is a more direct way to Jounpore. To Chappergat [1] is 12 c. Here is one of the fairest saraies in India, liker a goodly castle then a inne to lodge strangers; the lodgings very faire of stone, with lockes and keyes, able to lodge a thousand men. A man can scarse shoote from side to side with an arrow; neere to it is a faire bridge; both built by one man; the way perillous for theeves. Itay [Etāwa] is thence 12 c.; anciently the seate of a Potan king, but now ruined. On the height of the hill, cut steepe downe, is seated a strong castle double walled, having at the entrance the figure of a mans face, which the Indians much worship, powring abundance of oyle upon it. To Amedipore [Itimādpur] is 48 c.; a plentifull countrey, full of good saraies for caravans. Much indico called *cole*,[2] of a grosse sort, is made in this way, which is spent in India or transported for Samercand [Samarkand], Cascat [Kashgar], and those parts; none passing into Christendome, except mixed with that of Biana. Hence to Agra is 7 c., passing Gemini close to the citie.

Lands lying Easterly from Lahor, with their Lords.

Alongst the Ravee easterly lyeth the land of Rajaw Bossow [Rāja Bāso], whose chiefe seate is Tem-mery,[3] 50 c. from Lahor. He is a mighty prince, now subject to the Mogol, a great minion of Sha Selim. Out of this and the adjoyning regions come most of the Indian drugges, growing on the mountaines, spikenard, turbith,[4] miras kebals,[5] gunlack [gumlac], turpentine, costus,[6] etc. This Raja confines the Kings land easterly. Bordering to him is another great Rajaw, called Tulluck-Chand [Tilok Chand], whose chiefe city is Negercoat [Nagarkot, now Kāngra], 80 c. from Lahor and as

[1] Chaparghata, on the Sengur. Mundy praises the *sarāi*.

[2] Koil (now Alīgarh) was the centre for an inferior kind of indigo.

[3] Dhameri, the old name of Nūrpur, near Pathānkot, in Kāngra.

[4] Indian jalap, the root of *Operculina turpethum*.

[5] Apparently chebulic myrobalans.

[6] The root of *Saussurea lappa*, valued both for medicinal purposes and as a perfume.

much from Syrinan [Sirhind]; in which city is a famous pagod called Je or Durga,[1] unto which worlds of people resort out of all parts of India. It is a small short idoll of stone, cut in forme of a man; much is consumed in offerings to him, in which some also are reported to cut off a piece of their tongue and, throwing it at the idols feet, have found it whole the next day (able to lye, I am afraid; to serve the father of lyes and lyers, how ever); yea, some out of impious piety heere sacrifice themselves, cutting their throats and presently recovering. The holyer the man, the sooner forsooth he is healed; some (more grievous sinners) remaining halfe a day in paine before the divell will attend their cure. Hither they resort to crave children, to enquire of money hidden by their parents or lost by themselves; which, having made their offerings, by dreames in the night receive answere, not one departing discontented. They report this pagan deity to have beene a woman (if a holy virgin may have that name); yea, that shee still lives (the divell shee doth) but will not shew her selfe. Divers Moores also resort to this peer [Pers. *pīr*, a saint]. This Raja is powerfull, by his mountaines situation secure, not once vouchsafing to visite Sha Selim.

On this Rajaw easterly confineth another, called Deccampergas,[2] a mightie prince; his chiefe seat Calsery, about an 150 c. from Agra; his countrey held 500 c. long north and south, 300 c. broad, populous, able to raise upon occasion five hundred thousand foot, but few or no horse; the land plentifull in it selfe, but sends forth little. To the eastward of this Rajaw, betwixt Jemini and Ganges lyeth the land of Rajaw Mansa,[3] a mighty prince and very rich, reported to be served all in vessels of massie gold; his countrey 300 c. long

[1] The temple of Bajreswari Devi: see the *Tūzuk*, vol. ii, p. 224, and Terry (*infra*).

[2] It has been suggested that this is meant for Ude Chand Parkāsh, Rāja of Sirmūr; but he had not yet come to the throne, and, bearing in mind that Finch's *r* is often mistaken for a *c*, it appears more likely that the earlier Rāja, Dharm Parkāsh, is intended. It is true that the latter had been dead for over forty years; but Finch's hearsay information is often inaccurate in such matters. 'Calsery' is Kālsi, the ancient capital of Sirmūr.

[3] Garhwāl. Here again Finch seems to be referring to a chief (Rāja Mān Sāh) long dead.

and one hundred and fifty broad ; his chiefe seat Serenegar [Srīnagar] ; the mountaines called Dow Lager [*Dhaulāgiri*, White Mountain], upon which in time of winter falls such extreame snowes that the inhabitants are forced to remoove into the valleyes. Yet doe I not thinke that any of these lands extend northerly above forty degrees, but the height of the mountaines causeth this extremity of cold. This Rajas land extendeth within some 200 c. of Agra, part within 50 c. of Syrinan ; very plentifull.

On the further side of Ganges lyeth a very mightie prince, called Rajaw Rodorow,[1] holding a mountainous countrey ; his chiefe seat Camow ; his territories extend 400 c. long and not much lesse in breadth, abounding with graine, have many goodly cities ; thence commeth much muske, and heere is the great breed of a small kind of horse called gunts [*gūnth*], a true travelling scalecliffe beast. This prince is puissant in foot, but hath few horse or elephants, the mountaines not requiring the one and the cold excluding the other ; his lands thought to reach neare China. To the south of this Raja, thwart the streames of Ganges, is seated another, Raja Mugg,[2] very powerfull in horse, foote, and elephants. In his land is the old rocke of naturall diamonds, which yeelds him no small benefit. His lands extend east, somewhat south, 700 c. from Agra. Beneath him amongst the streames of Ganges keepeth a Potan prince of the Dely-kings race, whom the King cannot subdue, by reason of the streames and ilands of Ganges.[3] He confineth upon Purrop, and makes often inroades upon the Kings lands, enforcing Sha Selim to maintaine a frontire army. Hence to the mouth of Ganges all is the Kings land ; only in the mouth the Portugall out-lawes hold a small fort, and doe much mischiefe, living in no forme of subjection to God or man.[4]

[1] This seems to be the Rāja Rudra Chand of Kumāon, though he had been dead some years when Finch wrote. By 'Camow' (Kumāon ?) is probably meant Almora.

[2] A vague reference to the Maghs or Mugs (see p. 26). The *Āīn* (vol. ii, p. 120) alludes to their contentions with the Arakanese over certain mines of diamonds, &c.

[3] Possibly Isa Khān (see p. 28) is meant.

[4] These were the Portuguese pirates who had settled on the island of Sandwīp and elsewhere.

On the further side of Ganges is the mightie king of Arracan, enjoying a large territory and infinite numbers of small barkes. Eastward from him is the kingdome of Siam; behind it Ova[1] and Jangoma [see p. 38]. Betweene Tanassar [Tenasserim] and Arracan is the kingdome of Pegu; the land now lyeth waste. To the south is the kingdome of Queda, Malacca etc. On the sea-coast of Bengala this King hath two chiefe ports, Ougolee [Hūgli] (tyrannized by the Portugals) and Pipilee [Pippli]; passing which and the land of Orixa [Orissa] you enter into the lands of Goloconda, on whom Sha Selim maketh warres, and hath forcibly taken much of his land. His chiefe port is Masulipatan, and his royall seat Braganadar [see p. 131] and Goloconda, that late builded. Alongst the seaside toward the Cape is the mightie king of Bezeneger [Vijayanagar], under whom the Portugals hold Saint Thome and Negapatan, but are not suffered to build a castle. But I let passe these neighbouring Indies and returne to Agra, the Mogols royall residence.

Agra hath not been in fame above fiftie yeeres, being before Acabars time a village; who removed (as you have heard) from Fetipore for want of good water. It is spacious, large, populous beyond measure, that you can hardly passe in the streets, which are for the most part dirty and narrow, save only the great bazar and some few others, which are large and faire. The citie lyeth in manner of a halfe-moone, bellying to the land-ward some 5 c. in length, and as much by the rivers side, upon the bankes whereof are many goodly houses of the nobility, pleasantly over-looking Gemini, which runneth with a swift current from the north to the south, somewhat easterly, into Ganges. Upon the banke of this river stands the castle, one of the fairest and admirablest buildings of the East, some three or foure miles in compasse,[2] inclosed with a faire and strong wall of squared stone; about which is cast a faire ditch, over it draw-bridges. The walles are built with bulwarkes, somewhat defensible, regalled,[3] with a counter-scarfe or front without, some fifteene yards broad. Within this are two other

[1] Probably 'Ava' is intended.

[2] This is an exaggeration. The circuit of the walls is about a mile and a half.

[3] Battlemented; from 'regal', a groove or slot.

strong walls and gates. To the castle are foure gates, one to the north, by which you passe to a rampire with great peeces; another west to the Bazar, called the Cichery [*Kachahri*, court house] gate, within which, over against the great gate, is the Casi [*kāzi*, a judge] his seat of Chiefe-Justice in matters of law, and by it two or three murtherers very great (one three foot in the bore and fifteene long) of cast brasse. Over against this seat is the Cichery or Court of Rolls, where the Kings Viseer sits every morning some three houres, by whose hands passe all matters of rents, grants, lands, firmans, debts, etc. Beyond these two gates you passe a second gate [the Hāthi Pol], over which are two Rajaws in stone,[1] who were slaine in the Kings derbar before the Kings eyes, for being over-bold in speech; they selling their lives bravely, in remembrance of which they are heere placed. Passing this gate you enter into a faire streete, with houses and munition all alongst on both sides. At the end of this street, being a quarter of a mile, you come to the third gate, which leads to the Kings Derbar; alwayes chained, all men but the King and his children there alighting. This gate is to the south, called Acabar Drowage,[2] close within which is the whores child,[3] many hundreds of which attend there day and night, according as their severall turnes come every seventh day, that they may bee ready when the King or his women shall please to call any of them to sing or dance in his moholl, he giving to every one of them stipends according to their unworthy worth. The fourth gate is to the river, called the Dersane,[4] leading into a faire court extending alongst the river, in which the King lookes forth every morning at sun-

[1] 'It is said that they were two brothers, Resboots, tutors to a prince their nephew, whom the King demaunded of them. They refused and were committed, but drew on the officers, slew twelve, and at last by multitudes oppressing were slain; and here have elephants of stone and themselves figured' (*marginal note*). It is uncertain whether this note is by Finch or by Purchas, but the former seems more likely. The figures stood on raised platforms on either side of the gate, but both men and animals have long since disappeared, though the pedestals of the elephants are still to be seen.

[2] *Darwāza* (gate). This is now known as the Amar Singh Gate.

[3] Probably a misreading of *chauk*, meaning 'square'.

[4] *Darshani* (see p. 151). Mr. Havell, in his *Handbook to Agra* (p. 45) says that this was near the old disused watergate.

rising, which hee salutes, and then his nobles resort to their tessillam.[1] Right under the place where he lookes out is a kind of scaffold whereon his nobles stand, but the addees with others awayt below in the court. Here also every noone he looketh forth to behold Tamashan [see p. 176] or fighting of elephants, lyons, buffles, killing of deare with leopards; which is a custome on every day of the weeke, Sunday excepted, on which is no fighting; but Tuesday on the contrary is a day of blood, both of fighting beasts and justiced men, the King judging and seeing execution.

To returne to the thirde gate: within it you enter into a spacious court with atescanna's round about, like shops or open stalls, wherein his captaines according to their degrees keep their seventh day chockees [watch: *chauki*]. A little further you enter within a rayle into a more inward court, within which none but the Kings addees and men of sort are admitted, under paine of swacking by the porters cudgells, which lay on load without respect of persons. Being entred, you approach the Kings derbar or seat, before which is also a small court inclosed with railes, covered over head with rich semianes to keepe away the sunne; where aloft in a gallery the King sits in his chaire of state, accompanied with his children and Chiefe Vizier (who goeth up by a short ladder forth of the court), no other without calling daring to goe up to him, save onely two punkaw's to gather wind; and right before him below on a scaffold is a third, who with a horse taile makes havocke of poore flies. On the right hand of the King, on the wall behind him, is the picture of our Saviour; on the left, of the Virgin. Within these railes none under the degree of foure hundred horse are permitted to enter. On the further side of this court of presence are hanged golden bels, that if any be oppressed and can get no justice by the Kings officers, by ringing these bels when the King sits, he is called, and the matter discussed before the King. But let them be sure their cause be good, least he be punished for presumption to trouble the King. Here every day, betweene three and foure a clocke,

[1] Explained in the margin as 'a gesture of humiliation'. It is the *taslīm*, or salute made by touching the ground with the back of the right hand and then rising and bringing the palm up to the crown of the head.

the King comes forth (and many thousands resort to doe their duties, each taking place according to his degree); where hee remaines hearing of matters, receiving of newes by letters read by his Vizier, graunting of suites, etc., till shutting in of the evening, the drumme meanewhile beating, and instruments playing from a high gallery on the next building opposite; his elephants and horses passing by in brave fashion, doing their tessillam and being perused by officers to see if they prosper. In the castle are two high turrets, over-laid with pure massie gold, which may be seen from farre, one over his mohol, the other over his treasury. After his going in from the derbar in the evening, some two houres after he comes out againe, sitting forth in a small more inward court behind the other, close to his moholl, into which none but the grandes, and they also with tickets to be renewed with every moone, are permitted to enter; where he drinkes by number and measure, sometimes one and thirtie, and running over, mixing also among severe judicatures. From this court is his privy passage into a curious garden, and to his barge, by which he often passeth the river to an other garden opposite. It is remarkeable that, both in court and here in these gardens, no courtiers or gardeners are tied to attendance, but by their seventh dayes turne.

Some adde [1] that the citie hath no walls, but a ditch round about, not broad, and dry also; adjoyning to the ditch without the citie are very large suburbs. The city and suburbs are one way seven mile in length, three in breadth. The noble mens houses and merchants built with bricke and stone, flat roofed; the common sort, of mudde walls, covered with thatch, which cause often and terrible fires. The citie hath sixe gates. The adjoyning river Gemini being broader then the Thames at London, on which are many boats, some of one hundred tunnes, but these cannot returne against the streame. Most of the noble mens houses are by the rivers side. From Agra to Lahor

[1] 'A written booke entituled *A Discourse of Agra and the foure principall waies to it*; I know not by what author, except it be Nic. Uphlet' (*marginal note*). This must be Purchas's note, not Finch's; and consequently the paragraph to which it refers must have been interpolated by the former. Ufflet's work does not seem to have been published.

sixe hundred miles.[1] The way is set on both sides with mulbery-trees.

King Acabars sepulchre is 3 c. distant from Agra in the way to Lahor; nothing neere finished as yet, after tenne yeares worke.[2] It is placed in the midst of a faire and large garden inclosed with bricke walls, neere two miles in circuit; is to have foure gates (but one of which is yet in hand), each, if answerable to this foundation, able to receive a great prince with a reasonable traine. Alongst the way side is a spacious moholl for his fathers women (as is said) to remayne and end their dayes in deploring their deceassed lord, each enjoying the lands they before had in the Kings time, by the pay or rents of five thousand horse the principall; so that this should be to them a perpetuall nunnery, never to marry againe. In the center of this garden stands the tombe foure square, about three quarters of a mile in compasse. The first inclosure is with a curious rayle, to which you ascend some sixe steps into a small square garden quartered in curious tankes, planted with variety of sweets; adjoyning to which is the tombe, rounded with this gardenet, being also foure square, all of hewne stone, with faire spacious galleries on each side, having at each corner a small beautifull turret, arched over head and covered with various marble. Betwixt corner and corner are foure other turrets at like distance. Here, within a faire round coffin of gold, lieth the body of this monarch, who sometimes thought the world too little for him. This tombe is much worshipped both by the Moores and Gentiles, holding him for a great saint. Some tenne or twelve foot higher you ascend by staires to another gallery (like, but narrower, to the former, as are also the rest that follow), containing onely three of those turrets betweeen corner and corner. Here in the midst is his wardrobe for a memoriall. The third story hath but two of those middle turrets on a side; the fourth one; the fifth hath only the corner turret and a small square gallery. The tombe[3] was not finished at my departure, but lay in manner of a coffin,

[1] An overstatement. The distance is about 440 miles by road.

[2] Hawkins (p. 120) says fourteen; but there is some doubt whether it was really begun before Akbar's death in 1605.

[3] By this Finch seems to mean the cenotaph on the top story.

covered with a white sheet interwrought with gold flowers. By his head stands his sword and target [shield], and on a small pillow his turbant, and thereby two or three faire gilded bookes. At his feet stand his shooes, and a rich bason and ewre. Every one approaching neere makes his reverence and puts off his shooes, bringing in his hand some sweete smelling flowers to bestrew the carpets or to adorne the tombe.

At my last sight thereof, there was onely over head a rich tent, with a semiane over the tombe. But it is to be inarched over with the most curious white and speckled marble and to be seeled all within with pure sheet-gold richly inwrought.[1] These foure last turrets, also inclosing the sepulchre, are of most rich curious marble and the ground underfoot paved with the like. There are in continuall worke about this and other buildings about it, the moholl and gate, not so few as three thousand. The stone is brought from à rich quarrey neere Fetipore, which (wee have said) may be cut in length and forme as timber with sawes, and plankes and seelings are made thereof.

[1] This plan was never carried out; but Fergusson notes that there are traces in the structure of such an intention.

1612–16

NICHOLAS WITHINGTON

When, in February 1612, Sir Henry Middleton sailed away from Surat, with Captain Hawkins aboard his flagship, all prospect of the English obtaining permission to trade in India seemed gone for ever; and Middleton's subsequent exactions from the Indian junks in the Red Sea were likely in any case to make the breach irreparable. This later development, however, was not yet known at Surat when, early in September 1612, Captain Thomas Best arrived at the river's mouth from England with the *Dragon* and *Hosiander*. Middleton had left behind him letters describing the way he had been treated, and these made Best very doubtful of the possibility of trade; but the merchants he had brought were eager for further experiment, and upon landing they were received with such apparent cordiality that they determined to stay ashore and test the value of the promises made to them. Even when, towards the end of the month, one of the junks that had suffered at Middleton's hands arrived at the port, the chief officials assured the English factors that what had occurred would make no difference in their attitude. In point of fact, the leading merchants were much impressed by this proof of the power of the English, and recognized that the intercourse with Mokha, which was the mainstay of the trade of Surat, was at the mercy of any nation that was strong in shipping; while the absence of Mukarrab Khān, who was now at court, also facilitated the establishment of improved relations. To remove the doubts still felt by Best, the local authorities on October 21 entered into a written agreement for English trade in Gujarāt, and promised that a *farmān* confirming it should be procured from the Emperor within forty days.

The news of this unexpected development roused the Portuguese Viceroy to action, and at the end of November a fleet of four galleons, with a swarm of frigates, under the command of Nuno da Cunha, attacked Best's two ships, only to be repelled with heavy loss. Soon after this the English, anxious to have sufficient sea room, left the shallows of the Gujarāt coast for the opposite side of the Gulf; and after some hesitation the Portuguese followed. On December 23 and 24 two more fights took place, ending in the defeat of

Da Cunha's squadron. Having driven off his assailants, and finding his stores and ammunition running low, Best returned to Swally. The expected *farmān* had not arrived, and, as the attitude of the Mughal authorities seemed less cordial, the English commander thought they were deluding him, and accordingly resolved to break off relations. Instructions were sent to Thomas Aldworth, the chief of the factors left at Surat, to wind up his business and repair aboard with all his companions. To this summons, however, Aldworth turned a deaf ear; he was convinced that a factory could be maintained and, whether the *farmān* was forthcoming or not, he was determined to make the experiment. His confidence appeared to be justified when, on January 7, 1613, the expected document arrived. A few days later it was delivered in state to Best, accompanied with fresh assurances of good treatment for any merchants he might leave in the country. His doubts thus removed, he consented to Aldworth remaining with a small staff; and, these things settled, he departed with his two ships for Sumatra, promising to return in the autumn to fetch away any goods that might then be ready for England.[1]

It had been decided already that Paul Canning, one of the factors, should be sent to court, to present to the Emperor a fresh letter which the fleet had brought from King James; and Aldworth's first task, after the departure of the fleet, was to provide the envoy with suitable articles to offer to His Majesty and to equip him for his journey to Agra. In addition to two English attendants, Canning had as companions a couple of musicians who had apparently been sent out for the purpose—one, his cousin, Lancelot Canning, who played on the virginals, and the other, Robert Trully, whose instrument was the cornet. After meeting with various troubles on the way, the envoy reached Agra in April 1613, and duly delivered the royal letter and the present. As regards the demands he had been instructed to make—which included the cession of a place on the Kāthiāwār coast which the English might fortify, to secure their ships against the Portuguese—he was referred to Mukarrab Khān, who raised some difficulties yet held out hopes that his requests would be granted. The two musicians displayed their skill before the assembled court. The virginals made no impression, whereupon (according to Trully) the unfortunate player 'dyed with conceiptt' (*O. C.* 110). Trully's cornet, on the other hand, created an immense sensation. Jahāngīr himself attempted to blow the novel instrument, and at once ordered his workmen to make six more, which,

[1] For all this see the narratives by Best and others in *Purchas His Pilgrimes*; Cross's account in *Lancaster's Voyages*; and various documents in *Letters Received*, vols. i–iv.

however, turned out to be failures. Trully was then directed to instruct one of the Emperor's chief musicians, who took such pains that in five weeks he was able to perform satisfactorily. However, his exertions brought on an illness which proved fatal a fortnight later; so Trully was left the only cornet player in the kingdom, though a very discontented one, seeing that Jahāngīr, while often calling upon him to play, rewarded him only with fifty rupees in all. The Jesuits, we are told, endeavoured to induce Trully to teach the art to a couple of their servants, but this he absolutely refused to do.

It is time now to introduce Nicholas Withington, the author of the ensuing narrative. This individual had come out in the fleet as an attendant upon Captain Best—a not uncommon method of getting a free passage to the Indies when unable to secure direct employment from the East India Company. At Surat he was taken into the service of that body, on the plea of a deficiency of factors and (as he tells us) because of his linguistic attainments; probably he was acquainted with Arabic, since it appears that he had been in Morocco a few years previous (British Museum, Egerton MS. 2086, f. 10). For a time he remained at Surat, helping in the ordinary business and learning the language; but on intelligence arriving from Agra that Canning needed an assistant, it was decided to send him thither. Before he could make a start, however, news arrived that Canning was dead; whereupon Thomas Kerridge, one of the senior factors and afterwards President at Surat, was dispatched to Agra instead. It was next proposed to send Withington to England by way of the Red Sea, carrying letters for the Company; but this plan fell through, owing to a fear that it would prove impossible for a Christian to pass unmolested through the Hejaz; and in October 1613 Withington proceeded with Aldworth to Ahmadābād to assist in the purchase of indigo. Thence he visited Cambay and Sarkhej, of each of which he finds something interesting to relate. From Ahmadābād he wrote in November a long letter to the Governor of the East India Company, which is to be found in original in the British Museum manuscript alluded to above.

In December 1613 Withington was called upon to undertake the remarkable journey which forms the chief attraction of his narrative. News had reached Ahmadābād that an English ship had arrived at Lahrībandar, the port town of Tatta, in Sind, and, as it was evidently desirable to communicate at once with any merchants she might have left there, it was resolved that Withington should proceed thither overland. He was not the first Englishman to go that way, for immediately after Best's departure Anthony Starkey, steward of the *Dragon*, had been dispatched by that route to Persia and Aleppo, carrying letters for England[1]; but he was certainly the last for many a long day to venture in that direction—a fact not surprising, in view of his unhappy experiences. Travelling by way of Rādhanpur and Nagar Pārkar, in company with some Indian merchants, Withington had nearly reached Tatta when the whole party was seized by a local chief who had undertaken to act as its guide and protector. The merchants were hanged out of hand and their property appropriated; while Withington and his attendants only escaped the same fate owing to the interest felt by the chief in the adventurous Englishman. As it would not do to allow them to continue their journey and give information of the crime, they were taken up into the hills for some weeks; then they were released and sent under escort back to Nagar Pārkar. On the way their guardians robbed them afresh, and they reached their destination in the greatest misery. Fortunately, Withington found there a Hindu merchant whom he had known at Ahmadābād; and, generously assisted by him, he was able to set out for the latter city, where he arrived early in April 1614. Finding none of his compatriots there, he continued his journey by way of Cambay to Surat.

After a short rest Withington was dispatched to Agra to make an investment in indigo and to report upon the proceedings of John Mildenhall, whose reappearance in India has already been dealt with on p. 51. The capital was reached on June 7, 1614, and during the next four months or so Withington was busy in providing the desired goods. The position of the English had been much improved, commercially and otherwise, by the breach which had now occurred between the Emperor and the Portuguese. The latter, resenting the admission of the English despite the promises of Jahāngīr to the contrary, had in the autumn of 1613 seized the largest of the Surat vessels trading to the Red Sea and carried her off as a prize with her valuable cargo and all the passengers she had on board, disregarding the fact that she had a Portuguese pass guaranteeing her against molestation. This high-handed proceeding excited great indignation at court, especially as the ship belonged to the Emperor's mother; and when it

[1] Starkey reached Tatta safely with his Indian attendant, and wrote thence in hopeful terms concerning the prospects of trade in Sind. Both, however, died in that city shortly after, their deaths being ascribed (probably without any foundation) to their being poisoned by two Portuguese friars. The letters they were carrying fell into the hands of the Portuguese (the only Europeans there resident) and were sent to Lisbon; translations of them will be found in *Documentos Remettidos*, vol. iii, pp. 71–88. No account of Starkey's journey is extant.

was found that the Portuguese had no immediate intention of restoring their booty, Mukarrab Khān was dispatched to Surat with orders to stop all traffic and to lay siege to the Portuguese town of Damān by way of reprisals. At the same time the Jesuit church at Agra was closed, and the Fathers were deprived of the allowances they had hitherto received. There was thus every hope that the Portuguese would be permanently excluded from the trade of Mughal India, to the benefit of their English rivals.

A letter from Withington at the end of October 1614 (*Letters Received*, vol. ii, p. 140) tells us that he had succeeded in getting together the desired indigo and was only waiting to receive and dispose of some expected broadcloth and other English goods before starting for Surat. Now, however, everything went wrong with him. First, his indigo was seized by the Governor of Agra, who had been blamed by the Emperor for allowing some Portuguese to carry off their belongings, and who, in his anxiety to avoid further censure, would not allow the Englishman to touch his property until a *farmān* to that effect was obtained by Kerridge, who was now with Jahāngīr at Ajmer (*ibid.*, p. 298). Then Withington received a letter informing him that the promised remittance of money from Surat to pay for his indigo could not be made, and he was obliged in consequence to return the indigo to those from whom it had been bought. This occasioned much dispute and worry, and was only effected by the interposition of the Governor of Agra, who thus made some amends for his former treatment of the unfortunate merchant. Next, the broadcloth, when it came to hand, proved to be so damaged as to be almost unvendible, while the other goods could only be sold at prices lower than those they would have fetched at Surat (*ibid.*, vol. iii, pp. 15, 63). These trials and vexations proved too much for Withington, and for some time he was 'distracted'.

Meanwhile, in October 1614, Captain Downton had reached Swally with a fleet of four ships, bringing William Edwards to be chief of the Company's affairs in India. Aldworth, however, protested so vigorously against being superseded that the matter was compromised by dispatching Edwards to Ajmer instead, to present another letter from King James, and to look after English interests at court. The Company had expressly forbidden any of their servants to imitate Hawkins in assuming the title of ambassador; but inasmuch as there was a general agreement at Surat that some higher status than that of a merchant was necessary to secure attention from the Emperor, Edwards was authorized to represent himself as 'a messenger' sent expressly by the English king; and under this title he set out from Surat in December 1614. That he should be regarded at court as an ambassador was natural enough in the circumstances, and probably Edwards was at no pains to disavow the rank assigned to him ; but Withington's charge that he arrogated that title to himself without authority seems to be baseless.

The news of the arrival of another English fleet spurred the Portuguese to fresh efforts. As soon as he could collect all his available forces, the Viceroy himself sailed to the northwards to crush the intruders and afterwards to punish their Indian allies. Alarmed at the prospect, Mukarrab Khān, who had in vain demanded that the English ships should aid in the siege of Damān by attacking that fortress from the sea, now applied to Downton to co-operate actively in the defence of Surat against the Viceroy's armada. Downton, however, was too cautious to pledge himself to anything of the kind, and resolved to remain strictly on the defensive. Not unnaturally, this attitude was warmly resented by the Mughal authorities, who considered that the war was solely due to their reception of the English ; and for a time relations were strained. These bickerings were hushed by the near approach of the Portuguese squadron, which on January 20, 1615, made a vigorous attack upon Downton's ships, ensconced behind the sandbanks at Swally. Attempts to carry by boarding one of the smaller vessels were defeated with the loss of three of the Portuguese ships and a large number of men. Endeavours were then made to burn the English fleet by means of fireships, but these failed entirely ; and at last the Viceroy returned to Goa utterly baffled and with great loss of credit. Downton remained at Swally until the beginning of March, and then departed for the Far East.

Withington was ill, he tells us, for three months, and did not completely recover until he had proceeded from Agra to Ajmer. In July 1615 he was again at the former city, Edwards having sent him and Robert Young thither to transact some business. A few months later Withington was surprised by the arrival of a party of Englishmen from Ajmer with orders from Edwards for his apprehension on a charge of defrauding the Company. In his narrative he of course makes out that he had done nothing to deserve such treatment ; but that there was something to be said on the other side seems evident, not only from the subsequent attitude of his employers, but also from the correspondence contained in Kerridge's letter-book, now in the British Museum (Addl. MS. 9866). Kerridge, who was then stationed at Ahmadābād, had certainly no animus against Withington and was not at all well-disposed towards Edwards ; yet he nowhere hints any doubt as to [illegible] of the latter's treatment of the former. Writing [illegible] ber 16, 1615, to Captain Keeling (who had reac[illegible] two months earlier with a fresh fleet, bringing Sir Th[illegible] on his memorable embassy), Kerridge forwards a letter from Edwards, which, he says, accuses Withington of having 'not only wronged the Company by peculiar stealths and other villanyes, but donn them an infinitt wronge in their investmentts'; and in another letter, addressed to Edwards, he expresses a perfunctory regret that the offender's 'youthfull imperfections' had apparently developed into 'vilde conditions' which were 'nowe past hope of remeady'.

The factors sent to secure Withington performed their duty promptly, and he was carried to Ajmer, according to his own account, in irons. At that place, he would have us believe, he answered satisfactorily all the charges made against him; whereupon Edwards, not to be baffled, trumped up a false charge of drunkenness, imprisoned him, and a little later sent him down to Surat in chains. Here again Kerridge's letters put a different complexion on the matter. In one of these, dated December 22, 1615, he writes: 'Last night late, Withington one horsbacke came to our dore drunke, but would not com in, fearinge apprehention; cryenge out *Jaylors, stand of, jaylers,* more like a maddman farr then when you sawe him last. None of his gardiants would laye hold one him, all of them denyeng, as not beinge comitted to their charge. Such a confused sending of a prisoner I have not seen. And retorninge to Dergee Seraw, wher he gott his liquour, fell out with Magolls on the waye, that unhorste, beat, and deliverd him prisoner to the Cutwall, who this morninge (to ad to our nations disgrace) hath carried him to Sarder Chan.' In another letter of the same date Kerridge says that Withington had escaped from his escort about sixteen days before. This is a rather different picture from that drawn in the text of an innocent prisoner lumbering meekly along the road in chains.

While still under confinement by the local authorities, Withington seems to have found means to write to Sir Thomas Roe, then newly arrived at Ajmer. In a letter to Kerridge, of January 13, 1616 (British Museum, Addl. MS. 6115, f. 67), Roe says: 'I am sorry to heare of such disorder in the factoryes . . . and particularly for Withington, who hath written me a strange complayning lettre, prayeing me to moove the King; but I hav busines of other importaunce now then to trouble him with his debaushednes. I shalbe ashamd the King know I have such a countryman. But least necessity force desperat courses, I have advised the Generall [i. e. Keeling] to redeme him (so it be not much to the prejudice of the Company [and] so as his wages in England may answer), only for our nations reputation. Hee foolishly threatens to curse me, if I redeeme him not. I will doe what is fittest, but care not for his blessings nor execrations.' The reference to 'desperat courses' is explained in Roe's letter to Keeling, in which a fear is expressed that Withington may either 'turne Moore' or commit suicide.

Shortly afterwards, Kerridge reported to Keeling that, after allowing Withington to remain in prison for a while, he had, at some expense, procured his release, and was now dispatching him in irons to Surat under the charge of some seamen who had been sent up to Ahmadābād with treasure. At Surat Withington evidently failed to convince Keeling of his innocence, in spite of his assertion in the text that he was there cleared of owing anything to the Company; for, although his period of service was not half completed, he was put on board the *Lion*, which sailed for England in February 1616, and reached her destination in the middle of the following September. Immediately on his arrival he was arrested at the suit of the East India Company, and remained in prison for over a month, when he was released on bail. The Court Minutes for the period are missing; but when, towards the end of 1617, they once more become available, we find the Company firmly convinced that they had been wronged by Withington. In December of that year a physician named Percival applied to the Court for payment of his bill against their late servant, 'for cure of his phrensy'; he had been told, he said, that his patient's goods and money were in their hands. This was indignantly denied, and the doctor was assured that in reality Withington was in the Company's debt, as had been proved before 'some noble personages'. Thereupon Percival declared that he would take other means to recover his fee; but he was warned not to make his patient mad again, 'because it is not unknowne that he can be mad and well againe when hee pleaseth.'

Early in 1618 Withington commenced an action against the Company, in which he failed completely. A little later he brought another against Edwards, the result of which is not known. At length, despairing of success by legal means, in November 1619 he made overtures to the Company for the relinquishment of his claims; but on its being found that he still expected to receive some compensation, the Committees decided to have nothing more to do with him. Sir Thomas Roe, who was present at the meeting, denounced Withington in severe terms, declaring that he was guilty of 'mere cousonage in the countrye, affirming he was never otherwise then a drunckard and of a most dissolute life, keping six or seven whores still in house, and ever a most wicked and deboyst fellow'. Of course this condemnation was not based upon personal knowledge, for the two had never met, at least in India; but it may be taken as representing the reputation Withington had left behind him in that country. With this we may take our leave of him, merely noting that he must have died before April 1624, when it was reported to the Company that his executor (probably the brother he mentions) had presented a petition to Parliament on the subject of his claims. Apparently nothing came of this.

From internal evidence it is concluded that Withington's narrative was compiled from his journal not long after his return—probably at the time of his suit against the Company. A copy of the 'tractate' (as he terms it) came into the possession of Purchas, who printed a much condensed version of it in his *Pilgrimes* (part i, book iv, chap. 8). More than a century later the story was printed in much fuller form, in a volume entitled *A Journey over Land from the Gulf of Honduras to the Great South-Sea, performed by John Cockburn and five other Englishmen. . . . To which is added a curious piece, written in the Reign of King James I and never before printed, intitled A Brief Discoverye of some Things best worth noteinge in the Travells of Nicholas Withington, a Factor in the East Indiase* (London, 1735). This appendix (itself dated 1734) is stated to have been printed from the original MS.; but the unnamed editor, in his preface, tells us nothing of the way in which he acquired the document. Nor has it since been traced.

The present reprint follows the text of the 1734 version, which is about three times as long as that given by Purchas. It is evident, however, that the eighteenth-century editor imitated his predecessor in omitting details which he judged to be unimportant, although Purchas had included some of them. The passages given by the latter have now for the most part been restored, either in notes or as interpolations (between square brackets) in the text. On the other hand, part of Withington's account of the outward voyage has been omitted here, as unnecessary for our present purpose.

. . . The 28th of June, 1612, wee departed from the Baye of Saldania [i. e. Table Bay] with prosperous wyndes, saylinge on in our voyage untill the 13th day of Auguste, when wee crossed the Equinoctiall Lyne. And the 30th daye wee sawe snakes swyminge in the sea, beeinge in the height of eighteene and a halfe degrees to the norward of the Equinoctiall.[1] And soe wee sayled on untill the fourth of September, when wee

[1] 'The first of September they saw land; the second anchor against Daman towne, inhabited and conquered by Portugalls. The fluxe infested them all that remained on land at Surat; Master Aldworth was sicke forty dayes' (*Purchas*).

came within foure leagues of the barr of Suratt, where wee mett with the *Ozeander*, beeinge one of our fleete, whoe was rydinge at an anchoure there ; havinge gotten a pilott out of a boate of the countrye and lefte one of our carpenter's mates in hostage for him, whoe unwiselye carryinge some moneye aboute him, when the Moores were from the shippe, they cutt his throate and tooke what hee had, as afterwards wee were certaynlye informed. Uppon the 7th of the same moneth wee arrived at the barre of Suratt in the East-Indeases, and the thirteenth day wee came to Suratt and were kyndlye entertayned of the Governor and the chiefes of the cittye. There is an order in this cuntrye that strangers cominge to visite an inhabitante (bee hee a man of anye fashion) doe presente him with somethinge or other, and not to come to him emptye-handed ; insomuch that our people which wee sente firste on shore, having nothing but money aboute them to give for presents, were fayne to presente the Governor of the cittye and other chiefe men with each a royall of eight, which they kyndlye accepted, takinge yt for a greate honour to bee presented, though the presente bee but small.

[Notwithstanding Sir Henry Middleton taking their ships in the Red-sea, yet they promised us good dealing, considering else they must burne their ships (said Mill Jeffed [Mīr Jafar], one of the chiefe merchants of Surat) and give over their trade by sea. Impossible it was to have any trade at Surat, by reason of Portugall frigats in the rivers mouth ; therefore the Generall repaired with his ships to Swally, whence he might by land go and come without danger. The third of October Sheke Shuffe,[1] Governour of Amadavar, chiefe citie of Guzerat, came to Surat and so to Swally, and agreed upon articles. Master Canning had been taken by the Portugals, but the Vice-Roy commanded to set him ashoare at Surat, saying : Let him goe helpe his country-men to fight, and then we will take their ship and the rest of them altogether. But the purser made an escape and so came to us on land. Master Canning was set on shoare at Surat, according to promise, and so went aboord.]

[1] Shaikh Safi. He appears to have been the Dīwān, not the Governor.

Here wee remayned trading untill the 29th of November, when the same daye, our shippes lying in the mouth of the river of Suratt, fower Portungale gallionns, with a whole fleete of frigotts, came in sight of our two shippes (or rather one shippe and a pynnace). Then our Generall (in the *Dragon*) presentlye wayed anchoure, and worthelye encouraged our men not to feare them nor the greatnesse of theire shippes or fleete, but to shew themselves true Englishmen; and soe mett theire admirall and vize-admirall, and shott not one shoote till hee came betweene them, and then gave each of them a broad syde and a brave volleye of shott, which made them give way and come noe more neare her that daye. The other shippes were not as yett come uppe, and the *Ozeander* could not gett cleare of her anchours, soe shee shott not one shoote that daye; but the *Dragon* supplyed her wante verye well and, it drawinge neare night, they all came to anchoure within sight of each other; and the next morninge wayed anchours againe and begann theire fight, in which the *Ozeander* bravely redeemed the tyme shee loste the daye before. The fyrye *Dragon*, bestiringe herselfe, in some three howers hott feight drove three of the gallions on the sands, and then the *Ozeander*, drawinge little water, daunced the haye [1] aboute them, and soe payed them that they durste not shewe a man on theire deckes, killinge and spoylinge their men, and battered theire shipps exceedinglye. In the afternoone, the flud beeinge come, the gallionns, with the helpe of the friggots, were aflote agayne, and receaved a brave welcome of our shippes; with whom they continued feight about foure howers, but much to theire disadvantage and our greate honour. It beeinge nowe night, wee came to our anchours, and theire rode that night and all the nexte daye without meddling each with other. And the daye after, the *Dragon* drawinge much water, and the baye shallowe, the Generall wente from thence and rode on the other syde of the baye, at a place called Mendofrobag [2]; where all that tyme Sardar Chaune,[3] a great nobleman of the Mogull's, with

[1] A country dance, in which the performers wound in and out.

[2] Muzaffarābād (generally contracted to Jāfarābād), a town on the coast of Kāthiāwār, about twenty-five miles east of Diu.

[3] Sardār Khān, the title given by Jahāngīr to Khwāja Yādgār, brother of Abdullah Khān.

2000 horses, was beseidginge a castle of the Rasbooches [Rājputs], a caste of Gentills and formerly (before the conqueste of Guyseratt by the Mogull) greate nobles of the cuntrye, but nowe live by robbinge and spoylinge poore passengers by the waye. Of this nobleman was our Generall verye honourablye entertayned, and presented with a gallante horse and furniture; which horse our Generall afterwards presented to the Governour of Goga [see p. 62], a porte-towne to the westward of Suratt.

About ten dayes after the shippes staye, where they had trade and commerce with this people, the Portungale shippes and friggots, havinge replenished theire wants with store of freshe men, came thether to our shippes; which made Sardar Chaune, allthough he had heard wee had put them to the worste on the other syde in our former fighte, yet, seeinge theire greate odds, bothe in bignesse and quantitye, through his love to our Generall was verye fearfull of the [e]vente of the fighte and counselled our Generall to flye; which hee smyling at, tould him that (God willinge) hee should see theire greate number should not avayle them against him. And soe, havinge all his men aboard, wayed anchoure and with a brave resolution sett on them, beatinge and spoylinge them in such fashion that theire whole defence was in flyinge away; and in fower houres space wee drove them cleane out of our sight, and retorned and anchored with perpetuall honoure; this fight beeing before thowsands of the countrye people, whoe (to our nation's greate fame) have devulged the same farr and neare. Sardar Chann, after the rasinge of his castle and takinge the rebbells, repayringe to the Greate Mogull, related to him at large the discourse of this fighte; which made the Kinge admire much, formerlye thinkinge there had bin noe nation comparable to the Portungale by sea.

The 27th of December, 1612, our shippes retorninge againe came to Suallye, havinge loste in all the fightes with the four Portungales only three men, and those saylors; and one man loste his arme, shott off with a greate shott; not anye else of our companye either hurte or wounded (thanks bee to God). But the Portungales on the contrarye (as wee have ben since certaynlye informed by those that sawe moste of them buryed) had slayne 160 men. Some reporte 300 and odd, but themselves confesse 160; but sure theire losse was more then they will confesse.

The 13th of Januarye, 1612 [1613], I (beeinge in Suratt) was sente for aboard by the Generall; where by a counsaile I was entertayned, and bounde to the Worshippfull Companye of Marchaunts, and in regard of my languadge (which others of theire factors wanted) I was appoynted to remayne in Suratt as a factor. And having entred into a bonde of 400*l.* for the accomplishment of my service, I was this day dispeeded from the Generall and retorned to Suratt. Theis and manye other things accomplished, wee for the cuntrye were set on shore, and the 18th of Januarye, 1612, the shippes departed for England,[1] the gallionns never offering one shott at them, havinge ridden manye dayes in sight of them. [Anthony Starkey was sent for England.]

Beeinge at Suratt, the 29th day of Januarye wee dispeeded Mr. Paule Caninge for Agra, havinge provided all things necessarye for his voyage to contentment; but he had a tedious and hard journey of yt, beeinge 70 dayes on the waye betweene Suratt and Agra, and underwente manye troubles, beeinge sett on by the ennemye on the waye, whoe shott him through the bellye with an arrowe and likewise one of his Englishmen through the arme, and killed and hurte manye of his pyonns [peons]; but, God bee thanked, hee loste not any thinge, but before his arrivall in Agra hee was well cured of his hurte. Soone after this, two of his Englishe[2] fell out with him and soe lefte him on the waye, retorninge to Suratt; one of them brought away his beste horse and furniture, which coste 20*l.* Soe Mr. Caninge proseeded on his journey, onlye attended with two musitians; and the 9th day of Aprill arrived in Agra. And the nexte day was called before the Kinge, to whom hee delivered the Kinge of England's letters and a presente, which was of noe greate vallue; which made the Kinge aske him if our Kinge sente him that presente; he answer'd our Kinge sente him the letter, but the marchaunts sente him that presente. The Kinge graced him by givinge

[1] Really for Achin and Bantam, before returning to England.
[2] Richard Temple and Edward Hunt.

him a cuppe of wyne with his owne hande (as Mr. Caninge wrote to us), and further toulde him that all his requests should bee graunted, willinge him to write home for all rich novelties, wherin hee much delighted; and in fyne referred him, for dispatch of his businesse, to Mochrobo Chaune [Mukarrab Khān], a greate nobleman; whoe objected, first, some five or sixe marchaunts to reside in Agra, and wee should have a castle builte for us at Mendofrobag: secondlye, hee alledged, if noe marchaunts should bee in Agra, then another Generall might take theire goods, as Sir Henry Middleton had don: thirdlye, if for our sakes they should breake peace with the Portungales, and then wee to have noe more shippe come in three or fower yeares, what satisfaction wee could make them for wrongs receaved by them from the Portungales? To all which Mr. Caninge answer'd to contente; and Mochrobo Chaune imparted his answere to the Kinge, whoe rested well contente therewith.

Soone after his cominge to Agra, one of his musitians [i. e. Lancelot Canning] dyed (which was the chiefest presente sent to the Kinge). Aboute the buriall of him Mr. Caninge had much trouble with the Portungale Fathers, whoe would not suffer him to bee buried in theire church-yarde (a place which the Kinge gave the Portungales for buriall of Chrystians); yet at laste Mr. Caninge buried him there. But the Portungales tooke him upp againe, and buried him in the heighway; which the Kinge hearing of, made them take him upp againe and bury him in the former place, threatninge them not onlye to turne them out of his kingdom, but allsoe theire dead bodies, theire countriemen, out of theire graves.[1]

Presentlye after, Mr. Caninge wrote to us of the daunger and feare hee lived in of beeinge poysoned by the Jesuitts, and therefore desired that I, Nich. Withington, might come upp to him, as well to assiste him in his presente affares as allsoe to

[1] Kerridge (*Letters Received*, vol. i, p. 283) gives a different account. He says that the Jesuits disinterred the body of Lancelot Canning without the knowledge of his cousin; and that, on the death of the latter, Trully buried both bodies together on one side of the Christian cemetery, at a good distance from the other tombs—an arrangement to which the Jesuits made no objection.

followe our suite at courte in case of his mortalletye; wheruppon it was concluded amongste us at Suratt, by a counsell, that I should departe with all conveniente speede for Agra. Presentlye after this, there came a pattamar[1] with letters from Agra, certifyinge us of the death of Mr. Caninge,[2] and allsoe howe the Kinge had taken order that all his goods should bee kepte safe till some of our Englishmen came thether to take charge of them; wheruppon yt was still agreed that I should proseede on my purposed journey to Agra; but exceptions was taken by one Thomas Kyrridge, whoe alledged that, Mr. Caninge beeinge dead, the place belonged to him. In fyne hee was dispeeded for Agra; but before his departure it was concluded amongste us that some one of us should goe for England overlande from Mocha, with letters to advise the Worshippfull Companye of our proseedings. And now in regard that within some eighte or ten dayes there was a shippe of this place bounde for Mocha in the Redd Sea, in which shippe one goinge might well in twoe moneths travell bee in Allexandria in Turkye: so that by all likelihood hee might bee sooner in England then if hee should goe by the way of Aleppo: in fyne our Agente propounded this journey to mee, N.W.; which I, seeinge the necessitye of sendinge one, and that none other would attempte the journey, gave waye to undertake. Soone after wee sente for the master of the shippe that was bounde for Mocha and acquaynted him with our intente; whoe tould us that it was impossible for a Chrystian to passe that way, unlesse hee were circumsized, noe Christian beeinge suffred to come neare Mocha,[3] where theire prophett Mahomet was buried; by which place I muste of force passe to goe to Allexandria. The like wee heard allsoe of divers others; which made us (but especiallye myself, not havinge a desier to bee cutt) to give over our determination. Yet notwithstandinge, wee hyred a fellowe, that understoode the Arabian tonge and had formerlye ben that way, to carrye our

[1] 'Or foote poste' (*marginal note*).

[2] Purchas says that Canning died May 29, 1613, and that Kerridge started for Agra on the 22nd of the following month. The date of Canning's death is also given as May 12 (*O. C.* 117) and May 27 (*O. C.* 116).

[3] Purchas has 'Mecca', which is evidently intended, though Muhammad's tomb is really at Medina

letters to Allexandria by that conveyance; whoe departed in the shippe, and at his arrivall in Mocha, hee hearinge newes that all our Englishmen were imprisoned and our goods confiscated for the late facte of Sir Henry Middleton, whoe not longe before had robbed divers in those parts, hee therefore durste not prosecede, but retorned our letters in the shippe, which arrived at the barre of Suratt the 13th of September, 1613, and was taken by the Portungales armado of friggotts, notwithstandinge theire passe which they had of the Portungales. This shippe [1] was verye richlye laden, beeinge worth a hundred thowsand pounde; yet not contented with the shippe and goods, but tooke allsoe 700 persons of all sorts with them to Goa; which deede of theires is nowe growne soe odious that it is like to bee the utter undoing of the Portungales in their parts, the Kinge takinge yt soe haynosly that they should doe such a thinge, contrarye to theire passe; insomuch that noe Portungale passeth that waye without a suertye, neither can anye Portungale passe in or out. [Merchants of Surat are by this meanes impoverished, and our goods left in our hands; with which we went to Amadabar.]

Not longe after, there came one [2] to us whoe had rune awaye from Sir Henry Middleton to the Portungales and with them had continued till his cominge to us. He informed us of the estate of the Portungales, which hee affirmed to bee verye weake, and at that time had divers of theire townes beseeged by the Decannes and other Moores theire neighbours, insomuch that they were fayne to sende out of theire townes manye hundreds of poore labouring people and others that dwelte amongste them, for wante of victualls; [three barkes of which came to Surat and divers others to Cambaya. Their weaknesse in fight with us caused all this.]

There came likewise unto us one [3] that had formerlye rune awaye from our shippes to the Portungales, and agayne from them to us; and in his waye passinge through the Decannes countrye, he was perswaded by another Englishman (that was turned Moore and lived there) to turne Moore; which hee

[1] The *Rahīmi*, belonging to the Queen Mother.

[2] Purchas gives his name as John Alkin.

[3] Purchas gives his name as Robert Johnson.

did and was circumsized, the Kinge allowinge him *7s. 6d.* per daye and his diett at the Kinge's own table ; but within eighte dayes after his circumsizion he dyed. Lykewise another of our companie, called Robert Trullye, which was an attendante to Mr. Caninge, whome hee lefte and wente to Decanne to the Kinge thereof, carryinge along with him a Germayne for his interpritor that understoode the language ; and cominge there, offred bothe to turne Moores, which was kyndlye accepted by the Kinge. So Trullye was circumsized, and had a newe name given him and greate allowance given him by the Kinge, with whom hee continued. But they cominge to cutt the Germayne, founde that hee had ben formerlye circumsized (as he was once in Persia), but thought nowe to have deceaved the Decanne, whoe, fyndinge him allreddye a Moore, would not give him entertaynment ; soe hee retorned to Agra and gott himselfe into the service of a Frenchman, and is turned Chrystian againe, goinge usuallye to Masse with his master. Another allsoe, called Robert Claxton,[1] whom wee had entertayned, hearinge reporte how Trullye was made of in the Decanns courte, lefte us and wente thether allsoe and turned Moore, havinge verye good allowance ; yet, not contente therewith, after the Englishe shippes came to Suratt, hee came thether, shewinge himselfe verye pennytente for what hee had don, and carried himselfe in such manner that everye man pittied him. At the laste hee gott into his hands some fortye and odd pounds, under pretence of helpinge them to buye commodyties, and then gave them the slippe and retorned from whence hee came, and there remaynes still, for ought wee knowe. So there is with the Kinge of Decanne fower Englishemen which are turned Moores, and divers Portungales allsoe.

Aboute the 12th of October, 1618, Mr. Aldworth (our Agente), myselfe, and Mr. Aldworth's man,[2] and a Germayne began our journey for Amadavar ; and travellinge alonge the cuntrye, the 18th daye wee came to a prittie village called

[1] Or Clarkson (*Letters Received*, vol. i, pp. 299, 304).

[2] John Young. The German was named Jacob. He had been captured by the Turks in Hungary and remained a slave for seven or eight years, when, after several changes of masters, he managed to escape to the Portuguese at Goa, from whom he fled to Surat (*Letters Received*, vol. i, pp. 299, 304).

Sarron,[1] and lodged in the Governor's yarde, where wee were safe from theeves. In the morninge wee beeinge reddye to departe, the Governor sente his men to us to begge somethinge of us; whoe were contente with 8 pites [pice], which is aboute 3*d.* Englishe. And travellinge yet further on our journey, wee came to a cittye called Brothra [Baroda], which is but a little cittye, yet of fyne buyldings; where wee bought some commodities for our trading. And about ten courses from thence wee came to a river called Wasseth,[2] where wee fownde Mussulph Chane [Musaff Khān ?], Governor of Brodra (and a friend to our Englishe), with his armye, beeinge reddye to fighte with the Rasbooches that laye on the other syde of the river, to the number of 2000 horses and manye foote. Wee vizitted him and presented him with cloth; and towards night peace was concluded betweene him and the rebbells. The cheife of them (beeinge the captain, and of the rase of the ould kinges of Suratt) came over the river to vizitt the Governor; but before hee came, hee sente over his whole armye, whoe put themselves in battell array, for feare of anye trecherye; for the yeare before, the brother of this rebbell cominge in the same manner to visite Mussulph Chane, whoe caused his throate to bee cutt, and after slewe manye of his souldiers. Soe this rebell, to prevente the like, sente over his whole armye first, and then came armed himselfe, beeing compassed with some fortye of his chiefest souldiers, all armed compleate, and soe presented himselfe before Mussulph Chane, giveinge him a white bowe, witnessinge (as wee conceaved) his innocencye; and soe, kissinge the hande of the Governor, presentlye departed. Mussulph Chane likewise the same night wente to Brodra, and lefte us twentie of his horsemen to accompanye us on our waye.

[1] Purchas gives the intermediate stages: 'From Surat I went to Periano [Variāo], three course. To Cosumbay [Kosamba], a little village, 10 c. Barocho [Broach], 10 c.: a prettie citie on a high hill, compassed with a wall, a great river running by, as broad as Thames; divers shippes of two hundred tunnes and odde there riding; best calicoes in the kingdome; store of cotton. To Saringa [Sārang], 10 c. To Carron [Kārvān] 10 c.' Sārang is about four miles north of Shāhābād.

[2] The Mahi. 'Wasseth' is really Vāsad, the place where the highroad crossed the river.

and allsoe lente us one of his ellephants to transporte our goods over the river, the water beeinge heighe. [To Niriand [Nariād], 14 c. ; a great towne where they make indico.]

The twenty-second daye wee came to Amadavar, which is the cheifest cittye of Guysseratt, and is verye neare as bigge as London, walled rounde with a verye stronge wall, scituate in the playne by the river-syde. Here are marchaunts of all places resydinge, as well Chrystians as Moores and Gentills. The commodities of this place are cloth of gould, silver tissue, vellvets (but not comparable to ours), taffetase and other stuffes, and divers druggs, with other commodities.[1] Here wee tooke a howse to hier in a place where divers Armenian marchaunts lye and other Chrystians. The nexte daye wee vizited Abdolla Chan,[2] Governor of this place (a nobleman of 5000 horse paye), and presented him with a veste of cloth[3] and other trifles of small vallue ; but hee expected greater matters, which wantinge, hee presentlye dismissed us without any grace.

Shortelye after, our Agente sente mee to Cambaya, givinge mee 200 rupeias, everye rupie containinge 2*s.* 6*d.*, to buye of all sorts of commodities which I should fynde there fitt for our tradinge, and to informe myselfe of the place ; which I thanke God I did, though with greate daunger of robbinge. [Seven course to Barengeo [Bareja], where every Tuesday the cafily [see p. 143] of Cambaya meete and so keepe company for feare of theeves. Hence sixteene course to Soquatera [Sojitra], a fine towne well manned with souldiers. Departed at midnight, and about eight of the clocke next morning came 10 c. to Cambaya.] And the 30th daye, havinge bestowed my 200 rupeias in such commodities as I founde for our turne, in the afternoone beeinge reddye to departe, the Governor sente for mee and shewed mee our King's letter of England, which General Beste brought ; tellinge mee it was sente him downe from the Kinge to have it translated, and intreated mee to doe yt ; but I excused myselfe, urginge the necessitie of my

[1] Purchas specifies 'gumbuck' [gumlac] and 'coloured baffataes'.
[2] Abdullah Khān, Fīrūz-jang, was Viceroy of Gujarāt from 1611 to 1616.
[3] 'Viz three yards and a half' (*marginal note*).

presente departure, and withall tould him that yt was a matter of more importance then for mee to doe yt alone, without the knowledge of our Agente, and desired him to sende yt to Amadavar to our Agente, and hee without doubte would translate yt; which the Governor did. Soe accordinglye it was translated.

Havinge well overcome our businesse and but little to doe, wee rode to Serkesse [Sarkhej; see p. 174] (some three courses from Amadavar), which is the cheife place where they make theire flatte indico; and there wee spente twoe or three dayes in seeinge the makinge therof. In this towne are the sepulchers of the Kings of Guyseratt, a verye dellicate churche and fayer toumbes, which are kepte verye comelye; whither there is much resorteinge from all parts of the kingdome to vizitt theis toumbes. Allsoe aboute a myle and a halfe off there is a verye fayer and pleasante garden of a myle aboute, which compasseth a verye fayer and statelye howse, seated dellicately by the river-side; which howse Chou Chou,[1] now the cheifeste nobleman of the Mogull's, builte in memoriall of the greate victorye which hee gott of the laste Kinge of Guyseratt, takinge him prisoner, and likewise brought all his whole kingdome in subjection of the Greate Mogull, as yt still continueth; in memoriall wherof, the battell beeinge fought in this place, hee builte this howse and planted the orchard, raysinge the heigh wall rounde aboute yt. Noe man dwelleth in this howse; onlye a fewe poore men that are hyred to keepe the orchard cleane. Wee lodged in yt one night, and sente for sixe fishermen, that in lesse then halfe an hower tooke more fishe then all our companye could eate; and soone after retorned to Amadavar agayne.

Here in Amadavar is a Jesuite[2] remayninge to converte

[1] The Khānkhānān (see p. 71) is meant. The remains of his *Fateh Bāgh*, or Garden of Victory (laid out in 1584), are still to be seen near the lake at Sarkhej.

[2] This was probably Jean de Seine, who is described by Pyrard de Laval in one place as belonging to Nancy, in another place to Verdun. When Pyrard left Goa (early in 1610) Father de Seine had gone to reside at Chaul. Kerridge mentions him in September 1615 (Letter-book, f. 5) as having gone to court with Mukarrab Khān. For other information see Father Hosten's article on Jesuit missionaries in the *Journal of the Bengal Asiatic Society*, 1910, p. 530.

heathens to Chrystianitie, though hee hath little proffit therebye hetherto; yet still resteth in his vocation. Hee tould us that they were a people absolutelye predestinated for hell. Hee, beeinge a Frenchman, was verye open to our Agente in all matters; and likewise made knowne unto him his owne poore estate, protestinge hee had nothinge to eate, by reason of the imbarquement of the Portungales and theire goodes; and in fyne intreated our Agente to lende him some money or give him some for God's sake. Our Agente, seeinge the povertye of the poore man, gave him tenn rupeias, viz. 25*s.* sterlinge; for the which afterwards hee wrote to him a thankful letter, but withall desired him to burne yt; whereby I note his pride of harte, to bee willinge to receave a good turne but not openlye to acknowledge that hee had neede of yt.

The 12th of December[1] wee had certayne intelligence by divers that there were English shipps arrived in Synda at Lowrybander[2]; wheruppon yt was thought fitt by our Agente (myselfe thereto consentinge) that I should instantlye take my journey thether to them, to informe them of our settled factorye and to advise them of other things conveniente for our and theire tradinge. Whereuppon I prepared all things necessarye, and the nexte daye departed on my journey. And the firste night I fell acquainted with certayne marchaunts bounde for Synda, of which acquayntance wee were all well pleased and glad, keepinge companye together till yt pleased God to parte us by death.[3] Keepinge on our waye, the 15th of December, 1613, wee came to a village called Callwalla. This towne the King's father (ould Accabaa) after the conqueste of Guyseratt, cominge thether, gave to a company of women and theire posteritie for ever, uppon condition to teache and bringe upp theire children in theire owne profession, which is dauncinge, etc. At our beeinge here, the women of the towne came into our caravan and daunced, everye man givinge them some-

[1] Purchas says November 28.

[2] Printed (here and elsewhere) 'Eowrybander'. It is Lahrībandar, the old port of Tatta, near the Piti mouth of the Indus.

[3] Purchas's version has: 'The thirteenth of December came to Cassumparo, where I overtooke a caphilo travelling to Radenpare [Rādhanpur], six dayes journey on my way. Fourteene, to Callitalowny, a faire castle. Thirteene [i. e. 15th], 7 c. to Callwalla,' &c.

thinge ; and afterwards they asked openlye : Whoe wants a bedfellow ? Soe shamelesse they were. Wee departed from thence the nexte day. [The sixteenth, 8 c. to Carrya [Khawad ?], where is a well-manned fortresse ; and the eighteenth (till which, for feare of theeves, wee stayed for another caravan) to Deccanaura [Dekawara]; our camell stolne and a man slaine.] And the 19th day wee came [10 c.] to Bollodo, a forte kepte by Newlocke Abram [1] (a brave souldier) for the Mogull ; whoe was that day retorned from battell, bringinge home with him 169 heads of the Coolies [Kolis], a theevish caste of moutteners [mountaineers ?] that live by robbinge and spoylinge poore passengers on the heighwaye. [The twentieth, 18 c. to Sariandgo, a fort.] Wee still kepte on our journey, and the 21st daye wee came [10 c.] to Raddinpoore [Rādhanpur], a bige towne, havinge a forte kepte in yt and a companye of brave souldiers. Wee stayed here twoe dayes to provide ourselves of provision for the desarte journey, there beeinge nothinge to bee had on the way, not soe much as freshe water for our cammells, nor anye other victualls for them or ourselves. The 23d day wee travelled [7 c.], and at night laye in the feilds. [Met a caravan robbed of all, from Tutta. The foure and twentieth 12 c. Dispeeded one of my pions to Lowribander with a letter ; which promised to doe it in ten dayes, but I thinke was slaine. The five and twentieth 14 c.] Lodged in the feilds, by a well of water, but yt was soe salte that wee could not use yt. [The six and twentieth 10 c. to such another well.] This daye wee gave our cammells water which wee brought from Raddinpoore, they not havinge dranke of three dayes, which is usuall with them there in their travell. Soe wee travelled the 27th day [14 c.] and laye in the feilds as before, havinge nothinge but what wee brought with us. And the 28th day [10 c.] wee came to Negar Parker [Nagar Pārkar], a poore towne, yet with good store of provision for travellers. In the deserte that wee had passed wee sawe greate aboundance of wilde asses, redd deare, foxes, and other wild beasts. This towne [2] (wherein wee

[1] Purchas calls him Newlock Abram Cabrate. This may be intended for Nūrullah Ibrāhim Kābuli.

[2] Purchas adds that here they 'met with an other caravan, robbed within two dayes journey of Tutta'.

stayed a daye to refreshe ourselves and then departed, payinge a toule [toll] for our cammells ladinge) payeth a yearelye tribute to the Mogull. All the reste betweene that and Juno,[1] which is halfe a day's journey from Tutta, paye none, neither acknowledge any kinge but themselves, robbinge and sparinge whom they liste. When an armye of the Mogull's cometh againste them, they fyer theire howses and flye into the mountayns, theire howses beeinge made of strawe and morter, in the fashion of beehives, which are soone burnte and soone upp agayne. They have a custome to guard passengers (when they have taken from them what they please, under culour of custome) till they be fourth of theire territoryes, takinge it in fowle disgrace to have anye other but themselves to robb anye man within theire command.

[We travelled 6 c. and lay by a tanke or pond of fresh water. The thirty one, 8 c., and lay in the fields by a brackish well. The first of January [1614][2] we went 10 c. to Burdiano.] Here wee payed custome for our goods, stayinge there a daye and better, manye of our companye beeinge sicke with drinking of theire water, which is brackish. And my owne provision of water beeinge spente, I was forced to drink this of theirs, but I mingled yt with buttermilke, wherof there is good store. Of this water, as bad as yt was, wee laded our cammells for four dayes journey, theire beeinge none to bee had in all that way. [Travelled more the second 18 c., all night. The third, in the afternoone till midnight, 10 c. The fourth, 12 c. Here I fell sicke and vomited, by reason of the water. The fifth, 7 c., and came to three wells, two salt, one sweetish. The sixth, to Nuraquimire, a pretie towne, 10 c. Here our Raddingpoore company left us. We remained two merchants, my selfe, five of their servants, foure of mine, with tenne camels, five camel-men. This towne is within three dayes of Tutta, and seemed to us after our desart a Paradise. We agreed with one of the Ragies or Governours kinred for twenty laries (twenty shillings) to conduct us; who departed with us the eighth,

[1] Possibly Juma, on the Indus, eight miles below Tatta.

[2] The later version says that it was on January 2 that they reached 'a little village called Burdiaws, seated on a hill'. Withington's stages, at this portion of the journey, cannot be identified.

and we travelled 10 c. to Gundajaw, where we had beene robbed but for our guard. The 9th wee departed from Gundayaw (a little towne full of robbers), and setting forwards from thence about nine of the clocke, wee were sett on by theeves; but havinge some warninge therof, wee shifted as well as wee could, bringinge our cammells rounde about us in a ringe and makinge them sitt downe (which they would doe with a commandinge word), and soe were within them as in a forte, plyinge our bowes and arrowes, yet not to hitt the ennemyes, for soe our guyde had given us charge. I discharged my pistoll twice at them. At the laste, through our guyde's perswasions, they were contente to take of us five layers,[1] and soe to lett us passe. Some three howers after, wee were sett on agayne by manye more, and soe were driven to our former shifts; and in fyne, as the former did, soe did theise, wee givinge them the like as to the firste. Soe this night wee came to Sarrunne, a greate towne of the Rasbooches, with a castle in yt, some 14 course from Tutta. Wee visited the Governor, called Ragee [2] Bowma, the eldest sonne of Sultan Bull Bull of the caste of the kings of Synda, untill Synda was conquered from his predecessors by the Persians. This Sultan Bull Bull was latelye taken prisoner by the Mogull, whoe pulled out his eyes; yet not longe after [3] hee escaped thence and came hether, livinge now uppon the mountaynes, and hath given his sonnes and kyndred charge to revenge the losse of his eyse of all passengers they can light on belonginge to the Mogull (but this I heard not of till afterwards). Soe this Ragee entertayned us verye kyndlye, sayinge hee was glad wee had escaped from them that would have troubled us; biddinge us take heede, for though wee were but 14 course from our journeyes end, yet there was much daunger on the way. Hee was especiallye kynde to mee, seeinge mee a white man and of a farr cuntrye (as my interpriter tould mee); and asked me manye questions of the state of my countrye, takinge much delight to heare therof; and at my

[1] 'Or lareese, which are made of silver, like a poynt tagg, worthe 12*d.* per peese' (*marginal note*). This is not a bad description of the *lāri*, a coin then much used in Southern Persia, Sind, and Western India.

[2] 'Or Rase' (*marginal note*). 'Bowma' and 'Bull Bull' cannot be identified.

[3] 'Two moneths before this', according to the version in Purchas.

companions departure willed mee to stay with him, makinge mee suppe there and givinge mee much wyne, drinkinge bothe together in one cupp till hee was allmoste stawed,[1] and then sente mee to my companye, and much victualls with mee.

Here wee remayned the nexte daye; and towards night I mett with a Banian,[2] whoe came that daye from Tutta, whoe tould mee that Sir Robert Sherley, with his wief and three or four English women, with seven or eight English men, were in Tutta. This Banian came in Sir Robert's companye from Lowryebander, in a shippe which sett them on shore at Tutta and so departed thence,[3] there beeinge noe English shippes, nor factorye seated there. Hee tould mee howe Sir Robert had ben much abused at Lowrybander, bothe by the Governor and the Portungales, and howe the Portungales came on shore in the night and fyred Sir Robert's house, hurtinge many of his men; and likewise at his arrivall at Tutta, three dayes journey from Lowrybander, Mersa Rusto,[4] then Governor of Tutta for the Mogull, used him verye unkyndlye and tooke from him jewells and what else soever pleased him, purposinge to sende him upp to the Mogull. In this estate hee lefte Sir Robert this laste night, when hee was at Sir Robert's house.[5] Hee advised mee to intreate the Governor of this place to lende us some of his souldiers to guard us to Tutta; which in fyne I did, and sente the Ragee for a presente 40 lareis, which hee tooke kyndlye, promisinge to bringe us himselfe, with 50 horsemen, to the gates of Tutta; and withall would make mee believe that yt was for my sake that hee wente himselfe;

[1] 'Stared' in Purchas.

[2] 'Baman' (here and elsewhere) in the printed version. It is explained in the margin as a 'pedlar'.

[3] This was the *Expedition*, commanded by Christopher Newport, in which Sir Robert Sherley, the celebrated adventurer, had returned from his long mission to various European courts as ambassador from the Persian Shāh. From Tatta he went up to Ajmer, to complain to the Emperor Jahāngīr. After a stay of about three months, he proceeded to Agra, and thence (Sept. 1614) overland to Persia.

[4] Mīrza Rustam (see p. 139) had recently been appointed Viceroy of Sind.

[5] The version in Purchas adds that the Banian 'told of the great trade of Tutta, the chiefe that he had seene, and that a shippe of three hundred tunne might come to Lowribander'.

which made my companions thinke themselves happie in my companye, and were more merrye then ever I sawe them before.

The 11th daye in the afternoone wee laded our cammells, the Ragee with his companye beeinge reddye to depart from Surrun; and that night rode five courses,[1] and rested by a river-syde. The Ragee sente for fishermen, whoe tooke more in halfe an hower then all the companye could eate. Wee supped that night with the Ragee, hee tellinge us that by nine of the clocke in the morninge hee would deliver us within the gates of Tutta; which made us all verye merrye. At two of the clocke in the morninge hee bad us lade our cammells, and then ledd us alonge by the river-syde aboute a myle and halfe, sayinge the river was too deepe for our cammells to passe; and then ledd us a cleane contrary way, as wee perceaved, which made us greatelye feare his intente. And aboute breakinge of day, wee came into a thicke valley of wood invironed about with hills, a place moste fitt for our bloudye guyde to acte his pretended [i. e. intended] tragedye. And beeinge in the middest of the thickett, hee bad us unlade our cammells, for he would see wherewithall they were laden; which beeing done, hee caused us all to bee bounde and our weapons to bee taken from us. Then opened the fardells [i. e. bales] and founde greate store of cloth of gould, silver, and tissue, and other commodities, which coste the marchaunts my companions in Amadavar twentye thousand rupiase (each rupia beeinge *2s. 6d.*), as they had formerly tould mee. The Ragee, seeinge this bootye soe rich, concluded to kill the marchaunts and all their servants; and his companye would have had him kill mee and my men allsoe, alledging as good save all as some; but by no meanes hee would therto consente, telling them I was of a verye farr countrye and would doe them noe hurte, wantinge language. In fyne hee promised his companye that I should not goe for Tutta to bewray this facte of theirs there, but hee would sende mee back againe to Amadavar from whence I came; so caused my four men presentlye to bee unbounde, making me sitt close by himselfe, and suddaynly caused his men to hange the three marchaunts

[1] 'A course is a mile and a halfe English' (*marginal note*).

and theire five men, tyinge theire cammells ropes about theire neckes and with a shorte truncheion twisted the ropes untill they were strangled, and then stripped them naked and made a greate hole in the earth and threwe them in all together; which done, hee tooke from mee my horse and gave mee twoe of my dead companions horses. Hee tooke from mee likewise eighty rupias of the Companies moneyes; and soe sente mee and my men, with four of his horsemen, to a brother's of his, which dwelte some twentye courses off the place, upp to the mountaynes; and soe aboute midday dispeeded mee from him.

Beeinge nowe on the way towards his brother, a newe feare fell on mee, for that my companions tould mee that the four horsemen that wente with mee had order to kill us all when wee were some twoe or three courses off; wheruppon they wept extreamlye and asked one another forgivenesse, making themselves reddye to dye; and the countenance of my guydes presaged little lesse, not once speaking to mee. Soe with a wofull harte, God knows, I rode till an hower within night; at which tyme wee came to a little village on the topp of a verye heigh hill, belonginge to the Ragee, where I lay that night, beeinge kyndlye welcomed by my guydes, giving mee and my men and horses vitles enough. The nexte day, beeinge the 14th of Januarye, 1613 [i. e. 1614] wee travelled all day longe without any baytinge, over terrible heigh hilles and rocks, and late at night came to the Ragee's brother's howse, to whom I was delivered and order given him by my guyde to keepe mee till hee heard farther newes from the Ragee. This man used mee kyndlye and gave mee a large place in his howse to lye in, and roome for my horses. The nexte morninge the four horsemen that brought mee thether retorned to their master, leavinge mee in this place; where I continued 22 dayes, beeinge never suffred to stir our of dores, nor none of my men, neither anye to come at us but those that brought us victuals twice a daye, which wee never wanted.

Notwithstandinge, I still feared I should never get thence with life; but yt pleased God, the 7th day of Februarye, order came from the Ragee to his brother to sende mee to Parker and there deliver mee to the Governor (which was likewise of theire kyndred) and hee should sende mee to Raddingpore.[1] This newes the Ragee's brother tould mee, and saide that the nexte daye I should goe, and hee would sende three of his horsemen with mee two dayes journey, and there hee had another brother that should bringe mee to Parker. Soe the eight day wee departed with our guydes, and that night rode sixteene course to a village called Nondogue, where wee were well entertayned of our guydes and lodged there that night. The ninth wee rode twentye course; but were till midnight before wee gott thether, and then came to the howse of him that I was consyned to bee delivered unto; and the nexte daye the men that brought mee thether retorned. This Ragee (for all the sonnes of the Sultan are called Ragees, or Commaunders) promised me within two dayes to goe with mee himselfe to Parker, haveinge (as hee said) businesse there. But hee kepte mee seven dayes, yet used mee kyndlye, and afterwards sente mee away with five of his souldiers to accompanye mee, not goinge himselfe. With theis I was ledd four terrible dayes journeye, which allmost killed mee and my poore men and horses. At the four dayes end they delivered mee to an other Ragee (of the kyndred of the firste of Sarrune), and hee kepte mee five dayes with him, not lettinge mee departe nor suffringe one of his men to goe with mee. Theis delayes made mee even wearye of my life. At the laste (through my importunitie) hee sente mee away the twentye-seventh day, and six of his souldiers to accompanye mee, who carried mee that night five courses to an aldeam,[2] and there gave mee noe victualls, as formerly I had; soe that I was fayne to sende my men into the village to begge; who brought mee a little rice sodd and some cammells milke, which, I eatinge, made mee extreame sicke that night; but for my horses they could gett nothinge, save onlye a little stubble and grasse, which they gott in the fields; which made them scarce able to travell. This night theis six rogues, seeinge I had verye good apparrell of the countrye fashion and a quilte of escete[3], with manye other things of worthe, determined with themselves to strippe mee of all; which they did, leavinge neither mee nor my men any thinge,

[1] 'Misprinted (here and elsewhere) 'Paddingpore'.

[2] 'A little village'; see p. 132.

[3] ? 'Cheete' (chintz).

save onlye our breeches; which done, they lefte us with our horses, which were not worth the taking. This miserye wente nearer my harte then all the former, beeinge nowe stripped of all and havinge nowe two third parts of my way to goe to Amadabar, not knowinge one foote of the way, and the wether could; which made mee allmoste wearye of my life, and my mens unhartinesse made me fuller of greefe. Yet comfortinge my selfe and men the beste I could, the firste of March, 1613 [1614] I wente on without a guyde, not knowinge one foote of the way but onlye by gesse, and travelled all day longe, and towards night came to two or three houses of poore cammel mens that kepte cammells in the mountaynes; to whom wee tould the mishapp which wee had receaved by our guydes thus leaving us. The poor people made much of us, givinge us such victualls as they had; and one of them promised to leade us into the way that goes to Parker, from thence some two dayes journey. In the morninge hee wente with us some three courses, puttinge us in the heigh way, and so lefte us; but wee, missinge our way, made four dayes journey to Parker. My horse tyringe, I was fayne to goe one foote, and, beeinge a bad footeman, travelled verye softlye. And everye night wee came to a little village and begged for our victualls, fyndinge all the inhabitants charitable people. So the sixth day at night we came to Parker, miserablye wearye and hungrye. I sente two of my men to proove what they could doe for mee with begging, but they brought me nothing; so I byded that night; and the nexte morninge I sente one of my horses to sell, but noe man would give above four mamoda's[1] for him. Yet I should have been forced to have sould him for that, but by greate chaunce I mett with a Banian marchaunte of Amadavar whom I had formerlye knowen; whoe wondred to see mee in that case, and after manye kynde salutations offred mee what money I would have, not suffringe mee to sell my horse. Thus it pleased God to sende mee releefe, when I was in greate necessitie, not knowinge what to doe to gett provision for my journey over the desarte to Amadaver, whither of force I muste have gone; but it pleased God to sende mee this succour. Hee furnished mee and my men with clothes and

[1] Mahmūdis (see p. 77). The margin explains the term as 'shillings'.

victualls sufficient to serve us in the deserte, and gave me nine mamoda's in my purse, payinge all my expences whileste I stayed heare, which was four dayes; and then, havinge good companye which wente to Radingpore, I wente alonge with them. The honest Banian commended mee unto them and brought mee one course on my way, and then retorned to Parker, where hee had businesse for ten dayes, as hee said.

Nothinge worth notinge passed in our way over the desart, onlye the superstitious customs of the people, which I will herafter expresse. Wee were six dayes betweene Parker and Raddingpore. And the nineteenth of March I came to Raddingpore, and there fell exceedinge sicke and remayned soe six dayes, liker to dye then live. And the twenty-sixth of March, 1614, beeinge somewhat amended, and good companye reddye to departe for Amadavar, I strayned curtesie with my sicknesse and departed with them, pawninge some of my clothes to one of the companye for five mamoda's, my monye formerlye borrowed beeinge spente in my sicknesse. And after seven dayes travell I arived in Amadavar (the Lord bee praysed), beeinge 111 dayes since my departure firste from thence into Synda. I founde noe Englishemen heare, onlye a letter which our Agente lefte with an Armenian for mee, advisinge mee of manye things. So I stayed heare two dayes, and provided my selfe of apparrell and money and a horse.

Soe the fifth of Aprill, 1614, I departed from Amadavar (Brodra way) to Suratt.[1] And the seventh day I came to Cambaya, where I fell sicke againe, and soe continued five dayes very ill. And beeinge somewhat recovered and able to travell, the twelfth day of Aprill I lefte Cambaya and passed the large river that night (which river is about seven course broad, verye dangerous to passe, and yearlye swalloweth upp manye hundreths) [to Saurau [Sārod]. On the other side the river is a towne and castle of the Razbootches. The sixteenth of Aprill I travelled 25 c. to Borocho [Broach]. The seventeenth passed that river, and 10 c. to Cassimba [Kosamba]. The eighteenth, 13 c. to Surat.]

[Concerning Sinda, no citie is by generall report of greater

[1] From Purchas we learn that his route was, as before (see p. 206), via Bareja and Sojitra to Cambay.

trade in the Indies then Tutta; the chiefe port Lowribander, three dayes journey from it; a faire roade without the rivers mouth, cleare of wormes, which, about Surat especially, and in other places of the Indies, after three or foure moneths riding, if it were not for sheathing, would hinder returne. The ports and roads of Sinda are free. In two moneths from hence by water they goe to Lahor, and returne in one downe. There are these commodities: baffitas, stuffes, lawnes,[1] indico course, not so good as Biana. Goods may be conveied from Agra on camels to Bucker [in] twenty dayes, which is on Sinda River; thence in fifteene or sixteene dayes aboord the ships. One may goe as soone from Agra to Sinde as Surat; but there is more theeving, which the Mogoll seekes to prevent.]

Nowe, as concerninge the inhabitants of Synda, they are for the moste parte Rasebooches, Banians, and Boloches [Balūchis]. In the citties and greate townes theire Governors are Mogores, appoynted to rule there for the Greate Mogull. The people of the cuntrye (I meane those which inhabitt out of the citties) are for the moste parte verye rude, and goe naked from the waste uppwards, with turbants on their hedds, made up of a contrarye fashon to the Mogull's. For armes, fewe of them use gunes, bowes, or arrowes, but sword, bucklar, and launce. Theire bucklar is made verye greate and in the fashion of a bee-hive; wherin, when occasion serves, they will give theire camells drinke or theire horses provander. They have exceedinge good horses, verye swifte and stronge, which they will ride moste desperatelye, never shooinge them. They begin to backe them at twelve monethes ould. The souldiers that have noe horses, if occasion serve, will ride on theire cammells (and enter into a battell), which they bringe upp for that purpose. Those are the Rasbooches, which, as the Mogull sayes, knowe as well howe to dye as anye men in the world, in regard of theire desperatenesse. They [the Banians] are partelye of Pigmalion's[2] opinion: they will eate noe beefe nor buffellow, but honor them and pray unto them. They will kill noe livinge thinge, nor eate anye fleshe, for all the goods in the world. There are 30 and odd severall casts[3]

[1] Fine cotton goods, or muslins. [2] A confusion with Pythagoras.

[3] 'Or generations' (*marginal note*). See note on p. 138.

of theis, that differ in some things in theire religeon and, by theire lawe, cannot eate one with another. Yet they all in generall burne theire dead, not buryinge them as the Moores doe.

When the Banian dies, his wife, after the burninge of her husband, shaves her head and weres noe more her jewells; in which estate shee continues till shee dye. When the Rasbooche dies, his wife, when his bodye goes to bee burned, accompanieth him, attyred with her beste arrayments and accompanyed with her frends and kyndred, makinge much joye, havinge musicke with them. And cominge to the place of burninge, the fyer beeinge made, sitteth downe, havinge twice or thrice incompassed the place. Firste, shee bewayleth her husband's death, and rejoycinge that shee is nowe reddye to goe and live with him agayne; and then imbraceth her frends and sitteth downe on the toppe of the pile of wood and dry stickes, rockinge her husband's head in her lappe, and soe willeth them to sett fyer on the wood; which beeinge done, her frends throwe oyle and divers other things, with sweete perfumes, uppon her; and shee indures the fyer with such patience that it is to bee admired, beeinge loose and not bounde. Of theis manner of burninge I have seen manye. The firste that ever I sawe was in Surratt, with our Agente and the reste of our Englishe. It was verye lamentable. The woman which was burnte was not above ten yeares of age and had never layen with her husband. But this yt was. Hee beeinge a souldier, and goinge uppon service, was slayne in the action, and there burned, but his clothes and turbante were brought home with newes of his death; wheruppon his wife would needes bee burnte, and soe made preparations for it. And beeinge reddye to sacrefise her selfe with her husband's clothes, which she had with her, order came from the Governor that shee should not dye, in regard she had never layen with her husband; which newes she took wonderfull passionately, desiringe them to sett fyer on the wood presentlye, sayinge her husband was a greate waye before her. But they durste not burne her, till her frends wente to the Governor and intreated him, givinge him a presente for the same; which when they obteyned, they retorned and (with greate joye to her, as she seemed) burnte her to ashes with her husband's clothes, and then caste the ashes into the river. This was the firste that ever I sawe; at the sight wherof our Agente was soe greeved and amazed at the undaunted resolution of the younge woman that hee said hee would never see more burnte in that fashion while hee lived. The kyndred of the husband that dies never force the wife to burne her selfe, but her owne kyndred, houldinge it a greate disgrace to theire familie if shee should denye to bee burned; which some have done, but verye fewe. And if they will not burne (yt beeinge in theire choyce), then shee muste shave her hayer and breake her jewells, and is not suffred to eate, drinke, or keepe companye with anye bodye, and soe liveth in this case, miserablye, till her death. Nowe, if any one of them purpose to burne and (after ceremonies done) bee brought to the fyer, and there, feelinge the scorchinge heate, leape out of the fyer, her father and mother will take her and bynde her and throwe her into the fyer and burne her per force; but such weaknesse seldome happeneth amongste them. For the reste of the ceremonies, theire washinge, honoringe of stocks, stones, and cowes, with a hundred other superstitious ceremonies, too large to reherce, I will here omitt. And thus much for the Rasbooches and Banians.

Nowe for the Boloches of Synda, inhabitinge nere the river, they are Moores of the religeon of Mahomett (as the Greate Mogull and King of Decan are). Theis are a people that deale much in cammells; and in those parts moste of them are robbers on the heigh way and allsoe on the river, múrdringe such as they robbe. Aboute the tyme that I was in Synda, the Boloches tooke a boate wherin were seven Itallians and one Portungale fryer, which fought with them and were slayne everye man; only the Portungale escaped alive, whoe beeinge verye fatt, they ripped upp his bellye and searched whether there were anye gould or pedareea [1] in his guts. Of likelyhood those Boloches living there are bloudye mynded villaynes; yet there are manye verye honeste men of that caste dwellinge about Guyseratt, but moste of them aboute Agra.

I had allmoste forgotte the custome of the Banian marriage.

[1] Explained in the margin as 'jewells'. It is the Portuguese *pedraria*.

They marrye their chilldren verye younge, about the age of three yeares and under. And some tymes they make promise to one an other that theire children shall marrye together, before they bee borne; as in example: if two neighbours wives bee with childe, they make a bargayne that if one bringe forthe a sonne and the other a daughter, they shall marrye together. They may not marrye but one of theire owne caste and religeon, and they muste bee likewise of one occupation or trade, as the sonne of a baker shall marrye a baker's daughter, provided they bee bothe of one caste and religeon. And when theire chilldren are three or four yeares ould, they make a greate feaste and sett the two children that are to bee married upon two horses, with a man before eache of them for feare of fallinge, havinge apparrelled them in theire beste clothes, all haunged aboute with flowers, and accompanied with the Brammans or priests and manye others, accordinge to the state of the parents of the children; and soe leade them upp and downe the cittye or towne where they dwell, and then to the pagod, and thence, after the ceremonies there done, they come home and feaste; and in the same manner continue feastinge certayne dayes, more or lesse, accordinge to the welthe of the parents. And when the children come to bee ten yeares ould, they lye together. The reason whye they marrye them soe younge, they say, is in regard they would not leave their children wiveless; if yt should please God to take the parents awaye of either of the children, yet (say they) they have other parents to ayde them till they come to yeares of discretion. Likewise the reason whye the Rasbooches wives burne themselves with theire husbands dead bodies is that yt hath ben an ould custome, and longe since ordeyned by a certayne kinge of theires, because hee had manye of his nobles and souldiers poysoned (as was supposed) by theire wives. Hee therefore ordeyned that, when anye husband dyed, his wife should bee burned with his corpes; and if hee had more wives then one, as manye as hee had should all burne together. But then they were forced unto yt; but nowe they have gotte such a custome of yt that they doe yt moste willinglye.

As concerninge theire preists, which they call Bramans, they keepe theire pagods and have allmes or tythes of theire parishionors, beeinge esteemed marvaylous holye. They are married as the reste are, and are of occupations and followe theire businesse close. They are for the moste parte verye good workemen, and apte to learne to make anye thinge that they see the patterne of before them. They eate but once a day, and before and after meate washe all theire bodie; allsoe, if they make water or goe to stoole, they carrye water with them, to washe when they have done.

Beeinge nowe at Suratt, our Agente havinge occasion to buye some rounde indicoe which was to bee had in Agra, which is about 40 dayes journey from Suratt [1]: which journey in fyne our Agente propounded to mee, N.W.; which I undertooke and (I thanke God) performed, although I passed through manye perills, but especiallye of drowninge, it beeinge in winter, wherin for the space of 4 monethes or there abouts yt continuallye rayneth. The 7th of June, 1614, I came to the cittye of Agra, havinge ben 37 dayes on my journey from Suratt thether, which is, as neare as I could guesse, 1010 English miles,[2] which I was fayne to travell daye and night.

The 9th of June, 1614, I visited the Jesuites which remayned in Agra; whoe have a verye fayer church buylte them by the Kinge, and a howse allsoe. The Kinge alloweth the cheifeste

[1] The version in Purchas gives a different reason for the dispatch of Withington to Agra: 'John Mildnall, an Englishman, had beene employed with three English young men, which hee poisoned in Persia to make himselfe master of the goods; but he was likewise poysoned, yet by preservatives lived many moneths after, but swelled exceedingly; and so came to Agra, with the value of twenty thousand dollers. Thither therefore, I went, May the fourth, 1614, from Surat. Came to Bramport, where Sultan Perves lies; situate in a plaine, the river of Surat running by in a great breadth; having a large castle. Hence to Agra twenty sixe dayes. Betweene Surat and Agra are seven hundred courses (1010 English miles), which I travelled in seven and thirty daies in winter, wherein it almost continually raineth. From Surat to Bramport is a pleasant and champion countrey, full of rivers, brookes, and springs. Betweene Bramport and Agra very mountainous, not passable for a coach, hardly for camels. By Mando is the nearest way. There are high hils and strong castles in the way; many townes and cities every dayes journey, well inhabited; the countrey peaceable and cleare of theeves. Mildnall had given all to a Frenchman, to marry his bastard-daughter in Persia and bring up an other.'

[2] This is a gross exaggeration.

of them [1] 7 rupeias a daye, and the reste three rupeias a daye. They have licence to turne as manye to Christianitie as they can, and they have allreddy converted manye ; but (alas) it is for money's sake, for the Jesuites give them 3d. a daye. And when the Jesuites (thro' the facte of the Portungalls) were debarred of theire paye from the Kinge, having noe moneye to paye theire newe Christians withall, they dayley came and offered the Jesuitts theire beads agayne, tellinge them they had ben longe without theire paye and therefore they would bee no longer Christians. And soone after this the Kinge, seeinge the Portungales would not deliver the goods which they tooke at Suratt back agayne, caused the church doore[s] to bee locked upp, and they have soe continued ever since. So the poore Jesuits are fayne to make a church of one of theire chambers, wherein they saye Masse twice a daye and preach everye Sundaye, firste in the Persian tonge, that the Armenians and Moores may understand, and afterwards in Portungale, for the Portungales, Itallians, and Greekes. [These told me the particulars of Mildnals goods, who gave all to a French Protestant, himselfe a Papist ; which he denying was put in prison. After foure moneths all were delivered.]

Havinge dispatched my businesse which I came in charge withall, I received a letter from our Agent, givinge mee notice of four English ships that were arrived in Suratt, under the commande of General Nicholas Dawnton (which joyed mee much) ; and withall willed mee to provide as much indicoe as came to twenty thousand mamodas ; which I did, takinge it upp uppon my credytt, he promissinge mee that I should receave money by exchange within fower dayes for the same. So as soone as I could make it upp in fardells, I hyred camells and dispeeded the indicoe for Suratt to our Agent ; and two dayes after the dispeedinge thereof I receaved other letters from our Agent, wherein hee advised mee not to deale in any more indicoes, for hee could make me upp noe money. This news made me in a pittifull case, because I had mingled the goods together, so that I could not returne everye one his owne againe ; yet I presentlye tooke horse and fetched backe the camels againe, seekinge to come to composition with my

[1] Jerome Xavier, of whom see p. 55.

creditors and my camellmen. But it was a laboure far greater then Hercules's; for they would heare noe reason, but came cryinge and yawlinge for theyre money, which I had not to give them. They put mee to soe much trouble and greife that made mee almost oute of my witts. But at laste the Governor, seeinge how I had ben deceaved in the expectation of money promised, hearinge some good excuse which I made for my moneys not cominge, in fyne forced the marchaunts to take theire goods agayne and soe parte them amongste them, accordinge to the quantitie I had bought of eache, and made the camelmen pay backe the moneye receaved, savinge onlye the earneste I gave them. So this kynde Governor ridd mee of a world of trouble, which had like to have killed mee, for I proteste I scarce slepte in 10 or 12 dayes and nights, neither eat anye thinge scarce: soe deeplye was this greife rooted in my harte, this beeinge my firste imployments and in these parts in soe shorte a tyme to have such creditt to take upp soe much goods on my bare worde and then to break yt and soe consequentlye my creditt, that I was ashamed to goe oute of doores; but yt was God's pleasure thus to punish mee for my synnes, and soe I take yt. But sure I will hereafter beware howe I truste to letters of advice while I live, havinge escaped this error. Here I continued sicke a long tyme, beeinge much distempered with the greife formerlye receaved, which distemp[er]ature kepte mee for the space of three monethes. At the length I was sent for to Agimere, where (God bee thanked) I recovered.

The General [i. e. Downton] departed the 2d of March, 1614 [i. e. 1615], leaving William Edwards cheif marchaunte, who tooke uppon him the state and title of an ambassador, as I have hereafter set down. The General departinge with his four shipps from Sualley had a greate feight with the Portungalls,[1] they cominge againste them with ten gallions, two gallies, and sixty friggotts; in which feight the General fyred three of theire greate shipps and slew a greate number of theire men, himselfe receavinge little or noe damage in the feight (the Lord bee praysed).

[1] As will be seen from p. 193, this fight took place some time before Downton's departure.

It was determyned by Mr. Edwards, cheife marchaunte for the Englishe in those parts (and not ambassador, as we formerlye supposed), to sende upp to Agra one Robert Younge and myself, N.W., to dispatche some businesse. Soe the 28th of Julye, 1615, wee arrived in Agra, beeinge in the middeste of wynter. Between Adgemere and Agra, at everye ten courses (which is an ordinarye dayes journeye) there is a serralia or place of lodging boothe for man and horse, and hostesses [1] to dresse our victuals if we please, paying a matter of 3*d*. both for horse and meate dressinge. Betweene these places (which is esteemed to be 120 courses) at everye course end there is a greate pillar erected; and at everye 10 course end a fayer howse, built by the Kinge's father, ould Accabar, when hee went in pilgrimage from Agra to Adgemere on foote, sayinge his prayers at everye course end, where hee caused the foresaid pillars to bee erected. And where hee laye still all night, there hee caused the aforesaid howses to bee builte; they onlye servinge for the Kinge and his women, none ellse ever lodginge or dwellinge in them.

This kinge which nowe raignes lyes in Adgemere, upon some occasion of warr which he hath against the Ranna [2] or Rasboatcha, inhabitinge in the mountaynes, whom this kinge's father nor this kinge could ever bringe to subjection; but nowe, by the Kinge's lyinge soe neare him and continually for two yeares space plyinge him with a world of souldiers, hee at laste sente his sonne to do homage to the Kinge, and soe a peace was concluded between the Kinge and Ranna.

As concerninge the greatnesse of this kinge, the Greate Mogul, his state is soe greate in comparison of most Christian kinges that the report would bee almoste incredible; therefore I will omitt yt with admiration, and referre the reporte therof to the would-bee ambassador Edwards. Nor will I speak at large of his greate justice, sittinge three tymes a day therin

[1] For the female attendants in the *sarāis* see *The Travels of Peter Mundy*, vol. ii, p. 121.

[2] The Rāna of Udaipur, Amar Singh (see p. 100). He had now been reduced to submission by an army headed by Prince Khurram. The reception by Jahāngīr of the Rāna's son, Karan, is described in the *Tūzuk*, vol. i, p. 277.

himselfe. Hee hath a bell hanging in his seralia[1] with a cord which reaches into an outer room, where, if anye of his subjects be wronged and cannot have justice of his nobles, they may repaire, and ringinge the bell, he looketh out, causinge them to bee brought before him, and examineth the matter; and if hee fynde that the poore man bee wronged in justice, be hee the greatest nobleman about him, he presentlye takes away all his meanes, puttinge him either into prison perpetually or cutts his throate. In fyne his greatness is such that I rather admire at yt than presume to write of yt. But I will retorne to the accidents in my owne occasions.

Havinge dispatched all my owne affaires and nowe at leasure, I rode to the river of Ganges, the famous river of that countrye, and from Agra is two dayes journey. Here[2] I stayed two dayes and observed divers customes and ceremonies of the caste of Banyam, the river-side being full of pagods kept by Bramans, the relation wherof would bee too tedious to reporte heare. The water of this river Ganges is carried manye hundred myles from thence by the Banyans, and, as they affirme, it will never stinke, though kepte never so longe, neyther will anye wormes or vermine breede therin. Alsoe by Agra runeth a verye large and deepe river called Gemmynys [Jumna].

This Agra is noe cittye, but a towne; yet the biggest that ever I saw. The faireste thing in yt is the castle, wherin the Kinge (when hee is in Agra) keepeth his court. The wall of this castle is some two courses in compase and the fayrest and heigheste that ever I sawe, and within well replenished with ordinants, one of the which, beeinge of brasse, is far bigger then ever I sawe anye in England. The rest of this towne (excepte some noblemens howses which are verye fayer and for the moste parte seated by the river-syde) is very ruinous. The auncient seate of the kings of this countrye, where they keepe [kept ?] theire courts, was in Fettepoore, 12 courses from Agra, and is a verye stronge cittye, situate uppon a mayne quarrye of rocke; but since the castle of

[1] 'A place which his women for his pleasure are kept in' (*marginal note*). The term is more familiar to English readers in its Levantine form of *seraglio*.

[2] Possibly Kanauj.

Agra was builte, this cittye hath gone much to decaye and is nowe verye ruynous. Between Fettipoore and Agra is the sepulcher of this king's father, which is a wonderful rich and curious buildinge, and to my judgment the faireste that ever I sawe in Christendome or elsewhere; and yet the churche of Fettipoore cometh verye neare yt, and is likewise builte by geometrie.

Beeinge nowe in Agra, there came to mee Mr. Rogers[1] (a preacher), Thomas Mitford, Phillip Baker, and Charles Clarke, and brought mee newes of the arrival of four English shipps at Suratt, under the commande of Captayne William Keelinge; and withall tould mee they were sente upp to apprehende mee by order from Mr. Edwards, whoe heard that I had much goods of my owne in the howse, and he not knowinge howe I came by them, and therefore caused mee to bee taken and put in irons, and withall gave order I should bee sente soe unto him to Agimere. This was a strange alteration to mee, and a wonder that this thunderclapp should fall so suddenlye and noe lightninge before. For my owne parte I tould them yt were a greate follye in mee if I could not give sufficient reasons howe I came by my goods. I tould them I had four fardells of indico, two chests of semiames, cheetes,[2] and such like, and they might well bee assured that if I had not come honestlye by them, but by knaverye deceaved the Companye, I shoud doubtlesse have had soe much cunninge in mee as to have bought some dyamonds, rubyes, or such like, or else have kept the monye wherewith I bought them and have turned it into commodities which would have been easilye carried and close from the eye of the world, where on the contrarye I had boughte nothinge but such things as could not possibly bee carryed but must bee knowne, beeinge the goods I mentioned before. Such was my playne and open dealinge, not caringe whoe knew therof. But they made slight of what I sayde to them; whereuppon I made it knowne unto

[1] The Rev. Peter Rogers, concerning whom see a note on p. 299 of *Letters Received*, vol. iii, and the references in the section dealing with Coryat (*infra*).

[2] 'Semiames' were fine cotton goods bought at Samâna (Patiâla State). 'Cheetes' = chintz.

them of whom I had taken upp my goods ; some I took uppon my owne creditt, to be payed at 24 monethes ; others I bought for reddye money, which I borrowed uppon my owne bonde, to be payed at the same tyme. I willed that my creditors might bee sente for and that they might justifye the truthe. But they tould mee they muste followe the stricke order of Mr. Edwards, which was to send mee downe in irons and to take all the goods, bothe of the Companyes and my owne, into theire possessions. Soe the nexte daye in the morninge Mr. Rogers and Phillipp Baker tooke charge of mee, and with my irons on my heels, waighinge 20 pound waight, they brought mee to Agimere, which was 10 dayes journey. But Mr. Rogers verye kyndlye, some three courses before I came to Agimere, tooke off my irons to prevente mee of open shame before my countrymen, and so brought mee to Mr. Edwards, whoe gave him little thanks for that kyndnesse hee showed to mee.

At my cominge to Mr. Edwards (our would-bee ambassador), His Honour entered into a stricte examination of mee howe I came by my goods which I had in Agra. But I proteste hee proceeded soe foolishlye and with such apyshe questions, accordinge to his common jesture and well-marked shamefull-nesse in his carriage, that I did almoste scorne to answer him. But havinge more respecte to the place hee was in then to his unworthy person, I tould him trulye howe and in what manner I came by the goods, and withall charged him with the abuse he had offred, not onlye to mee but consequentlye to our whole nation, consideringe the fashon I had carried myself in in Agra, soe disgracefullye puttinge me in chaines, his made factor in Agra divulginge abroad that I was behynde-hand in accompte forty thousand rupeias (or half-crowns), with manye other disgracefull speeches of mee ; to which Edwards swore he never gave them order to putt irons on mee, with some other excuses. But his mynde was not according to his words to me, for within 10 dayes after, uppon slight occation quarrell-inge with me, falselye charged mee to bee drunke, as glad of the leaste occation, and came with his pions (or hired servants) into my chamber, and there on a suddayne bounde mee and putt a fayer payre of boults on my leggs, swearinge hee would sende mee downe to the General, William Keelinge, to Suratt in that fashion. The cheifest cause of his soe base usage of mee was in regard I went with Mr. Rogers, our preacher, to visit Mochrobochane (a great nobleman), I beeinge Mr. Rogers his interpriter for that tyme ; Mr. Rogers onlye purposinge to take his leave of him. But Mochrobochane, heringe that hee would departe for England, tould Mr. Rogers hee muste needes see the Kinge before hee wente, and willed him to come the nexte morninge and hee would presente him before the Kinge. Mr. Rogers allso visited the Prince Sultan Cusserow [Khusrau], whoe receaved him verye gratiouslye, givinge him a letter to the Governor of Suratt for his good entertainment there, which letter stoode us in good stead in Suratt. Nowe Mr. Edwards, hearinge howe Mr. Rogers had been entertayned by the Prince, and allsoe had agreed (at Mochorobochane's motion) to goe with him to the Kinge, he stormed extremelye and fell into filthy uncivill tearmes with Mr. Rogers the preacher, and caused him to bee kepte prisoner by his pions in his chamber, not sufferinge him to stire out of doores to the Kinge ; which was (especially by the Jesuytts) laughed at, to see how baselye wee esteemed our countrymen, and taken notice of by the Moores and Christians, much to his hindrance, for it was thought, the Kinge being soe bountifull to all strangers, would have given our preacher some good reward ; which Mr. Edwards fearinge, and in regard himselfe was soone to departe from hence, hee thought the King's bountye would bee lesse to him, not beeinge contente with all the former giftes, which amounteth in my knowledge to the some of 6000 rupeias, which is 700*l.* English and odd.[1] Soe the carravan cominge from Agra, wee departed from Adgemere towards Suratt, viz. Mr. Rogers, preacher, and others, and myselfe, N.W., in chaynes.

And nowe I cannot but somewhat touch the businesse and the carriage of our would-bee ambassador, Mr. Edwards, whoe, cominge into the Easte-Indeas, tooke the title and state of an ambassador uppon him ; and havinge the Kinge of England's letter delivered him by General Downton to deliver to the

[1] A more authoritative account makes the total 11,000 or 12,000 *mahmūdis* (*Letters Received*, vol. iv, p. 295).

Greate Mogull, did open the same, addinge and diminishinge what seemed beste for his owne purpose and commoditie, either to or from yt, and soe presented his translation to the Great Mogull, with the present sente him by the marchaunts; and the Kinge bestowed on him 3000 rupeias (or half-crownes) for horse-meate. After this hee continued in Adgemere, and sometymes went to the court, where behavinge himselfe not as beseeminge an ambassador, especiallye sente from soe worthye and greate a prince as the Kinge of England (beeinge indeede but a mecannycal fellowe and imployed by the Companye into those parts), was kicked and spurned by the King's porters out of the courte-gates, to the unrecoverable disgrace of our Kinge and nation, hee never speakinge to the Kinge for redresse,[1] but carryinge those greate dishonours like a good asse, makinge himselfe and our nation a laughing stock to all people in general, to the greate rejoycinge of the Portungales, whoe openlye divulged the disgrace of the English ambassador receaved, by letters throughout all the countrye. After this our honourlesse ambassador, William Edwards, petitioned to the Great Mogull to obtayne licence from him to inflicte justice uppon all Englishmen (malefactors) in his dominions, by execution to death or other bodilye punishmente, according to our English lawes; which the Mogull denyed him. And uppon this a quarrell arrose betweene him and the companye of English factors lyinge in Agimere; soe that the said Edwards was by one Thomas Mittford (a factor) stabbed into the shoulder with a dagger. And after the shipps arrival at Suratt which brought over an ambassador trulye sente frome the Kinge of England, as we then heard yt reported, which was Sir Thomas Roe, Edwards, nowe fearinge the disgrace of his knaverye would light uppon him, and beeinge asked what the ambassador was which was arrived at Suratt, made answer that he was a man subdare, which is a common souldier of fower horse paye, and of no reputation.[2] Theis and manye more I could sett downe, but for brevetye sake. And if hee should denye the leaste tittle I have heare written, I will

[1] This accusation is corroborated by Roe (*Embassy*, p. xiii).

[2] The comparison was an unfortunate one, but a *mansabdār* was generally of much higher rank than is suggested in the text.

bringe good proofes to mayntayne yt, not onlye before' our worthye imployers, but also before the King's Majesty and Counsell. I omitt his determination of cozenninge the Companye, with his factor Yonge in Agra; but when occation shall be offred, I will likewise bringe sufficient prooffe of that; but till then this shall suffise. But I hope the Companye will take warninge howe they imploy such mechannick fellowes about such businesse; and I likewise hope that Sir Thomas Roe, nowe ambassador, by his worthye carriage will redeeme the great dishonour that Edwards hath raised to our Kinge and nation by his ill carriage, and testifye the same by some relations.

But nowe to returne to my owne wrongs; beeinge nowe dispeeded in chaynes from Agimere towards Suratt, which I passed thro' with execeedinge payne (havinge never been used to such hard garteringe), it beeinge a thousand and tenne miles from Agra (where I was first chayned) to Suratt, where, I thanke our General, they were taken off. The people of the countrye that knewe mee (and indeede for the beste sorte of them respected mee) manye of them followed mee downe the countrye, wonderinge what I had done that they should use mee in that manner; and if they had knowne the cause to be noe otherwise then yt was, they would not have suffered mee to have been soe used; for some of them offred me that, if I would at any tyme (when they offred me wronge) but hould upp my fingar or sende the leaste boye to them, they would deliver me from them and (yt may bee) have cutte the throats of them all. But knowinge myselfe to bee soe free from deceavinge the Companye, and allsoe to regayne the goods which Edwards had taken from mee, I came with them most willinglye, hopinge to purge myselfe of theire accusations. But in fyne I was brought aboard the shippe to our General [i. e. Keeling], whoe promised that when Edwards came downe I should have free speeche to cleare myselfe, which as yet I could never have. So my accompts were audited and I cleared not to owe the Companye anye thinge, and soe was dispeeded for England.[1] And at my arrival at Lyon-Key in

[1] He sailed in the *Lion*, on February 19, 1616, the other passengers including Edwards and the Rev. Peter Rogers (*Letters Received*, vol. iv,

London,[1] I was entertayned by some of the Companye, with whom I went presentlye to Sir Thomas Smyth,[2] of whom I hoped to have redresse of all my wrongs, with restitution of my goods and wages due unto me for the tyme of my service; of whom, instead of kynde usage and thankes for all the paynes taken for him and the Companye, I receaved most ungratefull disgrace and vilde usage; which I founde to growe through the false suggestions of Mr. Edwards, who, beeinge set on shore at Dover, was at home longe before mee.

The fourth of October, 1616, which was four days before my arrival, the Companye, by false and frivolous suggestions, had procured a writt of *Ne exeat regnum* againste mee; whereuppon, after some conference with Sir Thomas Smyth, I was in his owne howse arrested and carried to the Compter of London, where I remayned 36 dayes, the Companye not allowinge one pennye to releeve mee, nor so much as clothes to my backe, but demaunded six and thirtye thowsand pounde bayle of mee, which (God knowes) I was farr unable to procure. I intreated a poore brother of myne (whoe came 100 myles to mee) to goe to Sir Thomas and the Companye, to knowe theire reasons for my hard usage; but they would give none. I wrote a letter to Sir Thomas, desyringe I might knowe my faltes and that I might answer to anye thinge which could bee objected againste mee. I likewise sente him my particular accomptes howe I came by my goods; to all which, and manye more petitions and letters which I sente to them (the coppies wherof I have herafter caused to bee sett downe),[3] I could never yet receave any answer, onlye this: that I had done the Companye much hurte, not showinge anye particular wherin.

p. 12 *n.*). The version in Purchas states that in the return voyage they reached Table Bay on May 24, 1616, finding there an outward bound fleet under Benjamin Joseph, and that they arrived at Dover on September 15.

[1] Lion Quay was in Lower Thames Street, about halfway between Billingsgate and London Bridge.

[2] Governor of the Company, whose offices were at this time in Smythe's house, situated at the Fenchurch Street end of Philpot Lane.

[3] Copies of three letters to Sir Thomas Smythe, and of a petition to the Company, are printed in the eighteenth-century version. They contain nothing of importance.

At the end of 36 dayes of my imprisonment, it pleased Theire Worshipps, through much intercession of myselfe and my poore brother (which is all the friends I have in the world, and on whose charge I still remayne) to take his bonde and another of my friends in a thowsand poundes, that I should not goe nor sende out of the kingdom without licence, according to the tenor of the writte ; wheruppon (payinge my charges) I was sett at libertye, although I was in very poore and weake estate, scarce able to go without helpe. But yt plesead God to sende me frends : one whoe tooke me into his howse, where ever since I have remayned, not knowinge howe to make him satisfaction for the trouble with mee in the tyme of my sicknesse ; the other was Doctor Eglisem,[1] whoe, takinge pittye on mee, in charitye hath cured mee of my great malladye and sicknesse, which grew on mee partlye through greife which I tooke at theire ungratefull oppression and wronge, and partlye through my loathsome imprisonment. But I hope God, whoe hath preserved mee in the greater, will likewise deliver mee from the lesse ; and I hope that our greate Kinge, of whom the world rings fame, grace, and justice, will not suffer the dove to be oppressed with the greatness of the eagle.

[1] 'One of His Majesty's doctors of phisicke' (*marginal note*). This was Dr. George Eglisham, the Scottish physician and poet.

1612–17

THOMAS CORYAT

TOM CORYAT, 'the Odcombian Gallo-Belgic leg-stretcher,' as he called himself (in allusion to his birthplace and his pedestrian feats in Western Europe), is a figure familiar enough to students of seventeenth-century literature, though his fame is based almost as much upon his eccentricities as upon the merits of his published works. Here we are concerned only with his remarkable journeys in Asia; and we may note in this connexion that, leaving out of account the Jesuit Stevens, he was the first Englishman to set out for India with no thought of trade, his motives being in the first place to see that strange country, and in the second to write a book about his experiences.

The son of a Somersetshire clergyman who had himself made some reputation as a writer of Latin verse, young Coryat was educated at Winchester and Oxford, leaving the latter with a great knowledge of the Classics, which his ready memory enabled him to turn to good account. After the accession of James I he obtained a small post in the household of Prince Henry and thus secured a footing in Court circles. Here he quickly made himself notorious by his irrepressible loquacity and his eagerness to push himself into notice; and he became in consequence a general butt, alike at Court and in the famous club that met at the Mermaid Tavern, where Ben Jonson and his associates diverted themselves hugely at his expense. Fuller tells us that Coryat served as 'the courtiers anvil to try their wits upon; and sometimes this anvil returned the hammers as hard knocks as it received, his bluntness repaying their abusiveness'. In general, however, Coryat put up very patiently with gibes and practical jokes, content to pay any price for the privilege of figuring on such a stage.

In his restless desire to distinguish himself, in 1608 he undertook a continental walking tour, traversing parts of France, Northern Italy, Switzerland, and Germany, and covering about two thousand miles—all on foot and in one pair of shoes. His account of his peregrinations appeared in 1611, dedicated to Prince Henry and bearing the characteristic title of *Coryats Crudities, hastily gobled up in five moneths travells*. A special feature of the book was an extraordinary number of commendatory verses and epigrams, contributed by the wits of the day, in which the traveller's peculiarities were not spared; but it had solid merits of its own, in its vivid and accurate descriptions of the places visited and the many shrewd observations scattered up and down its pages. Its success was so great that the author was encouraged to publish in the same year a supplement, entitled *Coryats Crambe, or his Colwort twise sodden*.

Elated by the notice taken of his travels, Coryat now determined upon a far greater enterprise. He would go overland to India, see the Great Mogul in all his glory, and ride upon an elephant. First, however, he visited his birthplace and, after delivering an elaborate oration, solemnly hung up in the church the pair of shoes he had worn during his continental journey. An ingenious commentator has found an allusion to this in Shakespeare's *Measure for Measure*, where 'brave Master Shoetie, the great traveller', is named among the inmates of the Duke's prison. This seems likely enough; but it may be added that, as the play was produced in 1604 (though not printed till 1623), the allusion must have been introduced afterwards—possibly by some player induced thereto by the attention excited by Coryat's perambulations.

The earlier stages of Coryat's journey are described, from his own notes, in *Purchas His Pilgrimes* (part ii, book x, chap. 12). He started in October 1612, just before the death of his patron, Prince Henry. His first objective was Constantinople, to which place he went by sea. On the way he visited the islands of Zante and Scio, and made an excursion, with some of his fellow voyagers, to the ruins of Troy; here the party indulged in some characteristic fooling, and Coryat was, by one of his companions, solemnly dubbed a Knight of Troy, to the astonishment—and perhaps disappointment—of some peasant onlookers, who imagined that he was about to be beheaded for some crime. Constantinople was reached in April 1613, and there the traveller found a hospitable friend in Mr. (afterwards Sir) Paul Pindar, the English Agent. Coryat tarried in the city and neighbourhood until the following January, and then, once again taking ship, he coasted down the shores of Asia Minor until he reached Scanderoon, where he disembarked and hastened up to Aleppo. After a fortnight's stay, he and another Englishman set out for Jerusalem by way of Damascus. The Holy City was reached in the middle of April, and there, after visiting all the sights, Coryat had his wrists tattooed with the Crusaders' fitched cross and other devices, as a memento of his visit (Terry's *Voyage*, ed. 1655, p. 64). This practice, by the way, is alluded to by Manucci as being a common one among Christians making the pilgrimage to Jerusalem; and it is said that the late King Edward VII had something of the kind tattooed on his arm when he visited that city in 1869. After a visit to the Jordan the two Englishmen retraced their steps to Aleppo.[1]

Coryat spent four months in Aleppo waiting for a caravan, and then started on his long tramp eastwards, apparently some time in September 1614. He travelled by way of Diarbekr (where a Turkish soldier robbed him of most of his money), Tabrīz, Kazvin, and Ispahān to Kandahār. Near the Indian frontier he met Sir Robert and Lady Sherley, coming in great state from the Mughal court (see p. 212). The former exhibited to the flattered author the *Crudities* and its supplement, which he had brought from London, and further excited Coryat's cupidity by promising to show them to the Persian Shāh and urge him to bestow a princely reward on the writer as he returned through his dominions. Lady Sherley, more practical or more generous than her husband, gave the traveller a sum of money to help him on his road.

Still making eastwards, Coryat proceeded, by way of Multān (where he had the altercation with a Muhammadan described on p. 271) to Lahore, and thence to Delhi and Agra. Even now his journey was not at an end, for he found that the Emperor was at Ajmer; so thither the indefatigable traveller turned his steps, arriving, it would seem, in the early part of July 1615. He had spent in all ten months in trudging from Aleppo; and not the least remarkable feature of his journey was that it was performed at an average cost of little more than twopence a day. The explanation is of course the hospitality and kindness of Eastern races, especially to wandering pilgrims; also the fact that Coryat travelled in Oriental dress, was always ready to rough it, and had learnt to content himself with Spartan fare. All the same, he must have experienced many a hardship; and it is much to his credit that he made so light of this aspect of his travels.

At Ajmer Coryat was comparatively in clover. He found there a little group of the East India Company's servants, ten in all, including William Edwards the agent, and a chaplain, Peter Rogers, who, later in the year, carried down to Surat and thence to England the first four of the letters here reprinted, and was commended in them by Coryat to the hospitality of the Mermaid Club. A travelling Englishman, especially one of some notoriety, was always welcome to a lodging in the Company's factory and a seat at the Company's table; and

[1] Terry states that Coryat sailed from Smyrna to Alexandria, went up the Nile to Cairo and back, and then took ship for Jaffa and so reached Jerusalem. This, however, is quite inconsistent with the traveller's own account, and evidently in this, as in other instances, the reverend gentleman's memory played him false.

so Coryat was able to rest himself in comfort after the fatigues of the journey, and enjoy at leisure the strange sights afforded by a city crowded with the retainers of the Great Mogul. Early in October came the news that Sir Thomas Roe had landed at Surat as ambassador from King James, much to the satisfaction of our traveller, who describes Roe as a 'deare friend' of his. Three days before Christmas the ambassador was met within a stage of Ajmer by Edwards and Coryat, and, sick and weary as he was, had to endure from the latter 'a long, eloquent oration' by way of welcome. However, Roe was not sorry, among the many troubles of the next few months, to distract himself with the conversation of Coryat, 'whom', he says in a letter to Lord Pembroke, 'the fates have sent hither to ease mee, and now lives in my house. He came heither afoote: hath past by Constantanople, Jerusalem, Bethlem, Damascus, and (breefly) thorowgh all the Turkes territory: seene every post and pillar: observed every tombe: visited the monuments of Troy, Persia, and this kings dominions, all afoote, with most unwearied leggs; and is now for Samarcand in Tartarya, to kisse Tamberlans tombe: from thence to Susa, and to Prester Jhac in Ethiopia, wher he will see the hill Amara, all afoote: and so foote it to Odcombe. His notes are already to great for portage: some left at Aleppo, some at Hispan—enough to make any stationer an alderman that shall but serve the printer with paper. And his excercise here, or recreation, is making or reapeating orations, principally of my Lady Hartford.'

In all, Coryat spent about fourteen months in Ajmer. Some account of his doings there, including the oration he one day made to Jahāngīr in Persian (which he had now acquired, in addition to some Turkish and Arabic), will be found in the letters that follow. At last the time came for him to resume his wanderings. Roe was to accompany the Emperor in his progress southwards, and, since the march was likely to be an arduous one, only the ambassador's immediate attendants were to be taken, while the factory at Ajmer was to be dissolved as soon as possible after the departure of the Court. The only plan Coryat had formed (besides one of visiting the Ganges) was to return overland in the same way as he had come; and for this Agra was a convenient stage. He therefore took the opportunity of the departure of two of the English merchants for that city on September 12, 1616, to accompany them thither. At the time of his arrival, Agra was in the grip of the plague, but of this the intrepid traveller says nothing. One incident of his stay there is referred to by Terry (*infra*, p. 315); and from the same authority we learn that Coryat visited Akbar's tomb at Sikandra.

At the end of October 1616, when he wrote the last of his

extant letters, Coryat was still at the capital, but was intending in about six weeks' time to make an excursion to Hardwār, on the Ganges, and then to set out for Lahore on his homeward journey. We now lose sight of him for several months; but we know from Terry that he carried out his intention of visiting Hardwār, and that his tour included the famous temple of Jawāla Mūkhi, in Kāngra. Evidently, however, he still lingered for some time at Agra after his return. Possibly his health had already been affected by the climate; and since he was enjoying, as at Ajmer, the hospitality of the Company's factors, he was in no hurry to face the hardships of the long overland journey to Europe. In this uncertainty arrived a letter from Roe, written from the imperial headquarters at Māndu to one of the Agra factors on July 20, 1617, in which he expressed a desire to learn Coryat's 'purpose, for England or stay; or, if I take any new course, whither hee will goe with mee' (Brit. Mus., Addl. MS. 6115, f. 205). At this time the ambassador was half expecting to receive by the next fleet instructions to proceed to Persia (the 'new course' to which he referred), and otherwise he hoped to sail for England early in 1618. His invitation offered Coryat the chance of either going with Roe to Persia in comfort by sea, and then resuming his land journey, or of taking a passage home in the same ship as the ambassador. Accordingly he made his way down to Māndu, and spent several weeks in Roe's temporary home there. During his time Coryat shared the quarters of Chaplain Terry, who tells us a good deal about his strange companion and his doings.

Evidently the rest at Māndu was very necessary, for hard living and much travelling had told severely upon Coryat's health. One day he fainted in the ambassador's presence and was with difficulty brought to his senses. Moreover, he was troubled with a presentiment—born doubtless of his enfeebled condition—that he would never live to reach England and give his expectant countrymen the promised account of the wonders he had seen. Soon his plans were deranged by a new turn of events. The letters from England absolved Roe from going to Persia, while the slow progress of his negotiations rendered it doubtful whether he would be able to return home for yet another year. All that was clear was that the ambassador must follow the Emperor wherever he went, whether (as was expected) to Ahmadābād or (as some of the courtiers hoped) to Agra. When Jahāngīr left Māndu on October 24, 1617, his real intentions were still uncertain; and, perhaps in the hope that his destination would prove after all to be the capital, whence Coryat could set out afresh on the overland journey to Europe, our traveller started with Roe on October 29 to overtake the Emperor. Before, however, the party had got as far as Dhār, it was known for certain that Gujarāt was their goal; and thereupon, it would seem, Coryat decided to make his way down to Surat, where he was sure of hospitality at the English factory and might rest while he matured fresh plans. The date of his quitting the ambassador's camp seems to have been on or about November 13, 1617.[1] Of the incidents of this last lonely tramp nothing is recorded. We only know that he managed to reach his destination, and that the English merchants there received him kindly—too kindly in fact, for they plied him with sack, which increased the dysentery from which he was suffering, with the result that he rapidly succumbed to the illness. The date of his death, at the early age of forty, was some time in December 1617.

There was then no regular English burying-ground at Surat; so the body was taken outside the city on the north and interred on the western side of the road leading to Broach. It is true that Terry, who, as Coryat's contemporary, might be supposed to know the facts (though he was not at Surat when the death occurred), declares that the traveller was buried at Swally, 'amongst many more English that lye there interred'; but he was writing nearly forty years later, and, as we have seen, his recollection was frequently in fault over matters of detail.[2] The evidence on the other side is strong. Thomas Herbert, who reached India only ten years after Coryat's death, says that the body of a Persian ambassador, who had died aboard the English fleet at Swally, was 'conveighed to Surrat (10 miles thence), where they intombed him, not a stones cast from Tom Coryats grave, knowne but by two poore stones, there resting till the resurrection' (*Some Yeares Travels*, p. 35); while Dr. John Fryer, when at Surat in 1675, was shown, just outside the Broach Gate, the tomb of the Persian ambassador, 'not far from whence, on a small hill on

[1] This is inferred from an entry in the accounts of the Court Factory (India Office *Factory Records*, *Miscellaneous*, vol. xxv, f. 9), which shows that on that date Coryat paid in thirty-five rupees in cash and received in exchange a bill on the factors at Surat for the same amount. Two of Roe's letters to Surat (probably carried by Coryat) are dated November 11 and 12 respectively.

[2] It should be mentioned that the Admiralty chart of the coast near Swally marks 'Tom Coryat's Tomb'; but this is probably the monument at Rājgari, 'consisting of a dome resting on circular pillars', in a Muhammadan style of architecture, which, in the absence of any inscription or other clue, has been supposed to be the resting-place of the traveller (*List of Tombs and Monuments in the Bombay Presidency*). We know, however, that originally the grave had merely two small stones at head and foot, without an inscription; and there is no reason to suppose that a later generation provided an elaborate monument.

the left hand of the road, lies Tom Coriat, our English fakier (as they name him), together with an Armenian Christian, known by their graves lying east and west' (*New Account*, p. 100). It may be added that some years ago Mr. (now Sir William) Morison, who was then Collector at Surat, made an unsuccessful search for traces of Coryat's grave, and came to the conclusion that it had either been swept away or silted over by the periodical floods of the Tāpti.

In conclusion, a few words may be said regarding the literature of Coryat's Eastern travels. As we have learnt from Roe, the pilgrim left one batch of notes at Aleppo and another at Ispahān; while presumably he had a third with him at the time of his death. The first instalment found its way to England and came into the hands of Purchas, who, as already noted, printed considerable extracts in the second volume of his *Pilgrimes*. Of the fate of the other two portions nothing is known. Their loss is much to be deplored, for Coryat had a true gift of observation and narrated fully and accurately what he saw, including many small details which other travellers have passed over as unworthy of notice. Had he lived to publish as full an account of his Indian journey as he had previously given of his travels in Europe, it would probably have ranked as high as the works of Fryer or Tavernier; but unfortunately, all that we have from his own pen are the five letters here printed. Apart from these, there are some notes given to Purchas by Roe (see p. 276), and a few details and anecdotes preserved by Terry (p. 282). Finally, we may trace in Roe's journal and correspondence, as also in the map of India which he assisted Baffin to compile, items of information supplied to him by Coryat concerning parts of India which Roe himself had not visited. We have thus mere scraps of what might have been a feast. Our consolation is that even these scraps are better than nothing, and that, slight as they are, they contain much to make us remember with gratitude the eccentric wanderer who sleeps in an unknown grave on the banks of the Tāpti.

Turning to the letters themselves, we may note that the first four were printed, almost immediately after their arrival in England, in a pamphlet entitled *Thomas Coriate, Traveller for the English Wits: Greeting*, illustrated with some rough woodcuts. Apparently this production excited considerable interest, for a reprint was issued with the same date.[1] The fifth letter was published in similar form two years later, under the title of *Mr. Thomas Coriat to his Friends in England sendeth Greeting*, adorned by a picture of the author riding on a camel.

[1] 1616. Of course this would extend to March 24, 1617, according to modern reckoning.

In 1625 Purchas, in his *Pilgrimes* (part i, book iv, chap. 17), reprinted large portions of the first, third, and fifth; and the fifth was again reproduced, five years later, in a volume containing the works of John Taylor, the Water Poet. The 1776 edition of Coryat's works gives the first four letters in full, while as regards the fifth it is content to follow the abbreviated version supplied by Purchas. Since then there has been no fresh edition of the letters from India, though Purchas's extracts from them were of course included in the recent reissue of the *Pilgrimes*. The text now given is from the British Museum copies of the 1616 and 1618 pamphlets, omitting the commendatory and other verses.

I

Most deare and beloved Friend, Maister L. W.,[1] *animæ dimidium meæ.*

Cordial salutations in the Author of Salvation, Jesus Christ. Where I writ unto you last I remember wel; even from Zobah, as the Prophet Samuel calleth it (2 *Booke*, 8 chap., ver. 3), that is, Aleppo,[2] the principall emporium of all Syria, or rather of the orient world; but when, in trueth I have forgotten, for I keepe not coppies of my letters, as I see most of my countrey-men doe, in whatsoever place of the worlde I finde them. Howbeit, if my conjecture doe not much faile me, I may affirme that it was about xv. moneths since, about a month after I returned unto Aleppo from Jerusalem; after which time I remained there three months longer, and then departed therehence in a caravan into Persia, passing the noble river Euphrates (the cheefest of all that irrigated Paradise wherehence, as from their original, the three other rivers were derived) about foure dayes journey beyond Aleppo; on the farther side of which I entered Mesapotamia, alias Chaldea, for the Euphrates in that place disterminateth Syria and Mesopotamia. Therehence I had two dayes journey to Ur [Orfah] of the Chaldeans, where Abraham was born, a very

[1] Laurence Whitaker, who (as shown by the next letter) was secretary to Sir Edward Phelips. He contributed some laudatory poems to the *Crudities*, as well as a prose eulogy.

[2] This identification is not accepted by modern commentators, who place Zobah farther south.

delicate and pleasant cittie. There I remained foure dayes; but I could see no part of the ruines of the house wher that faithful servant of God was borne, though I much desired it. From thence I had foure dayes journey to the river Tigris, which I passed also; but in the same place where I crossed it I found it so shallow that it reached no higher then the calfe of my legge; for I waded over it afoot. Now I wel perceive, by mine occular experience, that Chaldea is named Mesopotamia for that it is inclosed with the foresaid rivers. *Trajecto Tigride,* I entred Armenia the Greater; after that, Media the Lower, and resided six dayes in the metropolis therof, heretofore called Ecbatana, the sommer seate of Cyrus his court, a city eftsoone mentioned in the Scripture, now called Tauris [Tabrīz]. More wofull ruines of a city (saving that of Troy and Cyzicum [1] in Natolia) never did mine eies beholde. When I seriously contemplated those ἐρείπια [i. e. ruins], the doleful testimonies of the Turkish devastations, I called to minde Ovids verse:

***Ludit in humanis divina potentia rebus.*[2]**

And that of Hesiod,

τὰ δ' ὑπέρτερα νέρτερα θήσει Ζεὺς ὑψιβρεμέτης.[3]

From that I had two daies journey to a city that in Strabos time was called Arsacia, in Media the Higher, now Casbin, once the royall seate of the Tartarian princes, 4 daies journy from the Caspian Sea. From Casbin I had 23 daies to Spahan, in Parthia, the place of residence of the Persian K[ing]; but at my being there he was in the countrey of Gurgistan, ransacking the poor Christians ther with great hostility, with fire and sword.[4] There I remained 2 months, and so with a caravan travelled into the Easterne India, passing 4 months and odde daies in my travell betwixt that (through part of the true

[1] Now Kyzik, on the southern shore of the sea of Marmora.

[2] *Epist. ex Ponto,* lib. iv, epist. iii, l. 49.

[3] This is really from Aristophanes (*Lysistrata,* 772); but, as Dr. Thomas points out, Coryat was probably thinking of line 8 of Hesiod's *Works and Days.*

[4] The campaign of Shāh Abbās in Georgia is mentioned by Roe (*Embassy,* pp. 113, 121), but he doubtless had his information from Coryat.

Persia, and a large tract of the noble and renownd India) and the goodly city of Lahore in India, one of the largest cities of the whole universe, for it containeth at the least xvi. miles in compasse and exceedeth Constantinople itself in greatnesse. But a dozen dayes before I came to Lahore I passed the famous river Indus, which is as broad againe as our Thames at London, and hath his originall out of the mountaine Caucasus,[1] so much ennobled by the ancient, both poets and historiographers, Greeke and Latine; which Plato for curiosity sake, in his travelles of these parts, went to see. It lyeth not farre from that upon the confines of Scythia, now called Tartaria; my selfe also conceiving some hope of seeing it before my finall farewel of India.

I had almost forgotten one memorable matter to impart unto you: About the middle of the way, betwixt Spahan and Lahore, just about the frontiers of Persia and India, I met Sir Robert Sherley and his lady, travailing from the court of the Mogul (where they had beene verie graciously received, and enriched with presents of great value) to the King of Persia's court; so gallantly furnished with all necessaries for their travailes that it was a great comfort unto me to see them in such a florishing estate. There did he shew mee, to my singular contentment, both my bookes neatly kept; and hath promised me to shew them, especially mine itinerarie, to the Persian King, and to interpret unto him some of the principall matters in the Turkish tongue, to the end I may have the more gracious accesse unto him after my returne thither; for through Persia I have determined (by Gods helpe) to returne to Aleppo. Besides other rarities that they carried with them out of India, they had two elephants and eight antlops, which were the first that ever I saw; but afterwards, when I came to the Moguls court, I sawe great store of them. These they meant to present to the Persian King. Both he and his lady used me with singular respect, especially his lady, who bestowed forty shillings upon me in Persian mony; and they seemed to exult for joy to see mee, having promised me to bring mee in good grace with the Persian King, and that

[1] The range of the Hindu Kush was known to ancient geographers as the Indian Caucasus.

they will induce him to bestow some princely benefit upon me. This I hope will be partly occasioned by my booke, for he is such a jocond prince that he will not be meanlie delighted with divers of my facetious hieroglyphicks, if they are truelie and genuinely expounded unto him.

From the famous citie of Lahore I had twentie daies journey to another goodly citie, called Agra, through such a delicate and eeven tract of ground as I never saw before, and doubt whether the like bee to be found within the whole circumference of the habitable world. Another thing also in this way beeing no lesse memorable then the plainenesse of the ground; a row of trees on each side of this way where people doe travell, extending it selfe from the townes end of Lahore to the townes end of Agra; the most incomparable shew of that kinde that ever my eies survaied. Likewise wheras ther is a mountaine some ten daies journey betwixt Lahore and Agra, but verie neere ten miles out of the way on the left hand, the people that inhabite that mountaine observe a custome very strange, that all the brothers of any familie have but one and the selfesame wife, so that one woman sometimes doth serve 6 or 7 men [1]: the like whereof I remember I have read in Strabo, concerning the Arabians that inhabited Arabia Felix. Agra is a verie great citie, and the place where the Mogul did alwaies (saving within these two yeares) keepe his court; but in everie respect much inferior to Lahore. From thence to the Moguls court I had ten daies journey, at a towne called Asmere, where I found a cape merchant of our English men, with nine more of my countrimen, resident there upon termes of negotiations for the Right Worshipfull Company of Merchants in London that Trade for East India. I spent in my journey betwixt Jerusalem and this Moguls court 15 moneths and odde daies; all which way I traversed afoot, but with divers paire of shooes, having beene such a propateticke (I will not call my selfe peripatetick, because you know it signifieth one that maketh a perambulation about a place, περιπατεῖν signifying to walk about), that is, a walker forward on foote, as I doubt whether

[1] Polyandry is still common in parts of the Dehra Dūn and other Himālayan tracts. For a discussion of the passage in Strabo, see Robertson Smith's *Kinship and Marriage in Early Arabia*, p. 133.

you ever heard of the like in your life; for the totall way betwixt Jerusalem and the Moguls court containeth two thousand and seaven hundred English miles. My whole perambulation of this Asia the Greater is like to bee a passage of almost sixe thousande miles, by that time that in my returne backe thorough Persia, afterward also by Babylon and Ninivie, I shall come to Cairo in Egypt, and from that downe the Nylus to Alexandria, there to be one daie (by Gods helpe) imbarqued for Christendome; a verie immense dimension of ground.

Now I am at the Moguls court, I think you would be glad to receive some narration thereof from mee, though succinctly handled: for I meane to be very compendious, lest I shold otherwise preoccupate that pleasure which you may here after this reape by my personall relation thereof. This present prince is a verie worthy person, by name Selim, of which name I never read or heard of any more then one Mahometan king, which was Sultan Selim of Constantinople, that lived about 80 years since; the same that conquered Jerusalem, Damascus, Aleppo, Cairo, etc., adding the same to the Turkish Empire. He is 53 yeares of age,[1] his nativitie daie having beene celebrated with wonderfull pompe since my arrivall here; for that daie he weighed himselfe in a paire of golden scales, which by great chance I saw the same day (a custome that he observeth most inviolablie every year) laying so muc golde in the other scale as countervaileth the weight of his body, and the same he afterward distributed to the poore. Hee is of complexion neither white nor blacke, but of a middle betwixt them; I know not how to expresse it with a more expressive and significant epitheton then olive; an olive colour his face presenteth. Hee is of a seemelie composition of bodie, of a stature little unequall (as I guesse, not without grounds of probabilitie) to mine, but much more corpulent then my selfe. The extent of his dominion is verie spacious, beeing in circuite little lesse then 4000 English miles, which verie neere answereth the compas of the Turks territories; or if any thing be wanting in geometricall dimension of ground, it is with a great pleonasme supplied by the fertility of his soyle. And in these two thinges hee exceedeth the Turks, in

[1] Jahāngir was really only forty-six, having been born in 1569.

the fatnesse (as I have said) of his land, no part of the world yeelding a more fruitfull veine of ground then all that which lieth in his empire, saving that part of Babylonia where the terrestriall paradise once stoode; whereas a great part of the Turks land is extreme barren and sterill, as I have observed in my peregrination thereof, especially in Syria, Mesopotamia and Armenia; many large portions thereof beeing so wonderfull fruitelesse that it beareth no good thing at all, or if any thing, there *infelix lolium et steriles dominantur avenæ*.[1] Secondly, in the conjunction and union of all his territories together in one and the same goodly continent of India, no prince having a foote of land within him. But many parcels of the Turkes countries are by a large distance of seas and otherwise divided asunder. Again, in his revenue he exceedeth the Turk and the Persian his neighbour by just halfe; for his revenues are 40 millions of crownes (of sixe shillings value) by the yeare,[2] but the Turkes are no more then fifteene millions (as I was certainly informed in Constantinople), and the Persians five millions, *plus minus* (as I heard in Spahan). It is saide that he is uncircumcised, wherein he differeth from all the Mahometan princes that ever were in the world.

Hee speaketh very reverently of our Saviour, calling him in the Indian tongue *Isazaret Eesa* [*Hazarat Īsa*], that is, the Great Prophet Jesus; and all Christians, especiallie us English, he useth so benevolently as no Mahometan prince the like. Hee keepeth abundance of wilde beasts, and that of divers sorts, as lyons, elephants, leopards, beares, antlops, unicornes; whereof two I have seene at his court, the strangest beasts of the world.[3] They were brought hither out of the countrie of Bengala, which is a kingdom of most singular fertilitie within the compasse of his dominion, about four moneths journey

[1] This is from Virgil's *Georgics*, bk. i, l. 154.

[2] Presumably his informant gave the amount as 120 millions of rupees, which Coryat converted at the rate of 2*s*. to the rupee (the value he adopts elsewhere). Even assigning a higher value to the rupee, and supposing the figure to relate to land revenue only, it is probably too low an estimate (cf. Hawkins, *supra*, p. 99, and Thomas's *Revenue Resources*, p. 26).

[3] In the original pamphlet a fanciful portrait of a unicorn is here inserted. The beasts mentioned by Coryat were of course rhinoceroses.

from this, the midland parts therof being watered by divers channels of the famous Ganges, which I have not as yet seene, but (God willing) I meane to visite it before my departure out of this countrie, the neerest part of it beeing not above twelve daies journy from this court. The King presenteth himselfe thrice every daie without faile to his nobles ; at the rising of the sunne, which he adoreth by the elevation of his hands ; at noone ; and at five of the clocke in the evening. But he standeth in a roome aloft, alone by him selfe, and looketh uppon them from a window that hath an embroidered sumptuous coverture, supported with two silver pillasters to yeeld shaddowe unto him. Twice every week elephants fight before him, the bravest spectacle in the worlde. Many of them are thirteene foot and a halfe high ; and they seeme to justle together like two little mountaines, and were they not parted in the middest of their fighting by certaine fire-workes, they would exceedingly gore and cruentate one another by their murdering teeth. Of elephants the King keepeth 30,000 in his whole kingdome at an unmeasurable charge ; in feeding of whom, and his lyons and other beasts, he spendeth an incredible masse of money, at the least ten thousand pounds sterling a day.[1] I have rid upon an elephant since I came to this court, determining one day (by Gods leave) to have my picture expressed in my next booke sitting upon an elephant.[2] The king keepeth a thousand women for his own body, whereof the chiefest (which is his Queene) is called Normal.

I thinke I shall here after this send another letter unto you before my departure out of this countrey, by a worthy man, which is the minister and preacher of our nation in this place, one M. Peter Rogers, a man to whom I am exceedingly obliged for his singular offices of humanity exhibited unto me. Pray use him kindly for my sake. Hee understanding that there is a certaine yong gentleman, called Maister Charles Lancaster, that serveth the M[aster] of the Rolles, intreated me to desire

[1] This appears to be an exaggeration (cf. *supra*, p. 104).

[2] Though Coryat did not live to issue another book, the publishers of the 1616 pamphlet remembered his wish and placed on the title-page a fancy sketch of him riding upon an elephant. This illustration appears three times.

you to recommend him very kindly unto him. Our cape-merchants name is M. William Edwards, an honest gentleman, that useth me with verie loving respect.

Dear M. L. W., conveigh these twoe letters that I have sent to you, to the parties to whom they are directed: my poore mother and mine unckle Williams. You may do me a kinde office to desire him (with such convenient termes and patheticall perswasions as your discretion shall dictate and suggest unto you) to remember me as his poore industrious peregrinating kinseman, neerest unto him in blood of all the people in the world; to remember me, I say, with some competent gratuitie, if God should call him out of the world before my returne into my native countrie. I praie you, if hee be living, and doth use to come to London as he was wont to doo, that you would deliver my letter to him with your owne hands, and not send it unto him.

You may remember to relate this unto your friends that I will now mention as a matter verie memorable: I spent in my ten moneths travels betwixt Aleppo and the Moguls court but three pounds sterling, yet fared reasonable well everie daie; victuals beeing so cheape in some countries where I travelled, that I oftentimes lived competentlie for a pennie sterling a day. Yet of that three pound I was cousened of no lesse then ten shillings sterling by certaine lewd Christians of the Armenian nation; so that indeed I spent but fiftie shillings in my ten moneths travailes. I have beene in a citie in this countrie, called Detee [Delhi], where Alexander the Great joyned battell with Porus, K[ing] of India, and conquered him; and in token of his victorie erected a brasse pillar, which remaineth there to this day.[1]

Pray remember my humblest service to the Right

[1] Terry, in his 1655 edition (p. 81), says: 'I was told by Tom Coryat (who took special notice of this place) that he, being in the city of Dellee, observed a very great pillar of marble, with a Greek inscription upon it which Time hath almost quite worn out, erected (as he supposed) there and then by great Alexander, to preserve the memory of that famous victory' [over King Porus]. Roe also mentions this monument (*Embassy*, p. 103), no doubt on Coryat's authority. The reference seems to be to the Asoka pillar described by Finch (*supra*, p. 156). It is of stone, not of brass as stated in the text.

P. 248

CORYAT ON AN ELEPHANT

Honourable, your Maister of the Rolles, *si superatque, et vescitur aura ætherea, nec adhuc crudelibus occubat umbris.*[1] And to Sir Robert Phillips, once my Mecænas, but how affected to me at this time I know not. Pray tell them that I meane to write to each of them before my departure out of India. Remember my duty also to their right vertuous ladies. About foure yeares hence looke for me, but not before. For if God grant me life and health, I meane to make it a voyage of full seaven yeares before I come home, whereof three are already spent. Commend me also, I pray you, to M. Martin,[2] though at a mans house in Woodstreet he used mee one night verie perversly before I came away; but you see that my being at Jerusalem dooth make me forget many injuries. Commend mee likewise to Maister H. Holland[3] and Inigo Jones.[4] At this time I have many irons in the fire; for I learne the Persian, Turkish, and Arabian tongues, having already gotten the Italian (I thank God). I have bene at the Moguls court three moneths already, and am to tarry heere (by Gods holy permission) five moneths longer, till I have gotten the foresaide three tongues, and then depart herehence to the Ganges, and after that directly to the Persian court.

Your assured loving friend till death,
THO. CORYATE.

From the court of the Great Mogul, resident at the towne of Asmere, in the Eastern India, on Michaelmas day, anno 1615.

I do enjoy at this time as pancraticall and athleticall a health as ever I did in my life; and so have done ever since I came out

[1] This is a combination of two passages from the *Aeneid*: *Superatne et vescitur aura?* (bk. iii, l. 339) and *Si vescitur aura aetheria, neque adhuc crudelibus occubat umbris* (bk. i, l. 546).

[2] Richard Martin, Recorder of London, still remembered as a wit and poet.

[3] Hugh Holland, poet and traveller. He wrote a sonnet prefixed to the first folio of Shakespeare.

[4] The celebrated architect. Both he and Holland wrote laudatory poems for the *Crudities*.

of England, saving for three dayes in Constantinople, where I had an ague, which with a little letting blood was clean banished; the Lord be humbly thanked for His gracious blessing of health that Hee hath given me. I was robbed of my money, both golde and silver (but not all, by reason of certaine clandestine corners where it was placed), in a cittie called Diarbeck in Mesopotamia, the Turks countrey, by a Spaheê [*Spāhi*], as they call him, that is, one of the horsemen of the Great Turke; but the occasion and circumstance of that misfortune would be too tedious to relate. Notwithstanding that losse, I am not destitute of money, I thanke God. Since my arrivall heere, there was sente unto this King one of the richest presents that I have heard to be sent to any prince in al my life time. It consisteth of divers parcels; one beeing elephants, whereof there were 31, and of those two so gloriously adorned as I never sawe the like, nor shal see the like again while I live. For they wore foure chaines about their bodies all of beaten gold; two chains about their legges of the same; furniture for their buttocks of pure gold; twoe lyons upon their heads of the like gold; the ornaments of each amounting to the value of almost eight thousand pound sterling; and the whole present was worth ten of their leakes [i.e. lakhs], as they call them (a leak being ten thousand pound sterling); the whole, a hundred thousand pounds sterling.[1]

Pray commend me to M[aster] Protoplast and all the Sireniacall[2] gentlemen; to whom I wrote one letter from Aleppo, after my being at Jerusalem, and another I intend to write before my going out of Asia. Their most elegant and incomparable safe-conduct that they have graciously bestowed upon me I have left at Aleppo, not having made any use of it as yet, neither shall I in all my peregrination of Asia; but when I shall one day arrive in Christendome, it will be very available to me.

[1] This embassy was from the King of Bījāpur, and reached Ajmer about the middle of August 1615 (see the *Tūzuk*, vol. i, p. 298).

[2] The members of the Mermaid Club called themselves Sireniacs (cf. p. 256)—a term due to the confusion of the mermaid with the Siren. Possibly there was also a playful allusion to the Cyrenaic philosophers, who held that pleasure was the chief aim of life. Who was meant by 'Master Protoplast' has not been ascertained.

I have heere sent unto you the coppy of certaine facetious verses that were lately sent to me to this court, from one of my countrimen, one M. John Browne,[1] a Londoner borne, now resident, with divers other English merchants, at a citie in India, five hundred miles from the place where I abide, called Amadavers, about sixe dayes journey from the sea; who, understanding of my arrivall at this court, and of my tedious pedestriall peregrination all the way from Jerusalem hither (understanding it, I say, by Latine and Italian epistles that upon a certaine occasion I wrote to some of that company), made these pretty verses, and sent them me. You may reade them to your friends, if you thinke fit, and especially to the Sireniacall gentlemen; for they are elegant and delectable. The superscription of his letter was this: To the painefull gentleman, M. Thomas Coryate. The title within, prefixed before the verses, this: To the Odcombian wonder, our laborious countriman, the generous Coryate. . . .[2]

Yet one post-script more by way of a corollary, and so with the same, beeing the fourth and the last, I will adde the final umbilicke to this tedious English-Indian epistle. I have written out two severall coppies of these verses, and included them within the letters which I have intreated you to distribute for me, but so that the letters are not scaled upon them, onely they lie loose within the letters; therefore they are subject to losing, except you have an extraordinary care of them. Wherefore I intreate you to deliver that to mine unkle with your owne hands, if he be in London, or to conveigh it to him by such a one as will not lose that loose paper of verses. The like care I desire you to have of that to my mother, and to send it unto her by some other man then a carrier, if you can jet [meet ?] with such an opportunity: for in truth I am afraide the carrier will lose the inclosed paper. Pray take advice of some of the M[aster] of the Rolles his people that are to ride to Euill.[3] Pray remember my commendations with all respect to M. Williams the goldsmith and his wife; and to Benjamin

[1] Went out to India in 1614. He was chief of the Ahmadābād factory from early in 1616 to his death in April, 1620.

[2] The verses have been omitted, as not worth quoting.

[3] Yeovil, the nearest town to Odcombe.

Johnson, and to reade this letter to them both; likewise to Mistris Elizabeth Balch, if shee continueth with your lady.

One appendix more, and so an end. There happened betwixt the day of the writing of this letter and the day of the sealing of it up, a memorable occurrent not to bee omitted. Wee received newes at this court the ninth day after the writing of this letter (for nine daies it was unsealed), being the eight of October, of the arrivall of foure goodly English ships at the haven of Surat in India, and in the same of a very generous and worthy English knight, a deare friend of mine, Sir Thomas Rowe, to come to the court with some mature expedition, as an ambassadour from the Right Worshipfull Company of London Merchants that Trade for India. He cometh with letters from our King and certaine selected presents of good worth from the Company; amongst the rest a gallant caroch, of 150 pounds price.[1] Also there came with him 15 servants, al Englishmen. Forty daies hence at the farthest, we expect (θεοῦ διδόντος [2]) his arrival at this court. This newes doth refocillate (I will use my olde phrase so well knowne to you) my spirits; for I hope he will use me graciously, for old acquaintance sake.

II

To The Right Honourable Sir Edward Phillips, Knight, and Maister of the Rolles, at his house in Chancery-Lane, or Wanstead.[3]

Right Honourable,

I am perswaded that if ever any accident worthy of admiration ever happened unto Your Honor in al your life time, it will be the receiving of this present letter from me out of the

[1] Particulars of this coach are given in *The Embassy of Sir Thomas Roe*, p. 322.

[2] 'God granting it.'

[3] Sir Edward Phelips, Speaker of the House of Commons (1604) and Master of the Rolls (1611), was the fourth son of Thomas Phelips, Coryat's godfather. The family seat was at Montacute, near Odcombe. In 1612 Sir Edward rented Wanstead House (afterwards the residence of Sir Josia Child), and there entertained King James, at a cost (it is said) of £700. He was dead at the time when Coryat was writing this letter.

Easterne India; yet perhaps it will seeme unto you so wondrous that I beleeve you will doubt whether this bee the true handwriting of your once Odcombian neighbor, Thomas Coryate. But Your Honour may soone very infallibly and apparantly perceive it to be true, partly by the forme of the style, which is just answerable to that manner of speech that you have heard and observed in me, sometimes in my linsie-woolsie orations and somtimes in my extravagant discourses; and partly by the testimony of the bearer heereof, M[aster] Peter Rogers, minister, at the time of his being in India, to the English merchants resident at the court of the most puissant monarch the Great Mogul, at a town called Asmere; whose comfortable and sweet company I enjoyed at the same court about the space of foure moneths.

Now, though there hath itched a very burning desire in mee, within these few yeares, to survay and contemplate some of the chiefest parts of this goodly fabricke of the world besides mine owne native country, yet never did I thinke it would have broken out to such an ambitious vent as to travell all on foote from Jerusalem so farre as the place where I wrote this letter. Howbeit since fortune, or rather (to speake more properly, in using a Christian word) the providence of the Almighty, (for *Fatuus est*, S. Augustine saith, *qui fato credit*) hath so ordained that I should securely passe so far into the orientall world, with all humilitie, upon the bended knees of my hart, I thank my Creator and merciful Redeemer, Jesus Christ (whose sacrosanct sepulcher I have visited and kissed, *terque quaterque*, in Jerusalem), and do very much congratulate mine owne happines that He hath hitherto endued mee with health (for in all my travels since I came out of England I have enjoyed as sound a constitution of body and firme health as ever I did since I first drew this vitall ayre), libertie, strength of limbs, agilitie of foot-manship, etc.

Neither do I doubt but that Your Honour it selfe will likewise congratulate the felicitie of our Sommersetshire, that in breeding me hath produced such a traveller as dooth, for the diversitie of the countries he hath seene and the multiplicitie of his observations, farre (I beleeve) out-strippe anie other whatsoever that hath beene bred therein since the blessed

Incarnation of our Saviour. Yea, I hope my generall countrie of England shall one day say that Odde-combe, for one part of the word, may truelie be so called (for Odde-combe consisteth of two words, odde and combe, which latter word in the olde Saxon tongue signifieth, besides the vertical point of a cocks head, the side of a hill, because the east side of the hill whereon Od-combe standeth is very conspicuous, and seene afar off in the country eastward) for breeding an odde man, one that hath not his peere in the whole kingdome to match him.

Three yeares and some few odde dayes I have spent already in this second peregrination, and I hope with as much profite (unpartially will I speake it of my selfe, without any overweening opinion, to which most men are subject), both for learning foure languages more then I had when I left my country (viz. Italian, Arabian, Turkish, and Persian) and exact viewing of divers of the most remarkeable matters of the universe; together with the accurate description thereof, as most of my countri-men that are now abroad. Yet such is my insatiable greedinesse of seeing strange countries (which exercise is indeede the very queene of all the pleasures in the world) that I have determined (if God shall say Amen) to spend full seaven yeares more, to the ende to make my voyage answerable for the time to the travels of Ulysses; and then with unspeakable joy to revisite my country, which I will ever entitle (notwithstanding all the goodly regions that I have seene in my two perambulations) with the stile of the true Canaan of the world, that flowes with milke and hony. Onely wish me good successe, I beseech Your Honour, as I will from my heart to you and all your familie; hoping to salute you after the finall catastrophe of my exoticke wanderings, when you shall bee in the great climacterical year of your age; you being about fifty three, if my conjecture doth not faile mee, when I tooke my leave of you; a thing verie likely, by the mercifull goodnesse of God, for your father, that was my god-father, who imposed upon me the name of Thomas, lived more then eightie yeares.

Honourable Sir, take it not (I beseech you) for a discourtesie, in that I write nothing in this letter of my past travels. I am certaine that a letter which I have written to M[aster] Whitaker, your learned and elegant secretary, wherein I have compendiouslie discoursed of some of my observations in Asia, will quicklie come to your hands, at least if hee remaineth still in your service; therfore it would be superfluous to have repeated the same things. Dutie joyned with the recordation of the manifold benefits and singular favours I have received from you, hath injoyned mee to send this letter to Your Honour, from this glorious court of the Mogul; wherein, seeing I relate not the singularities I have seene in those orientall regions, I will desist to be farther tedious; humbly recommending Your Honour, and vertuous lady: your well-beloved sonne and heire-apparant, Sir Robert[1] (to whom I have written a few times [lines ?] also) and his sweet lady: M. Martin [see p. 249] also: M. Christopher Brooke,[2] whom I thanke still for his no lesse elegant then serious verses: M. Equinoctiall Pasticrust, of the Middle Temple[3]: M. William Hackwell[4]: and the rest of the worthy gentlemen frequenting your honourable table, that favour vertue and the sacred Muses: to the most heavenly clientele of the Eternall Jehovah.

Your Honors most obsequious beadsman,

THOMAS CORYATE.

From the court of the Great Mogul, resident in the towne of Asmere, in the Easterne India, on Michaelmas day, Anno 1615.

I beseech Your Honour to speake courteously to this kind minister, M. Rogers, for my sake; for he ever shewed himselfe very loving unto me.

[1] Sir Robert Phelips, a prominent parliamentarian. He was knighted at the same time as his father (1603).

[2] Brooke was a lawyer and a friend of Ben Jonson. His poems were reprinted in 1872.

[3] John Hoskins (see p. 258) was another friend of Jonson and a well-known wit.

[4] William Hakewill, legal antiquary and parliamentarian.

III

To the High Seneschall of the Right Worshipfull Fraternitie of Sireniacal Gentlemen, that meet the first Fridaie of every moneth at the signe of the Mere-Maide in Bread-streete in London, give these.[1]

From the court of the Great Mogul, resident at the towne of Asmere, in the Easterne India.

Right generous, joviall, and mercuriall Sirenaicks, I have often read this Greeke proverb, χεὶρ χεῖρα νίπτει,[2] that is, one hand washeth another, and in Latine, *Mulus mulum scabit*,[3] one mule scratcheth another; by which the ancients signified that courtesies done unto friends ought to bee requited with reciprocall offices of friendship. The serious consideration heereof dooth make me to call to mind that incomparable elegant safe-conduct, which, a little before my departure from England, your Fraternity with a general suffrage gave me for the security of my future peregrination, concinnated by the pleasant wit of that inimitable artizan of sweet elegancy, the moytie of my heart, and the quondam Seneschall of the noblest Society, M[aster] L. W[hitaker]. Therefore, since it is requisite that I should repay some-what for the same, according to the lawes of humanity, such a poore retribution as I sent unto you from Aleppo, the metropolitan city of Syria, by one M. Henry Allare of Kent, my fellow-pilgrime therehence to Jerusalem (I meane a plaine epistle, which I hope long since came unto your hands), I have sent unto you by a man no lesse deare unto mee then the former, one M. Peter Rogers, a Kentish man also, from the most famigerated region of all the East, the ample and large India; assuring my selfe that because I am not able to requite your love with any essentiall gratulations, other then verball and scriptall, you wil as lovingly entertaine my poore letters, beeing the certaine manifestation of an ingenious minde, as if I should send unto you the minerall riches or drugges of the noble country.

[1] Purchas notes that Rogers delivered this letter to him.

[2] This proverb occurs among the fragments of Epicharmus, in the form χεὶρ τὰν χεῖρα νίζει.

[3] Ausonius (*Idyllia*, 12) has *Mutuum muli scabunt*.

Thinke it no wonder, I pray you, that I have made no use in all this space, since I left my native country, of the super-excellent *commeate* [passport; Latin *commeatus*]; for I have spent all my time hitherto in the Mahometan countries, and am like to spend three yeares more in these Musselman (as they call them) regions of Asia, after of Europe, before I shal arrive in Christendome. For this cause I left it in Aleppo, with my countrimen, there to receive it from them againe, after that I shall have ended my Indian and Persian perambulation; and therethence to carrie it once more to Constantinople, and that by the way at Iconium, Nicæa, Nicomedia, and in the country of Natolia, a journie of forty daies. From that finally through the heart of Greece, by the cities of Athens, Thebes, Corinth, Lacedæmon, Thessalonica, and to the citie of Ragouze, heretofore Epidaurus, so sacred for the image of Aesculapius in the countrie of Sclavonia, once called Illyricum; from thence, I have three daies journey to the inestimable diamond set in the ring of the Adriatique Gulfe (as once I said in the first harangue that ever I made to Prince Henry of blessed memory, translated, since my departure from London, from the terrestriall tabernacles to the cœlestial habitations), venereous Venice, the soveraign queen of the *Mare Superum*. If the great Jehovah shall be so propitious unto mee as to grant mee a prosperous arrivall in that noble cittie, I will there beginne to shew your safe conduct, and to decantate, yea, and blazon your praises for the same; and after in every other place of note, untill I shall arrive in glorious London, communicate it to the most polite, with that the cities will yeeld, thorough which my laborious feete shall carry mee.

It would be supervacaneous to commemorate unto you the almost incredible extent of land I traversed from Jerusalem to the court of the Great Mogul in India, where I now reside; with the variable regions and provinces interjacent betwixt them, and the manifold occurrences and observations of speciall worke [worth ?] in this vaste tract: for it wold be such a fastidious discourse that it could not be wel comprehended in a large sheete of paper. But M[aster] W[hitaker], I hope, will not faile to import unto you in a few compendious relations, which I have acquainted him with, in a particular letter to himselfe; of which if I should have written againe to you, it would have proved *Crambe bis Cocta*.

The gentleman that bringeth this letter unto you was preacher to the English merchants conversant at the court of the aforesaide mighty monarch in the towne of Asmere in this Easterne India; and in divers loving offices hath bene so kind unto me that I intreat your generosities to entertaine him friendly for my sake, to exhilarate him with the purest quintessence of the Spanish, French, and Rhenish grape which the Mermaid yeeldeth; and either one in the name of you all, or else the totall universalitie of the one after another, to thanke him heartily, according to the quality of his merits. Farewell, noble Sirenaicks.

Your Generosities most obliged countreyman, ever to be commanded by you, the Hierosolymitan-Syrian-Mesopotamian-Armenian-Median-Parthian-Persian-Indian Leggestretcher of Odcomb in Somerset,

THOMAS CORYATE.[1]

[1] In a postscript, dated 8 Nov., 1615, is given a list of persons to whom Coryat desired to be commended. This includes 'the two Ladies Varney, the mother and the daughter'; 'that famous antiquarie, Sir Robert Cotten'; 'Master William Ford Preacher to our nation at Constantinople'; George Speake, son of Sir George Speake; John Donne; Richard Martin, of the Middle Temple; Christopher Brooke, of York and Lincoln's Inn; John Hoskins, 'alias Æquinoctiall Pasticrust'; George Garrat; William Hackwell or Hakewill, of Lincoln's Inn; 'Benjamin Johnson, the poet, at his chamber at the Black-Friars'; John Bond, chief secretary to the Lord Chancellor; 'Master Doctor Mocket'; and Samuel Purchas. There is also a postscript containing a message to the Bishop of Bath and Wells [James Montague], promising to write him a letter which 'shall not bee unworthy to bee read to the Kings most excellent Majesty'.

Some of the persons mentioned require no introduction to the reader, and others have been already described on pp. 249, 255. Several of them had contributed laudatory verses to the *Crudities*. The Ladies Verney were Mary, third wife of Sir Edmund Verney the elder, and Ursula, her daughter by a former husband, wife of Sir Francis Verney. Bond was a physician and classical scholar, secretary to Lord Chancellor Egerton; and Dr. Richard Mocket was Warden of All Souls and a theologian of some repute.

IV

To his Loving Mother.

By this present letter I am like to minister unto you the occasion of two contrary matters, the one of comfort, the other of discomfort. Of comfort, because I have, by the propitious assistance of the omnipotent Jehovah, performed such a notable voyage of Asia the Greater, with purchase of great riches of experience, as I doubt whether any English man this hundred yeares have done the like ; having seene and very particularly observed all the cheefest things in the Holy-land, called in times past Palastina ; as Jerusalem, Samaria, Nazareth, Bethlehem, Jericho, Emaus, Bethania, the Dead Sea, called by the Ancients Lacus Asphaltites, where Sodome and Gomorrha once stood. Since that, many famous and renowned cities and countries ; Mesopotamia, in the which I entred by the passage of the river Euphrates, that watered Paradise ; in which the citty of Ur, where Abraham was borne ; both the Mediaes, the Higher and the Lower ; Parthia, Armenia, Persia ; through al which I have travailed into the Eastern India, being now at the court of the Great Mogull, at a towne called Asmere, the which from Jerusalem is the distance of two thousand and seaven hundred miles ; and have traced all this tedious way afoote, with no small toile of bodye and discomfort.

Because that beeing so exceeding farre from my sweet and most delicious native soyle of England you will doubt perhaps, how it is possible for me to returne home againe ; but I hope I shall quickly remove from you that opinion of discomfort (if at the least you shall conceive any such), because I would have you know that I alwayes go safely in the company of caravans from place to place. A caravan is a word much used in all Asia ; by which is understood a great multitude of people travelling together upon the way, with camels, horses, mules, asses, etc., on which they carry merchandizes from one country to another, and tents and pavillions, under which instead of houses they shelter themselves in open fields, being furnished also with all necessary provision, and convenient implements to dresse the same; in which caravans I have ever most securely passed betwixt Jerusalem and this towne, a journey of fifteene months and odde dayes; whereof foure (wanting a weeke) spent in Aleppo, and two and five and od dayes spent in Spahan, the metropolitan citty of Persia, where the Persian King most commonly keepeth his court. And the occasion of my spending of sixe moneths of the foresaide fifteene in those two citties, was to waite for an opportunity of caravans to travaile withall; which a traveller is not sure to finde presently when he is ready to take his journey, but must with patience expect a convenient time; and the caravan in which I travelled betwixt Spahan and India contained 2000 camels, 1500 horses, 1000 and odde mules, 800 asses, and sixe thousand people. Let this therefore (deer mother) minister unto you a strong hope of my happy returne into England.

Notwithstand all these lines for provision for your funerall, I hope for to see you alive and sound in body and minde, about foure yeares hence; and to kneele before you with effusion of teares, for joy. Sweet mother, pray let not this wound your heart, that I say four yeares hence, and not before; I humbly beseech you, even upon the knees of my heart, with all submissive supplications, to pardon me for my long absence; for verily, I have resolved, by the favour of the supernall powers, to spend 4 entire yeares more before my returne, and so to make it a pilgrimage of 7 yeares, to the end I may very effectually and profitably contemplate a great part of this worldly fabricke; determining, by Gods special help, to go from India into the countrey of Scythia, now called Tartaria, to the cittie Samarcanda, to see the sepulcher of the greatest conqueror that ever was in the worlde, Tamberlaine the Great; thither it is a journey of two months from the place I now remaine. From that I meane to return into Persia; and therethence, by the way of Babylon and Ninivy, and the mountaine Ararat, where Noahs arke rested, to Aleppo, to my countrymen. From that, by the way of Damascus, and once again to Gaza in the land of the Philistims unto Cairo in Egypt; from that downe the Nilus to Alexandria; and therehence finally I hope to be imbarked for some part of Christendome, as either

Venice, or etc. After mine arrivall in Christendome, I shall desire to travell two yeares in Italy, and both High and Low Germany, and then with all expedition into England, and to see you (I hope) with as great joy as ever did any travailer his father or mother. Going in that manner as I do, like a poore pilgrime, I am like to passe with undoubted securitie and very small charge; for in my tenne months travailes betwixt Aleppo and this Moguls court, I spent but three pounds sterling, and yet had sustenance enough to maintaine nature, living reasonably well, oftentimes a whole day for so much of their money as doeth countervaile two pence sterling. But least I be over tedious unto you, I will heere make an end, etc.

I will now commend you to the most blessed protection of our Saviour Jesus Christ; before whose holy sepulcher at Jerusalem I have poured foorth mine ardent orisons for you to the most sacrosanct Trinity, beseeching It, with all humilitie of heart, to blesse and preserve you in a solid health, etc.

Your loving sonne,

THO. CORYATE.

V

To His Mother.

From Agra, the capitall city of the dominion of the Great Mogoll, in the Easterne India, the last of October, 1616.

Most deare and welbeloved Mother,

Though I have superscribed my letter from Azmere, the court of the greatest monarch of the East called the Great Magoll, in the Eastern India, which I did to this end, that those that have the charge of conveiance thereof, perceiving such a title, may be the more carefull and diligent to convey it safely to your hands: yet in truth the place from which I wrote this letter is Agra, a city in the said Eastern India which is the metropolitan of the whole dominion of the foresaid

King Mogol, and 10 daies journy from his court at the said Azmere.

From the same Azmere I departed the 12 day of September, An. 1616, after my abode there 12 moneths and 60 daies; which though I confesse it were a too long time to remaine in one and the selfe same place, yet for two principall causes it was very requisite for me to remaine there some reasonable time: first, to learne the languages of those countries through which I am to passe betwixt the bounds of the territories of this prince and Christendome, namely these three, the Persian, Turkish, and Arab (which I have in some competent measure attained unto by my labour and industry at the said Kings court), matters as availeable unto me as mony in my purse, as being the cheifest or rather onely meane to get me mony if I should happen to be destitute, a matter very incidentall to a poore footman pilgrim as my selfe, in these heathen and Mahometan countries through which I travell; secondly, that by the helpe of one of those languages (I meane the Persian) I might both procure unto my selfe accesse unto the King, and be able to expresse my mind unto him about the matter for the which I should have occasion to discours with him. These were the reasons that moved me so long to tarry at the Mogols court; during which time I abode in the house of the English merchants, my deare countrimen, not spending one little peece of mony, either for diet, washing, lodging, or any other thing. And as for the Persian tongue, which I studied very earnestly, I attained to that reasonable skill (and that in a fewe moneths) that I made an oration unto the King before many of his nobles in that language, and, after I had ended the same, discoursed with His Majesty also in that tongue very readily and familiarly; the coppy of which speech, though the tong it selfe wil seem to an Englishman very strange and uncuth, as having no kind of affinity with any of our Christian languages, I have for novelty sake written out in this letter, together with the translation thereof in English, that you may shew it to some of my lerned friends of the clergy and also of the temporalty in Euil and elswere, who, belike, will take some pleasure in reading so rare and unusuall a tongue as this is. The Persian is this that followeth:

The Copie of an Oration that I made, in the Persian tongue, to the Great Mogoll, before divers of his Nobles.[1]

Hazaret Aallum pennah salamet, fooker Daruces ve tehaungeshta hastam kemia emadam az wellagets door, ganne az mulk Inglizan : ke kessanaion petheen mushacas cardand ke wellagets, mazcoor der akers magrub bood, ke mader hamma iezzaerts dunmast. Sabebbe amadane mari mia boosti char cheez ast auval be dedane mobarreck deedars. Hazaret ke seete caramat ba hamma Trankestan reeseedast ooba tamam mulk Musulmanan der sheenedan awsaffe. Hazaret daueeda amadam be deedane astawne akdas musharaf geshtam duum

[1] The Persian has been printed exactly as it appears in the original text, printer's errors and all. The late Sir Charles Lyall kindly furnished the following transcript, which does not, however, attempt to correct Coryat's wording or grammar :—

Ḥaẓarat-i 'ālam-panāh salāmat ! Faqīr darvīsh u jahāngashta hastam, ki īnjā āmadam az wilāyat-i dūr, ya'nī az mulk-i Inglistān, ki qiṣṣa-navīsān-i (?) pīshīn mushakhkhaṣ karda-and ki wilāyat-i mazkūr dar ākhir-i maghrib būd, ki mādar-i hamah jazā'ir-i dunyā-st. Sabab-i āmadan-i man īnjā ba-wāsiṭa-e (?) chār chīz ast : awwal ba-dīdan-i mubārak dīdār-i Ḥaẓarat, ki ṣīt-i karāmat ba-hamah Farangistān rasīdast u batamām mulk-i Musalmānān : dar shanīdan-i awṣāf Ḥaẓarat davīda āmadam : ba-dīdan-i āstān-i aqdas musharraf gashtam. Dūwam barā-e dīdan-i fīl-hā-e Ḥaẓarat, ki chunīn jānwar dar hīch mulk na-dīdam. Sīwam barā-e dīdan-i daryā-e nāmwar-i shumā Gangā, ki sardār-i hamah daryāhā-e dunyā-st. Chahārum īn ast, ki yak farmān-i 'ālī-shān 'ināyat farmāyand, ki bituwānam dar wilāyat-i Uzbak raftan ba-shahr-i Samarqand, barā-e ziyārat kardan-i qabr-i Ṣāḥib-Qirān ki awṣāf jang u musakhkhara-e ū dar tamām 'ālam mashhūr ast, balki dar wilāyat-i Uzbak īn-qadar mashhūr nīst chunān ki dar mulk-i Inglistān ast. Dīgar, bisyār ishtiyāq dāram ba-dīdan-i mubārak mazār-i Ṣāḥib-Qirān-rā barā-e īn sabab, ki ān zamān ki faqīr dar shahr-i Istambōl būdam, yak 'ajīb kuhna 'imārat dīdam dar miyān-i yak khush bāgh nazdīk-i shahr-i mazkūr, kujā ki pādshāh-i 'Īsā'iyān ki nāmash Manuel būd ki Ṣāḥib-Qirān-rā khush-mihmānī-yi 'aẓīm karda būd, ba'd az giriftan-i Sulṭān Bāyazīd-rā az jang-i 'aẓīm ki shuda būd nazdīk-i shahr-i Bursa, kiānjā ki Ṣāḥib-Qirān Sulṭān Bāyazīd-rā dar zanjīr-i ṭilā'ī bastand u dar ḳafas nihādand. Īn chār chīz marā az mulk-i man jumbānīd tā īnjā, az mulk-i Rūm u 'Irāq piyāda gashta, az dūr dar īn mulk rasīdam, ki chār hazār farsang rāh dārad : bisyār dard u miḥnat kashīdam, ki hīch kas dar īn dunyā īn qadar miḥnat na kashīdast, barā-e dīdan-i mubārak dīdār-i Ḥaẓaratat ān rūz ki ba takht-i shāhanshāhī musharraf farmūdand.

bray deedane feelhay Hazaret, kin chunm ianooar der heech mulk ne dedam seu in bray deedane namwer daryaee shumma Gauga, ke Serdare hamma daryaha dumiest. Chaharum een ast, keyec fermawne alishaion amayet fermoyand, ke betwanam der wellayetts Vzbeck raftan ba shahre Samarcand, bray zeerat cardan cabbre mobarrec Saheb crawncah awsaffe tang oo mosachere oo der tamam aallum meshoor ast belkder wellagette Vzbec eencader meshoor neest chunan che der mulc Inglisan ast digr, bishare eshteeac daram be deedanc mobarrec mesare Saheb crawnca bray een saheb, che awne saman che focheer de shabr Stambol boodam, ycaiaeb cohua amarat deedam dermean yecush bawg nasdec shaht mascoor coia che padshaw Eezawiawn che namesh Manuel bood che Saheb crawnca cush mehmannec aseem carda bood, baad as gristane Sulten Baiasetra as iange aseem che shuda bood nas dec shahre Bursa, coimache Saheb crawn Sultan Baiasetra de Zenicera tellaio bestand, oo der cafes nahadond een char chees meera as mulche man ium baneed tamia, as mulc Room oo Arrac peeada geshta, as door der een mulc reseedam, che char hasar pharsang raw darad, beshare derd oo mohuet casheedam che heech ches der een dunnia een cader mohuet ne casheedast bray deedune mobarrec dedare Haseretet awn roos che be tacte shaugh ne shaughee musharaf fermoodand.

The English of it is this.

Lord [1] Protector of the World, all haile to you. I am a poore traveller and world-seer, which am come hither from a farre country, namely England, which auncient historians thought to have been scituated in the farthest bounds of the West, and which is the queene of all the ilands in the world. The cause of my comming hither is for foure respects. First, to see the blessed face of Your Majesty, whose wonderfull fame hath resounded over all Europe and the Mahometan countries; when I heard of the fame of Your Majesty, I hastened hither with speed, and travelled very cherefully to see your glorious court. Secondly, to see Your Majesties elephants, which kind

[1] 'This is the ordinary title that is given him by all strangers' (*marginal note*).

of beasts I have not seen in any other country. Thirdly, to see your famous river Ganges, which is the captaine of all the riever[s] of the world. The fourth is this: to intreat Your Majesty that you would vouchsafe to grant mee your gracious passe that I may travell into the country of Tartaria to the city of Samarcand, to visit the blessed sepulcher of the Lord of the Corners [1] (this is a title that is given to Tamberlaine in this country in that Persian language, and wheras they call him the Lord of the Corners, by that they meane that he was lord of the corners of the world, that is, the highest and supreme monarch of the universe), whose fame, by reason of his warres and victories, is published over the whole world: perhaps he is not altogether so famous in his own country of Tartaria as in England. Moreover, I have a great desire to see the blessed toombe of the Lord of the Corners for this cause; for that when I was at Constantinople, I saw a notable old building in a pleasant garden neer the said city, where the Christian Emperor that was called Emanuell [Manuel Palaeologus] made a sumptuous great banquet to the Lord of the Corners, after he had taken Sultan Bajazet in a great battell that was fought neere the city of Bursia [Brusa], where the Lord of the Corners bound Sultan Bajazet in fetters of gold, and put him in a cage of iron.[2] These four causes moved me to come out of my native country thus farre, having travelled a foote through Turky and Persia. So farre have I traced the world into this country that my pilgrimage hath accomplished three thousand miles; wherin I have sustained much labour and toile, the like whereof no mortall man in this world did ever performe, to see the blessed face of Your Majesty since the first day that you were inaugurated in your glorious monarchall throne.

[1] *Sāhib Kirān* (properly *Qirān*), a title largely used by Tīmūr. Coryat is wrong as to its meaning, which is really 'Lord of the (auspicious) Conjunction'—alluding to the grand conjunction of the planets at the time of Tīmūr's birth. Coryat has evidently confused *qirān* with *karān* ('boundary' or 'limit').

[2] The reference is to the battle of Angora (1402), in which Tīmūr defeated and captured Bāyazīd I. The story of the iron cage is a myth (see Gibbon's *Decline and Fall*, chap. 65).

After I had ended my speech, I had some short discourse with him in the Persian tongue, who amongst other things told me that, concerning my travell to the city of Samarcand, he was not able to doe me any good, because there was no great amity betwixt the Tartarian princes and himselfe; so that his commendatory letters would doe me no good. Also he added that the Tartars did so deadly hate all Christians that they would certainely kill them when they came into their country; so that he earnestly diswaded me from the journy, if I loved my life and welfare. At last he concluded his discourse with me by a sum of mony that he threw downe from a windowe through which he looked out, into a sheete tied up by the foure corners, and hanging very neer the ground, a hundred peeces of silver, each worth two shillings sterling, which countervailed ten pounds of our English mony. This busines I carried so secretly, by the help of my Persian, that neither our English Ambassador, nor any other of my countrimen (saving one speciall, private, and intrinsical friend) had the least inkling of it till I had throughly accomplished my designe; for I well knew that our Ambassador would have stopped and barracadoed all my proceeding therein, if he might have had any notice thereof; as indeed he signified unto me after I had effected my project, aleaging this forsooth for his reason why he would have hindered me, because it would redound some what to the dishonour of our nation that one of our countrey should present himselfe in that beggarly and poore fashion to the King, out of an insinuating humor to crave mony of him; but I answered our Ambassador in that stout and resolute manner, after I had ended my busines, that he was contented to cease nibling at me. Never had I more need of mony in all my life then at that time; for in truth I had but twenty shillings sterling left in my purse, by reason of a mischance I had in one of the Turkes cities called Emert,[1] in the country of Mesopotamia, where a miscreant Turke stripped me of almost all my monies, according as I wrote unto you in a very large letter the last yeer, which I

[1] Coryat has already stated (p. 250) that this incident took place at Diarbekr. Apparently he is here giving that town its alternative name of (Kara) Amid.

sent from the court of this mighty monarch by one of my countrimen that went home by sea in an English shippe laden with the commodities of this India; which letter I hope came to your hands long since.

After I had been with the King, I went to a certaine noble and generous Christian of the Armenian race,[1] two daies journy from the Mogols court, to the end to observe certain remarkable matters in the same place; to whom by means of my Persian tongue I was so welcome that hee entertained me with very civill and courteous complement, and at my departure gave mee very bountifully twenty peeces of such kind of mony as the King had done before, countervailing 40 shillings sterling. About ten daies after that, I departed from Azmere, the court of the Mogol Prince, to the end to begin my pilgrimage after my long rest of fourteen moneths back againe into Persia; at what time our Ambassador gave mee a peece of gold of this Kings coine worth foure and twenty shillings,[2] which I will save (if it be possible) till my arivall in England. So that I have received for benevolences since I came into this country twenty markes sterling [13*s*. 4*d*. each] saving two shillings eight pence; and by the way uppon the confines of Persia a litle before I came into this country three and thirty shillings foure pence [3] in Persian mony of my Lady Sherly. At this present I have in the city of Agra, where hence I wrote this letter, about twelve pounds sterling, which, according to my maner of living uppon the way at two-pence sterling a day (for with that proportion I can live pretty well, such is the cheapnes of all eatable things in Asia, drinkable things costing nothing, for seldome doe I drinke in my pilgrimage any other liquor then pure water), will mainetaine mee very competently three yeeres in my travell with meate, drinke and clothes. Of these gratuities which have been given me, willingly would I send you some part as a demonstration of the filiall love and

[1] This was probably the well-known Mirza Zulkarnain, who farmed the salt works at the Sāmbhar Lake, about forty miles north-east of Ajmer. See Father Hosten's article on him in *Memoirs of the Asiatic Society of Bengal*, vol. v, no. 4, p. 122.

[2] A gold mohur, valued by Coryat at twelve rupees.

[3] Doubtless a hundred *shāhis* On p. 243 Coryat gives the sum as 40*s*.

affection which every child bred in civility and humility ought to performe to his loving and good mother; but the distance of space betwixt this place and England, the hazard of mens lives in so long a journey, and also the infidelity of many men, who though they live to come home, are unwilling to render an account of the things they have received, doe not a little discourage me to send any precious token unto you; but if I live to come one day to Constantinople againe (for thither doe I resolve to goe once more, by the grace of Christ, and therehence to take my passage by land into Christendom over renouned Greece), I wil make choice of some substantial and faithfull countriman, by whom I will send some prety token as an expression of my dutifull and obedient respect unto you.

I have not had the oppertunity to see the King of Persia as yet since I came into this country, but I have resolved to goe to him when I come next into his territories, and to search him out wheresoever I can find him in his kingdome; for, seeing I can discourse with him in his Persian tongue, I doubt not but that, going unto him in the forme of a pilgrime, he will not onely entertaine me with good words, but also bestow some worthy reward upon me, beseeming his dignity and person; for which cause I am provided before hand with an excellent thing, written in the Persian tongue, that I meane to present unto him. And thus I hope to get benevolences of worthy persons to maintaine me in a competent maner in my whole pilgrimage till I come into England; which I hold to be as laudable and a more secure course then if I did continually carry store of mony about mee.

In the letter which I wrote unto you by an English ship the last yeere, I made relation unto you both of my journy from the once holy Hierusalem hither, and of the state of this Kings court, and the customes of this country; therfore I hold it superfluous to repeat the same things againe. But what the countryes are that I meane to see betwixt this and Christendome, and how long time I will spend in each country, I am unwilling to advertise you of at this present, desiring rather to signify that unto you after I have performed my designe then before. Howbeit, in few words I will tell you of certaine cities of great renown in former times, but now partly ruined, that I resolve (by Gods help) to see in Asia, where I now am, namely, ancient Babilon and Nymrods Tower, some few miles from Ninive, and in the same the sepulcher of the prophet Jonas, spacious and goodly; Caire in Egypt, heretofore Memphis, upon the famous river Nilus, where Moises, Aron, and the Children of Israel lived with King Pharaoh, whose ruined palace is shewed there til this day, and a world of other movable things as memorable as any city of the whole world yeeldeth, saving only Jerusalem. But in none of these or any other cities of note do I determin to linger as I have done in other places, as in Constantinople, and Azmere in this Easterne India; onely some few daies will I tarry in a principall city of fame, to observe every principal matter there, and so be gone.

In this city of Agra where I am now, I am to remaine about six weekes longer, to the end to expect an excellent oportunity which then will offer it selfe unto me to goe to the famous river Ganges, about five daies journy from this, to see a memorable meeting of the gentle people of this country, called Baieans,[1] whereof about foure hundred thousand people go thither of purpose to bathe and shave themselves in the river, and to sacrifice a world of gold to the same river, partly in stamped mony, and partly in massy great lumpes and wedges, throwing it into the river as a sacrifice, and doing other strange ceremonies most worthy the observation.[2] Such a notable spectacle it is, that no part of all Asia, neither this which is called the Great Asia nor the Lesser, which is now called Natolia, the like is to be seen. This shew doe they make once every yeere, comming thither from places almost a thousand miles off, and honour their river as their God, Creator, and Saviour; superstition and impiety most abominable in the highest degree of these brutish ethnicks, that are aliens from Christ and the common-wealth of Israel. After I have seen

[1] A misprint for 'Banians', meaning Hindus.

[2] Coryat appears to be referring to the annual bathing festival at Hardwār, held on the first day of the Hindu sidereal year (in 1617 this would fall about the end of March). Terry (ed. 1665, p. 88) expressly states that Coryat visited Hardwār. The latter's informant seems to have exaggerated the amount of gold offered on such occasions, though Dr. William Crooke, C.I.E., tells me that he has known of small coins, and sometimes sand gold, being dropped into the pool.

this shew, I wil with all expedition repaire to the city of Lahore, twenty daies journy from this, and so into Persia, by the helpe of my blessed Christ.

Thus have I imported unto you some good accidents that happened unto me since I wrote a letter unto you the last yeere from the Kings court, and some litle part of my resolution for the disposing of a part of my time of abode in Asia; therefore now I will draw to a conclusion. The time I cannot limit when I shall come home, but as my mercifull God and Saviour shall dispose of it. A long rabble of commendations, like to that which I wrote in my last letter to you, I hold not so requisite to make at this present; therefore, with remembrance of some fewe friends names, I will shut up my present epistle. I pray you recommend me first in Odcombe to Master Gollop, and every good body of his family, if he liveth yet; to Master Berib, his wife and all his family; to all the Knights,[1] William Chunt, John Selly, Hugh Donne, and their wives; to Master Atkins and his wife at Norton. I pray commend me in Euill to these; to old Mr. Seward,[2] if he liveth, his wife and children, the poore Widow Darby, old Master Dyer, and his sonne John, Master Ewins, old and young, with their wives, Master Phelpes and his wife, Master Starre and his wife, with the rest of my good friends there. I had almost forgotten your husband[3]: to him also, to Ned Barber and his wife, to William Jenings. Commend me also, I pray you, and that with respectfull and dutifull termes, to the godly and reverent fraternitie of preachers that every second Friday meet at a religious exercise at Euill; at the least, if that exercise doth continue, pray read this letter to them, for I thinke they wilbe well pleased with it, by reason of the novelties of things. And so finally I commit you and all them to the blessed protection of Almighty God.

Your dutifull, loving, and obedient sonne, now a desolate pilgrim in the world.

THOMAS CORIAT.

[1] Probably Sir Edward and Sir Robert Phelips.

[2] The Rev. John Seward, of Yeovil, to whom Laurence Whitaker addressed a letter in praise of the *Crudities*, printed as an introduction to that work.

[3] Coryat's mother had evidently married again (see a passage in the commendatory verses prefixed to the 1618 pamphlet),

The copy of a speech that I made to a Mahometan in the Italian tongue.

The coppy of a speech that I made extempore in the Italian tongue to a Mahometan at a citie called Moltan, in the Easterne India, two daies journy beyond the famous river Indus, which I have passed, against Mahomet and his accursed religion, upon the occasion of a discurtesie offered unto mee by the said Mahometan in calling me Giaur,[1] that is infidell, by reason that I was a Christian. The reason why I spake to him in Italian was because he understood it, having been taken slave for many yeeres since by certaine Florentines in a galley wherein hee passed from Constantinople towards Alexandra; but being by them interrupted by the way, he was carried to a citie called Ligorne [Leghorn] in the Duke of Florences dominions, where after two yeeres he had learned good Italian; but he was an Indian borne and brought up in the Mahometan religion. I pronounced the speech before an hundred people, whereof none understood it but himselfe; but hee afterward told the meaning of some part of it as far as he could remember it to some of the others also. If I had spoken thus much in Turky or Persia against Mahomet, they would have rosted me upon a spitt; but in the Mogols dominions a Christian may speake much more freely then hee can in any other Mahometan country in the world. The speech was this, as I afterward translated it into English:

But I pray thee, tell me, thou Mahometan, dost thou in sadnes [i. e. in seriousness] call me Giaur? That I doe, quoth he. Then (quoth I) in very sobersadnes I retort that shamefull word in thy throate, and tell thee plainly that I am a Musulman and thou art a Giaur. For by that Arab word Musulman thou dost understand that which cannot be properly applied to a Mahometan, but onely to a Christian; so that I doe consequently inferre that there are two kindes of Muselmen, the one an orthomusulman, that is a true Musulman, which is a Christian, and the other a pseudo-musulman, that is, a false Musulman, which is a Mahometan. What thy Mahomet was,

[1] Giaour, an infidel, from the Persian *gaur* or *gabr*, through the Turkish *gyaur*

from whom thou dost derive thy religion, assure thy selfe I know better then any one of the Mahometans amongst many millions ; yea, all the particular circumstances of his life and death, his nation, his parentage, his driving camels through Egipt, Siria, and Palestina, the marriage of his mistris, by whose death he raised himselfe from a very base and contemptible estate to great honor and riches, his manner of cozening the sottish people of Arabia, partly by a tame pigeon that did fly to his eare for meat, and partly by a tame bull that hee fed by hand every day, with the rest of his actions both in peace and warre, I know aswell as if I had lived in his time, or had beene one of his neighbours in Mecca. The truth whereof if thou didst know aswell, I am perswaded thou wouldest spit in the face of thy Alcaron [*al-Kurān*], and trample it under thy feete, and bury it under a jaxe [i. e. privy], a booke of that strange and weake matter that I my selfe (as meanely as thou dost see me attired now) have already written two better bookes (God be thanked), and will hereafter this (by Gods gratious permission) write another better and truer. Yea, I wold have thee know (thou Mahometan) that in that renouned kingdome of England where I was borne, learning doth so flourish that there are many thousand boies of sixteene yeeres of age that are able to make a more learned booke then thy Alcaron. Neither was it (as thou and the rest of you Mahometans doe generally beleve) composed wholy by Mahomet, for hee was of so dull a wit as he was not able to make it without the helpe of another, namely a certaine renegado monke of Constantinople, called Sergis.[1] So that his Alcoran was like an arrow drawne out of the quiver of another man. I perceive thou dost wonder to see me so much inflamed with anger ; but I would have thee consider it is not without great cause I am so moved, for what greter indignity can there be offered to a Christian which is an Arthomusulman then to be called Giaur by a Giaur ; for Christ (whose religion I professe) is of that incomparable dignity that, as thy Mahomet is not worthy to be named that yeere wherein my blessed Christ is, so neither

[1] Sergius or Georgius, known to Muhammadans as *Bahīra* : see the *Encyclopaedia of Islam*, s. n., and Hughes's *Dictionary of Islam*, p.515. The assertion in the text is not accepted by modern scholars.

is his Alcoron worthy to be named that yeere wherein the Injeel[1] of my Christ is. I have observed among the Mahometans such a foolish forme of praier ever since my departure from Spahan (which I confesse was no novelty unto me, for that I had observed the like before, both in Constantinople and divers other Turkish cities) that what with your vain repeti[ti]ons and divers other prophane fooleries contained therein, I am certaine your praiers doe even stinke before God, and are of no more force then the cry of thy camell when thou doest lade or unlade him. But the praiers of Christians have so prevailed with God that in time of drougth they have obtained convenient aboundance of raine, and in time of pestilence a suddaine cessation from the plague, such an effect of holy and fervent praier as never did the *Scofferalahs*, or the *Allamisselalow*[2] of any Mahometan produce. Yet must wee, whose praiers like a sweete smelling sacrifice are acceptable to God, be esteemed Giaurs by those whose praiers are odious unto His Divine Majestie. O times! O maners!

Now, as I have told thee the difference betwixt the effect of our Christian and your Mahometan praiers, so I pray thee observe another difference betwixt you and us, that I wil presently intimate unto thee. Thou by the observation of the law of thy ridiculous Alcaron dost hope for Paradice, wherein thy master Mahomet hath promised rivers of rice, and to virgins the imbracing of angels under the shaddowe of spacious trees, though in truth that Paradice be nothing else then a filthy quagmire, so full of stincking dung-hils that a man cannot walke two spaces there but he shall stumble at a dung-hill and defile himselfe; but where this Paradice is, not one amongst a thousand of you knoweth; therefore I will tell thee. It standeth in a country scituate betwixt heaven and earth called Utopia, whereof there is mention in the third book of thy

[1] 'This doe all Mohametans call our Gospell or the History of our Saviour, written by the foure Evangelists' (*marginal note*). The word is *injīl* (=*evangelium*).

[2] 'Words that the Mahometans doe often repeat in their praiers' (*marginal note*). The first phrase is *Astaghfiru-l-lāh* ('I ask pardon'); the second may be all that Coryat could catch of the muttered formula *Lā ilāha illa-l-lāh, Muhammadur-Rasūlu-llāh* (see p. 315).

Alcaron and in the seven and thirty Asaria,[1] but expressed with those misticall and obscure termes that is very difficult to understand it. For this Utopian Paradice, I say, as the reward of al your superstitious mumbling in your praiers and the often ducking downe of your heads, when you kisse the ground with such a devoute humilitie forsooth, doe you Mahometans hope in another world! But wee Christians hope to live with God and His blessed angels for ever and ever in Heaven, as being a proper and peculiar inheritance purchased unto us by the precious blood of our Christ. Yet must wee be reputed Giaurs by those that are Giaurs?

One thing more will I tell thee (O thou Mahometan), and so I will conclude this tedious speech, whereunto thy discurtious calling of me Giaur hath inforced mee; and I prethee observe this my conclusion. Learning (which is the most precious jewell that man hath in this life, by which he attaineth to the knowledge of divine and humane things) commeth to man either by revelation, which we otherwise cal inspiration, or by industry. Learning by revelation I cal that which God doth infuse from above by His special grace, unto those whom He will use as the instruments of His glory; who without labour or travell doe aspire to a most eminent degree of knowledge. Learning by industry, I call it that which a man doth purchase to himselfe by continuall writing and reading, by practise and meditation. Now by neither of these meanes have the Mahometans acquired any meane, much less any singular, learning; for as Mahomet himselfe was a man of a very superficiall and meane learning, so never was there any one of his disciples in any part of the world that was indued with any profound knowledge. But wee Christians, by the one and the other meane, have attained to the most exquisite science that can be incident to man.[2] Some of our men that never were brought up in studies having been so expert in a generall learning (onely by Gods special illumination) as those have spent forty yeeres

[1] The Kurān is not divided into books but into chapters, known as *sūrahs*. 'Asaria' is apparently meant for some form of *al-sūrah* (*as-sūrah*), which, in the Latin translation of 1550, appears as 'azoara'. The 37th *sūrah* is the one describing Paradise.

[2] 'I mean the blessed Apostles of our Saviour' (*marginal note*).

in the practise thereof; and others, by continuall practise of writing and reading, have beene so excellent that they became the very lampes and stars of the countries wherein they lived. These things being so, it cannot possible come to passe that the Omnipotent God should deale so partially with mankind as to reveale His will to a people altogether misled in ignorance and blindnes as you Mahometans are, and conceale it from us Christians that bestowe all our lifetime in the practise of divine and humane disciplines, and in the ardent invocation of God's holy name with all sincerity and purity of heart. Goe to, then, thou pseudomusulman, that is, thou false-beleever, since by thy injurious imputation laid upon mee, in that thou calledst mee Giaur, thou hast provoked mee to speake thus. I pray thee, let this mine answere be a warning for thee not to scandalize mee in the like manner any more; for the Christian religion which I professe is so deare and tender unto mee that neither thou nor any other Mahometan shal scotfree call me Giaur, but that I will quit you with an answer much to the wonder of those Mahometans. *Dixi*.

I pray you, mother, expect no more letters from me after this till my arrivall in Christendom; because I have resolved to write no more while I am in the Mahometans countries, thinking that it will be a farre greater comfort, both to you and to all my friends whatsoever, to heare newes that I have accomplished my travelles in Mahometisme, then that I am comming up and down, to and fro in the same, without any certainty of an issue therof. Therfore, I pray, have patience for a time. About two yeers and a halfe hence I hope to finish these Mahometan travelles, and then either from the citie of Raguzi [Ragusa] in Sclavonia, which is a Christian citie and the first we enter into Christendome from those parts of Turky by land nere unto the same, or from famous Venice, I will very dutifully remember you againe with lines full of filiall piety and officious respect.

I have written two letters to my Uncle Williams since I came forth of England, and no more; whereof one from the Mogols court the last yeere, just at the same time that I wrote unto you; and another now, which I sent jointly by the same messenger that carried yours out of India by sea. Once more I recommend you and all our hearty wel-willers and friends to the gratious tuition of the Lord of Hosts. I pray you, remember my duty to Master Hancoke, that reverend and apostolicall good old man, and his wife, if they are yet living; to their sonnes Thomas and John, and their wives.

Certaine observations written by Thomas Coryat.[1]

Whereas the beggers begge in this countrey of a Christian in the name of Bibee [*Bībī*, Lady] Maria, and not of Hazaret Eesa [see p. 246], thereby we may gather that the Jesuits have preached Mary more then Jesus.

A great Raja, a Gentile, a notorious atheist and contemner of all deitie (glorying to professe he knew no other God then the King, nor beleeving nor fearing none), sitting dallying with his women, one of them plucked a haire from his brest; which, being fast rooted, plucked off a little of the skinne, that bloud appeared. This small skarre[2] festered and gangrened incurably; so that in few dayes he despaired of life. And beeing accompanied with all his friends and divers courtiers, he brake out into these excellent words: Which of you would not have thought that I, being a man of warre, should have dyed by the stroke of a sword, speare, or bow? But now I am inforced to confesse the power of that great God whom I have so long despised: that Hee needs no other lance then a little haire to kill so blasphemous a wretch and contemner of His majestie as I have beene.[3]

Ecbar Shaugh had learned all kind of sorcery; who, beeing once in a strange humour, to shew a spectacle to his nobles, brought forth his chiefest queene, with a sword cut off her head, and after the same, perceiving the heavinesse and sorrow of them for the death of her (as they thought), caused the head,

[1] From *Purchas His Pilgrimes*, part i, bk. iv, chap. 17.

[2] A term, now obsolete, for a crack or incision. It is quite distinct from our ordinary 'scar'.

[3] For an account of other versions of this story see *The Embassy of Sir T. Roe*, p. 311 *n*.

by vertue of his exorcismes and conjunctions, to be set on againe, no signe appearing of any stroke with his sword.

Sultan Cursaroo [1] hath but one wife ; for which one principall reason is that during his imprisonment the King, intending to make a hunting progresse of foure moneths, consulted how to keepe him safe in his absence ; at last resolved to build a towre and immure him within it, without gate, doore, or window, except some small holes to let in ayre, higher then he could come unto ; putting in all sorts of provision whatsoever, both fire, clothes, etc., with some servants to abide with him for that time. While this was building, his wife came and fell at the Kings feete, and never would let goe till shee had obtayned leave to bee shut up with him. The King much perswading to enjoy her libertie, she utterly refused any other comfort then to be the companion of her husbands miseries amongst which this was the greatest, that if any of those that were immured (beeing in number fiftie) should have dyed in the Kings absence, there was no meanes to burie them, for that no man was admitted to come neere the towre.

The fountaine found the first day by one of My Lords people, Master Herbert (brother to Sir Edward Herbert) [2] ; which if he had not done, he [i.e. Roe] must have sent ten course every day for water to a river called Narbode [Narbada], that falleth into the Bay of Cambaya at Buroch [i.e. Broach] ; the custome being such that whatsoever fountaine or tanke is found by any great man in time of drought, hee shall keepe it proper and peculiar to himselfe, without the interruption of any man whatsoever. The day after, one of the Kings haddys finding

[1] Khusrau's devotion to his wife (a daughter of Aziz Koka) is said to have cost him his chance of the succession and consequently his life. The story is that Nūr Mahal was willing to lend him her support against Khurram, on condition that he would also espouse her daughter by her former husband—a proposal he scornfully rejected (see *Della Valle*, Grey's edition, vol. i, p. 56, where also it is stated that his wife insisted on sharing his imprisonment).

[2] This is an incident of Roe's stay at Māndu : see *The Embassy*, p. 393. For the Thomas Herbert here mentioned, the *Dictionary of National Biography*, *Letters Received* (vol. v, p. 126), and Terry's *Voyage* (ed. 1655, p. 176) may be consulted.

the same, and striving for it, was taken by My Lords people and bound all, etc., a great controversie being about it, etc.

Remember the charitie of two great men that, in the time of this great drought,[1] were at the charge of sending ten camels with twentie persons every day to the said river for water, and did distribute the water to the poore; which was so deare that they sold a little skinne for eight pise.

Ecbar Shaugh a very fortunate prince, and pious to his mother; his pietie appearing in this particular, that when his mother was carried once in a palankeen betwixt Lahor and Agra, he, travelling with her, tooke the palankeen upon his owne shoulders, commanding his greatest nobles to doe the like, and so carried her over the river from one side to the other. And never denyed her any thing but this, that shee demanded of him, that our Bible might be hanged about an asses necke and beaten about the towne of Agra, for that the Portugals, having taken a ship of theirs at sea, in which was found the Alcoran amongst the Moores, tyed it about the necke of a dogge and beat the same dogge about the towne of Ormuz. But hee denyed her request, saying that, if it were ill in the Portugals to doe so to the Alcoran, being it became not a King to requite ill with ill, for that the contempt of any religion was the contempt of God, and he would not be revenged upon an innocent booke; the morall being that God would not suffer the sacred booke of His truth to be contemned amongst the infidels.

One day in the yeere, for the solace of the Kings women, all the trades-mens wives enter the Mohal [see p. 148] with somewhat to sell, in manner of a faire; where the King is broker for his women and with his gaines that night makes his supper, no man present.[2] (Observe that whatsoever is brought in of virill shape, as instance in reddishes, so great is the jealousie,

[1] At Māndu, caused by Jahāngīr's heedlessness in fixing his camp in this deserted city. Roe (*loc. cit.*) speaks of the pitiful misery caused by the scarcity of water.

[2] For accounts of these fairs see the *Āīn*, vol. i, p. 276, Constable's trans. of Bernier, p. 272, and *The Travels of Peter Mundy*, vol. ii, p. 238.

and so frequent the wickednesse of this people, that they are cut and jagged for feare of converting the same to some unnaturall abuse.) By this meanes hee attaines to the sight of all the prettie wenches of the towne. At such a kind of faire he got his beloved Normahal.

After Shaof Freed [Shaikh Farid] had wonne the battle of Lahor [1] by a stratagem, the captaines being taken by the King and hanged upon flesh-hookes and stakes made an entrance for the King to Lahor. His sonne Cursaroo being then taken prisoner and riding bare-footed upon an elephant, his father demanded him how hee liked that spectacle of his valiant and faithfull captaines hanging in that manner, to the number of two thousand. Hee answered him that hee was sorrie to see so much crueltie and injustice in his father, in executing them that had done nothing but their dutie, for that they lived upon his bread and salt; but hee should have done right if hee had saved them and punished him, which was their master and the authour of the rebellion.

For more cleere declaration of this excellent vertue, upbraiding the coldnesse of our charitie, you shall understand a custome of this King, who sleeping in his Gusle-can,[2] often when hee awakes in the night, his great men (except those that watch) being retired, cals for certaine poore and old men, making them sit by him, with many questions and familiar speeches passing the time; and at their departure cloathes them and gives them bountifull almes often, whatsoever they demand, telling the money into their hands.

For a close of this discourse, I cannot forget that memorable

[1] The victory by which Khusrau's rebellion was crushed. The stratagem seems to be that mentioned on p. 159, of pretending that Jahāngir had arrived on the scene with all his forces (see also Herbert's *Some Yeares Travels*, p. 73). The conversation between Khusrau and his father is recorded by Terry (ed. 1655, p. 430), doubtless on Coryat's authority. Manucci (vol. i, p. 131) has a similar story, but makes it relate to Jahāngir's rebellion against Akbar.

[2] *Ghusl-khāna*, 'bath-room', and hence a private apartment. For examples of Jahāngir's respect for such devotees, see Roe, pp. 366, 380

pietie, when at Asmere hee [1] went afoot to the tombe of the prophet Hod. Mundin there buried, and kindling a fire with his owne hands and his Normahal under that immense and Heidelbergian-aequipollent [2] brasse-pot, and made kitcherie [3] for five thousand poore, taking out the first platter with his owne hands and serving one; Normahal the second; and so his ladies all the rest. Cracke mee this nut, all the [4] Papall charitie vaunters.

An Armenian, desirous to turne Moore, procured a noble-man to bring him to the King; whom the King asked why hee turned Moore: whether for preferment? Hee answered: No. Some few monethes after, craving some courtesie of the King, hee denyed it him, saying that hee had done him the greatest favour that could bee, to let him save his soule; but for his bodie, hee himselfe should provide as well as he could.

The King likes not those that change their religion; hee himselfe beeing of none but of his owne making, and therefore suffers all religions in his kingdome; which by this notable example I can make manifest. The King had a servant that was an Armenian, by name Scander [5]; to whom, upon occasion of speech of religion, the King asked if hee thought either hee or the Padres had converted one Moore to bee a true Christian, and that was so for conscience sake and not for money; who answered with great confidence that hee had one which was a perfect Christian and for no worldly respect would bee other; whom the King caused presently to bee sent for, and, bidding his master depart, demanded why hee was become a Christian; who rendred certaine feeble, implicite, Jesuiticall reasons, and

[1] Jahāngīr. The reference is to the ceremony still observed during the *Urs Mela* festival at the shrine of Khwāja Muinuddīn Chishti at Ajmer, when, at the expense of some rich devotee, a gigantic mixture of rice, spices, &c., is cooked in a large cauldron and distributed to the pilgrims.

[2] Equal in capacity to the Great Tun of Heidelberg (a description of which was one of the features of Coryat's *Crudities*).

[3] *Khichri* (whence 'kedgeree'), the common Indian dish of rice, cooked with pulse and butter.

[4] Probably this should be 'ye'.

[5] Possibly this was Mirza Sikandar, father of Mirza Zulkarnain (see p. 267*n*.). Father Hosten takes this view.

avowed that hee would never be other. Whereupon the King practised by faire speeches and large promises to withdraw him to the folly of Mahomet, offering him pensions, meanes, and command of horse, telling him hee had now but foure rupias a moneth wages, which was a poore reward for quitting his praepuced faith; but if hee would recant, hee would heape upon him many dignities; the fellow answering it was not for so small wages hee became Christian, for hee had limbes and could earne so much of any Mahometan, but that hee was a Christian in his heart, and would not alter it. This way not taking effect, the King turned to threatnings and menacings of tortures and whippings; but the proselyte manfully resolving to suffer any thing, answered hee was readie to endure the Kings pleasure. Upon this resolution, when all men expected present and severe castigation, the King changed his tune, highly commending his constancie and honestie, bidding him goe and returne to his master, and to serve him faithfully and truely; giving him a rupia a day pension for his integritie. About two monethes after, the King, having beene a hunting of wilde hogges (a beast odious to all Moores), and accustomed to distribute that sort of venison among Christians and Razbootes, sent for this Armenian, master of this converted catechumen or Mahometan, to come and fetch part of his quarrie. The Armenian not beeing at home, this his principall servant came to know the Kings pleasure; who commanded him to take up a hogge for his master (which no Moore will touch); which hee did and, being gone out of the court-gate, was so hooted at by the Mahometans that hee threw downe his present in a ditch and went home, concealing from his master what had passed. About foure dayes after, the Armenian comming to his watch, the King demanded of him whether the hogge he sent him were good meat or no; who replyed hee neyther heard of nor see any hogge. Whereat the King, remembring to whom this hogge was delivered, caused the fellow to be sent for; and examining the matter, had it confessed how he threw away the hogge and never carryed it home. The King pressing to know the reason, the poore fellow answered how he was mocked for touching it, and (it being a thing odious to the Moores) for shame he threw it away. At which he replyed: By your law there is no difference of meats, and are you ashamed of your lawes? Or, to flatter the Mahumetans, doe you in outward things forsake it? Now I see thou art neither good Christian nor good Mahumetan, but a dissembling knave with both. While I found thee sincere, I gave thee a pension; which now I take from thee, and for thy dissimulation doe command thee to have a hundred stripes (which were presently given him in stead of his money); and bade all men by his example take heed that, seeing hee gave libertie to all religions, that which they choose and professe they may sticke unto.[1]

Terry's Account of Coryat.[2]

And now, Reader, I would have thee to suppose me setting my foot upon the East-Indian shore at Swally before named; on the banks whereof, amongst many more English that lye there interred, is laid up the body of Mr. Thomas Coryat, a man in his time *notus nimis omnibus*, very sufficiently known. He lived there, and there died while I was in those parts, and was for some months then with my Lord Embassadour; during which time he was either my chamber-fellow or tent-mate, which gave me a full acquaintance of him. . . . If he had lived, he would have written his last travels to and in and out of East-India; for he resolved (if God had spared him life) to have rambled up and down the world (as sometimes Ulysses did); and though not so long as he, yet ten full years at least before his return home; in which time he purposed to see Tartaria, in the vast parts thereof, with as much as he could of China and those other large places and provinces interposed betwixt East-India and China, whose true names we might have had from him, but yet have not. He had a purpose after this to have visited the court of Prester John in Æthiopia, who is there called by his own people *Ho Biot*, the King; and after this it was in his thoughts to have cast his eyes upon many

[1] This anecdote bears a strong resemblance to one recorded in a letter from Father Jerome Xavier in 1604, which is reproduced by Sir Edward Maclagan in his article on *Jesuit Missions to the Emperor Akbar*. In that version the present was a live pig and was intended for a Portuguese.

[2] From the 1655 edition of the *Voyage to East-India*, p. 57.

other places; which if he had done, and lived to write those relations, seeing (as he did or should) such variety of countries, cities, nations, things, and been as particular in them as he was in his Venetian journal, they must needs have swoln into so many huge volumns as would have prevented the perishing of paper. But undoubtedly, if he had been continued in life to have written them, there might have been made very good use of his observations; for, as he was a very particular, so was he without question a very faithful, relator of things he saw; he ever disclaiming that bold liberty which divers travellers have and do take by speaking and writing any thing they please of remote parts, when they cannot easily be contradicted, taking a pride in their feigned relations to overspeak things. . . . And because he could not live to give an account unto the world of his own travels, I shall here by the way make some little discovery of his footsteps and flittings up and down, to and fro; with something besides of him in his long peregrinations, to satisfie very many yet living, who, if they shall please to read this discourse, may recall that man once more into their remembrance; who, while he lived, was like a perpetual motion, and therefore now dead should not be quite forgotten. . . .[1]

From hence [Shīrāz] they journied afterwards to Candahor, the first province north east under the subjection of the Great Mogol; and so to Lahore, the chiefest city but one belonging to that great empire; a place (as I have been often told by Tom. Coryat and others) of very great trade, wealth, and delight, lying more temperately out of the parching sun than any other of his great cities do. And to this city he wanted not company, nor afterwards to Agra, the Mogol's metropolis or chief city. And here it is very observable that from Lahore to Agra it is four hundred English miles, and that the countrey betwixt both these great cities is rich, even, pleasant, and flat, a *campania*; and the rode-way on both sides all this long distance planted with great trees, which are all the year

[1] Terry's lengthy account of the earlier stages of Coryat's journey has been omitted, partly because they are sufficiently described in his letters and the introduction, and partly because the reverend gentleman's statements are unreliable.

cloathed with leaves, exceeding beneficial unto travellers for the shade they afford them in those hot climes. This very much extended length of way 'twixt these two places is called by travellers the Long Walk, very full of villages and towns for passengers every where to find provision.

At Agra our traveller made an halt, being there lovingly received in the English factory, where he staid till he had gotten to his Turkish and Morisco or Arabian languages some good knowledge in the Persian and Indostan tongues; in which study he was alwaies very apt, and in little time shewed much proficiency. The first of those two, the Persian, is the more quaint; the other, the Indostan, the vulgar language spoken in East-India. In both these he suddenly got such a knowledge and mastery that it did exceedingly afterwards advantage him in his travels up and down the Mogol's territories; he wearing alwaies the habit of that nation and speaking their language. In the first of these, the Persian tongue, he made afterwards an oration to the Great Mogol. . . . Then, larding his short speech with some other pieces of flattery, which the Mogol liked well, concluded. And when he had done, the Mogol gave him one hundred roopies, which amounts to the value of twelve pounds and ten shillings of our English money; looking upon him as a derveese or votary or pilgrim (for so he called him), and such as bear that name in that countrey seem not much to care for money; and that was the reason (I conceive) that he gave him not a more plentiful reward.

After this, he having got a great mastery likewise in the Indostan or more vulgar language, there was a woman, a landress belonging to my Lord Embassadors house, who had such a freedome and liberty of speech that she would sometimes scould, brawl, and rail from the sunrising to sun-set. One day he undertook her in her own language, and by eight of the clock in the morning so silenced her that she had not one word more to speak.

. . . He was a man of a very coveting eye, *that could never be satisfied with seeing* (as Salomon speaks, *Eccles.* i. 8.), though he had seen very much; and I am perswaded that he took as much content in seeing as many others in the enjoying of great and rare things. He was a man that had got the mastery of many hard languages (as before I observed) to the Latine and Greek he brought forth of England with him; in which, if he had obtained wisdome to husband and manage them as he had skill to speak them, he had deserved more fame in his generation. But his knowledge and high attainments in several languages made him not a little ignorant of himself; he being so covetous, so ambitious of praise that he would hear and endure more of it than he could in any measure deserve; being like a ship that hath too much sail and too little ballast. Yet if he had not fall'n into the smart hands of the wits of those times, he might have passed better. That itch of fame which engaged this man to the undertakings of those very hard and long and dangerous travels hath put thousands more (and therefore he was not alone in this) into strange attempts onely to be talked of. . . . 'Twas fame, without doubt, that stirred up this man unto these voluntary but hard undertakings, and the hope of that glory which he should reap after he had finished his long travels made him not at all to take notice of the hardship he found in them. That hope of name and repute for the time to come did even feed and feast him for the time present. And therefore any thing that did in any measure eclipse him in those high conceivings of his own worth did too too much trouble him; which you may collect from these following instances. Upon a time one Mr. Richard Steel[1], a merchant and servant to the East-India Company, came unto us from Surat to Mandoa, the place then of the Mogol's residence . . . at which time Mr. Coryat was there with us. This merchant had not long before travelled over-land from East-India through Persia and so to Constantinople, and so for England; who in his travel homeward had met with Tom. Coryat, as he was journeying towards East-India. Mr. Steel then told him that, when he was in England, King

[1] His journey in pursuit of Mildenhall has been mentioned on p. 51. From Surat he was sent back to Persia at the end of 1614, and proceeded thence overland to England, arriving in May, 1616. He came out again to India in the 1617 fleet, and was sent from Surat to Roe's camp, carrying with him some valuable pearls. He arrived on Nov. 2, and left again for Surat a few days later. For his subsequent proceedings see *The Embassy of Sir T. Roe.*

James (then living) enquired after him, and when he had certified the King of his meeting him on the way, the King replied: Is that fool yet living? Which when our pilgrim heard, it seemed to trouble him very much, because the King spake no more nor no better of him; saying that kings would speak of poor men what they pleased.

At another time, when he was ready to depart from us, my Lord Embassadour gave him a letter, and in that a bill to receive ten pounds at Aleppo when he should return thither. The letter was directed unto Mr. Libbeus Chapman, there consul at that time; in which that which concerned our traveller was thus: Mr. Chapman, When you shall hand these letters, I desire you to receive the bearer of them, Mr. Thomas Coryat, with curtesy, for you shall find him a very honest poor wretch. And further I must intreat you to furnish him with ten pounds, which shall be repayed, etc. Our pilgrim lik'd the gift well, but the language by which he should have received it did not at all content him; telling me that my Lord had even spoyled his curtesy in the carriage thereof; so that, if he had been a very fool indeed, he could have said very little less of him than he did (Honest poor wretch); and to say no more of him was to say as much as nothing. And furthermore he then told me that, when he was formerly undertaking his journey to Venice, a person of honour wrote thus in his behalf unto Sir Henry Wotton, then and there Embassadour: My Lord, Good wine needs no bush, neither a worthy man letters commendatory, because whithersoever he comes he is his own epistle, etc. There (said he) was some language on my behalf; but now for my Lord to write nothing of me by way of commendation but Honest poor wretch is rather to trouble me than to please me with his favour. And therefore afterwards his letter was phras'd up to his mind; but he never liv'd to receive the money. By which his old acquaintance may see how tender this poor man was to be touched in any thing that might in the least measure disparage him. O what pains this poor man took to make himself a subject for present and after discourse; being troubled at nothing for the present, unless with the fear of not living to reap that fruit he was so ambitious of in all his undertakings. And certainly he was surprized with some such thoughts and fears (for so he told us afterwards), when upon a time, he being at Mandoa with us, and there standing in a room against a stone pillar, where the Embassadour was and myself present with them, upon a sudden he fell into such a swoon that we had very much ado to recover him out of it. But at last come to himself, he told us that some sad thoughts had immediately before presented themselves to his fancy, which (as he conceived) put him into that distemper; like Fannius in Martial [1]: *Ne moriare mori*, to prevent death by dying. For he told us that there were great expectations in England of the large accounts he should give of his travels after his return home; and that he was now shortly to leave us, and he being at present not very well, if he should dye in the way toward Surat, whither he was now intended to go (which place he had not as yet seen), he might be buried in obscurity and none of his friends ever know what became of him, he travelling now, as he usually did, alone. Upon which my Lord willed him to stay longer with us; but he thankfully refused that offer, and turned his face presently after towards Surat, which was then about three hundred miles distant from us. And he lived to come safely thither; but there being over-kindly used by some of the English, who gave him sack which they had brought from England; he calling for it as soon as he first heard of it, and crying: Sack, sack; is there such a thing as sack? I pray give me some sack; and drinking of it, though, I conceive, moderately (for he was a very temperate man), it increased his flux which he had then upon him. And this caused him within a few daies, after his very tedious and troublesome travels (for he went most on foot) at this place to come to his journies end; for here he overtook Death in the month of December, 1617, and was buried (as aforesaid) under a little monument, like one of those are usually made in our church-yards.[2]

[1] *Epigrammata*, bk. ii, no. 80.

[2] Terry adds a poetical epitaph (from his own pen) which, he suggests, might have commemorated Coryat, 'if it could have been there engraved upon his tombe'.

1616–19

EDWARD TERRY

TERRY'S account of India, which, to adopt the quaint language of his editor Purchas, is here offered as 'a good fare-well draught of English-Indian liquor', was the outcome chiefly of his own observations during the two and a half years which he spent in that country as chaplain to Sir Thomas Roe. It owes something to Coryat, who, as we have seen, was the reverend gentleman's companion for a considerable period: something also to the gossip of other members of the ambassador's suite or of the merchants at Surat; but in the main it is a record of what the author himself had observed. It bears traces of a vigorous and penetrating mind, stimulated by a strong interest in its strange surroundings—an interest further evidenced by the fact that, although he had no intention of staying in the country, Terry took the pains to acquire some knowledge of the Persian language.

The opportunity of seeing the East at close quarters came to our author almost as a matter of chance. Born in 1590, and educated at Rochester School and Christ Church, Oxford, in the spring of 1616 he accepted an engagement for a voyage to the Indies and back as one of the chaplains in the fleet commanded by Captain Benjamin Joseph. On the way out a Portuguese carrack was overtaken and destroyed, after a smart encounter in which the English commander was slain; and Swally Road was safely reached on September 25, after a voyage of nearly eight months. Roe's chaplain had died a month earlier, and he had written to the Surat factors to provide him with another. As Terry was well commended and was willing to remain in India, he was engaged for the post. He joined the ambassador near Ujjain towards the end of February 1617, and accompanied him to Māndu, where the Emperor fixed his court until October of that year, when he removed to Ahmadābād. Roe and his suite followed him thither and spent about nine months in attendance upon him in that city. Then, in September 1618, the ambassador took his leave and proceeded to Surat to enjoy a few months' rest before embarking for England on February 17, 1619. Thus Terry had only himself seen parts of Mālwa and Gujarāt—a fact to be borne in mind when reading his generalizations about India.

EDWARD TERRY

P. 288

The *Anne*, in which the ambassador and his suite returned, anchored in the Downs about the middle of September 1619. The next we hear of Terry is on October 22, when he appeared before the Court of Committees of the East India Company to beg to be released from paying freight on a quantity of calicoes he had brought home. His action was, in fact, a breach of the regulations, since the trade in piece-goods was reserved to the Company; but on hearing Roe's commendations of Terry's 'sober, honest, and civill life' in India, the Committees 'were contented to pas over this fault' and to excuse him from any payment of freight. Further, on learning that he had spent about £14 on books, most of which he had given to the factors in India, they ordered that this sum should be made good to him.

The reverend gentleman now went back for a while to his Oxford college. Probably it was there that he wrote the results of his observations in India, as now reprinted. This document in 1622 he presented in manuscript to the Prince of Wales, afterwards King Charles I. How it came into the possession of the Rev. Samuel Purchas, who published it three years later in his *Pilgrimes* (part ii, book ix, chap. 6), is not known; but it is not unlikely that the Prince himself (to whom, by the way, the first volume of the *Pilgrimes* is dedicated) had made it over to that editor. That Terry himself was not consulted is suggested by the fact that, in the preface to his own edition of 1655, he makes no allusion to the previous appearance of the work in Purchas's volumes; and it may be that he was further aggrieved by the pruning (slight as it was) to which the editor had subjected his manuscript, on the plea that part of its contents had been anticipated in the narratives of Roe and others.

However this may be, Terry did not trouble about the matter, but settled down contentedly to his pastoral duties as Rector of Great Greenford, near London, a living which he held from 1629 till his death. There his ministrations appear to have afforded general satisfaction, to judge from the account given of him by Anthony à Wood in his *Athenae Oxonienses*, as 'an ingenious and polite man, of a pious and exemplary conversation, a good preacher, and much respected by the neighbourhood'. Only once, so far as we know, did the East India Company take any notice of their former chaplain. This was in 1649, when they paid him the compliment of asking him to preach before them on the occasion of the almost simultaneous return of no less than seven of their ships from the East Indies. The sermon was duly delivered at the Church of St. Andrew Undershaft in Leadenhall Street, on September 6, and was afterwards printed under the title of *The Merchants and Mariners Preservation and Thanksgiving*;

while the occasion was further celebrated by a dinner at a tavern in Bishopsgate Street, to which the preacher was doubtless invited.

Six years later Terry's account of his experiences reappeared in separate form as a dumpy volume of 571 pages, under the title of *A Voyage to East-India.* In the preface he tells us that the initiative in the matter had been taken by a printer, who had somehow acquired his original manuscript and had persuaded him to revise it. Terry certainly made the most of his opportunity, for, not content with amplifying his previous statements and adding fresh details (in some of which his memory evidently betrayed him), on all possible pegs he hung long moral and religious disquisitions, in the avowed hope that 'they who fly from a sermon and will not touch sound and wholesom and excellent treatises in divinity, may happily (if God so please) be taken before they are aware, and overcome by some divine truths that lie scattered up and down in manie places of this narrative'. With such zest did the reverend gentleman moralize that he expanded his work to seven or eight times the length of its original form as given by Purchas and made it exceedingly wearisome to readers who have no taste for seventeenth-century divinity. It is largely on this account, but partly also because the earlier text contains some interesting details which were struck out in the revised version, that we have here preferred to reprint the narrative as we find it in Purchas's collection. At the same time we have given in notes many extracts from the 1655 edition, where these correct or amplify in any important respect the author's earlier statements. The rather lengthy account of the voyage out, which appears in both versions, is here omitted, as having no bearing on Terry's experiences in India itself.

Despite its didactic prosiness, the work in its separate form attained a considerable degree of popularity, as was shown by its republication ten years later (slightly condensed and without the author's name) in a folio volume containing also Havers's translation of the letters of Della Valle; while long afterwards (1777) a reprint of the 1655 edition was issued. Terry himself lived on quietly at Great Greenford, just long enough to witness the restoration of the monarchy—an event he celebrated by the publication of *A Character of King Charles II*—and then died in October 1660. Under the portrait prefixed to his *Voyage* he had written:

> In Europe, Africk, Asia have I gonne;
> One journey more, and then my travel's donne.

And now he had set out on that long last journey.

THE large empire of the Great Mogol is bounded on the East with the kingdome of Maug [see p. 26]; west with Persia, and the mayne ocean southerly; north with the mountaynes of Caucasus and Tartaria; south with Decan and the Gulfe of Bengala. Decan, lying in the skirts of Asia, is divided between three Mahometan kings and some other Indian Rhajaes. This spacious monarchie, called by the inhabitants Indostan, dividing it selfe into thirtie and seven severall and large provinces, which anciently were particular kingdomes; whose names, with their principall cities and rivers, their situation and borders, their extent in length and breadth, I first set downe, beginning at the north-west.[1]

First, Candahor; the chiefe citie so called. It lyes from the heart of all his territorie north-west. It confines with the King of Persia, and was a province belonging to him. 2. Cabul; the chiefe citie so called; the extreamest north-west part of this emperours dominions. It confineth with Tartaria. The river Nilab[2] hath its beginning in it, whose current is southerly till it discharge it selfe in Indus. 3. Multan; the chiefe citie so called. It lyes south from Cabul and Candahor, and to the

[1] This list of provinces is closely related to the list given by Roe (*Embassy*, p. 531) and to the map of India (*ibid.*, p. 542) which was compiled and published in 1619 by William Baffin, the Arctic navigator, who was serving on board the ship in which the ambassador returned to England. That Terry had this map before him, when making his list, is evident from the general coincidence of the spelling of the names (often differing materially from Roe), and also from the fact that in both a province of 'Jeselmeere' (not mentioned by Roe) is inserted, while 'Roch' (i. e. Kuch Bihār), which was included by Roe, is omitted. On the other hand Terry was careful to keep the number of provinces the same as in Roe's list, from which he also copied some of his descriptions.

The list corresponds but slightly with the familiar one of the various *sūbahs* of the Mughal Empire. It is in fact a rough enumeration of the various states which had fallen under the sway of Akbar and his successor, and this accounts in part for its errors and want of proportion. The reader will find it fully discussed in *The Embassy of Sir Thomas Roe* (*loc. cit.*). Here it is only possible to give brief identifications of the more obscure names.

The map given in the 1655 edition of Terry is a poor version of Baffin's, on a reduced scale.

[2] Properly the upper Indus, but apparently here the Kābul River is meant.

west joynes with Persia. 4. Hajacan,[1] the kingdome of the Baloches (a stout warlike people). It hath no renowned citie. The famous river Indus (called by the inhabitants Skind) borders it on the east; and Lar (a province belonging to Sha-Abas, the present King of Persia) meetes it on the west. 5. Buckor[2]; the chiefe citie called Buckorsuccor. The river Indus makes a way through it, greatly enriching it. 6. Tatta; the chiefe citie so called. The river Indus makes many ilands in it, exceeding fruitfull and pleasant. The chiefe arme meetes with the sea at Synde,[3] a place very famous for curious handicrafts. 7. Soret [Sorath, in Kāthiāwār]; the chiefe citie is called Janagar [Jūnāgarh]. It is a little province, but rich, lyes west from Guzarat, and hath the ocean to the south. 8. Jeselmeere [Jaisalmer, in Rājputāna]; the chiefe citie so called. It joyneth with Soret, Buckor, and Tatta, lying to the west of it. 9. Attack [Attock]; the chiefe citie so called. It lyeth on the east side of Indus, which parts it from Hajacan. 10. Penjab, which signifieth five waters, for that it is seated among five rivers, all tributaries to Indus, which somewhat south of Lahor make but one current. It is a great kingdome, and most fruitfull, etc. Lahor, the chiefe citie, is well built, very large, populous, and rich; the chiefe citie of trade in all India. 11. Chishmeere [Kashmīr]; the chiefe citie is called Siranakar [Srīnagar]. The river Phat [Bihat: see p. 169] passeth through it, and so, creeping about many ilands, slides to Indus. 12. Banchish; the chiefe citie is called Bishur.[4] It lyeth east southerly from Chishmeere, from which it is divided by the river Indus. 13. Jengapor;[5] the chiefe citie so called. It lyeth upon the river Kaul, one of the five rivers that water

[1] Baluchistān, or more specifically the lower Derājāt, ruled by the descendants of Hāji Khān, whose overlordship was recognized by all the Baloch tribes.

[2] The district round the fortress of Bukkur, on the Indus. It was a *sarkār* of the province of Multān.

[3] 'Sindee' (i. e. Diul-Sind, or Lahrībandar) in the 1655 edition.

[4] Professor Blochmann identified Banchish with Bangash, in N.W. Kohāt, and Bishur with Bajaur, a district still farther north. Possibly, however, Peshāwar is intended.

[5] Roe's 'Jenupar'. It is probably Jaunpur. The 'Kaul' (i. e. Kāli) is the Gogra, a tributary of the Ganges; but Jaunpur is on another tributary (the Gūmti).

Penjab. 14. Jenba ;[1] the chiefe citie so called. It lyeth east of Penjab. 15. Delli ; the chiefe citie so called. It lyeth twixt Jenba and Agra. The river Jemni (which runneth through Agra, and falleth into Ganges) begins in it. Delli is an ancient great citie, the seate of the Mogols ancestors, where most of them lye interred. 16. Bando ;[2] the chiefe citie so called. It confineth Agra on the west. 17. Malway [Mālwa], a very fruitfull province ; Rantipore[3] is the chiefe citie. 18. Chitor, an ancient and great kingdome ; the chiefe citie so called. 19. Guzarat, a goodly kingdome and exceeding rich, inclosing the Bay of Cambaya. The river Tapte watereth Surat. It trades to the Red Sea, to Achin, and to divers other places. 20. Chandis [Khāndesh] ; the chiefe citie called Brampoch [Burhānpur], which is large and populous. Adjoyning to this province is a petie prince called Partapsha [see p. 136], tributarie to the Mogol ; and this is the southermost part of all his territories. 21. Berar ; the chiefe citie is called Shapore,[4] the southermost part whereof doth likewise bound this empire. 22. Narvar ;[5] the chiefe citie called Gehud. It is watered by a faire river which emptieth itselfe in Ganges. 23. Gwaliar ; the chiefe citie so called, where the King hath a great treasury of bullion. In this citie likewise there is an exceeding strong castle, wherein the Kings prisoners are kept. 24. Agra, a principall and great province ; the chiefe citie so called. From Agra to Lahor (the two choise cities of this empire) is about foure hundred English miles ; the countrey in all that distance even without a hill, and the high way planted on both sides with trees, like to a delicate walke. 25. Sanbal ;[6] the chiefe citie so called. The river Jemni parts it from Narvar ; and after, at the citie Helabass [Allahābād], falls into Ganges, called by the inhabitants Ganga.

[1] Chamba, one of the Punjab hill states.

[2] Banda district in the United Provinces, south-west of the Jumna.

[3] Ranthambhor seems to be meant ; but it is not in Mālwa.

[4] Shāhpur, about eleven miles south of Bālāpur (see p. 16). After the annexation of Berār to the Mughal Empire in 1596, Prince Murād established his quarters there, and, according to Abūl Fazl, the place grew into a fine city. It is now quite insignificant.

[5] Narwar, in Gwalior territory. 'Gehud' seems to be Gohad.

[6] Sambhal, in Moradābād district, United Provinces.

26. Bakar [Bīkaner, in Rājputāna]; the chiefe citie called Bikaneer. It lyeth on the west side of Ganges. 27. Nagracutt [see p. 179]; the chief citie so called, in which there is a chappel most richly set forth, both seeled and paved with plate of pure gold.[1] In this place they keepe an idoll, which they call Matta, visited yeerly by many thousands of the Indians, who out of devotion cut off part of their tongues to make a sacrifice for it.[2] In this province there is likewise another famous pilgrimage to a place called Jallamakae,[3] where out of cold springs and hard rocks there are dayly to be seene incessant eruptions of fire, before which the idolatrous people fall downe and worship. 28. Syba;[4] the chiefe citie is called Hardwair, where the famous river Ganges seemed to begin, issuing out of a rocke which the superstitious Gentiles imagine to bee like a cowes head,[5] which of all sensible creatures they love best. Thither they likewise goe in troopes daily for to wash their bodies. 29. Kakares;[6] the principall cities are called Dankalee [Dangāli] and Purhola [Pharwāla]. It is very large and exceeding mountaynous, divided from Tartaria by the mountaynes of Caucases. It is the farthest part north under the Mogols subjection. 30. Gor [Gaur, in Bengal]; the

[1] In his 1655 edition (p. 86), Terry substitutes 'silver' for 'gold', and adds: 'most curiously imbossed over head in several figures, which they keep exceeding bright by often rubbing and burnishing it'. Coryat was his authority for these statements, as also for his account of Jawāla Mukhi and Hardwār.

[2] The reference is to the famous temple of Māta Devi or Bajreswari Devi at Bhawan, a suburb of Kāngra. For the sacrifice of tongues, see Finch (*supra*, p. 180), the *Āīn*, vol. ii, p. 313, and the account published by John Oranus in 1601 of the labours of the Jesuits in India, China, and Japan.

[3] Jawāla Mukhi ('she of the flaming mouth'), a temple built over some jets of combustible gas, believed to be a manifestation of the goddess Devi. See the *Āīn*, vol. ii, p. 314.

[4] Sība, now part of the Kāngra district, but formerly an independent principality. The town of that name is about seventeen miles S.W. of Kāngra. Baffin in his map wrongly extended Sība to include Hardwār, and Terry improved upon this by making the latter the capital of the former.

[5] The *gau-mukh*, or cow's mouth, is the glacier cavern from which the head-waters issue. It is at Gangotri, in the state of Tehri.

[6] The country of the Ghakkars, in the north of the Punjāb.

chiefe citie so called. It is full of mountaynes. The river Persilis,[1] which dischargeth it selfe in Ganges, beginnes in is 31. Pitan;[2] the chiefe citie so called. The river Kanda watert it, and falls into Ganges in the confines thereof. 32. Kanduana;[3] the chiefe citie is called Karhakatenka. The river Sersily parts it from Pitan. That and Gor are the north-east bounds of this great monarchie. 33. Patna [Bihār]; the chiefe citie so called. The river Ganges bounds it on the west, Sersily on the east. It is a very fertile province. 34. Jesual;[4] the chiefe citie called Rajapore [Rajpūra, near Amb]. It lyeth east of Patna. 35. Meuat;[5] the chiefe citie called Narnol. It is very mountaynous. 36. Udessa [Orissa]; the chiefe citie called Jokanat [Jagannāth]. It is the most remote part east of all this kingdome. 37. Bengala; a most spacious and fruitfull kingdome, limited by the gulfe of the same name, wherein the river Ganges, divided in foure great currents, loseth it selfe.

And here a great errour in our geographers must not escape mee; who in their globes and maps make India and China neighbours, when many large countries are interposed betwixt them; which great distance will appeare by the long travell of the Indian merchants, who are usually in their journey and returne more then two yeeres from Agra to the walls of China. The length of those forenamed provinces is, north-west to south-east, at the least one thousand courses, every Indian course being two English miles. North and south, the extent thereof is about fourteene hundred miles; the southermost part lying in twentie degrees, the northermost in fortie three of north latitude.[6] The breadth of this empire is, north-east to south-west, about fifteene hundred miles.

Now, to give an exact account of all those forenamed

[1] As shown by Baffin's map, this is an error for 'Sersily' [i. e. the Saraswati], as under no. 32.

[2] Paithān or Pathānkot, in Kāngra. The Gandak river runs nowhere near it.

[3] Gondwāna, in the Central Provinces. It is absurdly misplaced in the text. 'Karhakatenka' is Garhakatanka, near Jabalpur.

[4] Jaswān, in Hoshiārpur district (Punjab).

[5] Mewāt, lying to the south of Delhi. Nārnaul was its chief town

[6] This is quite wrong, but he is following Baffin's map.

provinces were more then I am able to under-take; yet out of that I have observed in some few I will adventure to ghesse at all; and thinke for my particular that the Great Mogol, considering his territories, his wealth, and his rich commodities, is the greatest knowne king of the East, if not of the world. To make my owne conjecture more apparent to others. This wide monarchie is very rich and fertile; so much abounding in all necessaries for the use of man as that it is able to subsist and flourish of it selfe, without the least helpe from any neighbour. To speake first of that which nature requires most, foode. This land abounds in singular good wheate, rice, barley, and divers other kindes of graine to make bread (the staffe of life). Their wheate growes like ours, but the graine of it is somewhat bigger and more white; of which the inhabitants make such pure well-relished bread that I may speake that of it which one said of the bread in the Bishoprick of Leige; it is *panis pane melior*.[1] The common people make their bread up in cakes, and bake it on small iron hearths, which they carry with them when as they journey, making use of them in their tents; it should seeme an ancient custome, as may appeare by that president of Sarah, when shee entertayned the angels (*Genes.* 18). To their bread they have great abundance of other good provision, as butter and cheese, by reason of their great number of kine, sheepe, and goats. Besides they have a beast very large, having a smooth, thicke skinne without haire, called a buffelo, which gives good milke; the flesh of them is like beefe, but not so wholsome. They have no want of venison of divers kinds, as red deare, fallow deare, elkes, and antelops; but nowhere imparked. The whole kingdome is as it were a forrest, for a man can travell no way but he shall see them, and (except it bee within a small distance off the King) they are every mans game. To these they have great store of hares; and, further to furnish out their feasts, varietie of fish and fowle. It were as infinite as needlesse to relate particulars: to write of their geese, duckes, pigeons, partridges, quailes, peacockes, and many other singular good fowle, all which are bought at such easie rates as that I have seene a good mutton [i.e. a sheep] sold for the

[1] A super-bread, in the jargon of the present day.

value of one shilling, foure couple of hennes at the same price, one hare for the value of a penie, three partridges for as little, and so in proportion all the rest. There are no capons amongst them but men. The beeves [oxen] of that countrey differ from ours, in that they have each of them a great bunch of grisselly flesh which growes upon the meeting of their shoulders. Their sheepe exceed ours in great bob-tayles, which cut off are very ponderous. Their wooll is generally very course; but the flesh of them both is altogether as good as ours.

Now, to season this good provision, there is great store of salt; and to sweeten all, abundance of sugar growing in the countrey, which, after it is well refined, may be bought for two pence the pound or under. Their fruits are very answerable to the rest; the countrey full of musk-melons, water-melons, pomegranats, pome-citrons,[1] limons, oranges, dates, figs, grapes, plantans (a long round yellow fruit, in taste like to a Norwich peare), mangoes (in shape and colour like to our apricocks, but more luscious), and, to conclude with the best of all, the ananas or pine,[2] which seemes to the taster to be a pleasing compound made of strawberries, claret-wine, rose-water, and sugar, well tempered together. In the northermost parts of this empire they have varietie of apples and peares; every where good roots, as carrets, potatoes,[3] and others like them as pleasant. They have onions and garlicke, and choyce herbs for salads; and in the southermost parts, ginger growing almost in every place. And here I cannot choose but take notice of a pleasant cleere liquor called Taddy [toddy], issuing from a spongie tree that growes straight and tall, without boughs to the top, and there spreads out in branches (some-

[1] The lime, or possibly the pomelo. In his later edition Terry added to this list of fruits 'prunelloes' [i. e. dried plums], almonds, coco-nuts, and myrobalans.

[2] The pine-apple (*ananas*), which had been introduced into India from America by the Portuguese.

[3] In the 1655 edition Terry mentions (p. 210) 'potatoes excellently well dressed' as having been served at a banquet given by Āsaf Khān to Sir Thomas Roe in Nov. 1617. According to Sir George Watt (*Commercial Products of India*, p. 1028), this is the first mention of the ordinary potato in connexion with India. It is, however, possible that Terry was referring to the sweet potato, which was common in India at that time and was well known in England under the name of 'potato'.

what like to an English colewort), where they make incisions, under which they hang small earthen pots to preserve the influence.[1] That which distills forth in the night is as pleasing to the taste as any white wine, if drunke betimes in the morning; but in the heat of the day the sunne alters it so as that it becomes heady, ill relished, and unwholsome. It is a piercing medicinable drinke, if taken early and moderately, as some have found by happie experience, thereby eased from their torture inflicted by that shame of physicians and tyrant of all maladies, the stone.

At Surat, and to Agra and beyond, it never raines but one season of the yeere, which begins neere the time that the sunne comes to the Northerne Tropicke, and so continues till his returne backe to the Line. These violent raines are ushered in, and take their leave, with most fearefull tempests of thunder and lightning, more terrible then I can expresse, yet seldome doe harme. The reason in Nature may be the subtiltie of the aire, wherein there are fewer thunderstones made then in such climates where the aire is grosse and cloudy. In those three moneths it raines every day more or lesse, sometimes one whole quarter of the moone scarce with any intermission; which aboundance of raine, with the heat of the sunne, doth so enrich the ground (which they never force) as that, like Egypt by the inundation of Nilus, it makes it fruitfull all the yeere after. But when this time of raine is passed over, the skie is so cleere as that scarcely one cloud is seene in their hemisphere the nine moneths after. And here the goodnesse of the soyle must not escape my pen; most apparent in this, for when the ground hath beene destitute of raine nine moneths, and lookes like to barren sands, within seven dayes after the raine begins to fall it puts on a greene coate. And further to confirme this, amongst many hundred acres of corne I have beheld in those parts, I never saw any but came up as thicke as the land could well beare it. They till their ground with oxen and foot-ploughs. Their seed-time is in May and the beginning of June; their harvest in November and December, the most temperate moneths in all their yeere. Their ground is not enclosed, unlesse it be neere townes and villages, which (though not

[1] i. e. that which flows in.

expressed in the map, for want of their true names) stand very thicke. They mowe not their grasse (as we) to make hay, but cut it either greene or withered on the ground as they have occasion to use it. They sowe tobacco in abundance; but know not how to cure and make it strong, as those in the Westerne India [*i.e.* the West Indies].

The countrey is beautified with many woods and great varietie of faire goodly trees; but I never saw any there of those kinds which England affoords. Their trees in generall are sappie, which I ascribe to the fatnesse of the soyle. Some of them have leaves as broad as bucklers; others are parted small as ferne, as the tamarine trees, which beare a sowre fruit that growes somewhat like our beanes, most wholesome for to coole and cleanse the bloud. There is one tree amongst them of speciall observation, out of whose branches grow little sprigs downeward till they take root, and so at length prove strong supporters unto the armes that yeeld them; whence it comes to passe that these trees in time grow unto a great height and extend themselves to an incredible bredth.[1] All the trees in those southerne parts of India still keepe on their greene mantles. For their flowres, they rather delight the eye then affect the sense; in colour admirable, but few of them, unlesse roses and one or two kinds more, that are any whit fragrant.

This region is watered with many goodly rivers. The two principall are Indus and Ganges. Where this thing remarkable must not passe: that one pinte of the water of Ganges weigheth lesse by an once then any in the whole kingdome[2]; and therefore the Mogol, wheresoever hee is, hath it brought to him that he may drinke it.[3] Besides their rivers, they have store of wells, fed with springs, upon which in many places they bestow great cost in stone-worke. To these they have many ponds, which

[1] Needless to say, this is the Banyan or Indian Fig-tree.

[2] Ovington (*Voyage to Suratt*, 1689) says that 'a quart of it is lighter by much than any other water' (p. 209).

[3] The 1655 edition adds: 'The water is brought to the King in fine copper jars, excellently well tin'd on the inside, and sealed up when they are delivered to the water-bearers for the King's use; two of which jars every one carries, hanging upon slings fitted for the porter's shoulders.'

they call tankes; some of them more then a mile or two in compasse, made round or square, girt about with faire stone-walls, within which are steps of well-squared stone which encompasse the water, for men every way to goe downe and take it. These tankes are filled when that abundance of raine falls, and keepe water to relieve the inhabitants that dwell farre from springs or rivers, till that wet season come againe. This ancient drinke of the world is the common drinke of India. It is more sweet and pleasant then ours, and in those hot countries agreeth better with mens bodies then any other liquor. Some small quantitie of wine (but not common) is made among them. They call it Raack [arrack], distilled from sugar and a spicie rinde of a tree, called Jagra.[1] It is very wholsome, if taken moderately. Many of the people who are strict in their religion drinke no wine at all. They use a liquor more healthfull then pleasant, they call Cohha [coffee : Arabic *kahwa*] : a blacke seed boyled in water, which doth little alter the taste of the water. Notwithstanding, it is very good to helpe digestion, to quicken the spirits, and to clense the bloud. There is yet another helpe to comfort the stomacke for such as forbeare wine, an herbe called Beetle or Paune [see p. 148]. It is in shape somewhat like an ivie leafe, but more tender. They chew it with an hard nut some-what like a nut-megge, and a little pure white lime among the leaves; and when they have sucked out the juyce, put forth the rest. It hath many rare qualities; for it preserves the teeth, comforts the braine, strengthens the stomacke, and cures or prevents a tainted breath.

Their buildings are generally base, except it be in their cities, wherein I have observed many faire piles. Many of their houses are built high and flat on the toppe, from whence in the coole seasons of the day they take in fresh ayre. They have no chimnies to their houses, for they never use fire but to dresse their meate. In their upper roomes they have many lights and doores to let in the ayre, but use no glasse. The materials of their best buildings are bricke or stone, well squared and composed; which I have observed in Amadavar

[1] Jagra is a coarse sugar made from the sap (not the rind) of various palms (see p. 13).

(that one instance may stand for all), which is a most spacious and rich citie, entred by twelve faire gates, and compassed about with a firme stone wall. Both in their villages and cities are usually many faire trees among their houses, which are a great defence against the violence of the sunne. They commonly stand so thicke that, if a man behold a citie or towne from some conspicuous place, it will seeme a wood rather then a citie.

The staple commodities of this kingdome are indico[1] and cotton-wooll. For cotton-wooll they plant seedes which grow up into shrubs like unto our rose-bushes. It blowes first into a yellow blossome, which falling off, there remaynes a cod about the bignesse of a mans thumbe, in which the substance is moyst and yellow, but, as it ripens, it swels bigger till it breake the covering, and so in short time becomes white as snow, and then they gather it. These shrubs beare three or foure yeares ere they supplant them. Of this wooll they make divers sorts of pure white cloth, some of which I have seene as fine, if not purer then, our best lawne. Some of the courser sort of it they dye into colours, or else stayne in it varietie of curious figures.

The ship that usually goeth from Surat to Moha [Mokha] is of exceeding great burthen. Some of them, I beleeve, at the least fourteene or sixteene hundred tunnes; but ill built, and, though they have good ordnance, cannot well defend themselves. In these ships are yeerely abundance of passengers; for instance, in one ship returning thence, that yeere we left India, came seventeene hundred, the most of which number goe not for profit but out of devotion to visite the sepulchre of Mahomet at Medina, neere Meche, about one hundred and fiftie leagues from Moha. Those which have beene there are ever after called Hoggeis [Hāji], or holy men. The ship bound from Surat to the Red Sea beginnes her voyage about the twentieth of March, and finisheth it towards the end of September following. The voyage is but short and might

[1] Purchas omitted Terry's account of indigo culture, referring the reader instead to Finch's narrative (see p. 153). The omitted portion will be found in the 1655 edition (p. 113), but it scarcely merits quotation here.

easily bee made in two moneths; but in the long season of raine, and a little before and after it, the winds are commonly so violent that there is no comming, but with great hazard, into the Indian Sea. The ship returning is usually worth two hundred thousand pounds sterling, most of it in gold and silver. Besides, for what quantitie of monies comes out of Europe by other meanes into India, I cannot answere; this I am sure of, that many silver streames runne thither, as all rivers to the sea, and there stay, it being lawfull for any nation to bring in silver and fetch commodities, but a crime not lesse then capitall to carry any great summe thence. The coyne or bullion brought thither is presently melted and refined, and then the Mogols stampe (which is his name and title in Persian letters) put upon it. This coyne is more pure then any I know, made of perfect silver without any allay; so that in the Spanish riall (the purest money of Europe) there is some losse. They call their pieces of money roopees, of which there are some of divers values; the meanest worth two shillings,[1] and the best about two shillings and nine pence sterling. By these they account their estates and payments. There is a coyne of inferiour value in Guzarat called mamoodies [see p. 77], about twelve pence sterling. Both the former and these are made likewise in halfes and quarters;[2] so that three pence is the least piece of silver currant in the countrey.[3] That which passeth up and downe for exchange under this rate is brasse[4] money, which they call pices; whereof three or thereabouts countervaile a peny. They are made so massie as that the brasse in them, put to other uses, is well worth the silver they are rated at. Their silver coyne is made either round or square, but so thicke that it never breakes nor weares out.[5]

Now, farther for commodities, the countrey yeelds good store of silke, which they weave curiously, sometimes mingled with silver or gold. They make velvets, sattins, and taffataes; but not so rich as those of Italy. Many drugs and gummes are

[1] This is amended in the 1655 edition to *2s. 3d.*

[2] 'Some few in quarters' (1655 edition).

[3] 'And very few of them to be seen' (*ibid.*).

[4] 'Or copper' (*ibid.*).

[5] 'They have pure gold coyn likewise, some pieces of great value; these are not very ordinarily seen amongst them' (1655 edition).

found amongst them, especially gum-lac, with which they make their hard wax. The earth yeelds good minerals of lead, iron, copper, and brasse, and they say of silver; which, if true, they neede not open, being so enriched by other nations. The spices they have come from other places, from the ilands of Sumatra, Java, and the Moluccoes. For places of pleasure they have curious gardens, planted with fruitfull trees and delightfull flowers, to which Nature daily lends such a supply as that they seeme never to fade. In these places they have pleasant fountaynes to bathe in and other delights by sundrie conveyances of water, whose silent murmure helps to lay their senses with the bonds of sleepe in the hot seasons of the day.

But lest this remote countrey should seeme like an earthly Paradise without any discommodities, I must needes take notice there of many lions, tygres, wolves, jackals (which seeme to be wild dogs), and many other harmefull beasts. In their rivers are many crocodiles, and on the land over-growne snakes, with other venimous and pernicious creatures. In our houses there we often meete with scorpions, whose stinging is most sensible and deadly, if the patient have not presently some oyle that is made of them, to anoint the part affected; which is a present cure. The aboundance of flyes in those parts doe likewise much annoy us; for in the heate of the day their numberlesse number is such as that we can be quiet in no place for them. They are ready to cover our meate assoone as it is placed on the table; and therefore wee have men that stand on purpose with napkins to fright them away when as wee are eating. In the night likewise we are much disquieted with musquatoes, like our gnats, but somewhat lesse.[1] And in their great cities there are such aboundance of bigge hungrie rats that they often bite a man as he lyeth on his bed.

The windes in those parts, which they call the Monson, blow constantly, altering but few points; sixe moneths southerly, the other sixe northerly. The moneths of Aprill and May, and the beginning of June till the rayne fall, are so extreme hot as that the winde, blowing but gently, receives such heate from the parched ground that it much offends those that receive

[1] The 1665 edition adds that 'chinches' (i. e. bugs) were a further nuisance.

the breath of it. But God doth so provide for those parts that most commonly he sends such a strong gale as well tempers the hot ayre. Sometimes the winde blowes very high in those hot and drie seasons, raysing up thick clouds of dust and sand, which appeare like darke clouds full of rayne. They greatly annoy the people when they fall amongst them. But there is no countrey without some discommodities; for therefore the wise Disposer of all things hath tempered bitter things with sweet, to teach man that there is no true and perfect content to be found in any kingdom but that of God.

But I will returne againe whence I disgressed, and looke farther into the qualitie of the countrey; that affords very good horses, which the inhabitants know well to manage. Besides their owne, they have many of the Persian, Tartarian, and Arabian breede, which have the name to be the choise ones of the world. They are about the bignesse of ours, and valued among them as deare, if not at a higher rate then we usually esteeme ours. They are kept daintily, every good horse being allowed a man to dresse and feede him; their provender a kind of graine, called Donna [*Dāna*, grain], somewhat like our pease, which they boyle, and when it is cold, give them mingled with course sugar; and twise or thrise in the weeke butter to scoure their bodies. Here are likewise a great number of camels, dromedaries, mules, asses, and some rhynocerots, which are large beasts as bigge as the fayrest oxen England affords; their skins lye platted, or as it were in wrinkles upon their backs. They have many elephants; the King for his owne particular being master of fourteene thousand, and his nobles and all men of qualitie in the countrey have more or lesse of them, some to the number of one hundred. The elephants, though they bee the largest of all creatures the earth brings forth, yet are so tractable (unlesse at times when they are mad) that a little boy is able to rule the biggest of them. Some of them I have seene thirteene foot high; but there are amongst them (as I have beene often told) fifteene at the least. The colour of them all is black; their skins thick and smooth without haire. They take much delight to bathe themselves in water, and swim better then any beast I know. They lye downe and arise againe at pleasure, as other beasts doe. Their pace is not swift, about three mile an houre; but of all beasts in the world are most sure of foot, for they never fall nor stumble to endanger their rider. They are most docile creatures and, of all those we account meerely sensible, come neerest unto reason. Lipsius [1] in his *Epistles* (1 *Cent. Epist.* 50) out of his observations from others writes more of them then I can confirme, or any (I perswade my selfe) beleeve; yet many things remarkable, which seeme indeed acts of reason rather then sence, I have observed in them. For instance, an elephant will doe any thing almost that his keeper commands him; as, if he would have him affright a man, he will make towards him as if hee would tread him in pieces, and when he is come at him, doe him no hurt; if he would have him to abuse or disgrace a man, he will take dirt or kennell water in his trunke and dash it in his face. Their trunks are long grisselly snouts hanging downe twixt their teeth, by some called their hand, which they make use of upon all occasions.

An English merchant of good credit upon his owne knowledge reported this of a great elephant in Adsmeere (the place then of the Mogols residence), who being brought often through the bazar or market place, a woman who sate there to sell herbs was wont usually to give him a handfull as he passed by. This elephant afterward, being mad, brake his fetters and tooke his way through the market place. The people, all affrighted, made haste to secure themselves; amongst whom was this herbe-woman, who (for feare and haste) forgat her little child. The elephant, come to the place where shee usually sate, stopt, and, seeing a child lie about her herbs, tooke it up gently with his trunke, not doing it the least harme, and layed it upon a stall under a house not farre off; and then proceeded in his furious course. Acosta (a travelling Jesuite) relates the like of an elephant in Goa, from his owne experience.[2] Some elephants the King keeps for execution of malefactors; who being brought to suffer death by that mightie beast, if his keeper bid him dispatch the offender speedily, will presently with his foot pash him into pieces; if otherwise he would

[1] Justus Lipsius (Joest Lips), the Dutch humanist, 1547–1606.

[2] See Christoval Acosta's *Tractado de las Drogas y Medecinas de las Indias Orientales* (Burgos, 1578), p. 417.

have him tortured, this vast creature will breake his joynts by degrees one after the other, as men are broken upon the wheele.

The Mogol takes much delight in those stately creatures, and therefore oft when hee sits forth in his majestie calls for them, especially the fairest; who are taught to bend to him as it were in reverence, when they first come into his presence. They often fight before him, beginning their combat like rams, by running fiercely one at the other; after, as boares with their tusks, they fight with their teeth and trunks. In this violent opposition they are each so carefull to preserve his rider, as that very few of them at those times receive hurt. They are governed with an hook of steele, made like the iron end of a boat-hook, with which their keepers, sitting on their neckes, put them back or pricke them forward at their pleasure. The King traines up many of his elephants for the warre; who carrie each of them one iron gunne about sixe foot long, lying upon a square strong frame of wood, fastned with girts or ropes upon him, which like an harquebuse is let into the timber with a loop of iron. At the foure corners of this frame are banners of silke, put upon short poles;' within sits a gunner to make his shot according to his occasion. The peece carrieth a bullet about the bignesse of a little tennis-ball. When the King travels, he hath many elephants thus appointed for guard. Hee keeps many of them for state to goe before him, who are adorned with bosses of brasse, and some of them are made of massie silver or gold, having likewise divers bells about them, in which they delight. They have faire coverings, either of cloth or velvet or cloth of silver or gold; and for greater state, banners of silke carried before them, in which is the ensigne of their great king (a lion in the sunne) [1] imprinted. These are allowed each three or foure men at the least, to waite upon them. Hee makes use of others to carrie himselfe or his women, who sit in pretie convenient receptacles fastned on their backes (which our painters describe like to castles), made of slight turn'd pillars, richly covered, that will hold foure sitters. Others he employes for carriage of his necessaries.

[1] See *The Embassy of Sir Thomas Roe*, vol. ii, p. 563.

Onely he hath one faire elephant, which is content to be fettered, but would never indure man or other burthen on his backe.

These vast beasts, though the countrey be very fruitfull and all provision cheape, yet by reason of their huge bulke are very chargeable in keeping; for such as are well fed stand their masters in foure or five shillings each of them the day. They are kept without doores, where by a sollid chaine upon one of their hind legges they fasten them to a tree or some strong post. As they stand in the sunne, the flyes often vex them; wherefore with their feete they make dust, the ground being very dry, and with their truncks cast it about their bodies to drive away the flyes. Whenas they are mad (as usually the males are once a yeare for their females, when they are lustie, but in few dayes after come againe in temper), they are so mischievous that they will strike any thing (but their keeper) that comes in their way; and their strength is such as that they will beate an horse or camell dead with their truncke at one blow. At these times, to prevent mischiefe, they are kept apart from company, fettered with chaines. But if by chance in their phrensie they get loose, they will make after every thing they see stirre; in which case there is no meanes to stop them in their violent course but by lighting of wild-fire, prepared for that purpose, whose sparkling and cracking makes them stand still and tremble. The King allowes every one of his great elephants foure females, which in their language they call wives. The males testicles lye about his fore-head; the females teates are betwixt her fore-legges. Shee carrieth her young one whole yeare ere she bring it forth. Thirtie yeares expire ere they come to their full growth, and they fulfill the accustomed age of man ere they dye. Notwithstanding the great plentie of them, they are valued there at exceeding great rates; some of them prized at one thousand pounds sterling and more.

Now, for the inhabitants of Indostan, they were anciently Gentiles, or notorious idolaters, called in generall Hindoos; but ever since they were subdued by Tamberlaine, have beene mixed with Mahometans. There are besides many Persians and Tartars, many Abissines and Armenians, and some few almost of every people in Asia,[1] if not of Europe, that have residence here. Amongst them are some Jewes, but not beloved, for their very name is a proverbe or word of reproch. For the stature of these Easterne Indians, they are like us, but generally very streight, for I never beheld any in those parts crooked. They are of a tawnie or olive colour; their haire blacke as a raven, but not curl'd. They love not a man or woman that is very white or faire, because that (as they say) is the colour of lepers (common amongst them). Most of the Mahometans, but the Moolaes (which are their priests) or those that are very old and retyred, keepe their chinnes bare, but suffer the haire on their upper lip to grow as long as Nature will feed it.[2] They usually shave off all the haire from their heads, reserving onely a locke on the crowne for Mahomet to pull them into Heaven. Both among the Mahometans and Gentiles are excellent barbers. The people often wash their bodies, and anoint themselves with sweet oyles.

The habits both of the men and women are little different, made for the most part of white cotton-cloth. For the fashion, they are close, streight to the middle, hanging loose downward below the knee. They weare long breeches underneath, made close to their bodies, that reach to their ankles, ruffling like boots on the smal of their legs. Their feet are bare in their shooes, which most commonly they weare like slippers, that they may the more readily put them off when they come into their houses, whose floores are covered with excellent carpets (made in that kingdom, good as any in Turkie or Persia) or somwhat else (according to the qualitie of the man) more base, upon which they sit, when as they conferre or eate, like taylors on their shop-boards. The mens heads are covered with a long thinne wreathe of cloth, white or coloured, which goes many times about them; they call it a shash. They uncover not their heads when as they doe reverence to their superiours, but in stead of that bow their bodies, putting their right hands to the top of their heads, after that they have touched the earth

[1] In the later edition Terry avers that he saw some Chinese and Japanese in India.

[2] The 1655 edition says that the hair is kept black 'by combing it continually with black lead combes'.

with them; as much as to say, the partie they salute shall, if he please, tread upon them. Those that bee equals take one the other by the chinne or beard, as Joab did Amasa (2 *Sam.* 20), but salute in love, not treacherie. They have good words to expresse their wel-wishes, as this: *Greeb-a Nemoas*; that is: *I wish the prayers of the poore*;[1] and many other like these most significant.

The Mahometan women, except they bee dishonest or poore, come not abroad. They are very well favoured, though not faire; their heads covered with veiles. Their haire hangs down behind them twisted with silke. Those of qualitie are bedecked with many jewels about their neckes and wrists. Round about their eares are holes made for pendants; and every woman hath one of her nostrils pierced, that there, when as shee please, shee may weare a ring. It should seeme an ancient ornament (*Es*[*aiah*] 3. 21). The women in those parts have a great happinesse above all I know, in their easie bringing forth of children; for it is a thing common there, for women great with childe one day to ride, carrying their infants in their bodies, the next day to ride againe, carrying them in their armes.

For the language of this empire, I meane the vulgar, it is called Indostan; a smooth tongue, and easie to be pronounced, which they write as wee to the right hand.[2] The learned tongues are Persian and Arabian, which they write backward, as the Hebrewes, to the left. There is little learning among them; a reason whereof may be their penury of bookes, which are but few, and they manuscripts. But doubtlesse they are men of strong capacities, and, were there literature among them, would be the authors of many excellent workes. They have heard of Aristotle (whom they call Aplis[3]), and have some

[1] The phrase is really a form of address: *gharib-nawāz*, 'considerate to the poor'. Sir Charles Lyall points out that Terry has confused *nawāz* with *namāz* (prayers).

[2] 'It is expressed by letters which are very much different from those alphabets by which the Persian and Arabian tongues are formed' (1655 edition, p. 232). Terry is referring to either Hindi or Gujarātī, written in the *nāgarī* characters.

[3] Possibly Terry had heard him referred to as *al failsūf*, i. e. the philosopher.

of his bookes translated into Arabian. Avicenna, that noble physician, was borne in Samarcandia, the countrey of Tamerlaine; in whose science they have good skill. The common diseases of the countrey are bloudie fluxes, hot fevers and calentures; in all which they prescribe fasting as a principall remedie. That filthy disease, the consequence of incontinencie, is common amongst them. The people in generall live about our ages; but they have more old men. They delight much in musicke, and have many stringed and wind instruments, which never seemed in my eare to bee any thing but discord. They write many wittie poems, and compose stories or annals of their owne countrey; and professe themselves to have good skill in astrologie. And in men of that profession the King puts so much confidence that hee will not undertake a journey, nor yet doe any thing of the least consequence, unlesse his wizards tell him tis a good and prosperous houre.

The Gentiles beginne their yeare the first of March. The Mahometans theirs at the very instant (as the astrologers ghesse) that the sunne enters into Aries; from which time the King keepes a feast that is called the Nooros,[1] signifying *nine dayes*, which time it continues (like that Ahasuerus made in the third yeare of his raigne: *Ester* the first); where all his nobles assemble in their greatest pompe, presenting him with gifts, hee repaying them againe with princely rewards; at which time being in his presence, I beheld most immense and incredible riches to my amazement in gold, pearles, precious stones, jewels, and many other glittering vanities. This feast I tooke notice of at Mandoa [Māndu], where the Mogol hath a most spacious house, larger then any I have seene; in which many excellent arches and vaults speake for the exquisite skill of his subjects in architecture. At Agra hee hath a palace wherein two large towers, the least ten foot square, are covered with plate of the purest gold.[2]

There are no hangings on the walls of his houses, by reason

[1] See p. 117. Terry's explanation of the term is of course wrong. He has confused *nau* (new) with *nuh* (nine).

[2] In the 1655 edition Terry adds: 'this I had from Tom Coriat, as from other English merchants who keep in a factory at that place'.

of the heate; the wals are either painted or else beautified with a purer white lime then that we call Spanish. The floores, paved with stone or else made with lime and sand, like our playster of Paris, are spred with rich carpets. There lodge none in the Kings house but his women and eunuches, and some little boyes which hee keepes about him for a wicked use. Hee alwayes eates in private among his women upon great varietie of excellent dishes, which dressed and prooved by the taster are served in vessels of gold (as they say), covered and sealed up, and so by eunuchs brought to the King. He hath meate ready at all houres, and calls for it at pleasure. They feede not freely on full dishes of beefe and mutton (as we), but much on rice boyled with pieces of flesh or dressed many other wayes. They have not many roast or baked meats, but stew most of their flesh. Among many dishes of this kinde Ile take notice but of one they call Deu Pario,[1] made of venison cut in slices, to which they put onions and herbs, some rootes, with a little spice and butter: the most savorie meate I ever tasted, and doe almost thinke it that very dish which Jacob made ready for his father, when he got the blessing.

In this kingdome there are no innes to entertaine strangers. Onely in great townes and cities are faire houses built for their receit (which they call Sarray), not inhabited; where any passengers may have roome freely, but must bring with him his bedding, his cooke, and other necessaries wherein to dresse his meate; which are usually carried on camels, or else in carts drawne with oxen, wherein they have tents to pitch when they meete with no Sarras. The inferior sort of people ride on oxen, horses, mules, camels, or dromedaries (the women like the men); or else in slight coaches with two wheeles, covered on the top and backe, but the fore-part and sides open, unlesse they carrie women. They will conveniently hold two persons, beside the driver. They are drawne by oxen, one yoake in a coach, suted for colour, but many of them are white, not very large. They are guided with cords, which goe through the parting of their nostrils and so twixt their hornes into the coach-mens hand. They dresse and keepe them clothed as

[1] This seems to be meant for *dopyáj* or *dupiyázah*, for which see the *Áin*, vol. i, p. 60.

their horses. They are naturally nimble; to which use makes them so fitting to performe that labour, as that they will goe twentie miles a day or more with good speed. The better sort ride on elephants, or else are carried upon mens shoulders alone, in a slight thing they call a palankee [palanquin], which is like a couch or standing pallat, but covered with a cannopie. This should seeme an ancient effeminacie sometimes used in Rome, Juvenal [1] thus describing a fat lawyer that fil'd one of them: *Causidici nova cum veniat lectica Mathonis plena ipso*——.

For pastimes they delight in hawking, hunting of hares, deere, or wilde beasts. Their dogs for chase are made somewhat like our gray-hounds, but much lesse; they open not [2] in the pursuite of the game. They hunt likewise with leopards, which by leaping sease on that they pursue. They have a cunning device to take wild-fowle; where a fellow goes into the water with a fowle of that kind he desires to catch, whose skinne is stuffed so artificially as that it appeares alive. He keepes all his body but the face under water, on which he layes this counterfeit; thus comming among them, plucks them by the legs under water.[3] They shoote for pastime much in bowes, which are made curiously in the countrey of buffeloes hornes, glewed together; to which they have arrowes made of little canes, excellently headed and feathered. In these they are so skilfull that they will kill birds flying. Others take delight in managing their horses on which they ride, or else are otherwise carried, though they have not one quarter of a mile to goe; the men of qualitie holding it dishonorable to goe on foote.

In their houses they play much at that most ingenious game we call chesse, or else at tables.[4] They have cardes, but quite different from ours. Sometimes they make themselves merry

[1] 'In his first Satire', adds the 1655 edition; where the following translation is given:

'Matho the pleader comes in his new chaire,
Fild with himself, when he takes the air.'

[2] Do not give tongue.

[3] This practice is described in the *Āīn* (vol. i, p. 295); also by Ovington (*Voyage to Suratt*, p. 274).

[4] The old English name for backgammon. The Indian equivalent here referred to, viz. the game of *chaupar*, is described in the *Āīn* (vol. i, p. 303). An account of Indian cards will be found at p. 306 of the same volume.

with cunning jugglers or mountebankes, who will suffer snakes they keepe in baskets to bite them, and presently cure the swelling with powders; or else they see the trickes of apes and monkeyes.

In the southerne parts of Indostan are great store of large white apes; some, I dare boldly say, as tall as our biggest gray-hounds. They are fearefull (as it should seeme) to birds that make their nests in trees; wherefore Nature hath taught them this subtiltie, to secure themselves by building their little houses on the twigs of the utmost boughs, there hanging like purse-nets, to which the apes cannot possibly come.[1]

Every great towne or citie of India hath markets twice a day: in the coole season presently after the sunne is risen, and a little before his setting. They sell almost every thing by weight. In the heate of the day they keepe their houses; where the men of better fashion, lying on couches or sitting on their carpets, have servants stand about them who, beating the ayre with broade fannes of stiffe leather or the like, make winde to coole them. And taking thus their ease, they often call their barbers, who tenderly gripe and smite their armes and other parts of their bodies, instead of exercise, to stirre the bloud. It is a pleasing wantonnesse, and much used in those hot climes.

I must needes commend the Mahumetans and Gentiles for their good and faithfull service; amongst whom a stranger may travell alone, with a great charge of money or goods, quite through the countrey and take them for his guard, yet never bee neglected or injured by them. They follow their masters on foote, carrying swords and bucklers or bowes and arrowes for their defence; and by reason of great plentie of provision in that kingdome, a man may hire them upon easie conditions, for they will not desire above five shillings the moone, paide the next day after the change (*Quibus hinc toga, calceus hinc est; et panis fumusque domi*[2]), to provide themselves all necessaries, and for it doe most diligent service. Such

[1] He is describing the nest of the weaver bird.

[2] Another quotation from Juvenal's *Satires*. The 1655 edition translates the passage thus:

'Their coat, their shooes, their bread, their fire,
And all besides, bought with this hire.'

is their pietie to their parents that those which have no greater meanes will impart halfe of it at the least to releeve their necessities, choosing rather for to famish themselves then to see them want.

There are, both among the Mahumetans and Gentiles, men of undaunted courage. Those of note among the Mahumetans are called Baloches,[1] inhabiting Hajacan, adjoyning to the kingdome of Persia ; or else Patans, taking their denomination from a province in the kingdome of Bengala.[2] These will looke an enemie boldly in the face and maintaine with their lives their reputation of valour. Among the many sects of Gentiles there is but one race of fighters, called Rashbootes, a number of which live by spoyle ; who in troopes surprize poore passengers, cruelly butchering those they get under their power. Those excepted, all the rest in the countrey are in generall pusilanimous, and had rather quarrell then fight ; having such poore spirits in respect of us Christians that the Mogol is pleased often to use this proverbe : that one Portugal will beate three of them, and one English-man three Portugals.

Touching their munition for the warre, they have good ordnance, made (for ought I could gather) very anciently in those parts. Iron peeces carried upon elephants (before described), and lesser gunnes made for foot-men, who are somewhat long in taking their ayme, but come as neere the marke as any I ever saw. They fire all their peeces with match. As for gun-powder, they make very good. They use lances and swords and targets [shields], bowes and arrowes. Their swords are made crooked like a faulchion, very sharpe, but for want of skill in those that temper them, will breake rather then bend ; and therefore wee often sell our sword-blades at high prices that will bow and become streight againe. I have seene horse-men there, who have carried whole armories about them, thus appointed : at their sides good swords ; under them sheves of arrowes ; on their shoulders bucklers, and upon their backs guns fastned with belts ; at the left side bowes hanging in cases, and lances about two yards and a halfe

[1] The Balūchis were scattered all over Northern and Western India, owing to the general use of their camels for the transportation of goods.

[2] This is, of course, a mistake.

long (having excellent steele heads), which they carrie in their hands. Yet for all this harnesse, the most of them dare not resist a man of courage, though he have for his defence but the worst of those weapons. The armies in those easterne warres oftentimes consist of incredible multitudes ; they talke of some which have exceeded that mightie host which Zerah, King of Ethiopia, brought against Asa (2 *Chron.* 14). The musicke they have when they goe to battell is from kittle-drums and long winde instruments. The armies on both sides usually beginne with most furious onsets ; but in short time, for want of good discipline, one side is routed and the controversie, not without much slaughter, decided.

The Mahometans have faire churches, which they call Mesquits, built of stone. The broade side towards the west is made up close, like a wall ; that towards the east is erected on pillars ; so that the length of them is north and south, which way they burie their dead. At the corners of their great churches which stand in cities are high pinacles, to whose tops the Moolaas ascend certain times of the day and proclaime their prophet Mahomet thus in Arabian : *La Alla illa Alla, Mahomet Resul-Alla* ;[1] that is : No God but one God, and Mahomet the ambassadour of God. This in stead of bells (which they endure not in their temples) put the most religious in minde of their devotion. Which words Master Coryat often hearing in Agra, upon a certaine time got up into a turret, over against the priest, and contradicted him thus in a loude voyce : *La Alla, illa Alla, Hazaret-Eesa Ebn-Alla* :[2] No God but one God, and Christ the Sonne of God ; and further added that Mahomet was an impostor ; which bold attempt in many other places of Asia, where Mahomet is more zealously professed, had forfetted his life with as much torture as tyrannie could invent. But here every man hath libertie to professe his owne religion freely and, for any restriction I ever observed, to dispute against theirs with impunitie.

Now concerning their burials. Every Mahometan of qualitie in his life time provides a faire sepulcher for himselfe and

[1] The proper form is: *Lā ilāha illa-l-lāh, Muhammadur-Rasūlu-llāh.*

[2] *Ḫazarat Īsā Ibn Allāh.*

kindred, encompassing with a firme wall a good circuit of ground, neere some tanke (about which they delight for to burie their dead) or else in a place nigh springs of water that may make pleasant fountaynes; neere which hee erects a tombe, round or square, vaulted upon pillars, or else made close, to be entred with doores; under which are the bodies of the dead interred. The rest of the ground they plant with trees and flowers, as if they would make Elysian fields such as the poets dreamed of, wherein their soules might take their repose. They burie not within their churches. There are many goodly monuments of this kinde, richly adorned, built to the memorie of such as they have esteemed saints, of which they have a large kalender. In these are lamps continually burning, whither men transported with blinde devotion daily resort, there to contemplate the happines these Pieres [see p. 180] (for so they call them) enjoy. But among many faire piles there dedicated to this use, the most excellent is at Secandra, a village three miles from Agra. It was beganne by Achabar-sha, this Kings father, who there lyes buried, and finished by this present King, who meanes to lye beside him.

Their Moolaas imploy much of their time like scriveners, to doe businesse for others. They have libertie to marrie as well as the people, from whom they are not distinguished in habite. Some live retyred, that spend their dayes in meditation or else in giving good morall precepts unto others. These are of high esteeme; and so are another sort called Seayds [see p. 171], who derive themselves from Mahomet. The priests doe neither reade nor preach in their churches;[1] but there is a set forme of prayer in the Arabian tongue, not understood by most of the common people, yet repeated by them as well as by the Moolaas. They likewise rehearse the names of God and Mahomet certayne times every day upon beads, like the misse-led Papist, who seemes to regard the number rather

[1] In the 1655 edition this statement is corrected to one that the mullahs 'read some parcells out of their *Alcoran* upon Frydays (which are their Sabboths or days of rest) unto the people assembled in their mosquit or churches, and then further deliver some precepts, which they gather out of it, unto their miserably deluded hearers'.

then the weight of prayers. Before they goe into their churches they wash their feete, and entring in put off their shooes. As they beginne their devotions, they stop their eares and fixe their eyes, that nothing may divert their thoughts. Then in a soft and still voyce they utter their prayers; wherein are many words most significantly expressing the omnipotencie, greatnesse, eternitie, and other attributes of God; many words full of humiliation, confessing with divers submissive gestures their owne unworthinesse; when they pray, casting themselves low upon their faces sundrie times, and then acknowledge that they are burthens to the earth and poison to the aire, and the like, and therefore dare not so much as looke up to heaven, but at last comfort themselves in the mercies of God through the mediation of Mahomet. And many amongst them (to the shame of us Christians), what impediment soever they have, either by pleasure or profit, pray five times every day, at six, nine, twelve, three, and six of the clock. But, by the way, they distinguish their time in a different manner from us, dividing the day into foure and the night into as many parts, which they call Pores [*pahar*]. These are againe subdivided each into eight parts, which they call Grees [*ghari*], measured according to the ancient custome by water dropping out of one little vessell into another, by which there alwayes stand servants appointed for that purpose,[1] smiting with an hammer a concave piece of pure metall, like the inner part of an ordinarie platter, hanging by the brim on a wyre, the number of Grees and Pores as they passe.

For the temperance of many, both among the Mahometans and Gentiles, it is such as that they will rather die (like the mother and her seven sonnes: 2 *Mac*[*cabees*] 7) then eate or drinke any thing their law forbids. Such meate and drinke as their law allowes they use onely to satisfie nature, not appetite; hating gluttonie, and esteeming drunkennesse (as indeed it is) a second madnesse, and therefore have but one word in their language (*mest*) for a drunkard and a mad-man.[2] They keepe a solemne Lent, which they call the *Ram-Jan*,

[1] 'To turn that vessell up again when it is all dropped out, and then to strike', &c. (1655 edition).

[2] This is an overstatement, though *mast* has a wide connotation.

about the moneth of August,[1] which continues one whole moone; during which time those that bee strict in their religion forbeare their women, and will take neither meate nor drinke so long as the sunne is above their horizon; but after he is set, eate at pleasure. Towards the end of this Lent they consecrate a day of mourning to the memorie of their dead friends; when I have beheld divers of the meaner sort make bitter lamentation. (Beside this common sadnesse, there are many foolish women who often in the yeere, so long as they survive, moysten the graves of their husbands or children with affectionate teares.) But when the night begins to cover the day of generall mourning, they fire an innumerable companie of lamps and lights, which they set on the sides and tops of their houses and all other most conspicuous places; and when these are extinguished, take foode. The *Ram-Jan* fully ended, the most devout Mahometans assemble to some famous misquit, where by a Moola some part of the *Alcoran* (which they will not touch without reverence) is publikely read. They keepe a feast in November, called *Buccaree* [*Bakarah-ĭd*], signifying the Ram-feast, when they solemnely kill a ram, and roast him in memorie of that ram which redeemed Ishmael (as they say) when Abraham was readie to make him a sacrifice. Many other feasts they have in memorie of Mahomet and their Pieres.

They have the bookes of Moses, whom they call *Moosa Carym-Alla*: Moses the righteous of God. *Ibrahim Calim-Alla*: Abraham the faithfull of God.[2] So Ishmael, the true sacrifice of God; *Dahoode* [*Dāūd*], David the prophet of God; *Selimon* [Sulaimān], Salomon the wisedome of God; all expressed, as the former, in short Arabian words. To whose particular remembrances they daily sing ditties. And more-

[1] Terry was misled by the fact that both in 1617 and in 1618 the beginning of Ramazān fell within the month of August. The 1655 edition substitutes: 'which begins the first new moon which happens in September'; but this is also wrong. As the Muhammadan year is lunar, any given month in time moves round the calendar of the solar year.

[2] These epithets should be: *Mūsa Kalīmullāh*, Moses, the man who conversed with God: *Ibrāhīm Khalīlullāh*, Abraham, the friend of God.

over, there is not a man amongst them (but those of the ruder sort) that at any time mentions the name of our blessed Saviour, called there *Hazaret-Eesa*, the Lord Christ, without reverence and respect, saying that He was a good man and a just, lived without sinne, did greater miracles then ever any before or since Him. Nay farther, they call Him *Rhahow-Alla* [*Rûhullâh*], the breath of God; but how He should be the Sonne of God cannot conceive, and therefore will not beleeve. Notwithstanding this, the Mahometans in generall thinke us Christians so uncleane they will not eate with us, nor yet of any thing is dressed in our vessels.

Among the Mahometans are many called Dervises, which relinquish the world and spend their dayes in solitude, expecting a recompence in a better life; whose sharpe and strict penances they voluntarily under-take farre exceede all those the Romanists boast of. For instance, there are some that live alone upon the tops of hills remote from companie, there passing their time in contemplation, and will rather famish then move from these retyred cells; wherefore the people that dwell neerest to them, out of devotion, releeve them. Some againe impose long times of fasting upon themselves, til nature be almost quite decayed. There are many other among them they call religious men, who weare nothing about them but to hide their shame; and these, like the Mendicant Friars, begge for all they eate. Usually they live in the suburbs of great cities or townes, and are like the man our blessed Saviour mentions, about the citie of the Gadarens, which had devils and ware no clothes, neither abode in any house but in the tombes. They make little fires in the day, sleeping at night in the warme ashes, with which they besmeare their bodies. These ashmen suffer not the rasor at any time to come upon their heads, and some of them let their nayles grow like birds clawes, as it is written of Nabuchadnezzar, when hee was driven out from the societie of men. And there are a sort among them, called Mendee,[1] who, like the priests of Baal,

[1] Sir Charles Lyall suggests that this term may represent *Mahdawi*, a sect of Shiah devotees in Gujarât. In India *Mahdi* is popularly pronounced *Menhdi*. During the Muharram such devotees often gash their bodies.

often cut their flesh with knives and launcers. Others I have seene who out of devotion put such massie fetters of iron upon their legs as that they can scarce stirre with them; and so,[1] as fast as they are able, goe many miles in pilgrimage barefoote upon the parching ground, to visit the sepulchres of their deluding saints; thus taking more paines to goe to hell (*tantum relligio potuit suadere malorum*[2]) then any Christian I know doth to goe to heaven. These marry not. Such as doe, Mahomet allowes foure wives. Besides they take libertie to keepe as many women as they are able. Only the priests content themselves with one. Notwithstanding this polygamie, the hot jealousies of the lustfull Mahometans are such that they will scarce endure the brothers or fathers of their beloved wives or women to have speech with them, except in their presence; and Time, by this restraint, hath made it odious for such women as have the reputation of honestie to be seene at any time by strangers. But if they dishonour their husbands beds or, being unmarried, are found incontinent, professing chastitie, rather then they shall want punishment, their owne brothers will bee their executioners; who for such unnaturall acts shall be commended rather then questioned. Yet there is toleration for impudent harlots, who are as little ashamed to entertayne as others openly to frequent their houses. The women of better fashion have eunuchs in stead of men to wait upon them; who in their minoritie are deprived of all that may provoke jealousie.

Their marriages are solemnized in great pompe. For after the Moola hath joyned their hands, with some other ceremonie and words of benediction, the first watch of the night they begin their jollitie; the man on horse-backe, be he poore or riche, with his friends about him, many cresset lightly[3] before him, with drums and wind instruments and other pastimes. The woman followes with her friends in coaches, covered; and after they have thus passed the most eminent places of the citie or towne they live in, returne home and there part with a banquet, the men and women separated. They marry for

[1] The 1655 edition adds (p. 283): 'covered with blew mantles'.

[2] A well-known quotation from Lucretius. The 1655 edition gives the whole passage.

[3] Lights?

the most part at the ages of twelve or thirteene, their mothers most commonly making the matches.

Now more particularly of the Gentiles, which are there distracted in fourscore and foure severall sects, all differing mainly in opinion ; which had oftentimes fild me with wonder, but that I know Satan (the father of division) to be the seducer of them all. Their illiterate priests are called Bramins ; who, for ought I could ever gather, are so sottish and inconstant in their grounds that they scarce know what they hold. They have little churches which they call Pagodes, built round, in which are images for worship made in monstrous shapes. Some of them dreame of Elysian fields, to which their soules must passe over a Styx or Acharon, and there take new bodies. Others hold that ere long the world shall have a period ; after which they shall live here againe on a new earth. Some Bramins have told me how that they acknowledge one God, whom they describe with a thousand hands, with a thousand feete, and as many eyes, thereby expressing his power. They talke of foure books, which about six thousand yeeres since were sent them from God by their prophet Ram ; whereof two were sealed up and might not be opened ; the other to be read onely by themselves.[1] They say that there are seven orbes, above which is the seate of God : that God knowes not petie things, or, if He doe, regards them not. They circumscribe God unto place, saying that He may be seene, but as in a mist

[1] The version in the 1655 edition (p. 349) is as follows: 'Those Bramins talk of two books, which, not long after the Creation, when the world began to be peopled, they say were delivered by Almighty God to Bramon . . . one of which books (they say), containing very high and secret and mysterious things, was sealed up and might not be opened ; the other to be read, but onely by the Bramins or priests. And this book thus to be read came after, as they further say, into the hands of Bremaw . . . and by him it was communicated unto Ram and Permissar, two other fam'd prophets amongst them, which those heathen do likewise exceedingly magnifie, as they do some others whose names I have not. Now that book, which they call the *Shester*, or the book of their written word, hath been transcribed in all ages ever since by the Bramins, out of which they deliver precepts unto the people.' In this 'Bramon' is *Brahma*, the primeval spirit: 'Bremaw', the god *Brahma*: 'Ram', *Râma*: 'Permissar', *Parameshvra* (i. e. *Shiva*): and 'Shester' the *Shâstra*.

afarre off, not neere. They beleeve that there are devils, but so bound in chaines that they cannot hurt them. They call a man Adam [Hind. *admi*], from our first father Adam, whose wife, tempted with the forbidden fruit, tooke it (as they say) and eate it downe ; but as her husband swallowed it, the hand of God stopped it in his throat ; whence man hath a bunch there, which women have not, called by them Adams apple. As anciently among the Jewes, their priesthood is hereditarie ; for every Bramins sonne is a priest, and marries a Bramins daughter. And so among all the Gentiles the men take the daughters of those to bee their wives which are of their fathers tribe, sect, and occupation ; for instance, a merchants sonne marries a merchants daughter. And every mans sonne that lives by his labour marries the daughter of him that is of his owne profession ; by which meanes they never advance themselves. These Gentiles take but one wife ; of which they are not so fearefull as the Mahometans of their multitude, for they suffer them to goe abroad. They are married yong, at six or seven yeeres old (their parents making the contracts), and about twelve come together. Their nuptials, as those of the Mahometans, are performed with much pompe and jollitie.

For their habit, it differs little from the Mahometans ; but many of the women weare rings upon their toes, and therefore goe barefoote. They have likewise broad rings of brasse (or better metall according to the qualitie of the woman) about the small of the legges to take off and on ; haply such as the Prophet meant by the tinkling ornaments about the feete, or the ornaments of the legs, which the Jewish women were wont to put on (*Esay* 3). And such as these they have about their armes. The flaps or nether part of their eares are boared when they are yong, which hole, daily stretched and made wider by things kept in it for that purpose, at last becomes so large that it will hold a ring (I dare boldly say) as large as a little sawcer, made hollow on the sides for the flesh to rest in. Both men and women wash their bodies every day before they eate ; which done, they keepe off their clothes (but the covering of modestie) till they have fed. This outward washing appertaines, as they thinke, to their clensing from sinne ; not unlike the Pharisies, who would not eate with unwashen hands (*Mar*. 7). Hence they ascribe a certaine divinitie to rivers, but above all to Ganges; daily flocking thither in troopes, and there throw in pieces of gold or silver, according to their devotion and abilitie; after which they wash their bodies.[1] Both men and women paint on their fore-heads or other parts of their faces red or yellow spots.

Now farther for their grosse opinions, they beleeve not the resurrection of flesh; and therefore burne the bodies of their dead neere some river (if they may with conveniencie), wherein they sowe the ashes. Their widowes marrie not; but, after the losse of their husbands, cut their haire and spend all their life following as neglected creatures; whence, to bee free from shame, many yong women are ambitious to die with honor (as they esteeme it), when their fiery love brings them to the flames (as they thinke) of martyrdome most willingly; following their dead husbands unto the fire, and there imbracing are burnt with them; but this they doe voluntary, not compelled. The parents and friends of those women will most joyfully accompanie them, and when the wood is fitted for this hellish sacrifice and begins to burne, all the people assembled shoute and make a noyse, that the screeches of this tortured creature may not bee heard. Not much unlike the custome of the Ammonites, who, when they made their children passe through the fire to Moloch, caused certaine tabret or drums to sound, that their cry might not be heard; whence the place was called *Tophet*, a tabret (2 *Kings*, 23. 10). There is one sect among the Gentiles which neither burne nor interre their dead. They are called Parcees; who incircle pieces of ground with high stone walls, remote from houses or roade-wayes, and therein lay their carkasses wrapped in sheetes; thus having no other tombes but the gorges of ravenous fowles.[2]

The Gentiles for the most part are very industrious. They till the ground or else spend their time otherwaies diligently

[1] 'And the nearer they can come to the head of that river, the more virtue they believe is in the water' (1655 edition, p. 348).

[2] In the 1655 edition this account of the Parsees is much enlarged from the Rev. Henry Lord's *Display of Two Forraigne Sects in the East Indies*, 1630

in their vocations. There are amongst them most curious artificers, who are the best apes for imitation in the world; for they will make any new thing by patterne. The Mahometans are generally idle; who are all for to morrow (a word common in their mouthes). They live upon the labours of the Gentiles. Some of which poore seduced infidels will eate of nothing that hath life; and these live upon herbs and milke and butter and cheese and sweet-meates, of which they make divers kindes, whereof the most wholsome is greene ginger, as well preserved there as in any part of the world. Others will eate fish, and no living thing else. The Rashbootes eate swines-flesh, most hatefull to the Mahometans. Some will eate of one kinde of flesh, some of another; but all the Gentiles abstaine from beefe, out of the excellent esteeme they have of kine; and therefore give the King yeerly (beside his other exactions) great summes of money as a ransome for those creatures; whence among other good provision we meete there but with little beefe. Those most tender hearted idolaters are called Banians; who hold Pithagoras his μετεμψύχωσις as a prime article of their faith. They thinke that the soules of the best men and women, when their bodies let them out of prison, take their repose in kine, which in their opinion are the best of all creatures. So the soules of the wicked goe into viler beasts; as the soules of gluttons and drunkards into swine; the soules of the voluptuous and incontinent into monkies and apes; the soules of the furious, cruell, and revengefull into lyons, tygers, and wolves; the soules of the envious into serpents; and so into other creatures according to their qualitie and disposition, successively from one to another of the same kinde, *ad infinitum*; by consequence beleeving the immortalitie of the world. So that there is not a silly flie but, if they may bee credited, carries about some soules (haply they thinke of light women) [1]; and will not be perswaded out of these grosse opinions, so incorrigible are their sottish errours; and therefore will not deprive the most offensive creatures of their life (not snakes, that will kill them),

[1] The 1655 edition adds that 'probably they further believe that the souls of froward, peevish, and teachy [i. e. touchy] women go into waspes'.

saying it is their nature to doe harme: how that they have reason to shunne, not libertie to destroy them.

For their workes of charitie many rich men build Sarraas, or make wells or tankes neere to high-wayes that are much travelled, where passengers may drinke; or else allow pensions unto poore men, that they may sit by the high-way sides and offer water unto those that passe.

Their day of rest is Thursday; as the Mahometans Friday. Many festivals they have which they keepe solemne; and pilgrimages, whereof the most famous are specified in the briefe descriptions of Negracut and Cyba; where people out of devotion cut off part of their tongues, which (if Master Coryat, who strictly observed it, may be beleeved) in a few daies became whole againe. It were easie to enlarge, but I will not cast away inke and paper in a farther description of their stupid idolatries. The summe is that both Mahometans and Gentiles ground their opinions upon tradition, not reason; and are content to perish with their fore-fathers, out of a preposterous zeale and loving perversenesse, never ruminating on that they maintayne, like to uncleane beasts which chew not the cud.

Now both these Mahometans and Gentiles are under the subjection of the Great Mogoll, whose name signifieth a circumcised man,[1] and therefore he is called the Great Mogoll, as much as to say: *the Chiefe of the Circumcision*. He is lineally descended by the father from that famous conquerour of the East, called in our stories Tamberlaine, in theirs Temar [Tīmūr]; who towards his end, by an unhappie fall from his horse, which made him halt to his grave, was called Temar-lang, or Temar the Lame. The present King is the ninth in a direct line from that his great ancestor. The Emperour stiles himselfe: *the King of Justice, the Light of the Law of Mahomet, the Conquerour of the World*.[2] Himselfe moderates in all matters

[1] The same statement is made by Salbank (*Letters Received*, vol. vi, p. 184), by Roe (*Embassy*, p. 312), and by Bluteau (*Vocabulario*, 1712–21): but there is no ground for it.

[2] The original of the first epithet can only be guessed at, though it may be a perversion of *Ghufrān panāh* ('the asylum of pardon'), which appears as one of the Emperor's titles on his tomb. The rest is Nūr-ud-

of consequence which happen neere his court, for the most part judging *secundum allegata et probata*. Tryals are quicke, and so are executions: hangings, beheading, impaling, killing with dogges, by elephants, serpents, and other like, according to the nature of the fact. The execution is commonly done in the market place. The governours in cities and provinces proceed in like forme of justice. I could never heare of law written amongst them; the King and his substitutes will is law. His vice-gerents continue not long in a place, but, to prevent popularitie, receive usually a remoove yearely. They receive his letters with great respect. They looke for presents from all which have occasion to use them, and if they be not often visited will aske for them; yea, send them backe for better exchange. The Cadee [*Kāzi*] will imprison debtors and sureties, bound with hand and seale; and men of power for payment will sell their persons, wives, and children; which the custome of the land will warrant.

The King shewes himselfe thrice a day; first, at sun-rising at a bay-window[1] toward the east, many being there assembled to give him the salam, and crying *Padsha salament* [*Pādshāh salāmat*], that is: *Live, O King*. At noone he sees his elephants fight or other pastimes. A little before sun-set he shewes himselfe at a window to the west, and, the sunne being set, returneth in with drums and wind instruments, the peoples acclamations adding to the consort. At any of these three times, any sutor, holding up his petition to be seene, shall be heard. Betwixt seven and nine he sits privately, attended with his nobles.

No subject in this empire hath land of inheritance, nor have other title but the Kings will; which makes some of the grandes to live at the height of their meanes; merchants also to conceale their riches, lest they should be made spunges. Some meane meanes the King allowes the children of those great ones; which they exceed not, except they happily

dīn Muhammad Jahāngīr; but in this 'Muhammad' is a personal name and has no relation to the preceding word, as Terry supposed.

[1] 'In a place very like unto one of our balconies, made in his houses or pavilions for his morning appearance directly opposite to the east, about seven or eight foot high from the ground' (1655 edition, p. 389).

succeed in their fathers favours. His pensions are reckoned by horse, of which hee payeth a million in his empire, for every horse allowing five and twentie pound yearely,[1] raised from lands thereunto designed. There are some twentie in his court which have pay of five thousand horse: others of foure thousand or three thousand: and so downward. Hee which hath pay of five thousand is bound to have two thousand [2] at command, and so in like proportion others. This absolute dependance makes them dissolute parasites. When he giveth advancement, he addeth a new name (as Pharao did to Joseph), and those pithily significant; as *Mahobet Chan*, the *Beloved Lord*; *Chan Jahaun*, the *Lord of my Heart* [3]; *Chan Allau*,[4] the *Lord of the World*; etc. The chiefe officers of state are his Treasurer, the Master of his Eunuches (who is Steward and Comptroller of his House), his Secretarie, the Master of his Elephants, the Tent-master, and Keeper of his Wardrobe. These [There ?] are subordinate titles of honour, as *Chan*, *Mirza*, *Umbra* [see p. 147] or Captaine, *Haddee* [see p. 99], a souldier or horseman.[5] Gorgeous apparell is prohibited by the sunnes heate; the King himselfe being commonly vested with a garment, as before described, of pure white calico lawne. Blue may not be worne in his presence (the colour of mourners), nor the name of death sounded in his eares; but such casually is mollified by tearmes to this purpose: *Such an one hath made himselfe a sacrifice at Your Majesties feet.* That heate of the countrey makes little sale for English cloth, most used there for coverings of elephants, horses, coaches. Yet may this king be thought to exceed any other

[1] In the 1655 edition Terry reduces this sum to £18.

[2] 'One thousand or more' (1655 edition).

[3] Mahābat Khān means 'the lord who inspires awe'; while Khān Jahān is 'the lord of the world'. Sir Charles Lyall points out that Terry, whose smattering of Persian often misled him, has confused the one term with *maḥabbat* (affection) and the other with *jān* (the soul).

[4] Corrected in the 1655 edition to 'Chan-Allaam' (for whom see p. 99).

[5] The later edition amplifies this paragraph into: 'All the Kings children are called Sultans or princes: his daughters Sultanaus or princesses. The next title is Nabob, equivalent to a duke; the next Channa, a double lord, or earle; the next Chan, a lord. So Meirsa signifies a knight that hath been a general or commander in the wars: Umbra, a captain: Haddee, a cavalier or souldier on horse-back.'

in glorious thrones and rich jewels. Hee hath a throne in his palace at Agra, ascended by degrees [steps], on the top whereof are foure lions made of massie silver, gilded, set with precious stones, supporting a canopie of massie gold.[1] By the way I may mention a tame lion living in his court while I was there, going up and downe without hurt like a dogge. His jewels, wherewith hee is daily adorned about his head, necke, wrists, and hilts of his sword and dagger, are invaluable. He is on his birthday, the first of September, (now sixtie times renewed) yearely weighed, and account kept thereof by his physicians, thereby ghessing at his bodily estate.[2]

Part of two letters to His Majestie is here translated out of Persian; sent by Sir Thomas Roe, but written one a yeare before the other.[3]

'When Your Majestie shall open this letter, let your royall heart be as fresh as a sweet garden; let all people make reverence at your gate; let your throne be advanced higher amongst the greatnesse of the kings of the Prophet Jesus. Let Your Majestie be the greatest of all monarches, who may derive their counsell and wisedome from your brest as from a fountayne, that the law of the majestie of Jesus may revive and flourish under your protection. The letters of love and friendship which you sent me, and the presents (tokens of your good affection toward mee), I have received by the hands of your embassadour Sir Thomas Roe, who well deserveth to be your trusted servant; delivered to me in an acceptable and happie houre. Upon which mine eyes were so fixed that I could not easily remoove them to any other object, and have accepted them with great joy,' etc.

The last letter hath this beginning :—

'How gracious is Your Majestie, whose greatnesse God preserve. As upon a rose in a garden, so are mine eyes fixed upon you. God maintayne your estate, that your monarchie may prosper and be augmented, and that you may obtayne

[1] In the 1655 edition Terry says that he had this information from English merchants who had been at Agra. He adds that the lions stood on pedestals of curiously coloured marble.

[2] See notes on pp. 118, 245, *supra*.

[3] Both letters are given at full length in *The Embassy* (pp. 557, 559).

all your desires, worthy the greatnesse of your renowme. And as your heart is noble and upright, so let God give you a glorious raigne, because you strongly defend the majestie of Jesus, which God yet made more flourishing, because it was confirmed by miracles,' etc.

That which followeth in both letters is to testifie his care and love toward the English. These letters being written, their copies were sent to the Lord Embassadour, and the originals, rolled up and covered with cloth of gold and sealed up at both ends ; which is the letter-fashion of those parts.

We travelled two yeares with the Great Mogoll in progresse, in the temperate moneths twixt October and April, there being no lesse then two hundred thousand men, women, and children in this leskar or campe (I am hereof confident), besides elephants, horses, and other beasts that eate corne ; all which notwithstanding, wee never felt want of any provision, no, not in our nineteene dayes travell from Mandoa to Amadavar, thorow a wildernesse, the road being cut for us in the mayne woods. The tents were of divers colours, and represented a spacious and specious citie. The Kings tents red, reared on poles very high, and placed in the midst of the campe, covering a large compasse, incircled with canats [*kanāt*, a screen] (made of red calico stiffened with canes at every breadth, standing upright about nine[1] foot high), guarded round every night with souldiers. He remooved ten or twelve miles a day, more or lesse, according to the convenience of water. His wives and women of all sorts (which are one thousand at least, provided for in his tents) are carryed in palankas or upon elephants, or else in cradles hanging on the sides of dromedaries, covered close and attended by eunuches. In wiving, he respects fancie more then honour, not seeking affinitie with neighbour princes, but to please his eye at home. Noore-Mahal, the name of his best beloved, signifieth *the Light of the Court*. Shee hath much advanced her friends, before meane, and in manner commands the commander of that empire by engrossing his affections. The King and his great men maintayne their women, but little affect them after thirtie yeares of their age.

[1] 'Ten' in the 1655 edition.

This multitude of women notwithstanding, the Mogoll hath but sixe children: five sonnes and a daughter. All his sonnes are called Sultans or Princes: the eldest Sultan Cursero, the second Sultan Parveis, Sultan Caroon the third, Sultan Shahar the fourth. The last is Sultan Tauct, which word in the Persian signifieth *a throne*; so named by the King, who the first houre of his quiet possessing the throne had newes of his birth, about nineteene yeares since.[1] The first sonne, by any of his marryed wives, by prerogative of birth inherits; the elder brother beeing there called the *Great Brother*.[2] Although the younger be not put to death, as with the Turkes, yet it is observed that they survive not long their father, employed commonly in some dangerous expedition. Achabar-sha had threatned to disherit the present King, for abuse of Anar-kalee (that is *Pomegranate Kernell*), his most beloved wife [see p. 166]; but on his death-bed repealed it. This Achabars death is thus reported. He was wont upon displeasure to give pils to his grandes to purge their soules from their bodies; which intending against one, and having another cordiall pill for himselfe, whiles hee entertayned the other with faire flatteries, by a happie-unhappie mistake hee tooke the poyson himselfe; which with a mortall fluxe of bloud in few dayes killed him.[3] *Neque enim lex justior ulla est quam necis artifices arte perire suâ.*[4]

This Kings disposition seemes composed of extreames: very

[1] Jahāndār (see note on p. 100) was born in 1605.

[2] 'Budda Bij, their great brother' (1655 edition). This phrase stands for *buddha bhāi*, 'old brother'.

[3] This story of Akbar's death, though not accepted by modern historians, had evidently a wide currency in India at this time. It is to be found also in the Chronicle appended to De Laet's *De Imperio Magni Mogolis*, and in Peter Mundy's journal under date of 1632 (vol. ii, p. 103). In both of these the intended victim is identified as Mirza Ghāzi, son of Mirza Jāni Beg, ruler of Sind; though the tradition among the Rājputs was that he was Rāja Mān Singh of Amber (see Tod's *Rajasthan*). Herbert (*Some Yeares Travell*, p. 72) has a somewhat different version; and yet another is given by Manucci (vol. i, p. 150).

[4] In the 1655 edition Terry translates the couplet thus:

'When some to kill most deadly engines frame,
Tis just that they themselves be caught i' th' same.'

It is from Ovid's *Art of Love* (i, 655).

cruell, and otherwhiles very milde; often overcome with wine, but severely punishing that fault in others. His subjects know not to disobey; Nature forgetting her private bonds twixt father and sonne to fulfill that publike. He daily relieves many poore, and will in pietie helpe to carrie sometimes his mother in a palanka on his shoulders. He speakes respectively of our Saviour, but is offended at His crosse and povertie; thinking them incompetible to such majestie, though told that His humilitie was to subdue the worlds pride.

All religions are tolerated, and their priests in good esteeme. My selfe often received from the Mogoll himselfe the appellation of Father,[1] with other many gracious words, with place amongst his best nobles. The Jesuites have not only admittance into his presence but incouragements from him by many gifts, with libertie of converting to them; and to the subject, to be without losse of favour converted. He made tryall of one convert[2] with many threats to deterre him from his new profession; and finding him undauntedly resolute, he assayed by flatteries and promises to re-gaine him; but therein also failing, hee bade him continue, and with a reward discharged him; having told him that if he could have frayed [i. e. frightened] or brought him from his religion, he would have made him an example for all waverers. The chiefe Jesuite was Franciscus Corsi,[3] a Florentine by birth, living at the Mogolls court agent for the Portugals. I would I were able to confirme the reports of their conversions. The truth is they have spilt the water of baptisme upon some faces, working on the necessities of poore men, who for want of meanes, which they give them, are content to weare crucifixes, but for want of instruction are only in name Christians. I observed that of the poore there, five have begged in the name of Marie for one in the name of Christ [cf. p. 276]. I also desired to put my hand to this holy worke, but found it difficult, both

[1] *Padre*—a term which, introduced by the Jesuit missionaries, still does duty in India for a chaplain or minister of any Christian denomination.

[2] 'A gentleman of quality and a servant of the Great Mogol' (1655 edition). This tale was derived from Coryat (see p. 280, *supra*).

[3] For an account of him see *The Embassy*, p. 314.

by Mahumetane libertie for women and the debauched liv of some Christian-unchristian men amongst them, *per quoru latera patitur Evangelium.*[1] Hee which hath *the Key of Davi open their eyes*, and in His good time *send labourers into th vineyard. Amen.*

[1] 'By whom the Gospell of Jesus Christ is scandalized and exceeding suffers' is the translation given in the 1655 edition.

INDEX

'Abashed', 138.
Abbās, Shāh. *See* Persia, King of.
Abdullah Khān, 17 *n*., 98, 198 *n*.; Viceroy of Gujarāt, 206.
Abdurrahīm, Mīrza, 71, 78, 80, 98, 106, 108, 131 (3), 137–8, 155 *n*., 162, 207; influence of, 165, 207; his gardens, 138, 207.
Abdurrahīm, Shaikh, 72–3, 77, 126 (2).
Āb-i-bārīk, 168.
Abraham, the Patriarch, 47, 241–2, 259, 318 (2).
Abūlbi Uzbeg, 99.
Abūlfath Dekhani, 99.
Abūl Hasan, Khwāja, 66–8, 85, 87–95, 99, 146–7.
Abu Rīsh, 9.
Abyssinians, 138, 307.
Achin, 35, 41, 128, 200 *n*., 293.
Acosta, Christoval, 305.
Ada, 21.
Adam, 177, 322.
Aden, 60–2, 68.
Ādil Shāh, 14, 15.
Agates, 22, 27, 174.
Agra, 47, 59, 278, 293, 295; Fitch at, 5, 17; Mildenhall at, 55–9; Hawkins at, 64–5, 80–95, 192; Finch at, 146–8; Canning at, 189, 200–2; Withington at, 191–3, 222–8; Sherley at, 212 *n*.; Coryat at, 236–7, 244, 261, 267, 283, 315; described, 17, 182–5, 226; centre of the Mogul's dominions, 100; palace-fortress at, 100, 182–5, 226, 310, 328; black throne at, 115; stone figures at, 183; Jesuits at, 49, 55, 222; Christian cemetery at, 201; fires at, 146, 185; plague at, 237; Governor of, 192, 224.
Ahadi, 99, 164, 184 (2), 277, 327.
Ahmadābād, 76, 100, 106, 170, 193–5, 213, 216–17; described, 173, 206, 300; English at, 190, 203–4, 206–7, 251; Jesuit at, 207; Jahāngīr at, 288, 329; Governor of, 133; Dīwān of, 197.
Ahmadnagar, city of, 130, 146.
Ahmadnagar, King of, 13, 15, 130–1, 138, 291; subdued by Akbar, 130 *n*.
Ajmer, 51–2, 225, 305; described, 170–1; Akbar's pilgrimage to, 148, 150, 171, 225; Jahāngīr at, 192, 225, 236–7, 280; English at, 192 (2), 230, 236, 244, 253; Edwards at, 192, 227–31, 236; Withington at, 193–4, 224, 228; Sherley at, 212 *n*.; Roe at, 194, 237; Coryat at, 236–7, 244, 256, 259, 262, 267; factory closed, 237.
Ajodhya, 176 (2).
Akbar, the Emperor, 2, 3 *n*., 4 *n*., 16–18, 62 *n*., 85, 107, 139 *n*., 142, 168, 170; his conquests, 13, 17, 23–4, 26, 28, 106, 130, 140, 208; defeats Sher Shāh, 152; builds Allahābād castle, 177; founds Fatehpur Sīkri, 149, 160; leaves it, 150, 182; his pilgrimage to Ajmer, 148, 171, 225; Jahāngīr's rebellion, 107, 159, 177, 279 *n*.; deals with the succession, 107–8, 159, 330; Bairām Khān and, 165; Partab Shāh and, 137; Anārkikali and, 166, 330; Fitch and, 5, 17, 18; Mildenhall and, 49, 50; pictures of, 163–4; his magic powers, 276; his piety towards his mother, 278; his death, 49, 330; his widows, 186; his tomb: *see* Sikandra.
Akbarpur (Mālwa), 140.
Akbarpur (Muttra District), 155.
Akbarpur (Oudh), 176.
Albuquerque, Mathias de, 11, 12
Alcaron. *See Kurān*.

Aldea, 132, 134, 136–7, 140, 143 (3), 151, 215.
Aldworth, Thomas, Chief at Surat, 189–90, 192, 202, 219–20, 222–3; ill, 196 *n.*; at Ahmadābād, 204–8, 217.
Aleppo, 2, 3, 6, 7, 9, 18, 47–8, 53, 57, 124–5, 191, 202; Coryat at, 235–7, 241, 243, 250, 256–7, 260–1; consul at, 7, 286.
Alexander the Great, 177, 248.
Alexandria, 202–3, 245, 260, 271.
Alfandega, 128, 134.
Aliad indigo, 153.
Ali Akbar Kuli, Mīrza, 99.
Ali Boghan, 168.
Ali Mardān Khān Bahādur, 99.
Ali Masjid, 168.
Alkin, John, 203.
Allahābād, 5, 19, 107, 177–8, 293; the castle at, 159, 177–8.
Allare, Henry, 256.
Ally Pomory, 77.
Almonds, 297 *n.*; used as money, 25.
Almora, 181 *n.*
Alūwa sarāi, 158.
Amara, 237.
Amar Singh of Udaipur, 100, 107, 114, 170, 225; his son, 225.
Ambāla, 123, 158.
Amber, 22, 47, 67 *n.*
Ambere, 167.
Amīnābād, 167.
Amīrulumara, the, 98.
Ām-Khās, 159.
Anah, 9 *n.*
Anānas, 297.
Anang Pāl, Rāja, 155 *n.*
Anārkikali, 166, 330.
Ana Sāgar, the, 171.
Angeli, 25–6.
Anil, 40.
Anne, the, 289.
Antelopes, 243, 246, 296.
Antri, 144.
Anūp Rāi, 154.
Apes, 313.
Aplis, 309.
Apples, 297.
Arabia. *See* Mesopotamia, Red Sea, etc.
Arabic language, the, 249, 254, 284, 309–10, 315–16, 318.
Arāil, 178.
Arakan, 26, 29, 182.
Ararat, mt., 260.
Arāvad, 137.
Areca nuts, 38, 300.
Aristotle, 309.
Armada, 76 (2), 139.
Armenia, 1, 10, 47, 242, 246, 259.
Armenians, 53, 57, 64, 85, 133, 138–9, 167, 206, 217, 223, 240, 248, 267, 280–1, 307, 331.
Arrack, 300.
Arrows, 218, 312–14.
Arsacia, 242.
Arz, 56, 91.
Asafetida, 18.
Āsaf Khān (Itikād Khān), 68, 94 *n.*, 297 *n.*
Āsaf Khān (Jafar Beg), 98, 139, 163, 165.
Ascension, the, 64–5, 85; wrecked, 86, 132; survivors of, 65, 86, 132–3, 155 *n.*; her pinnace, 85, 131–2.
Ashrafi, 101.
Asīr, 100, 140.
Asoka pillars, 156 *n.*, 157, 177, 248 *n.*
Asses, 209, 304.
Astrology, 310.
Atescanna. *See Yātish-khāna.*
Attock, 168, 292.
Austin of Bordeaux, 51–2.
Ava, 39, 182.
Avicenna, 310.
Ayuthia, 33.
Azīz Koka, 59, 98 (2), 155, 162, 277 *n.*; his son, 173.

Babel, Tower of, 10.
Bābur, the Emperor, 164–5, 168.
Babylon. *See* Bagdad.
Badakhshān, 87 *n.*, 168.
Bād-ki-sarāi, 155.
Baffin's map of India, 240, 291 *n.*, 294 *n.*, 295 *n.*
Bāfta, 175, 206 *n.*, 218.
'Bag and baggage', 130.
Bagdad, 2, 9–11, 47, 59, 124–5, 245, 260, 269; described, 9; Bāsha

of, 124–5; Venetian vice-consul at, 125.
Bāglān, 78 *n.*, 136.
Bahādur, Sultān, 12.
Bahādurpur, 138.
Bahādur Khān of Khāndesh, 140.
Bahādur Shāh of Gujarāt, 100, 133, 136, 142, 173.
Bahīra, 272.
Bahrein, 11, 44, 47.
Bairām Khān, 71 *n.*, 165 (2).
Bajaur, 292.
Bajreswari Devi, 180, 294 *n.*
Bakar, 294.
Bakarah-īd, 318.
Baker, Philip, 227–8.
Bākla, 27–8.
Bālāpur, 16, 293 *n.*
Balass rubies, 87, 89, 93, 102–3, 112, 115.
Balbi, Gasparo, 8, 9 *n.*
Balkh, 114.
Balkhar, 140.
Baltistān, 170.
Baluchis, 210, 218, 220, 292, 314.
Bamboos, 25, 30, 32, 47.
Banchiah, 292.
Banda, 293.
Bandar Sindri, 170.
Bandas, the, 41, 46.
Banderamde, 170.
Bangash, 292.
Bangham, Nicholas, 93.
Banians, *passim*.
Banian-tree. *See* Fig-tree.
Bantam, 61, 63, 69, 73, 97, 200 *n.*
Barbers, 308, 313.
Bareja, 206, 217 *n.*
Barīd, 16 *n.*
Bariku, 168.
Barley, 296.
Baroda, 205.
Barrai, 143.
Basāwal, 168.
Bāso, Rāja, 98, 163, 179.
Basra, 1, 2, 6, 8, 46–7; described, 10, 11.
Bassein (India), 13.
Bassein (Pegu). *See* Kusima.
'Bath', Prince, 100.
Bâtmān, 102–3.
Bats, 135.
Bāwa Farīd Shakarganj, 166.
Bayāna, 123 (2), 148–52; indigo, 151–2, 174, 179.
Bāyasanghar, Prince, 154; made a Christian, 86, 116, 147–8.
Bāyazid I, 265.
Bazaar, 135, 149, 151, 167, 174, 182–3, 305.
Beads, prayer, 114–5, 316.
Bears, 246.
Belgaum, 15.
Bells, 315; of justice, 113, 184, 226.
Benares, 5, 20, 176.
Bengal, 100, 114, 246, 295; Fitch in, 5, 6, 18, 24–8, 43; Portuguese in, 5, 25, 181–2; goods from, 34, 43–4, 46; Pathān kings of, 26, 28 *n.*
Benzoin, 35, 38, 46.
Berar, 293.
Best, Thomas, 188–90, 197–200, 206; defeats the Portuguese, 68, 198–9.
Betel, 143, 300.
Bhadwar, 136–7.
Bhāgnagar, 131, 182.
Bhagwān Dās, Rāja, 164 *n.*
Bhāo Singh, Rāja, 163.
Bhimbar, 169.
Bhīnmāl, 173.
Bhutān, 27.
Biana. *See* Bayāna.
Bibi, 276.
Bīdar, 16.
Bihār, 295, 314.
Bihār Bānu Begam, 101 *n.*
Bihāri Mal, Rāja, 98 *n.*, 105 *n.*
Bihat, River, 169, 292.
Bījāpur, city of, 4, 14, 15.
Bījāpur, kingdom of, 4, 14, 15; King of, 131, 204, 220, 291; embassy from, 250.
Bīkaner, 294.
Bikrāmi, 168.
Bima, 43.
Biot, *Ho*, 282.
Bir, 9, 47, 53.
Birds' nests, 313.
Bishur, 292.
Bitlis, 53.
Blue the colour of mourning, 327.

Bollodo, 209.
Bond, John, 258 *n*.
Book calicoes, 175.
Bora, 143.
Bore at Cambay, 174, 217.
Borgāon, 139.
Borneo, 35, 40.
Bottia, 27.
Bowma, Ragee, 211.
Bows, 312–14.
'Boy', 231.
Boys, Thomas, 124, 146, 167.
Brahma, 321.
Brahmans, *passim*; their doctrines and ceremonies, 18, 19, 21–2, 226, 321.
Brama (Burma), 39, 40.
Brass, 21, 22, 34–5, 40, 183, 226, 248, 302–3, 306, 322.
Bread-making, 296.
Broach, 140, 174, 205 *n*., 217, 277.
Broadcloth, 35, 64, 192, 205–6, 306, 327.
Brokers in Pegu, 35.
Brooke, Christopher, 255, 258 *n*.
Brown, John, 251.
Buck, Francis, 70, 74, 126 (2).
Budde-Charbag, 168.
Buddha Bhai, 330 *n*.
Buffaloes, 17, 24, 38, 104, 184, 218; described, 296; horns of, 312.
Bukkur, 155 *n*.
Bukkur-Sukkur, 161, 218, 292.
Bull Bull, Sultān, 211.
Bulsār, 134.
Buray, River, 137.
Burdiano, 210.
Burhānpur, 5, 16, 71 *n*., 78, 93, 100, 131, 133–4, 136–7, 143, 146–7, 222 *n*., 293; Hawkins at, 79, 80; Finch at, 138–9; castle at, 138, 222 *n*.; elephant rock at, 138; Governor of, 139.
Burials, 315.
Burma, 39, 40. *See also* Pegu.
Bushire, 2.
Butkhāk, 168.
Butter, 19, 152, 296, 304, 324.
Byāval, 138.

'Cabie', 18.
Cacchegate, 25
Cairo, 48, 245, 260, 269.
Calentures, 310.
Calicoes, 175, 205 *n*., 289, 327, 329.
Calicut, 44–5; King of, 45, 129.
Calivers, 45.
Callitalowny, 208 *n*.
Callwalla, 208.
Cambals (camboline), 27, 36.
Cambay, 12, 62–3, 84, 130, 173, 203; Finch's account of, 174; sacked, 133, 173; Portuguese trade with, 76 *n*., 174; bore at, 174, 217; Jesuits at, 88, 95–6; Hawkins returns via, 67–8, 93, 95–6; Mukarrab Khān in charge of, 71–2, 87 *n*.; Withington at, 190–1, 206, 217; Governor of, 206.
Camels, *passim*.
Camla, 140.
Camphor, 35, 46.
Candere, 151.
Canning, Lancelot, 189, 200–1.
Canning, Paul, 189, 197, 200–1; death of, 190, 201 *n*., 202.
Canton, 41.
Caplan, 39.
Capons, 297.
Caraemit, 53.
Caravallo, Albert, 28.
Caravans described, 259.
Cards, 312.
Careless, R., 127 (2).
Carpets, 18, 177, 308, 311.
Carrots, 297.
Cartaz, 129–31, 135.
Cartwright, John, 53–4.
Cassumparo, 208 *n*.
Caste, 138, 218, 220–1, 226, 322; caste-marks, 19, 20, 323.
Cathaia, 102.
Cats, 25, 33.
Caucasus, the Indian, 243 *n*., 291, 294.
Cavalero, 147.
Ceylon, 28, 43–5; King of, 43–4.
Chabūtara, 158 *n*.
Chalani rupees, 101 *n*.
Chaldea, 241–2.
Chamba, 293.
Chambal, R., 145.
Chandangāon, 170.

Chandeau, 26.
Chānd Rai, 28.
Chaparghata, 179.
Chapman, Libbeus, 286.
Chārīkār, 168.
Charke, Charles, 155.
Charles, Prince, 289.
Chātsu, 170.
Chauk, 183 *n*.
Chauki, 144, 184.
Chaul, 6, 13, 46, 129, 207 *n*.
Chāush, 53.
Chautri, 158 *n*.
Chay-root, 34.
Cheese, 152, 296, 324.
Cheetahs, 17, 104, 312.
Chenāb, R., 167.
Chess, 312.
Chia-yü-kuan, 169 *n*.
Childbirth easy, 309.
Chīma Gakkhar, 167.
China, 1, 2, 25 *n*., 27, 47, 181, 282, 295; goods from, 13, 34, 38, 41, 46, 102; trade with India, 169; account of, 41–2.
China dish, story of a, 109.
China-Machina, 109 (2).
Chinches, 303.
Chinese in India, 308 *n*.
Chingas Sarāi, 169.
Chīn Kilij, Mīrza, 99.
Chintz, 16, 34, 43, 215, 227, 301.
Chitor, 170, 293.
Chittagong, 5, 26–7.
Chitthi, 130.
Chopra, 137.
Chounter, 158, 162–6.
Chunām, 42.
Cinnamon, 44–5.
Clarke, Charles, 227.
Clarkson, Robert, 204.
Claxton, Robert, 204.
Cloves, 46. *See also* Spices.
Coaches, Indian, 311, 320, 327; English coach for Jahāngīr, 252.
Cochin, 6, 14, 43–6, 129; King of, 45.
Cochin-China, 25, 42, 46.
Coco-nuts, 11, 13, 29, 38, 297 *n*. *See also* Palmeiro.
Coffee, 300.
Cogi Alli, 45.
Coir, 11.
Colombo, 43.
Comorin, Cape, 44, 131, 182.
Conowa, 169.
Consent, the, 61–2.
Constantinople, 1, 18, 48, 53, 58, 258 *n*., 271; Coryat at, 235, 243, 250, 257, 265, 268, 273.
Coolies. *See* Kolis.
Cope, Sir Walter, 50.
Copper, 22, 34–5, 38, 41, 299 *n*., 303; ornaments, 11, 22–3, 28; coins, 302 *n*.
Coral, 102, 115.
Corn, 11, 13, 16, 20–1, 38, 44, 296, 298.
Cornelians, 102.
Cornet-player. *See* Trully.
Corsi, Francisco, 55, 148 *n*., 331.
Coryat, Thomas, 157 *n*., 315; account of, 234–41; his letters, 241–76; notes by, 276–82; his address to Jahāngīr, 263, 284; his speech to a Muhammadan, 271; King James and, 258 *n*., 280; Terry and: *see* Terry; his death, 239, 287; his place of burial, 239–40, 282, 287; his mother, 248, 251, 259, 261; his stepfather, 270; his uncle, 248, 251, 275.
Costus, 179.
Cotton, Sir Robert, 258 *n*.
Cotton, 17, 24; goods, 16, 17, 20, 24–6, 28, 34, 218, 301; yarn, 34; the shrub, 301.
Coulthrust, Richard, 53.
Course. *See* *Kos*.
Covert, Robert, 49, 65, 65 *n*., 67 *n*., 122, 155 *n*.
Cows venerated, 14, 22, 133, 218, 220, 294, 324.
Crocodiles, 30, 175, 303.
Crusado, 41.
Curdes, 161.
Curka, 136 (2).
Cypress trees, 158 (2), 178.
Cyrus, King, 242.

Dābhol, 96.
Da Cunha, Nuno, 188.
Daka, 168.

Dalin, 30.
Damān, 13, 77–8, 134, 192–3, 196 *n*.
Dāna, 304.
Danak, 10.
Dancing girls, 183, 208.
Dangali, 294.
Dāniyāl, Prince, 108, 147, 162; his mother, 166.
Dārāb, Mirza, 99.
Darbār, 162, 164, 178, 183–5.
Darīkhāna, 17.
Darshani, 151, 163, 177, 183, 326.
Darwāza, 166, 183.
Darwīz, 284, 319.
Dates, 11, 297; date-trees, 175.
David, King, 318.
De Castro, Martin Affonso, 128.
Deccan, the, 100, 114, 291; wars in, 79, 94–5, 113, 130–1, 137–9, 143, 146–7, 154–5, 155 *n*. *See also* Ahmadnagar, Bījāpur, etc.
Deer, 17, 25, 104, 157, 184, 209, 296, 312.
De Feyra, Conde, 88 *n*., 129–31.
Dekawara, 209.
Dela, 29, 30.
De Laet, Johannes, 122.
Delhi, 47, 236, 248, 293; the capital of India, 100, 156; Finch's account of, 155–7; Asoka pillars at, 156 *n*., 157, 248; early kings of, 152 *n*., 155 *n*., 156–7, 172, 181; Faujdār of, 157.
Delout, 143.
De Mascarenhas, Francisco, 12.
De Mendoça, André Furtado, 128–31.
De Menezes, Aleixo, 128, 130.
Deo, 134, 163.
Dergee Seraw, 194.
Dermain, 27.
Dervishes. *See Darwīz*.
De Seine, Jean, 207–8.
Deura, 155.
Dhāita, 78–9, 136–7.
Dhameri, 179.
Dharm Parkāsh, 180 *n*.
Dhaulāgiri, 181.
Dholpur, 145.
Dhooly, 172.
Diamonds, 15, 18, 41–2, 47, 111; the Mogul's, 102–3, 111–12, 115; mines, 15, 47, 181.
Diarbekr, 53, 236, 250, 266.
Dipālpur, 142.
Diu, 12, 68, 84, 94, 129 (2).
Diul Sind, 292.
Dīwān, 125.
Dīwān-i-ām and *Dīwān-i-khās*, 81 *n*., 159 *n*.
Dīwānkhāna, 151, 155, 162–5, 172, 178.
Doāba, 168.
Dogs, 22, 25, 33, 104, 312, 326.
Donne, John, 258 *n*.
Dopyāj, 311.
Dorāha, 158.
Dorchester, John, 127.
Downton, Nicholas, 84 *n*., 192–3, 223–4, 229; defeats the Portuguese, 68, 193, 224.
Dragoman, 57, 72, 78–9.
Dragon, the, 61–2, 188, 191, 198 (4).
Dress of Indians, 308.
Dromedaries, 104 *n*., 105–6, 304, 311, 329.
Drugs, 11, 13, 17, 41, 47, 174, 179, 206, 302.
Ducats, 15, 31, 57.
Ducks, 296.
Durga, 180.
Dutch, the, 6, 97, 127, 146; English declared to be, 74, 125–6; war with the Portuguese, 128–31.

East India Company, the, 1, 7, 48, 50, 60, 289 (2); and Withington, 195–6, 232–3; their offices, 232 *n*.
Ecbatana, 242.
Edwards, William, at court, 192, 227–31, 236–7, 248; beaten, 230; stabbed, 230; his title, 192, 224–5, 229; Withington and, 193–5, 225, 227–8; his donation from Jahāngīr, 229–30; goes home, 231 *n*., 232.
Eglisham, George, 233.
Eldred, John, 2.
Elephantiasis, 44.
Elephants, in Pegu, 27, 30–3, 35, 38, 44; in Ceylon, 43–4; in India, *passim*; the Mogul's,

104-6, 108, 184-5, 246-7, 304-7, 314, 326, 329; punishment by, 108-9, 305; fights of, 177, 184, 247, 306, 326; white, 31; described, 304-7; value of, 307; age of, 307.
Elizabeth, Queen, 1, 2, 5, 48, 55, 58.
Elks, 296.
Elmer, John, 132.
Emeralds, 102-3, 112, 115.
Emert, 266.
Emmets, 140.
Eshim, 102-3, 115.
Etāwa, 179.
Ethiopia, 237, 282.
Eunuchs, 18, 297, 311, 320, 327, 329.
Euphrates, R., 9, 10, 53, 241 (2), 259.
Eve, 177, 322.
Expedition, the, 97, 212 *n*.

Fairs at court, 278.
Fakir, 135, 150 *n*., 164.
Falcons (cannon), 132.
Famines, 12.
Farīdābād, 155.
Farīd Bukhāri, Shaikh, 99, 127 (2), 159, 163, 166, 279.
Farmān, 65, 68, 183, 188-9, 192.
Farrāsh, 99.
Fatehpur (Vairowāl), 158, 160.
Fatehpur Sīkri, 3 *n*., 4 *n*., 5, 170; described, 17, 18, 149, 226-7; built by Akbar, 149, 160; deserted, 150, 182; quarries at, 157, 187, 226; pillar found at, 157.
Faujdār, 157.
Feasts at court, 117-18, 120, 245.
Federici, Cesar, 8.
Feluja, 9.
Fenton, Edward, 1, 61.
Fevers, 310.
Figs, 29, 38, 166, 297; fig-trees, 29, 178, 299.
Finch, William, account of, 122-5; his narrative, 62 *n*., 125-87; at Surat, 63-4, 75-8, 81, 85-6, 122-3, 125-33; his route to Agra, 133-46; at Agra, 146-8; at Bayāna, 123; at Lahore, 67, 123-4, 155-60; Hawkins and, 70, 122-5, 146; goes home, 67, 124; dies, 124.
Firoz Shāh, 156 *n*., 157 *n*.
Fishes ringed, 168.
Fitch, Ralph, account of, 1-8; his narrative, 8-47; the journey out, 8-12; in India, 12-29; in Pegu, 29-43; his return journey, 43-7.
Flies, 303, 307.
Flowers, 166, 299, 303.
Flux, the, 76, 127, 137, 196 *n*., 310.
Foist, 28, 45.
Ford, William, 258 *n*.
Fowls, 297.
Foxes, 22, 28, 209.
Frain, Hugh, 96.
Frankincense, 35.
Frencham, John, 155.
Frenchmen in India, 146, 204, 207-8, 222 *n*., 223.
'Frigates', 63.
Fruits in India, 166, 297.
Fryer, John, 239.

Ganaur, 157.
Gandak, 295.
Gandamak, 168.
Gandevi, 65, 131, 134.
Ganges, R., 19, 20, 23-4, 26, 28-9, 175, 177-8, 180-1, 226, 247, 265, 269, 295, 299, 323; its name, 293; its source, 294; water, 226, 299.
Gansa, 35.
Garao, 171.
Garhakatanka, 295.
Garhwāl, 180.
Garlic, 297.
Garrat, George, 258 *n*.
Gaur, 24-5, 294-5.
Geese, 20, 296.
Gelole, 161.
Genefro, 131.
Gentiles, 11, 307, *and passim*.
Georgia, 242.
German swordblades, 103.
Germans in India, 204 (2).
Ghakkars, 294.
Ghari, 317.
Ghāzi, Mirza, 330 *n*.
Ghazni Khān, 172, 174.
Ghiyās Beg, 68, 94 (2), 99, 101.
Ghorband, 168.

Ghusl-khāna, 279.
Giaour, 271–5.
'Ging', 126.
Ginger, 46, 297, 324.
Glass, 23; not used, 300.
Goa, 8, 12, 63–4, 92–3, 127, 129, 131 (2), 135, 203, 305; described, 14; customs dues at, 12; trade with Cambay, 76 *n*., 174; Fitch at, 3, 6, 14, 15, 46; Viceroy of, 3–5, 12, 14, 15, 83–4, 88–9, 92, 95, 128–31, 146, 188, 193, 197; Mukarrab Khān's mission to, 66, 85, 87–90, 93.
Goats, 11, 25, 296.
'Gobins', 155.
Godown, 30.
Gogha, 62, 130, 199.
Gogra, R., 292 *n*.
Gohad, 293.
Gojri, 135 *n*.
Golconda, city of, 4, 182.
Golconda, kingdom of, 15, 182; King of, 15, 131, 182, 291.
Gold, 15, 33–6, 38, 41, 180, 185, 187, 269, 294, 302, 310–11, 323, 328; ornaments, 12, 250, 306; digging and washing for, 23, 42, 176; coins, 101, 159, 267, 302 *n*.
Gold, cloth of, 117, 206, 213, 306, 329.
Gondoree, 135.
Gondwāna, 295.
Goobade, 158.
Gopi Talāo, the, 132, 134.
Gosains, 155 *n*.
Grapes, 166, 297.
Grassias, the, 143.
Gravener, Stephen, 84.
Greeks, 223.
Greet, Hugh, 96.
Gujarāt, 8, 12–14, 34, 47, 64–5, 100, 114, 173, 293; the ancient dynasty, 100, 205; conquered by Akbar, 106, 207–8; Viceroy of, 76. *See also* Ahmadābād, Cambay, etc.
Gujarāti language, the, 309 *n*.
Gūjars, 152 (2), 156–7.
Gujrāt (Punjāb), 167, 169.
Gumlac. *See* Lac.
Gundajaw, 211.
Gunpowder, 314.
Guns, 28, 32, 43, 45, 218, 314 . *also* Ordnance.
Gūnth, 181.
Gwalior, 293; castle at, 100, 1 293; Finch describes, 1 Governor of, 145 (2).

Haggatt, Bartholomew, 124–5.
Hai-nan, 47.
Hāji, 301.
Hāji Khān, 292, 314.
Hakewill, William, 255, 258 *n*.
Hakluyt, Richard, 6–8, 40 *n*., 5
Hardwār, 238, 269 *n*., 294.
Hares, 296–7, 312.
Hasan Abdāl, 168.
Hasan Ali, Khwāja, 77.
Hassward, King, 172.
Hast Caunk, 169.
Hatya, 168.
Hawkins, William, account 60–70; his narrative, 70–12 at Surat, 70–9, 125–9; journey to court, 78–80; Agra, 65–8, 80–95, 146–8; return, 95–7; Finch and, 122–5, 146; his wife, 64, 67– 84–5, 92–3, 96, 133.
Hawks, 17, 104, 312.
Hay, the, 198.
Hazarat Isa, 246, 276, 315, 319.
Hector, the, 52, 60–3, 68–9, 122.
Henri IV of France, 167.
Henry, Prince, 234–5, 257.
Herba cloth, 26.
Herbert, Sir Edward, 277.
Herbert, Thomas, 122, 239, 277
Hermodactyle, the, 150.
Hijili, 25–6.
Hindaun, 170.
Hindi language, the, 309 *n*.
Hindustani language, the, 284, 3
Hing, 18.
Hira Nand, 111.
Hit, 10.
Hodal, 155.
Hoghe Moheede, 160.
Holland, Hugh, 249.
Horses, in India, *passim*; in Tib 27; none in Ceylon, 44; Persia 12, 304; Tartarian and Arabia

304; special breeds of, 174, 181, 218, 304; the Mogul's, 103, 104 *n.*, 105–6, 137, 185.
Hoshang, Prince, 154; made a Christian, 86, 116, 147–8.
Hoshang, Shāh, 141 *n.*
Hosiander, the, 188, 197–8.
Hoskins, John, 255, 258 *n.*
Howdahs, 306.
Hūgli, 5, 18 *n.*, 25, 182.
Humām, Hakīm, 101.
Humāyūn, the Emperor, 142 *n.*; Sher Shāh and, 141–2, 161, 165; his tomb, 156, 156 *n.*, 164–5.
Hunt, Edward, 200.
Hyderābād, 131 *n.*, 182.

Ibrāhīm Lodi, 165.
Idris Khān, 98.
Indigo, 40, 92, 149, 151–2, 155, 206, 227, 301; how made, 152–4; purchase of, 148, 190–2, 222–3; Bayāna, 151–2, 174, 179; Koil, 179; Sarkhej, 174, 207; Sind, 218.
Indus, R., 161, 168, 243, 291–2, 299.
Injīl, 273.
Īraj, Mīrza, 99.
Iron, 72, 303, 306, 314, 320.
Isa Khān, 28, 181.
Ishmael, 318 (2).
Ispahān, 51, 54; Coryat at, 236–7, 242, 260, 273.
Italians in India, 3, 59, 220, 223.
Itibār Khān, 99.
Itikād Khān, 68, 94 *n.*, 297 *n.*
Itimādpur, 179.
Ivory, 13, 22, 28.

Jackals, 303.
Jacob (a German), 204.
Jacobuses, 69.
Jade. *See* Eshim.
Jafar, Mīr, 197.
Jafarābād, 198, 201.
Jafar Beg. *See* Āsaf Khān.
Jagannāth, 295.
Jagannāth, Rāja, 105, 163.
Jagdalak, 168.
Jāghāl-āghli, 161 *n.*
Jāgīr, 161.
Jagra, 13, 300.
Jahān, Khwāja, 90, 99.
Jahāndār, Sultān, 100, 330.
Jahāngīr, the Emperor, 52, 63, 179–82, 189–90, 299; Mildenhall and, 58–9; his birth-name, 102; rebels against his father, 107, 159, 177, 279 *n.*; succeeds to the throne, 108, 330; his daily routine, 114, 183–5, 247, 311, 326; birthday festivities, 118, 245, 328; his income, 99, 246, 324; his treasures, 101–3; his chief officials, 327; his emblem, 306; his titles, 325; his age, 245, 328; his dress, 327–8; his appearance, 245; unpopular, 108; his cruelty, 108–11, 113, 184–5, 279, 326, 331; a drunkard, 67, 116, 185, 331; unorthodox, 147; uncircumcised, 246; his trust in astrologers, 310; his fondness for hunting, 154; his predilection for devotees, 279; his intended place of burial, 316; rumours of his death, 157; pictures of, 162–4; his memoirs, 65; Khusrau rebels against him, 82 *n.*, 108, 158–60, 178 *n.*, 179, 279; his relations with Anārkīkali, 166, 330; he makes his nephews Christians, 86, 116, 147–8; attacked by a lion, 154; his relations with the Jesuits, 192, 201, 222–3, 280, 331; story of an Armenian and, 280, 331; his wives, 90 *n.*, 94, 101, 118, 164, 170, 178, 247, 278, 306, 329; his mother, *see* Maryam; his sister, 94, 107; his children (*see also* Khusrau etc.), 98, 100–1, 184, 330; royal letters to and from: *see* James I.
Jahāngīrī rupees, 102.
Jahāngīr Kuli Khān, 99, 173.
Jaisalmer, 291 *n.*, 292.
Jaju, 146.
Jalālābād, 167–8.
Jalāl-uddīn Firoz, 172 *n.*
Jalap, 179.
Jālnapur, 131, 137.
Jālor, 171–2, 174.

Jamālpur, 155 *n.*
Jamba, 42.
Jāmbusar, 174.
James I, letters to the Mughal Emperor from, 61–3, 67, 70–4, 80–2, 132, 189, 192, 200, 206, 229, 252; answer refused, 92, 95; replies to, 328; abused by the Portuguese, 74–5, 78; Coryat and, 258 *n.*, 286.
Jampda, 170.
Jangoma, 38, 46, 182.
Jāni Beg, Mīrza, 330 *n.*
Japan, 41–2.
Japanese in India, 308 *n.*
Jari indigo, 153.
Jaswān, 295.
Jaunpur, 176–7, 179, 292 *n.*
Java, 303. *See also* Bantam.
Jawāla Mūkhi, 238, 294.
Jaxe, 272.
Je, 180.
Jenba, 293.
Jengapor, 292.
Jerusalem, 235, 241, 244–5, 249, 253, 256, 259, 261, 268.
Jesuits at Goa, 3, 15; at Surat, 64; at Agra, 190, 192, 201, 222–3; at court, 49–52, 55–9, 64, 83–4, 229, 276, 280, 331. *See also* Corsi, De Seine, Pinheiro, Xavier, etc.
Jesus Christ, 276, 328–9; reverenced in India, 246, 319, 331; pictures of, 115, 163, 184.
Jews in India, 308.
Jhūsi, 178.
Joagek Hately, 169.
Sogikāgāon, 171.
Johnson, Robert, 203.
Johnson, —, 122.
Johor, 128 (2).
Jonas, the Prophet, 269.
Jones, Inigo, 249.
Jonson, Ben, 234, 252, 255 *n.*, 258 *n.*
Joseph, Benjamin, 232 *n.*, 288.
Jourdain, John, at Surat, 148; his narrative, 64–7, 70, 85 *n.*, 91 *n.*, 95 *n.*, 96 *n.*, 104 *n.*, 109 *n.*, 111 *n.*, 112 *n.*, 123–4, 127 *n.*, 132 *n.*, 154 *n.*
Julfa, 54.
Juma, 210.
Jumna, R., 17–19, 156, 177–80, 182, 185, 226, 293 (2).
Jūnāgarh, 292.
Junkseylon, 41.
Junnar, 131 *n.*
Juno, 210.

Kābul, 100, 114, 154, 159–60, 167–8, 291; route to, 166–8.
Kābul R., 168, 291.
Kachahri, 183 (2).
Kacha Sarāi, 167.
Kachner Sarāi, 143.
Kachua, 5, 28 *n.*
Kāfila, 63 *n.*, 143, 206, 208 *n.*
Kahwa, 300.
Kāim Khān, 101.
Kakarwar, 143.
Kālabāg, 143.
Kalandar, 150, 164.
Kālapāni, 168.
Kālsi, 180.
Kanasia, 142.
Kanāt, 329.
Kanauj, 175.
Kandahār, 48, 54, 100, 114, 161, 167, 236, 283, 291; King of: *see* Rustam.
Kāngra, 179, 238, 294 *n.*
Kānwal kakri, 150 *n.*
Karan, Prince, 225.
Karnāl, 158.
Karod, 133, 136.
Karoli, 78.
Kārvān, 205 *n.*
Kashān, 54.
Kāshgar, 166, 168–9, 179.
Kashmīr, 104, 169, 292; shawls, 169.
Kāsim, Mīrza, 99.
Kāthiāwār, 189, 198 *n.*, 292.
Kaul or Kāli, R., 292.
Kāzi, 183, 326.
Kāzmi Khān, 99.
Kazvin, 48, 50, 54, 59, 236, 242.
Keeling, William, 61–2, 62 *n.*; at Surat, 193, 227, 229; and Withington, 193–5, 231.
Kermān, 54.
Kerridge, Thomas, 51–2, 193–5; sent to court, 190, 192, 202;

at Ahmadābād, 193–5; letters from, 124 *n.*, 193–4.
Keshu Dās, Rāja, 163.
Khalji kings, 141 *n.*, 142 *n.*, 172 *n.*
Khān, meaning of, 65, 83, 98, 327 *n.*
Khān Alām, 99, 327.
Khān Azam. *See* Aziz Koka.
Khandap, 171.
Khān Daurān, 98.
Khāndesh, 144, 293; Kings of, 140 *n.*, 141 *n.*, 142 *n.*
Khān Jahān Lodi, 98, 143, 163, 327.
Khān Jahān of Khāndesh, 141 *n.*, 142 *n.*
Khān-khānān: *see* Abdurrahīm; meaning of the term, 71 *n.*, 162, 165.
Khānkhānān Sarāi, 160.
Khānwa, 148, 151.
Khargon, 140.
Khawad, 209.
Khawāsspur, 167.
Khichri, 280.
Khumbaria, 136.
Khurram, Sultān, 67 *n.*, 98, 100, 154, 162–3, 330; subdues Udaipur, 225 *n.*
Khūshkhabar Khān, 82.
Khusrau, Sultān, 100, 163, 229, 330; Akbar and, 107–8, 159; rebels, 82 *n.*, 108, 158–60, 279; a prisoner, 98 *n.*, 108, 277; reported blinded, 108, 160; his mother, 164, 178; his wife's devotion, 277.
Khutiyāl indigo, 153.
Kiack, 36–7.
Kiang-mai, 5, 38, 46, 182.
Kilīj Khān, 98, 163.
Kiyāra Sundar, 100 *n.*
Koil indigo, 179.
Kolis, the, 143 *n.*, 173, 209.
Kos, *passim*; length of, 142, 144, 213 *n.*, 222 *n.*, 295; ten a day's journey, 225.
Kos pillars, 149, 225.
Kosamba, 205 *n.*, 217.
Kotwāl, 159, 194.
Kror, 99, 102.
Kuch Bihār, 5, 24–5, 27, 291 *n.*
Kulhāras, 143.
Kum, 54.
Kumāon, 181, 181 *n.*
Kurān, the, 278, 316, 318; Coryat on, 272, 274.
Kurds, the, 47, 53.
Kusima, 5, 29, 34, 43.
Kutbuddīn Khān Koka, 162.
Kyatpyin, 39.

Labuan, 42.
Lac, 35, 179, 206 *n.*, 303.
Ladāna, 170.
Lahore, 18, 48, 54, 91, 100, 159, 167, 179 (3), 185, 218, 279; castle at, 104, 159, 161–6; importance of, 123, 283, 292–3; Jesuits at, 55 *n.*, 124; Finch at, 67, 92, 123–4, 155–67; his description of, 161–6; Coryat and, 236, 243–4, 270, 283.
Lahrībandar, 209, 292; English at, 190, 208, 212; Portuguese at, 212; trade of, 212 *n.*, 218.
Lakh, 99, 101, 176, 250.
Lāl Bāg, 138.
Lāla Bīr Singh Deo, 99, 163.
Lancaster, Charles, 247.
Lancaster, Sir James, 6.
Lan-chan, 38–9.
Lar, 292.
Lari, 210–12; described, 211 *n.*
Lashkar, 329.
Lashkari, Mīrza, 99.
Law, no written, 326.
Lawns (muslins), 218, 301, 327.
Lead, 18, 33, 35, 40, 72, 303.
Leeds, William, 2, 3, 4 *n.*, 5, 8, 18.
Lemons, 166, 297.
Leopards, 17, 184, 246, 312.
Lepers, 308.
Levant Company, 6, 7.
Lignum aloes, 46, 115.
Lillo, Sir Henry, 53.
Limes, 297 *n.*
Linschoten, John Huyghen 2–4.
Lion, the, 195, 231 *n.*
Lion Quay, 231, 232 *n.*
Lions, 110, 174, 184, 246–7, 303; tame, at court, 104, 111, 328; Jahāngīr attacked by a, 154.
Lipsius, Justus, 305.
Literature, Indian, 309–10.

London, Treaty of, 60.
'Long Walk', the, 244, 283–4, 293.
Loure-Charebage, 168.
Lucknow, 175.
Lunera, 142.

Macao (China), 41.
Macao (Pegu), 5, 30
Mace, 46. *See also* Spices.
Machado, Anthony, 55.
Madder, Indian, 34.
Magarmachh, 175.
Mahābat Khān, 98, 155, 159, 163, 327.
Mahal, 148–9, 151, 156 (2), 158 (2), 163–6, 178, 183, 185–7, 278.
Mahdawi, 319.
Mahdi Kuli, 72, 125–6.
Mahi, R., 205.
Mahmūd I, 141, 142 *n*.
Mahmūdis, 127, 129, 131, 146, 216–17, 223; coinage of, 136; value of, 77 *n*., 216, 302.
Maidān, 134.
Makām, 138, 142–3.
Malabars, the, 43–5; pirates, 126, 129; and the Portuguese, 128–9, 139.
Malacca, 8, 26, 28, 30, 34, 182; Fitch at, 5, 41, 43; siege of, 128 (2), 130–1; Captain of, 41.
Malays, the, 41.
Malik Ali, Khwāja, 159.
Malik Ambar, 100, 130, 138.
Malik Shāh, 172 *n*.
Mālwa, 100 (2), 107, 142, 293.
Manār pearl fishery, 44, 47.
Māndu, 17, 152, 222 *n*.; palace at, 310; Finch's account of. 140–2: Jahāngīr at, 238, 277–8, 285, 288, 329; Roe at, 238–9, 277, 285, 287–8; Coryat at, 238, 285, 287.
Mango trees, 134, 144.
Mangoes, 297.
Manihpur, 178.
Manillas, the, 128.
Mansabdār, 98, 230.
Mān Sāh, Rāja, 180.
Mān Singh, Rāja, 98, 162, 164 *n*., 170, 179, 330 *n*.; sent to the Deccan, 131, 138–9, 143; his palace, 145
Mardin, 47.
Markets, 26, 313.
Marlow, Anthony, 62 *n*., 63, 73–4, 126.
Marriage ceremonies, 16, 22, 220–1, 320, 322.
Martaban, 34, 41, 43.
Martin, Richard, 249, 255, 256 *n*.
Mārwār, 170.
Mary, the Virgin, 276, 331; pictures of, 115, 163, 184.
Maryam-zamāni. 98 (2), 107, 118, 148, 331; her trading operations, 123, 129, 191, 203.
Mashak, 147.
Mashalchi, 162.
Massage, 313.
Mast, 317.
Masulipatam, 16, 34, 95, 133, 182; Dutch at, 97, 127.
Māta Devi, 294.
Maund, 102–3, 105.
Mecca, 14, 35, 165, 202, 301.
Media, 242, 259.
Medina, 202 *n*., 301.
Medinea, 9.
Medon, 29.
Melons, 297.
Mendaker, 145.
Mendee, 319.
Menhapoore, 148.
Mermaid Club, the, 234, 236, 250–1, 256.
Merta, 171.
'Meskites', 140–2, 144, 149, 166, 172, 176, 316 *n*., 318; described, 315.
Mesopotamia, 9–11, 47, 241–2, 246, 259, 266.
Mewāt, 295.
Mhowa trees, 136; wine, 136, 143.
Michelborne, Sir Edward, 72, 125.
Middleton, Sir Henry, 85, 95; at Surat, 68, 94, 96, 124 *n*., 203; is ordered to leave, 68, 188; retaliates in the Red Sea, 68, 96, 188, 197, 201, 203; goes east, 68, 96–7.
Mildenhall, John, 191, 222 *n*., 223; account of, 48–52; his letters, 52–9.
Mīnār, 157.

Mirrors, Venetian, 164.
Mīrza, title of, 98, 327.
Mitford, Thomas, 227, 230.
Mithkāl, 111–12.
Mocket, Richard, 258 *n*.
Modra, 173.
Mogargāon, 140.
Mogen, the, 26, 29.
Mogul, the Great: *see* Akbar, Jahāngīr, etc.; origin of the term, 325.
Mohurs, 101, 159, 267.
Mokha, 202–3; the English and, 68, 93, 96, 132; Indian trade with, 68, 76, 123, 129, 135, 197, 202, 301. *See also* Red Sea.
Moluccas, the, 41, 46, 303.
Monkeys, 174, 313.
Monsoon, the, 135, 303.
Montague, Bishop, 258 *n*.
Moses, 269, 318 (2).
Mosques. *See* Meskites.
Mosquitoes, 303.
Mosul, 47.
Mota, 136.
Mozābād, 170.
Mozambique, 129–30.
Mubārak Shāh, 84–5.
Mughalsarāi, 170.
Mugs, the, 26, 181, 291.
Muhammad, the Prophet, 202, 301, 308, 316–18, 320; Coryat on, 271–2, 274, 315.
Muhammadan devotions, 273–4.
Muhammad Hakīm, Mīrza, 101; his son, 148.
Muīnuddīn Chishti, 148, 171, 280.
Mukarrab Khān, 631, 31, 163, 188–9; and Hawkins, 63–4, 66, 71–3, 75–80, 85–7, 95, 127, 146–7; and Finch, 127, 130, 132; his negotiations with the English, 68, 189, 201; at court, 65, 86, 188, 229; complaints against, 65–6, 86–7; sent to Goa, 66, 85, 87–90, 93; favours the Portuguese, 83–4, 88–90; sent against them, 93; his brother, 63.
Mulberry trees, 186.
Mules, 104–5, 304, 311.
Mulher, 136.
Mullahs, 308, 315–16, 318, 320.
Multān, 114, 161 (2), 236, 271, 291.
Mundiākhera, 145.
Mundiāpura, 148 *n*.
'Munition', 183.
Murād, Sultān, 108, 162, 293 *n*.
'Murtherers', 183.
Musaff Khān, 205.
Muscovy. *See* Russia.
Musical instruments, 103, 310, 315.
Musk, 25, 27, 35, 38, 41, 46–7, 169 (2), 181.
Muzaffarābād, 198, 201.
Muzaffar Shāh III, 100, 133.
Myrobalans, 179, 297 *n*.

Nagarkot, 179, 294.
Nagar Pārkar, 191, 209, 214–17.
Nairs, the, 44–5.
Naites, the, 135.
Nakchivan, 54.
Nakodar, 158.
Nandurbār, 137.
Nārāyanpur, 136–7.
Narbada, R., 140, 277.
Narela, 156.
Nariād, 206.
Nārnaul, 295.
Narwar, 100, 144, 293.
Nāsiruddīn Ghāzi, 157.
Naubat, 166.
Nauroz feast, 117, 310.
Nausāri, 134.
Nāwab, title of, 132, 327 *n*.
Negapatam, 26, 44, 182.
Negrais, 29, 34.
Newbery, John, 1–6, 8, 18.
Newman, Richard, 51–2.
Newport, Christopher, 97 *n*., 212*n*.
New Year's feast. *See Nauroz*.
Nicobars, the, 6.
Nilāb, R., 291.
Nimgul, 137.
Nīmla, 168.
Nineveh, 47, 245, 260, 269.
Nizām, Khwāja, 76.
Noah, the Patriarch, 177, 260.
Nondogue, 215.
Nonnigong, 170.
'Notee' indigo, 153.
Nuraquimire, 210.

Nūr Jahān, 101, 247, 277 *n.*, 279–80; married to Jahāngīr, 68, 94; her great influence, 329.
Nūr Mahal. *See* Nūr Jahān.
Nūrpur, 179.
Nūruddīn, Governor of Surat, 70–1, 73–4, 77, 79, 126–7, 131–3.
Nūrullah Ibrāhīm, 209.
Nutmegs, 46. *See also* Spices.

Odcombe, 234, 237, 254, 258, 270.
Onions, 297, 311.
Opium, 18, 24, 34–5, 71, 116; how made, 142.
Oranges, 29, 166, 297.
Ordnance, 133, 141, 183 (2), 226, 301, 306, 314.
Orfah, 47, 53, 241, 259.
Orissa, 25–6, 182, 295.
Ormus, 1, 8, 12, 14, 129, 135, 278; described, 11, 12; Fitch at, 1, 3, 6, 11, 46; Captain of, 11, 12.
Osborne, Sir Edward, 1, 2, 9.
Ounces, 17, 104.
Oxen, 104–5, 297–8, 311.

Padre, the term, 331 *n.*
Pādshāh, 85, 326.
Pādshāh Bānu Begam, 101.
Pagodes (idols), 15, 31, 33–4, 155, 158, 177.
Pagodes (temples), 15 *n.*, 35 *n.*, 36, 134, 142, 171–2, 221 (2), 226, 321.
Pahar, 317.
Paithān, 295.
Pakhli, 169.
Pakka, 168.
Palanquin, 108, 154, 278, 329, 331; described, 312.
Palmeiro (palm tree), 10, 13, 14, 29, 31, 44–5, 175, 297.
Palwal, 155.
Pāmri, 169.
Pān, 143 *n.*, 300.
Pānīpat, 157.
Pankha, 164, 184, 313.
Paradise, 241, 246, 250, 273–4.
Paraich, 144.
Parameshvra, 321.
Parão, 29, 30, 45.
Pargana, 170.
Parsees, the, 323.
Parsons, Richard, 52.
Partab Shāh, 136–7, 293.
Parthia, 259.
Partridges, 296–7.
Parwīz, Sultān, 98 (2), 100, 110, 162–3, 222 *n.*, 330; sent to the Deccan, 131 *n.*, 138–9; Finch and, 139.
Pathānkot, 295.
Pathān Kings, 26, 152, 155 *n.*, 156–7, 161, 170, 172, 176–9, 181.
Pathāns, 78–9, 136, 141 *n.*, 144, 167, 314; story of a, 110.
Patna, 5, 295; described, 23–4; disturbances at, 113, 147.
Pattamar, 202.
'Pawn', 36.
Peacocks, 21, 174, 296.
Pearl, the, 69.
Pearls, 11, 18, 44–7, 102–3, 112, 115, 118, 310.
Pears, 297.
Pedraria, 220.
Pegu, city of, 5, 29, 30, 43.
Pegu, kingdom of, 5, 6, 8, 16, 18, 27, 34, 35, 46–7, 182; Fitch visits, 29–43; King of, 31–4.
Penang, 6.
Peons, 129, 200, 209, 228–9.
Pepper, 14, 16, 25–7, 35, 41, 44–5; shrub, 45–6.
Pepper, long, 26, 35, 46.
Percival, Dr., 195.
Persia, 1, 10 18, 27, 259; the Turks and, 161, 167; Mildenhall in, 51, 54, 59; revenues of, 246; trade between India and, 167; ambassadors from (*see also* Sherley), 161, 212 *n.*; King of, 110, 161 (2), 167, 236, 242–3, 260, 262, 268, 291–2. *See also* Ispahān, etc.
Persian language, the, 57, 249, 254, 262–3, 268, 284, 288, 309.
Persians in India, 307.
Peshāwar, 168, 292 *n.*
Peyton, Walter, 97 *n.*
Pharwāla, 294.
Phelips, Sir Edward, 241 *n.*, 247, 249, 251, 270; letter to, 252.
Phelips, Sir Robert, 249, 255, 270.

Philip II of Spain, 1, 4, 6, 126, 128; at war with England, 49, 55, 60.
Philippines, the. *See* Manillas.
Phillaur-ki-sarāi, 158.
Pice, 205, 278, 302.
Piehuna, 151.
Pigeons, 104, 296.
Pigot, Laurence, 124.
Pindar, Sir Paul, 235.
Pineapples, 297.
Pinheiro, Father Manoel, 55, 75, 77–9, 83, 89, 90, 127, 146.
Pīpar, 171.
Pipliagāon, 143, 143 *n.*
Pippli, 182.
Pīr, 180, 316, 318.
Pirates, 45, 181 *n.*
Pīr Panjāl pass, 169.
Piscaria, the, 47.
Piyāli, 164.
Plague at Agra, 237.
Plantains, 297.
Plaster of Paris, 311.
Polle-Medomy, 175.
Polyandry, 244.
Pome-citrons, 297.
Pomegranates, 166, 297.
Pomelo, 297 *n.*
'Ponde' (pundit), 155 *n.*
Porcelain, 34, 41, 169.
Porgos, 26.
Porto Grand, 26, 29.
Porto Piqueno, 18, 25.
Portuguese, 148, 203, 278, 282 *n.*, 331; at Surat, 75–7, 126, 129, 197–9; at Tatta, 191 *n.*; on the Coromandel Coast, 182; in Bengal, 5, 25, 181–2; their trade in India, 14, 63, 76 *n.*, 174; demand *cartaz* money, 129–30, 135; oppose the admission of the English, 1–3, 49, 50, 55, 60, 64–8, 83–4, 88–9, 132, 146, 230; intrigue against Hawkins, 75–8, 83–4, 88, 95; their war with the English, 49, 60, 68, 73–5, 96, 126, 188, 193, 198–9, 224, 288; with the Dutch, 128–131; with the Indians, 130–2, 191–3, 201, 203, 208, 223; and with Malabar pirates, 128–9, 139. *See also* Goa, Ormus, Malacca, etc.
Porus, King, 248.
Post, 145.
Potatoes, 297.
Prayāga, 19, 20, 177.
Prester John, 237, 282.
Priaman, 73.
'Prigonies', 170.
Prithwi Rāj, 156 *n.*
'Protoplast, Master,' 250.
Prunelloes, 297 *n.*
Punjāb, the, 100, 292. *See also* Lahore, etc.
Purb, 107, 147, 159, 181.
Purchas, Rev. Samuel, 62 *n.*, 70, 74 *n.*, 122, 125, 157 *n.*, 185 *n.*, 196, 235, 240–1, 258 *n.*, 289.

Quails, 296.
Queda, 130, 182.
Quicheu, 27.
Quilon, 44.
Quitasol, 103.

Rādhanpur, 173, 191, 208 *n.*, 209–10, 215, 217.
Rahīmi, the, 203.
Rainy season, 16, 17, 298.
Rai Pithora, 156 *n.*
Rai Singh, Rāja, 163.
Raisins, 9, 14.
Raīyat, 113.
Rāja, passim; term explained, 215.
Rāja, the atheistic, 276.
Rājpura, 295.
Rājputs, 106, 139, 154, 183 *n.*, 211, 217–21, 281, 324; their bravery, 106; freebooters, 143 *n.*, 199, 205, 314.
Ram, 19.
Rāma, 321.
Rāma Chandra, 176.
Ramazān, 317–18.
Rām Dās Kachhwāha, 98, 154, 163.
Rame, kingdom of, 26.
Rānder, 135.
Rankata, 155.
Ranthambhor, 100, 145, 293.
Rati, 89, 101 *n.*, 112.
Rats, 33, 303.
Rāver, 138–9.
Ravi, River, 161–4, 167, 179.
Rāwalpindi, 168.

Rāy Dūrga, 98.
Red rails, the, 91, 115, 120, 184.
Red Sea trade, 12, 14, 30, 35, 41, 191, 293; its importance to Surat, 188, 197. *See also* Mokha.
'Regalled', 182.
Renegades, English, 203–4.
Revett, William, 132.
Rhinoceroses, 246, 304; horns of, 176.
Rhubarb, Chinese, 169.
Rials of eight, value of, 77 *n.*, 109; purity of, 302.
Rice, 11, 13, 14, 16, 19, 20, 21, 26, 28, 35, 37–8, 44, 296, 311; wine from, 35.
Roe, Sir Thomas, 69, 70, 231, 291 *n.*, 297 *n.*, 328–9; at Surat, 193, 230, 237, 252; at Ajmer, 194, 237; at Māndu, 238, 277, 285, 288, 329; at Ahmadābād, 288, 329; returns, 288–9; Terry and, 288–9; Withington and, 194–5; Coryat and, 237–40, 252, 266–7, 282, 286.
Rogers, Rev. Peter, 227–9, 231 *n.*, 236, 247, 253, 255–6, 258, 267.
Rohri, 161.
Rohtās (Bihār), 100, 145.
Rohtās (Punjāb), 168.
Romeria, 165, 171.
Roses, 166, 299.
Rowli, 37.
Rubies, 15, 18, 33–5, 39, 44, 47, 66, 67 *n.*, 68, 87, 94, 102–3, 112, 115. *See also* Balass.
Rudra Chand, Rāja, 181.
Rūhullāh, 319.
Rupees, *passim*; value of, 16, 65, 83 *n.*, 99 *n.*, 102 *n.*, 109–10, 206, 208, 213, 228, 230, 246 *n.*, 250, 266–7, 284, 302; varieties of, 101–2; purity of, 302.
Russia, 1, 27, 59.
Rustam, Mīrza, 99, 139, 162, 212.

Sadullah, Mīrza, 99.
Saettia, 53.
Safar, 57.
Safawi, Kwāja Beg Mīrza, 99.
Saffron, 27, 169.
Safi, Shaikh, 197.
Sāhib Kirān, 265 *n.*
Saif Khān Barha, 99.
St. Augustine's Bay, 62, 135.
Saiyid, 171, 316.
Salām, 115, 326.
Sal-ammoniac, 158.
Salbank, Joseph, 100 *n.*, 101 *n.*
Saldania. *See* Table Bay.
Sālher, 136.
Salīm Shāh. *See* Jahāngīr.
Salīm Shāh (son of Sher Shāh), 142 *n.*, 152.
Salīm Chishti, Shaikh, 102 *n.*, 150.
Salt, 11, 18, 297.
Samarkand, 179, 237, 260, 265–6, 310.
Sambhal, 293.
Sandalwood, 13, 34, 46.
Sandwīp, 29, 181 *n.*
San Thomé, 34, 182.
Sapphires, 15, 33–5, 39, 44, 47.
Sarāi, 142–4, 148–9, 151, 158, 167–8, 179, 225, 311, 325; female attendants in, 225.
Sārang, 205.
Sarangpur, 143.
Saraswati, R., 295 (3).
Sardār Khān, 194, 198–9.
Sariandgo, 209.
Saris, John, 68, 96–7.
Sarkhej, 174, 190; described, 207.
Sārod, 217.
Sarpesh, 103.
Sarrunne, 211, 213, 215.
Sātgāon, 18, 25–6.
Sati, 14, 17, 22; described, 219, 323; Jahāngīr and, 119; reason for, 221.
Satin, 302.
Sawāi rupees, 102.
Scanderoon, 53, 235.
Scarlets, 35.
Schesche, 19.
Scio, 53, 235.
Scorpions, 303.
Seguro, 92–3.
Selwy, 40.
Semiames, 227.
Sequins, 9 *n.*, 83 *n.*
Seralia (seraglio), 226.
Sergius, 272.

Serpents, 33, 303, 324, 326; worship of, 173.
Serrion, 33, 37, 42.
Servants, fidelity of, 313; wages of, 313.
Servidore, 16.
Seward, Rev. John, 270.
Shāhābād, 158.
Shāhbandar, 71 *n.*
Shāh Begam, the, 164, 178.
Shāhdaura, 143.
Shāhi, 267 *n.*
Shāh Jahān. *See* Khurram.
Shāhnawāz Khān, 99 *n.*
Shāhpur, 293.
Shāhrukh Oglu, Mīrza, 99.
Shahryār, Sultān, 100, 330; anecdotes of, 105, 117.
Shakaru-n-nisa Begam, 94, 107.
Shamiyāna, 117, 156, 163, 184, 187.
Shamsuddīn, Mīrza, 99.
Sharīf Khān, 99 *n.*, 163.
Sharīf, Mīrza, 162.
Sharpeigh, Alexander, 96, 132.
Shashes, 20, 306.
Shāstra, 321.
Sheep, 25, 296-7.
Shemines, 33.
Sher Khān, 79.
Sherley, Sir Robert, 212; his wife, 236, 243, 267; Coryat and, 236, 243.
Sher Shāh, 141-2, 156 *n.*, 165.
Shikār, 154.
Ships, Indian, 301.
Shīrāz, 283.
Shwē Dagon, 36.
Siam, 33, 39, 46, 182. *See also* Kiang-mai.
Sība, 294.
Sigistam, 54.
Sikandar, Mīrza, 280.
Sikandarābād, 152, 170.
Sikandar Shāh Lodi, 152 *n.*, 165.
Sikandra, Akbar's tomb at, 120, 186, 227, 237, 316.
Silk, raw, 11, 13, 25, 27, 177, 302; goods, 11, 13, 18, 28, 302, 306; Chinese, 41, 169 (2).
Silver, 15, 33-5, 38, 40-1, 323, 328; ornaments of, 11, 12, 22-3, 28, 306; India rich in, 112, 302-3; its relation to gold, 101 *n.*
Silver tissue, 206, 213, 306.
Sind, 12; described, 217; conquest of, 211; outlaws in, 114. *See also* Tatta, etc.
Sindkhera, 137.
Singhāra, 150.
Sipri, 144.
Sirhind, 158, 180-1.
Sirmūr, 180 *n.*
Sironj, 17, 143.
Sistān, 54.
Sitpur, 161.
Slaves, 154.
Smyrna, 53.
Smythe, Sir Thomas, 70, 232 (4).
Snake-charmers, 313.
Snakes. *See* Serpents.
Soap, 9.
Sojitra, 206, 217 *n.*
Sokotra, 60, 62, 132.
Solomon, King, 318.
Solomon, the, 69, 97 (2).
Some, 9.
Sonārgāon, 5, 28, 100, 100 *n.*
Sorath, 292.
Soughtare, 100.
Spāhi, 250.
Spain, King of. *See* Philip II.
Speake, George, 258 *n.*
Spices, 11, 13, 16, 41, 46, 303.
Spikenard, 179.
Spinels, 33, 35, 39, 44, 47.
Spodium, 47.
Srinagar (Kashmīr), 169, 292.
Srīnagar (Garhwāl), 181.
Srīpur, 5, 28.
Stang, 30.
Staper, Richard, 1, 2, 9, 48, 50-2.
Starkey, Anthony, 190, 191 *n.*, 200.
'Stawed', 212.
Steel, Richard, 51-2, 285.
Stevens, Thomas, 3, 15, 234.
Stone quarries, 157, 187.
Story, James, 2-4, 8.
Strapado, 15.
Styles, Thomas, 124-5.
Suckel Counse, 25.
Sugar, palm, 13; cane, 24, 26, 35; price of, 297.
Sukesera, 143.

Sultān, 98, 327 *n.*, 330.
Sultāna, 327 *n.*
Sultanieh, 54.
Sultānpur, 123, 158.
Sultānunnisā, 101 *n.*
Sumatra, 16, 26, 28, 30, 41-2, 303. *See also* Achin *and* Tiku.
Sumbreiro, 29, 37.
Sunera, 142.
Sura, 175.
Sūrah, 274.
Surat, references to, *passim*; described, 62, 133; its trade, 293; customs dues at, 134; castle at, 133-4; bar of, 133, 148, 197; Dīwān of, 125; Governor of (*see also* Nūruddīn), 197, 219, 229; Shāhbandar of, 71-3, 77 *n.*, 131; English at, *passim*; English tombs at, 239-40; *farmān* for their trade, 188-9, 197; Portuguese at, 75-7, 126, 129, 148, 197; Jesuits at (*see also* Pinheiro), 132; threatened by Bahādur Shāh, 133.
Surgeons, 132.
Surkhāb, 168.
Sūrsing, Rāja, 98.
Susa, 237.
Suttee. *See Sati.*
Sutulāna, 171.
Swally, *passim.*
Swally Hole, discovery of, 96.
Swords, European, 314.
Syria, 241, 246.
Syriam, 30, 35.

Tabāshīr, 47 *n.*
Table Bay, 62, 69, 97, 196, 232 *n.*
Tables (backgammon), 312.
Taborer, Andreas, 15.
Tabrīz, 167, 236, 242.
Taffetas, 206, 302.
Tahmūras, Sultān, 154, 162; made a Christian, 86, 116, 147-8.
Takht, Sultān, 100 *n.*, 330.
Talikhān, 168.
Tallipoies, 36-9.
Tamarind trees, 144, 299.
Tamāsha, 176, 184.
Tamerlane. *See* Tīmūr.
Tanda, 5, 24-5.
Tanks, *passim*; term explained, 300.
Tapestry, 11.
Tapi Dās, 131, 146.
Tāpti, R., 62, 240, 293.
Tarapur, 140.
Tarbiyat Khān, 99.
Tareghe, 35.
Targets (shields), 187, 314.
Tāri, 175.
Tartars, 98, 168, 266, 307.
Tartary, 27, 46, 166, 169, 243, 260, 265, 282, 291, 294; Kings of, 242.
Tāsh Beg Khān, 99.
Taslīm, 184-5.
Tatta, 100, 161, 190-1, 191 *n.*, 209, 212-13, 292; trade of, 212 *n.*, 218; Governor of, 212; Sherley at, 212.
Tattooing, 40.
Tavoy, 41.
Temmery, 179.
Temple, Richard, 200.
Tenasserim, 41, 182.
Terry, Rev. Edward, notice of, 288-90; his account of India, 290-332; and Coryat, 236 *n.*, 238-40, 248 *n.*, 282-8, 310 *n.*, 325; and Roe, 288-9.
Teukes, 103.
Thālner, 137.
Thāna, 13.
Thānesar, 158.
Thomas, the, 69 (5), 97.
Tibet, 27.
Tibet, Little, 170.
Tiger, the, 2, 9.
Tigers, 17, 19, 24-5, 28-9, 174, 303.
Tigris, R., 10 (4), 242.
Tiku, 69, 97.
Tilok Chand, 179.
Time, measurement of, 317.
Timor, 41, 46.
Tīmūr, 165, 237, 260, 265, 307, 310, 325.
Tin, 22, 35, 41.
Tippera, 26, 29.
Tobacco, 299.
Toddy, 13, 175, 297.
Toddy-trees, 13, 175, 297.
Tola, 101-2.
Tongues, sacrifice of, 180, 294, 325.
Topaz, 102.

Towerson, Gabriel, 69 (2), 70.
Trade's Increase, the, 69, 97.
Trāj, 173.
Tree of life, 178.
Tripoli, 1, 9, 47.
Tripura Dās, 24.
Trully, Robert, 189, 190, 200, 201 *n*., 204.
Tuck (turban), 156.
Tucker, Thomas, 133.
Tughlakābād, 155 *n*.
Tughlak Shāh, 156 *n*.
Turbans, 20, 143, 156, 187, 218, 308.
Turbith, 179.
Turkey, 10, 11; Sultān of, 53; territories and revenues of, 245–6; English trade with, 1, 6. *See also* Constantinople, Aleppo. etc.
Turkey cock, 93 *n*.
Turkey Company, 1, 6.
Turks, the, 245, 330; and Persia, 161, 167.
Turpentine, 179.
Turquoises, 103.
Tūt, 166.
Typhoons, 135.

Uchen, 151.
Udaipur, Rāja Rāna of. *See* Amar Singh.
Ude Chand Parkāsh, 180 *n*.
Ufflet, Nicholas, 84–5, 92, 96, 123–4, 126 (2), 170; book by, 185 *n*.
Ujjain, 5, 17, 100, 142, 170, 288.
Umara, 147, 167, 327.
Unicorns, 246; horns of, 176.
Ur. *See* Orfah.
Urs Mela festival, 280.
Uzbeg Tartars, 98, 168.

Vairowāl, 158, 160.
Van, 53; Lake of, 53.
Varella, 35–6.
Variāo, 134, 175, 205 *n*.
Vāsad, 205.
Vechiete, João Battista, 59.
Velvets, 35, 117, 206, 302, 306.
Venereal disease, 310.
Venetian mirrors, 164.
Venetians, 124, 146.
Verney, the Ladies, 258 *n*.
Viāra, 136.
Vijayanagar, 8, 47, 182.
Virginals, 189.
Viss, 35.

Wasseth, 205.
Water-clocks, 317.
Waterfowl, device for taking, 312.
Wazīr, 68, 183–5.
Weaver bird, 313.
West Indies, 82, 299.
Wheat. *See* Corn.
Whitaker, Laurence, 241, 255–7, 270 *n*.
Wine, 35, 300.
Withington, Nicholas, 101 *n*.; account of, 188–96; his narrative, 196–233; Roe and, 194–5; the East India Company and, 195–6, 232–3; his brother, 196, 232–3.
Wolves, 303.
Women veiled, 309.
Wool, 27, 297.
Wotton, Sir Henry, 286.

Xavier, Jerome, 49, 55, 67, 80–1, 83, 85 *n*., 89, 90, 92, 148 *n*., 223, 282 *n*.
Xerafim, 101.

Yādgār, Khwāja, 198 *n*.
Yādgār Ali Sultān, 161.
Yaktails, 27.
Yamani, 102.
Yārkand, 169.
Yashm. *See* Eshim.
Yātish-khāna, 162 (2), 164, 184.
Year, beginning of, 310.
Yeovil, 251, 262, 270 (2).
Yead, 54.
Young, John, 204.
Young, Robert, 193, 225, 231.

Zafar Khān, 99.
Zāhid, Mirza, 99.
Zain Khān Koka, 101.
Zamāna Beg. *See* Mahābat Khān.
Zamorin, the, 45, 129.
Zante, 53, 235.
Zimmé. *See* Kiang-mai.
Zobah, 241.
Zulkārnain, Mirza, 267 *n*., 280 *n*.